The British Wool
Textile Industry
1770–1914

The British Wool Textile Industry 1770–1914

D. T. Jenkins
and
K. G. Ponting

Heinemann Educational Books
The Pasold Research Fund

Heinemann Educational Books Ltd
22 Bedford Square, London WC1B 3HH
LONDON EDINBURGH MELBOURNE AUCKLAND
HONG KONG SINGAPORE KUALA LUMPUR NEW DELHI
IBADAN NAIROBI JOHANNESBURG
EXETER(NH) KINGSTON PORT OF SPAIN

British Library Cataloguing in Publication Data

Jenkins, David
  The British wool textile industry. – (Pasold
  studies in textile history; 3)
  1. Wool trade and industry – Great Britain
  – History
  I. Title   II. Ponting, Kenneth   III. Series
  338.4'767731'0941   ND9901

  ISBN 0-435-32469-1

Typeset by Inforum Ltd, Portsmouth
Printed and bound in Great Britain by
Biddles Ltd, Guildford and King's Lynn

Contents

List of Tables

Preface

Over the last 25 years there has been a wealth of research on a very wide range of aspects of the history of the British textile industries. The wool textile industry has received its fair share of this attention. Studies of various regions, of the organisation of the industry, of the needs and supply of raw materials and factors of production and of the performance of the industry in a number of periods as well as histories of individual firms have together greatly contributed to our knowledge. In adding this volume to the literature we were conscious of two particular needs. We felt that it was time to attempt to draw together some of the findings of the various specialist studies, thus permitting an examination of the performance of the industry as a whole. Moreover it did seem necessary to attempt to redress a balance. Heaton's excellent painstaking study of the Yorkshire woollen and worsted industries and other more recent work have concentrated on the period up to and including the beginnings of factory production. Heaton unfortunately never brought his intended second volume on the nineteenth century to fruition. There have been important but far less comprehensive contributions on the heyday of the industry in the mid-nineteenth century but no overall survey has been attempted of its fortunes at that time nor of how it fared in the changing economic circumstances from the early 1870s.

Thus whilst reviewing the performance of and changes in the industry in the transitional decades to factory production, we concentrate our attention in particular on the period from 1835 to the First World War. Arguably there are two reasons for taking the early 1830s as the starting point for a closer assessment of what was happening. Although cyclical and other crises continued to occur and the industry, or branches of it, swung regularly from a state of excited activity to despondent depression and back again, that decade marked the beginning of a settling down, of expansion and new departures in such important branches as low woollens and cotton warp worsteds, and gloom, when it did occur, resulted perhaps less from periods of decline and more from the disappointment of failure to meet high expectations. For the industry as a whole the middle decades of the nineteenth century were ones of excitement, enthusiasm, dynamic activity and considerable success in markets both at home and abroad. After the short boost given by the Franco-Prussian war, fortunes changed but the evidence persuades us to take a still quite favourable view of its performance in the face of stiff protectionism in all its traditional major markets, and in the new markets it was successfully cultivating, although there undoubtedly were sections which responded less well to the activities of foreign adversaries.

The second reason for greater concentration on the post-1835 period is a more pragmatic one. A large and varied industry spread widely is by no means easy to generalise about. However, it is from the 1830s that both primary and secondary sources allow one to stand back more easily to assess as a whole what was happening. Various nationally collected statistics, evidence from parliamentary reports, contemporary comment in the form of regular trade reports and published works, and the availability of a wider and more representative range of business records allow a more comprehensive picture to be evolved. This is not to say that sources of information on the industry are perfect. Much that is available was generated by or within the industry itself. Comment and discussion was prone to much exaggeration at either end of the spectrum of boom and slump. And such was the diversity of the inputs and products of the industry and the markets that were being served that agreement was invariably impossible about the state of trade and the impact of world or home events. One region could fare well at the expense of another. Even within an area such was the range of product, and machinery and skill required, that some firms could be idle whilst others were overwhelmed with orders. War, in particular, could on the one hand boost, overnight, orders for blanket and uniform cloths to the benefit of low woollen manufacturers, yet on the other hand would curtail the normal trading relations of others.

These variations within the industry, not just between woollens and worsteds but also within each of these two major branches, often make sensible generalisation impossible. It was, for most of the century, heavily dependent on cotton as well as wool. Its product had a very wide range of uses and thus there were few major factors which affected all branches of the industry identically.

In the examination of the performance of the industry in the following chapters an attempt is made to strike a balance according to the importance of the output of the various sections of the industry and its relative size in the various parts of the country. What this means, of course, is that far more attention is given to the Yorkshire trades than to other areas and this is progressively more the case in the later chapters as a result of the increase in Yorkshire's domination. But it is also appropriate that relatively more attention should be given to Yorkshire because of previous studies. The Scottish, Welsh and West of England wool textile industries have all received recent attention in some detail. The Yorkshire industry has not been subject to such scrutiny.

This volume can make no claim to be a substitute for Professor Heaton's intended volume. Although its geographical spread is broader, the scope of the book has necessarily been limited to much narrower confines. We have purposely excluded many aspects of the history of the industry from our discussions. The social conditions of factories, the well-being of the work force, labour organisation and labour relations receive no attention from us. The struggle of labour to prevent the introduction of machinery gets only occasional mention. All these are areas which no doubt merit further study but the terms of reference that we set ourselves exclude them. We have also limited our attention in a number of other areas because of substantial new work at present being carried out. Dr P. Hudson's examination of the sources and adequacy of capital supply to the industry and Dr J. Malin's work on the contribution of shoddy and mungo to the low woollen trade are likely to quickly supersede anything we might have said. We have concerned ourselves more with the growth, organisation, factor supply, output, markets and performance of the industry. Even so, we are well aware of limitations in our consideration of many of these aspects. We have had less success than we would have liked in unravelling the fortunes of the industry in Lancashire which so successfully maintained its size when other minor areas were declining. Our discussion of the hosiery branch of the industry is limited on the whole to yarn supply. The trade in its final product receives only occasional comment. The same applies to the carpet trade, although here the gap is filled by Dr Bartlett's recent study.

We have enjoyed working together on this study. We feel our different backgrounds – one of us for many years a woollen cloth manufacturer, the other a university lecturer in economic history – and our different interests and perspectives have usefully melded together. We have learnt much from each other and have produced a work which is very much a joint enterprise. We have been very lucky also in having had close contact with many other historians working in the field of British textile history. Their published works and our discussions with them have aided our task immensely. Dr Julia de Lacy Mann's friendship, advice and wide knowledge of the history of the wool textile industry have been invaluable. Professor Donald Coleman has kindly read many sections of the manuscript and provided us with very apt comment. We would also like to gratefully acknowledge the friendly advice and assistance we have received from many scholars with specialist knowledge of aspects of the industry. Our understanding of the Yorkshire trade has been enhanced by the help of Dr R.G. Wilson, Dr J. Malin, Dr E.M. Sigsworth, and Dr P. Hudson. Mr K. Rogers' knowledge of the West of England, Dr C. Gulvin's work on Scotland and Dr J. Iredale's understanding of technical matters have proved very useful to us.

Staff at many museums and record offices have efficiently responded to our enquiries. There are so many of them that a full record is impossible here but we would make particular mention of Miss Natalie Rothstein at the Victoria and Albert Museum, whose unrivalled knowledge of many textiles and costumes has proved invaluable. Our understanding of technology has been aided by the staff of the industrial science museums at South Kensington, Manchester and Bradford, as well as by visits to working mills in many parts of the country. When we watch cashmere being processed at Kinross and shoddy at Batley the scope of the trade is vividly understood.

We would like to mention also that group of distinguished university and college staff whose work over the years has aided the progress of the industry and our understanding of it. The doyen of them all was Professor J.B. Speakman of Leeds University, so admirably succeeded by Professor Whewell.

There are many others we could mention. We have benefited from the advice and experience of relatives, friends, colleagues and business associates with very diverse interests and knowledge of the trade. We have had many friendly discussions and arguments with them. Although we have not always agreed with their views or taken their advice, our conversations have been enjoyable and ever informative.

Interest in the history of textiles and the textiles industries is very broad. We hope that this volume, besides being of value to those concerned with the economic history of industry, will also provide historians of fashion, fabrics and technology with a useful insight into the development of the British wool textile industry in the nineteenth century.

1 The Wool Textile Industry in 1770

Introduction: Wool Textile Manufacture in 1770

On the eve of the introduction of the factory system into the British wool textile industry, domestic spinning and weaving was taking place in every county in the realm. Throughout the middle of the eighteenth century the industry had undergone a phase of very rapid expansion and, with the cotton industry yet to catch the imagination of contemporary commentators, it figured large in the economic literature of the time. It has been estimated that between 1741 and 1772 raw material input to the industry increased by an average of 14 per cent per decade, far in excess of the rate of growth of the home population.[1] This rapid increase gave rise to much discussion and we have available a mass of estimates of the inputs and outputs of the industry, both as a whole and in its various regions. Much of this evidence was generated to exaggerate its importance for political and economic gain but it does allow us, in a rough and ready way, to take stock of its size and distribution before fundamental changes in organisation and production methods began to take place.

In the 1770s Arthur Young variously estimated the value of output of the wool textile industry at between £8 million and £10 million. A study of his methods has persuaded Phyllis Deane that the latter figure is the more realistic. The Leeds manufacturer, Thomas Wolrich, argued that in 1771/2, a fairly average year for the decade, the value of Yorkshire's wool textile output, including that of the Rochdale area of Lancashire, was about £3.3 million, of which over two-thirds was exported. He assessed that £1.9 million was the product of the woollen branch of the industry and £1.4 million accrued to worsteds. He, like others, had reasons to exaggerate the trade but it does not seem unreasonable to believe that by 1770 Yorkshire was accounting for about one-third of the value of the British wool textile industry and about one half of the value of wool textile exports.²

The worsted trade in Yorkshire was a relatively recent innovation. It seems to have established itself towards the end of the previous century and to have undergone a fairly steady progression. Defoe in the 1720s commented on the scale of the Yorkshire shalloon trade.³ By the 1740s complaints were emerging from Norfolk, the other main seat of the worsted industry, about Yorkshire competition. Throughout the middle of the century Yorkshire appears to have made steady inroads into the plainer parts of the home market as well as developing a substantial foreign trade. This manufacture was based primarily on the large parish of Halifax and the neighbouring area of Bradford but activity spread into the higher reaches of the Aire valley and into most of the other major textile centres of Yorkshire, including Leeds and Wakefield.

From 1726 records were kept of the amount of woollen cloth fulled in West Yorkshire, arising from an attempt to reduce fraud in the industry. Returns were made to the Quarter Sessions of the amount of broad and narrow cloth milled in each of the fulling mills of the county. There is, of course, no reason to believe that the figures were fully comprehensive. The record of lengths of cloth took no account of variation over the years of the average widths of the fabric. Moreover, occasional purges by the cloth searchers may have led to periods of more comprehensive recording, thus giving the false impression of higher output. However, with these reservations in mind, the statistics do enable some assessment of what was happening in the Yorkshire industry to be made. In the early 1740s narrow cloth pieces fulled outnumbered broadcloth by about three to two but by the end of the 1760s broadcloth had become the dominant product. Broadcloth output doubled in this period, narrow cloth output rose by about 25 per cent.⁴

There are many descriptions of the specialities of the various Yorkshire wool textile towns at the end of the eighteenth century. It is not necessary here to go into great detail. Moreover perhaps the locational differences between woollens and worsteds, broadcloths and narrow cloths, and white and coloured cloths have been over-stressed in the past. Saddleworth by the 1770s was developing a reputation for superfine broadcloth which, it was rather optimistically claimed, was beginning to rival those of the West of England.⁵ Huddersfield, immediately across the Pennines, gained its reputation from finer cloths also but it is apparent that the range of its woollen products was considerable and that it was active in the manufacture of narrow and broad cloths, of fancy cloths and kerseymeres. In

Table 1   *Broad and narrow cloth milled in the West Riding of Yorkshire*

Annual averages	Broad cloth (thousand pieces)	Narrow cloth (thousand pieces)
1740–44	46.5	61.8
1745–49	58.2	67.5
1750–54	58.7	73.7
1755–59	51.8	72.9
1760–64	50.0	73.9
1765–69	82.4	79.5
1770–74	101.1	71.8
1775–79	109.4	97.4
1780–84	115.6	101.4
1785–89	153.1	128.9
1790–94	191.3	153.3
1795–99	244.8	158.4
1800–04	276.1	146.6
1805–09	288.7	159.9
1810–14	313.8	145.5
1815–19	338.9	135.2

Halifax woollens were as important as worsteds with a large manufacture of kerseys, half thicks, bockings and baize. 'The whole of the British navy is clothed from this source' commented Aikin in 1795.[6]

The Leeds woollen trade was likewise very varied. Although its reputation was perhaps later built on lower and middle range cloth, in this period it would appear to have been engaged in a full variety of qualities. The town and neighbouring villages along the Aire Valley and its tributaries concentrated on coloured cloth, whereas the villages of the Calder Valley below Halifax were more concerned with white cloth, but the division was far from absolute.

Rochdale's reputation was built squarely on flannel and baize although the range of its products included kerseys, coatings and other cloths, and worsted shalloons. Flannels were relatively new to the town in the second half of the eighteenth century but an active export trade to most European countries rapidly emerged.[7] The wool textile trade was also established in many other parts of Lancashire. In Colne both woollen and worsted goods were manufactured, including serges, shalloons, calimancoes and tammies. An active woollen trade existed at Bury and flannel, baize and particularly bockings were made throughout Rossendale.

In the Northern Pennines, the Lake District and the Cheviots, domestic spinning and weaving or knitting were to be found in most towns and villages, providing primarily for local needs but sometimes giving rise to an export trade to other parts of the country and occasionally abroad. In Scotland in the 1770s the border woollen industry was on the brink of expansion. Its problems of wool supply, labour skills and access to markets were gradually being alleviated but at this stage it still remained dependent primarily on Scottish demand for coarse woollens, although yarn was spun for hosiery and for English manufacturers.[8]

Much has been written about the Norwich worsted trade and it is perhaps fair to say that there is still not total agreement about the fortunes and problems of that industry in the late eighteenth and early nineteenth centuries. Norwich's concentration on finer worsteds may have made the town more susceptible to market fluctuations. It traded with Northern European markets, with China through the East India Company, and with North and South America and the Mediterranean countries. Although the evidence seems to be that the Norwich trade was still expanding up to the 1770s and probably afterwards, its relative importance in worsted manufacture was clearly declining in the face of the rapid rise of the Yorkshire industry. Through some intricate and not very convincing calculations, Arthur Young valued the Norwich trade in 1772 at £1.2 million, rather less than the Yorkshire worsted trade at the same period.[9] Elsewhere in East Anglia the wool textile trade does not appear to have been sharing in the national expansion. Woollen manufacture in Essex was on the decline in the late eighteenth century. Josias Nottage, a manufacturer at Bocking, considered that the competition from Yorkshire, and specifically the Spanish war, had created the major problems for the local trade.[10]

In the eighteenth century the West of England cloth trade was a long established, rather traditional industry. Its early growth in late medieval and Tudor times, when the main product was undyed broadcloth for export, has been widely discussed. During the later years of the sixteenth century the trade began to decline as trade routes were disrupted during the war with Spain. But another trade in coloured broadcloth emerged which had its roots initially in the Stroud area where Stroudwater Scarlet had become famous in the sixteenth century. The cloth was improved and probably made lighter by such clothiers as William Brewer of Trowbridge, who, according to Aubrey, drove the greatest trade in medleys, and by the Methuen family of Bradford.[11] These coloured broadcloths were really the new

Fig. 1 British Wool Textile Manufacturing Centres

draperies of the West of England, and it was this same trade, producing cloth of various qualities, which remained the backbone of the West of England industry during the eighteenth century.

The Gloucestershire woollen trade experienced prosperity and expansion through the middle of the century. Its superfine cloths were in good demand in the 1760s but with depression setting in, in 1768, and prices beginning to fall, the 1770s were less prosperous. The coarser end of the trade suffered badly. The loss of the American market and the fluctuations in the East India Company purchases had widespread adverse consequences.[12] Further south in the Wiltshire/Somerset division of the traditional broadcloth area a somewhat similar pattern can be discerned. Trade in broadcloths followed much the same experience as in Gloucestershire and those areas that made cheaper cloths clearly suffered. Here, however, there was a balancing factor, namely the introduction of the fine cassimere which was just beginning to move ahead in the 1770s. More will be said later of this, amongst the finest woollen cloth ever made.

Finally a few other areas, some remnants of a past greatness, others new developments, remain to be summarised. For the Somerset/Devon industry, the other West of England trade, the great days had been in the seventeenth century but important sections remained in 1770 and some of them survived the industrial revolution even if what had been the main centre, Exeter, was no longer a cloth making or, rather, cloth finishing town. Indeed the area fragmented, with Wellington, near Taunton, having the main mills. One firm there, Fox Bros, ranked among the dozen most famous wool textile manufacturers in the country, making both woollens and worsteds and doing its own combing.[13] West of Exeter there were the remnants of the old established trade that had used the local wool to manufacture long ells and similar coarse cloths.

Quantitatively more important, the Welsh woollen trade, like the Scottish, had for centuries made fabrics from local wool for local purposes. For a period it looked almost as if a section of this trade would imitate the Scottish and have an important place in the national scene. During the middle years of the eighteenth century the Welsh flannel trade of Newtown expanded and supplied coarse plain weave flannels mainly used for shirts, to a large section of the population but for reasons which have not been clearly established, it lost some of its trade which passed rather oddly to Rochdale, in Lancashire.

Mention should also be made of the specialised London finishing trade, an interesting remnant of the long established clothworking trade of the capital. It remained quite common practice for cloths for export to be sent for what was called 'London finishing' or more usually, 'London shrinking'. The cloth was damped and allowed to relax naturally. In addition, these London shrinkers also examined the cloths for damages and their decision was often mutually accepted by British manufacturers and foreign buyers – a valuable service for all concerned.

Finally, emphasis must be placed on the large and increasing supplies of yarn which went to the expanding knitting and carpet trades which in many cases had their main centres away from the traditional weaving towns. Hand knitting had long been practised in most households in the country. Likewise machine knitting had had a long history, beginning with William Lee's invention of the knitting frame in about 1590. Based on it an important trade had grown up mainly centred on the Midland counties of Leicestershire, Nottinghamshire and Derbyshire, concentrating respectively on wool, cotton and silk. The late eighteenth and early nineteenth centuries saw many new inventions and knitting became a major industry – incidentally surpassing weaving in size in the twentieth century.

The carpet trade was also rather detached, geographically. Originally centred on such places as Axminster and Wilton, it became by the nineteenth century, fairly widespread, with a number of important mills in the West Riding. Two major centres, Kidderminster and Kilmarnock, were well away from what had become the main cloth weaving areas, although both these towns had had early textile trades which were largely submerged by the new development.

The estimates of output for the 1770s when compared with the official value of exports, which may somewhat underestimate the actual value, suggest that getting on for one-half of the output of wool textiles was exported. Almost one-quarter of the cloth was sent to America, one-third to Italy, Spain and Portugal. Europe as a whole was, of course, the major market, taking £2.8 million of the £4.3 million trade. The East India trade was valued at almost £0.5 million and major markets were being pursued also in Turkey, Africa and the West Indies. Trade to South America had yet to reach a significant level.

This short profile of the location and state of the wool textile industry in the 1770s contrasts the expansionary activities of northern manufacturers with the relative stagnation in some other areas. Clearly much of the expansion of the industry nationally in the third quarter of the eighteenth century is accounted for by the rise of Yorkshire and Lancashire. Only in a few relatively minor areas is it realistic to write of contraction but the beginning of the great divide between the fortunes of Yorkshire and the rest of the country may be dated from this time.

The Organisation of Domestic Manufacture

By the 1770s a quite complex system of organisation of domestic manufacture had emerged; a system which varied in different branches of the trade and in different areas. The regional and trade differences were to have significant implications for the establishment of factory production, its scale and organisation, its trading methods and its sources of capital. Whereas some parts of the trade were almost entirely organised by merchant-entrepreneurs putting out work, or even in some instances housing hand workers in mills and factories, other parts were based on unorganised, local, often part-time domestic workers working for themselves to provide for their local communities and marketing any production surplus further afield.

The more centrally organised production was in the West of England trade and in the Yorkshire worsted industry. A relatively few manufacturers controlled production on an outwork basis often distributing work for spinning or weaving over a large area. Robert Heaton of Ponden near Keighley in the 1750s was having some of his yarn spun in Lancashire villages almost 20 miles distant and in the 1760s he was sending his agent to deliver wool and collect yarn from Long Preston, Giggleswick and Rathmell, north west of Keighley and again up to 20 miles away.[14] Further north in the Yorkshire Dales, spinners were providing yarn for the Bradford worsted industry as well as for their own knitting needs. James provides perhaps the best description of this putting-out system, a description which he obtained from two manufacturers who had been involved in the domestic trade. He is worth quoting in some detail; he cites the case of Thomas Crosley of Bradford whose description of his domestic work was as follows:

> In putting out wool to spin we sent a pack of tops at once to Skipton by the canal. A boat came on purpose for the tops of various people. The pack was generally consigned to a shopkeeper or small farmer; the former the oftenest because it brought custom to his shop. He had for putting out a halfpenny per lb. We had spinning done in Lancashire as far as Ormskirk; in Craven, and at Kirby Lonsdale; in Wensleydale, Swaledale, and other parts of North Yorkshire. Much difficulty was experienced with the yarn; we had to sort it, and from the same top there would be yarn as

thick as sixteens and as small as twenty-fours, shewing the difference in the spinners.[15]

An even fuller description was provided by William Jennings of Windhill, relating to the end of the eighteenth century:

I went to York to buy wool, and at that time it averaged about a shilling per pound. I then came home, sorted, and combed it myself. After being combed it was oiled and closed, that is, the long end of the wool and the short end were put together to form a sliver. It took a number of slivers to make a top, each top weighing exactly a pound. Then I took it to hand spinners twenty or thirty miles distant. The mother or head of the family plucked the tops into pieces the length of the wool, and gave it to the different branches of the family to spin, who would spin about nine or ten hanks per day: for the spinning I gave a halfpenny a hank, and sometimes one shilling and two pence for every twenty-four hanks over. Sometimes I took the tops to shopkeepers in the spinning districts, and allowed them a sum of money per score for delivering the tops and receiving the hanks from the spinner. When I got it home I sorted the soft from the hard spun yarn, and made the former into weft, and the latter into warp. The weft was put upon a swift, and prepared upon a spool for the weavers.[16]

The Yorkshire worsted trade in the eighteenth century was therefore almost entirely organised by relatively few entrepreneurs who carried on their activity on a large scale, keeping close control of it. The small independent worsted clothier did not exist. Heaton points out that one of the results of this was that, whereas the woollen cloth halls had to provide sufficient accommodation for a host of other small clothiers, the Bradford Worsted Cloth Hall was much smaller. The latter accommodated only 258 manufacturers whereas the Leeds White Cloth Hall provided 1210 stands and the Leeds Mixed Cloth Hall could house 1770 stallholders.[17]

The more centralised organisation of domestic worsted manufacture in Yorkshire is realistically explained by Heaton in terms of the need of worsted entrepreneurs to fight their way into the wool textile trade, which could only be done 'by men who possessed some amount of capital, who were capable of defraying the initial costs, and willing to overcome many difficulties before they achieved success'.[18]

The worsted trade around Norwich was organised rather differently and in a less centralised way. The key figure was the worsted weaver, who bought yarn from independent spinners, wove it himself or had it woven by journeymen weavers who worked as independent craftsmen on commission or in direct employment to the master. The stuffs were then put out again to be dyed and finished, again by independent craftsmen. The finished cloth would then be sold locally to mercers or drapers or sent to London merchants.

It is less easy to generalise about the Yorkshire woollen industry as there were vast differences in the scale of domestic organisation. The Yorkshire woollen clothier was normally a small, independent man who purchased his raw material himself, and with the help of his family, and occasionally other employees, journeymen and apprentices, carried out the various stages of manufacture and then sold the fulled but unfinished cloth to a merchant, either directly or through one of the cloth halls. He used his own capital and enterprise and would have been aware that the quality and quantity of his work directly affected his financial return from it. Although the typical clothier was quite small, with limited capital and producing only one or two pieces a week, there were larger ones with many apprentices and a large workshop or loom shop. In 1806 Elijah Brooke of Morley gave evidence that he employed 12 journeymen who spun and wove for piece rates in their own homes. James Walker of Wortley, who became a mill owner, controlled 21 looms.[19] Many of these clothiers, as a result of the prosperity of the woollen industry in the last third of the eighteenth century were able to find sufficient resources to become mill entrepreneurs or partners in joint-stock mills. With the slower mechanisation in the woollen branch of the industry, clothiers survived until well into the nineteenth century. The 1851 census included 4878 people in Yorkshire who still described themselves as clothiers. Having had his cloth fulled, the woollen clothier then sold it and took no part in the finishing of it. This was undertaken by the merchant purchaser who had it finished in his own workshop, or put it out to commission cloth finishers.

Domestic organisation in the West of England was more akin to the Yorkshire worsted system. The West of England master clothier controlled all aspects of the manufacture of the cloth, even to the extent in some cases of owning the machinery worked by domestic outworkers. The clothiers' opulence is clearly indicated by their magnificent houses, many of which still survive. Most of the trade was in the hands of these wealthy entrepreneurs but there were also many smaller clothiers. Entry to the trade was not restricted and anyone who could amass a little capital could set himself up in business. Most of the cloth produced was sold to a London factor or merchant for resale, either at home or abroad. The clothiers sold some cloth direct to the final customer but normally the West of England clothier did not do his own merchanting.

Domestic organisation differed yet again in Wales and Scotland. The Welsh woollen industry was made up of the independent spinners and weavers working for themselves or on commission and, perhaps, putting out any work beyond their capabilities. In Merioneth, for example, specialist weavers wove their own yarn and worked on commission, keeping a proportion of the yarn entrusted to them as payment. The finished cloth would then have been marketed locally or sold to the Shrewsbury Drapers' Company, which up to the second half of the eighteenth century had a monopolistic control of the purchase of cloth from much of Wales.[20] In Scotland the domestic organisation varied in different parts of the country but most of it was in the hands of small, self-employed manufacturers catering mainly for local needs and marketing any surplus from time to time further afield. Merchant capitalists and larger domestic manufacturers were not common. But by the end of the eighteenth century some Border weavers were beginning to do commission work for English clothiers and weavers and spinners elsewhere were losing their independence, control over them being obtained by dyer-fullers, who purchased wool, distributed it and organised the finishing and marketing of the cloth. Dr Gulvin argues that this process of change was hastened by rising wool prices during the Napoleonic wars and the inability of spinners and weavers to afford their own materials.[21]

These distinctions in domestic organisation of the wool textile industry in the different parts of Britain were not, however, as clear cut at the end of the eighteenth century as has sometimes been suggested. Rapid alterations, that were taking place in all areas of the trade, were creating organisational changes and the embryonic factory system stimulated yet further alteration in the domestic system.

Raw Material Supply: Wool Qualities
The success of the wool textile trade depended upon the production of cloths with broad consumer appeal in both home and foreign markets. The manufacture of the necessary variety of cloths required the availability of a wide choice of raw materials. It is impossible to understand the problems of wool supply to the wool textile trade without an awareness of the wool qualities that clothiers were looking for. There were at least eleven qualities that affected a clothier's view of the suitability of the fibre for the type of cloth he was trying to manufacture. The fineness, the actual diameter of the wool, was the most important of all. A rather complicated system of numbering had been introduced to indicate this fineness. For example, 64s, a key type, meant that such wool could be spun into yarn of such a size that

64 × 560 (= 35,840) yards would weigh one pound. This strange figure came, apparently, from the English worsted trade, which at some early date had decided that a hank of worsted yarn should measure 560 yards. It should be remembered that a hank of yarn, familiar to all who hand knit, was the easiest way to transport yarn and consequently the spinner would pass his yarn forward to the weaver in this form. It followed that the thicker the yarn, the less the number of such hanks that would weigh one pound. A thick worsted yarn would have a count of 12s and a fine one of 48s. At some stage these count numbers were linked with the wools but in a rather odd way; not as indicating the actual size that was spun from wool of a certain fineness, but what was considered as the limit that could be spun. Whether any tests were ever carried out is not known and the figures are not logical. For example, a fine wool of say 70s quality would be used to produce a 48s worsted yarn, a coarse wool of 44s would be used for a 12s. Wool could be spun finer and there are records of hand spinning producing a 360s yarn from wool that could not have been finer than 60s. Thus the fineness of the wool did determine the fineness of the yarn and, as a general truth, fine yarns were required for fine cloths.

Length, the second quality of wool, was of secondary importance to fineness and to a considerable extent was relative. Three to four inches was long for a fine wool but short for a coarse wool. Most woolmen probably carried in their minds an ideal length for a wool of any specific type. Several important historical changes stand out and should be noted. Primitive sheep before they were domesticated certainly contained a fine inner and coarse outer fleece and this continued to be the case for many centuries after wool had become a recognised commodity for domestic use. Gradually, however, with most commercial breeds, certainly those in common use in Britain, the coarse wool had been bred out, most distinctly in the case of the merino, and also in most British breeds. The relatively fine wool of the Cheviot, the various Down breeds and the Dorset Horn and such similar sheep, could only have been achieved by this means. In the really coarse British breeds, the Blackface and the Devon Long Wool for example, it is more difficult to be sure. Particularly in the latter type of wool it is possible that the fine wool had been bred out. In some breeds, particularly the rarer ones such as the Shetland, distinct traces of both the finer and the coarser could be found.

The third quality of wool was the crimp, which was the natural wave occurring in the fibre. It has always been easy to recognise and ideally should make the wool fibre look something like a spring.

Crimp was one way of judging fineness, as the number of crimps per inch was usually proportional to the fineness. Crimp served several purposes, notably in giving bulkiness to the yarn, and has therefore always helped to make wool a warm fibre to wear.

Freedom from fault in the fibre structure was vital and was relatively easy to see. It arose from breaks caused by disease or drought or, in the case of the ewe, at lambing when diet deficiency led to a partial breakdown in the fibre structure. Sometimes this breakdown could cause cotting, where the fibres became almost ingrown with each other and when the separation, which had of course to be done before spinning could take place, caused great damage and loss of length.

Evenness in fineness and length was important. It should be remembered that wool from the same sheep varied considerably in length and to some extent in fineness in various parts of the fleece. The best and most level wool was found on the sides, the shortest on the neck and legs, the dirtiest on the belly, and it is this difference that necessitated classing on the farm or at the wool stapler, and later the sorting of the fleeces at the mill. Varieties in different parts of the fleece were particularly troublesome but unavoidable. There does not seem to be any real evidence that breeding over the centuries has done much to improve this fault. It could be put right by sorting but any variation in the same part of the fleece has always been undesirable and considerably lessened the value of the wool.

Colour was important and normally whiteness and freedom from coloured hair was of great value. A good wool scoured to a good white and was free from stain. Density of staple was another quality but is rather difficult to define. It can more easily be seen with merino wool than with any other. It was the tendency of a number of fibres to form clusters and the closeness with which they could be pressed together suggested how they would form in the cloth. Wool with really dense formation made fine cloths and would also felt well. Soft handling wool was of obvious value, as softness was usually sought after in the fabric and the one depended on the other. Basically, the finer the wool the softer the handle, but there were exceptions. Shetland wool, for example, was not as fine as Southdown but it handled softer and therefore gave a softer fabric. Woollen fabrics were particularly noted for their soft handle, even where there were some coarse fibres in the fleece, as the finer and shorter tended to go to the surface of the yarn, and this was further accentuated by the fulling. When we have examined eighteenth century patterns it has been noticeable that cloths have handled softer than the fineness of the wool would have led us to expect. The clothier could always improve the handle of the cloth by giving it more fulling if other factors, such as the weight required and the pattern, permitted it. A slight raising on a teazle gig would also bring the short, fine fibres to the surface and this effect was naturally most noticeable in the dress finish of the superfine broadcloth.

Felting was wool's most distinctive quality. No other fibre possessed it, not even the rarer hairs such as cashmere or camel hair. It depended mainly on the physical structure of the fibre which, on the surface, was covered with scales. Thus the fibre could only move in one direction, towards the tip, and consequently when cloth or wool was compressed into a smaller space, particularly under the influence of moisture and heat, it tended to remain there. The property of felting depended upon these outer scales and disappeared if they were removed.

Freedom from vegetable fault was important. The worst type of vegetable fault in the later nineteenth century was the burr which fortunately was not found in British wools. In some, notably those from Australia, it could be so bad as to necessitate removal either by mechanical means or by carbonising (that is, by destroying the vegetable matter with sulphuric acid) thereby causing some loss in the value of the wool. Linked with vegetable matter as a contamination were all the other impurities that the sheep collected, which together affected the yield of the wool, that is, the amount of clean wool that one obtained. Yields varied tremendously. Washed English wools could yield 85 per cent to 90 per cent; at the other extreme some South African wools heavily laden with sand, would only give a yield of 20 per cent. Most British wools yielded well, particularly those which were described as washed, which indicated that the sheep were washed in a stream shortly before shearing. During earlier times this would appear to have been the general custom and, remembering the freedom from vegetable contamination, which was and indeed remains a notable factor with British wools, these types could have been spun and were probably often spun without further scouring.[22]

During the early days of the cloth trade, and as far as woollens were concerned throughout the period, a considerable amount of wool did not fit into these categories. The most important exception was lambs' wool, which meant the four to six-months first growth. Such wools had many special qualities, notably soft handle and they would, of course, be shorter than full grown wools. Then there was skin wool, fell wool as it was sometimes called, which was removed from the skin of the sheep that had been killed for meat and consequently could be of any length. Its quality depended on the way it was removed from the skin. In Britain this was usually done by painting the skins with lime which was rather difficult to remove before processing could begin.

Raw Material Supply: Home Grown Wool

In 1770 the British wool textile trade depended mainly on home-grown wool. The exception was in the West of England where manufacturers of superfine broadcloths used some Spanish merino wool. The days when Britain had produced the finest wool were gone but she did grow the longest wool, of great importance to the worsted manufacture. Most of the complaints about wool smuggling related to long wool, for which the Continent had no adequate substitute.

Since Tudor days, sheep breeders had been aiming more and more at obtaining fatter sheep. In the eighteenth century, due to the work of such men as Bakewell, this effort was successful. As a by-product of the change, longer wool was grown on the low-lying, rich lands of the Midlands, but this increase in average quality longer wool should not be confused with the choice long wool which came from the specialised long breeds such as the Lincoln.

The pattern of the British wool trade and its distinctive sheep, which those who have known it in the twentieth century will well recognise, was already established. Although it is impossible to say what the early medieval sheep was like and difficult with the Tudor one, this is not the case with 1770, and it is possible to give a reasonably accurate picture of the types of wool available to the manufacturer. For long wool, the Lincoln was the most famous and the Leicester the most productive. Robert Bakewell had become involved in the Leicester breed after he had taken control of his father's farm in 1760 and he produced a good mutton sheep with long wool.[23] The effect of Bakewell's work was felt over large sections of British farming during the following 50 years; only the chalk downs to the south and the mountains and hills to the north and far west escaped its influence.

Two distinctive lines can be traced, first the one originating when the Leicester was taken north by the Culleys, who introduced it to Northumberland in 1767. They were very successful and in the Border Leicester gave the world a breed that was arguably, after the merino, the most important that has ever been produced. By crossing the Border Leicester with the native Cheviot the famous Scottish half-bred was evolved and the quantity of average long wool available to the industry was greatly increased. The importance of the availability of this wool in the North of England to the manufacturers of the West Riding has not been given the importance that it deserves. The tendency has been to stress the point that Bakewell, by making the sheep bigger, made the wool coarser but his work also meant that the weight of the fleeces was as much as doubled. Without this increase in wool supply it is difficult to see how the expanding West Riding industry could have found sufficient raw material to achieve its outstanding successes.

Back in the Midlands, near to its native breeding ground, the Leicester had its second and equally important effect. It was crossed with the native sheep of each area to produce slightly different breeds but all essentially mutton-producing animals giving long wool of basically the same type although in some instances with special features. The Leicester was crossed with the native sheep of Lincolnshire, famous for its long wool, to give the new Lincoln breed producing a better mutton sheep but one whose long wool was not as good. The Leicester was also crossed with the old-established and once famous Cotswold to give the modern Cotswold, a somewhat unsatisfactory product from the wool point of view. Further north, crossed with the old Teeswater it gave the distinctive Wensleydale with a wool that had a very spiral curl and was to find several speciality uses, notably for high class linings. Further away from its original centre the breed was used to improve the native Kent, so yielding the Romney Marsh which later became the most numerous sheep in New Zealand. Today the Romney, in its New Zealand version, produces the largest quantities of non-merino wool grown. To the west the Leicester was used with the native Bampton sheep of Devon to produce the Devon Longwool, the coarsest of all the descendants of Bakewell's Leicester. Finally, in Ireland, which had been and remained an important source of wool for much of the English cloth trade, it was used with the native breed to give the Roscommon – one of the few Irish breeds of importance later. All these descendants of the Leicester gave long, coarse wool varying in length from 6″ to 12″, and in quality from 36s to 48s. The worsted industry of the period was based upon them.

The second distinctive group came from the chalk downs which straddle England and had, during the great days of the English medieval wool trade, produced a considerable part of the wool that made the country famous. Just as Bakewell with his breeding experiments changed the Leicester and gave us long wool, so Ellman from 1780 onwards, with his experiments on the native sheep of the Sussex Downs, produced the modern Down sheep of which the typical type was the Southdown. Although the production of good mutton sheep was Ellman's main object he, like Bakewell, produced a new distinctive type of wool, finer in quality but shorter in length.

Just as the Leicester was used to change sheep over wide areas of the country, so with the Southdown. On the chalk downs of Oxford it was crossed with the native Cotswold to give the modern Oxford Down, a more successful cross than that of the Cotswold with the Leicester. In Wiltshire it was crossed rather unsuccessfully with the native sheep which had previously been mainly used for folding, that is manuring the chalk country, but had produced small weights of relatively fine wool. Later it was replaced in this area by the cross of the Southdown with the native Hampshire sheep to give the well known Hampshire Down. In Dorset the cross with the local sheep produced the so-called Dorset Down, perhaps the best of all these Down wools.

Like the Leicester, the new Southdown had some of its greatest success rather away from the original centre of its development, namely in Suffolk and Shropshire; the former originated about 1790 by crossing the old black-faced Norfolk Horn with the Southdown and the latter from crossing the old native sheep of the country of the Marches with the Southdown. All these sheep gave wools of varying fineness ranging from 50s to 58s; they were short, from three to five inches, not suitable for combing by the processes then known and were used for woollen cloths, notably the second-rate broadcloths.

It will be seen that, with the sheep deriving from these two groups, the woolmen of 1770 had a range of types capable of producing a wide variety of cloths. A third group comprised those wools that came from the hills and mountains. These sheep were basically unimproved and their wool suffered considerably from the fact that they were mixed in quality and length. The Blackface, which was to become the most numerous sheep of this group, had hardly started on its great expansion and shared the land with many other breeds – the Herdwick, the Lonk, and most numerous of all, the Welsh Mountain. These wools were used for making the coarser cloths – the Herdwick, for example, for Burns' Hodden Grey – and considerable quantities would have been used for purely domestic purposes.

This survey omits several important types difficult to fit in, above all the Cheviot, native to the hills of that name. This wool was the basis in the following century of the Lowland or Scottish tweed trade and its popularity was so great that the name was used to cover all sheep other than merinos, but during the late eighteenth century it had not emerged into fame. The same comments applied to the Dorset Horn, but in the Welsh Marches the Ryeland continued to produce the finest wool grown in the whole country. Under the name of 'Lemster Ore' it had been well known in Shakespeare's time and, probably due to careful breeding, gave a near 60s quality wool which was not that much different to merino. The West of England manufacturers used it for their best (not superfine) cloths and indeed may well have mixed some of it with the Spanish merino for the real superfines. The only wool the British manufacturer needed to import to have the full range of wools available for his use was the merino, and in 1770 the only source of supply was Spain. Spanish merino wool was of 64s quality. It was used for woollens and never combed.

Consequently, it follows that, compared with the range of wools of the nineteenth century, two important groups were missing. First, the really fine merino of 70s quality and upwards was simply not being produced. Secondly, there were no merino wools that were long enough to comb, partly because the merino wool from Spain tended to be shorter than this breed later became, and partly because hand combing could only deal with the longer wools. The filling of the first of these gaps represented the chief development of the following 50 years.

The Processes of Production

In 1770 the technology of manufacture in the wool textile industry was on the brink of very substantial change, but the coming of mechanisation did not basically alter the principles of production methods. The sequence of processes and ideas underlying them to all intents and purposes remained the same.

The processes of wool textile manufacture are conveniently divided into five groups. The first is the preparatory processes where the wool from the fleece is sorted, scoured and prepared for spinning. The second process involves the manufacture of the yarn with quite different technology required in the woollen and worsted branches of the industry. The third group encompassed the weaving of the cloth, a process basically the same for both woollens and worsteds. The final processes involve finishing where there were some differences between the treatment of woollens and worsteds, and dyeing a most important but somewhat neglected section of the industry.

The preparatory processes involved sorting, scouring, drying, picking, burring and blending. On the whole the differences that were due to breed, and to distinctly different sheep within one breed, were the problem of the grower who classed the fleeces he produced, but the great differences in a single fleece necessitated sorting by the manufacturer. The fleece was spread out on a table and divided into as many sorts as the nature of the wool demanded and the type of yarn or cloth being manufactured necessitated. Sorting was a skilled occupation and one that has never been mechanised. It is the only process in the whole sequence that has not been altered, although one would point out that now, in the latter part of the twentieth century, it is much less done than was the case formerly.

Scouring removed the natural fat that the sheep had deposited on the wool and most, but not all, of the impurity the animal had collected. It was imperative to do the operation efficiently. Scouring always involved treatment in water. The next process, unless the wool was dyed there and then, was drying, followed by picking to remove impurities such as seeds and other pieces of extraneous material such as vegetable matter and, in some cases, pieces of discoloured wool. As mentioned above, the burr, a seed covered with tiny hooks, caused much trouble during the second half of the nineteenth century. The preparatory processes concluded with the blending, where differing types of wool, occasionally material other than wool, or more often different colours of wool, were mixed together for a specific purpose. The best example was the mixing of white and black wool to make a grey. The blending process was more important in the woollen sequence, indeed with worsted combing it could be done after the top was made. During the blending, oil or fat was added to facilitate the opening that takes place during the carding in the woollen sequence and during the combing in the worsted.

The second main group of processes converted the mass of individual fibres into yarn and as these sections cover the great woollen-worsted divide, this is a convenient place to clarify the division. Woollen and worsted fabrics differed in four main respects. Woollens were made from short wool and worsted from long; the raw material for the former was carded, for the latter it was combed. This further accentuated the already established difference of short wool for woollens and long for worsteds because the combing process, in addition to disentangling the wool which was its main object, placed the fibres in a parallel fashion and removed the short ones. The third difference was more technical and involved two distinct ways of spinning. For woollen yarn drafting of the fibre was done while the twist was being inserted, whereas with the worsted yarn the long fibres allowed the drafting to be carried out without the insertion of twist. These technical differences had an important effect on the development of the mechanisation of the two methods of spinning. Finally, the fourth difference between woollen and worsted fabrics came in the finishing. Woollen cloth was fulled, worsted was not.

Obviously, differences of this nature are never quite clear cut. A few woollens were not fulled, a few worsteds – and this particularly applied to some of the worsted/warp, woollen/weft cloths that were made in the seventeenth century – were quite heavily fulled. These cloths which combined woollen and worsted yarns usually had the weaker woollen yarn in the weft. These half-worsteds, as they can conveniently be called, were important and included many of the New Draperies. Among them the serges in particular were heavily fulled.

The first process in the making of woollen yarn was carding which, it can be claimed with much justification, was the most important of all in the woollen sequence. Unless carding was properly done reasonable yarns could not be spun. The early history of carding is rather shrouded in mystery but need not concern us here because we know that by late medieval times so-called hand cards were made which consisted of wires inserted in a leather foundation and with them the wool was opened, that is, disentangled by working the material between the two cards. Christopher Sly in Shakespeare's *The Taming of the Shrew* was by birth a pedlar and by occupation a card maker. A preliminary opening of the wool was often obtained by beating it; the process was also known as bowing or willowing, and in some cases became, in practice, a part of the blending. It was also found better to use first a coarser card, that is one with the wires set further apart, and afterwards to remove the smaller entanglements with a card clothed with finer card wire; this led to the processes being given the different names of scribbling and carding but the latter term also continued to be used to cover the whole process. After the material had been completely opened it had to be separated into endless rovings in order to be spun. Originally this was part of the spinning process in so much that the carder produced small pieces of sliver, often called rolags, but later, in the early days of machine spinning, this preparation of endless rovings became part of carding with the new, distinctive name of slubbing. The rovings or the slubbings were then spun. In the woollen process of manufacture this had long been done on the spinning wheel; not, incidentally, on the type best known today with the flyer, but on the so-called big wheel, consisting simply of a driving wheel and a spindle.

In the worsted sequence, the raw material was combed; that is disentangled by drawing it through two combs with long metal teeth. The resulting long wool was made into a top and the short wool that was left on the comb was taken off, mixed with other wools and used for woollen spinning. This material, the so-called noils, has always been an important raw material for the woollen section of the trade. After the top had been made the thick sliver or roving was reduced in size so as to make it ready for spinning. This reduction which later became known as drawing, was accomplished on the spinning wheel and is therefore often reckoned as an adjunct of that process. With the actual spinning of worsted there was a problem. The spinning wheel as used for woollen yarn, which inserted twist with the drafting, was not suited for worsteds as the long wool was better drafted without twist. For this reason some writers have assumed that worsteds were often spun on the so-called Saxony wheel which had been invented in the late Middle Ages and had an ingenious device known as the flyer. This allowed twisting and winding to be done at the same time but also meant that drafting had to be done between the two hands, not between one hand and the spindle. This Saxony wheel was widely used for flax and was often called the flax wheel, but how far it was used for worsteds remains uncertain. There are many references to worsteds being spun on the old, simple spindle without the wheel but on the other hand the Saxony wheel does, from a technical point of view, appear a suitable apparatus for processing long wools and must surely have been used in this way, at least to some extent.

A considerable amount of yarn was used for weaving as it was spun but particularly with worsted yarn the twisting of two threads together to obtain a strong thread was widely practised. For ease of transport it was also common to wind the yarn into hank form. Both these processes, the twisting and the winding from the hank, were partly done on the simple wheel.

The weaving of woollens and worsteds involved the same basic principles, but before dealing with them let us look at the auxiliary processes, which may be divided into the preparation of the warp and of the weft. The former was the more complicated and normally consisted of the actual warping, sizing, the transfer of the warp on to the cloth beam, and the threading of the warp through the harness. If the yarn had been made up into hanks it also had to be rewound on to bobbins, which were set up in a warp creel, in the correct colour order if a fancy cloth was being made. Next, the necessary lengths of yarn were transferred to pegs fixed on a wall or on to a warp bar and there removed in the form of what was called the chain. To make the yarn strong enough to withstand the strain of weaving, it was often passed in chain form through a bath containing glue or some such substance that gave it additional strength. The next job was to spread the warp to the correct width, sometimes called raddling, and the winding of the chain on to the warp beam of the loom. Finally, each warp end had to be drawn through a heddle situated on a harness. This was relatively easy with the plain weave where there were only two harnesses and the ends were then drawn alternately through heddles on one and then the other, but rather more difficult with the common twill where four harnesses were needed and very time-consuming if fancy weaves were being made. Such fancy weaves were, in the woollen and worsted trade, much in the minority. It is well worth remembering that the preparation of the warp took up a considerable amount of the weaver's time, something like 25 per cent would be a reasonable estimate. The weft preparation was much easier; the yarn was transferred from the hank or other container on to the weaver's bobbins with the winding wheel once again the tool. In some cases the yarn could be spun direct on to the weaver's bobbins.

The loom as used for many centuries had reached its full development in the late medieval period. As far as our evidence goes, the classical civilisations had used both a horizontal and a vertical loom but for many centuries, especially in the more primitive societies, the vertical or so-called upright loom was more general. However, around 1050 in the great textile centres of Europe, the horizontal loom came into use in the form that is well known from many pictorial reproductions. There were two variations, the wide loom which wove cloth up to 100 inches wide and the narrow loom, which usually made cloth about half that width. There was also a much narrower loom used for weaving braid and ribbon, which need not concern us here as it was not much used in the woollen and worsted trade. The wide and narrow looms were similar in principle, the harnesses being raised and lowered by means of treadles operated by the weaver's feet. With the wide loom two operatives were needed; they sat at the end of the loom and usually wove plain weave cloth, that is cloth needing only two harnesses. With the narrow loom only one man was required; he sat in front of the loom and the majority of cloth woven in this type of loom was made in the twill weave, needing four harnesses. With fancy weaves a more complicated system of raising and lowering the harnesses was necessary. These two looms, the broad and the narrow, were the basic tools of the British wool textile industry in 1770. The only major invention had been Kay's flying shuttle. This was already being used but it is important to appreciate that it made comparatively little difference to the loom although it did increase production and, where adopted in broad loom weaving, did away with one of the weavers. After the fabric had been woven and before it was sent to be finished, the weaver, or more likely the weaver's wife, mended any weaving faults. Usually this involved the threading in of broken ends and picks.

A useful division of the finishing processes is into the wet and the dry, particularly as the main difference between the woollen and worsted sequences occurs in the former section. With woollen cloths the wet processes were first the cleaning or scouring, second the fulling, then the raising, followed by the drying and shearing. Sometimes the raising came after the drying but in the traditional broadcloth the raising and the shearing were done wet and were known as clothworking. The scouring cleaned the cloth by removing the oil inserted before carding, the size applied before weaving, and any other dirt that had been collected. This cleaning was done in the fulling stock, the one textile machine that had been successfully mechanised, using fuller's earth. This was a preliminary to the second fulling or thickening which, with the typical broadcloth, took many hours. Drying or tentering usually followed fulling and was done by stetching the cloth on open-air tenter racks which were well known landmarks around clothing towns. At some point during this finishing routine, perhaps most satisfactorily between scouring and fulling, burling was done. This involved the picking out from the cloth of any remaining small pieces of foreign matter, for example, small pieces of vegetable fibre that had been missed by the picker before spinning, small lumps of unopened wool, a particularly bad fault if one was making a mixture of, say, black and white and, of a rather different nature, any knots that had been tied to hold threads together during weaving. In the days when scouring and fulling were done together, this burling operation seems frequently to have been divided into two parts, the pieces of vegetable matter were removed before scouring but the knots were left until after the fulling. If they were removed before the cloth had been shrunk, the threads that had been tied with knots would tend to come apart and small holes be caused.

When making the best type of woollen cloth the two processes of raising and shearing were regarded as one. The cloth surface was raised by means of handles fitted with teasels and the nap was then cut down with large hand shears. This process could be done wet or dry. Different finishes were obtained. With wet raising the fibres tended to be laid in something like a skin fashion and, when repeated several times, resulted in the production of a fabric that resembled a fine skin, as is indicated by the names given to such cloths, for example doeskin, moleskin and bearskin. This finish was used on most types of broadcloth but it should be emphasised that not all woollen cloths had this complicated finish. The lower priced types, the kerseys and the northern dozens, were usually well fulled and often had some degree of clothworking, frequently with the raising done dry.

With worsteds the wet process sequence was much simpler; the cloth was scoured, tentered and sheared so as to remove uneven surface hair. It should be stressed that this shearing served a different purpose to that in the woollen sequence. With worsted cloth the object was to remove as much surface fibre as possible so that the weave would show clearly and distinctively. With the exception of this difference in purpose, the dry processes with woollen and worsted cloths were similar. There followed a further inspection to remove any pieces of foreign matter remaining; the degree to which this inspection was carried out depended on the quality of the fabric and of course the faults that remained. Finally, there was the pressing.

At some point during this long clothmaking routine the material had to be dyed, unless of course it was wanted white, which was not common. Dyeing could be done on the raw material, the yarn or the cloth, or with worsteds on the top, although there is little evidence that this procedure, which later became popular, was done around 1770. All the other three stages were used, with raw material and piece dyeing the most common. There were obvious advantages to doing the various manufacturing processes in the white and then finally dyeing. White wool processes better than coloured wool and the waste made can more easily be utilised again. Against this, a piece of cloth can only be dyed one shade. Fancy effects are not possible and this, in fact, was the dividing line. Plain cloths were dyed in the piece; fancy cloths were dyed earlier. The dyeing process involved two distinctly separate skills, the mechanical and the chemical. As far as the former was concerned a simple container heated by a fire was all that was needed. The chemical side was more complicated, although the early dyers did not know much about it. They used craft methods which had evolved over long periods involving chemical reactions, only understood many years later. Of all the craftsmen working in the wool textile trade, the dyers had perhaps the most difficult job, particularly as many of the materials, mainly vegetable dyes, that they used needed involved dyeing routines. It is arguable that the dyers never received the credit that they deserved for obtaining the beautiful colours that they, in fact, achieved.

When one turns to consider the way in which these many processes of textile manufacture were carried out around 1770, we know now that this was at the end of a great tradition. Only a few of the inventions that were destined to change the industry had been made. Two series were of crucial importance. In 1737 Lewis Paul and James Wyatt made their first invention, which included the former's revolutionary idea of roller drafting and ten years later Paul invented a

mechanical card. But a few months earlier Daniel Bourn had patented a better machine, and thus was the true discoverer of the circular
card. With regard to the second series the 1760s witnessed the
progress made by Hargreaves, Arkwright and Crompton. Hargreaves' jenny came in 1764, Arkwright's first invention in 1769. But
none of this new technology had yet had any significant impact on
traditional methods. The slow processes of hand carding, combing
and spinning continued. Production from the big wheel was such that
a spinner of average woollen yarn could do little more than one
pound per day. It has been said that one weaver needed ten spinners
to keep him going and this is probably an underestimate.

Many problems must have arisen from the wide area the weaver or
clothier had to cover to get his yarn spun. Although they would
obviously have tried to get definite standards with the yarn, they must
often have received back work that varied in the two vital properties
of size and twist. Heaton makes the point well: 'The clothier asked for
a definite standard when giving out the wool to be spun, but the
tendency would be for each house and each spinner to vary a little in
the thickness and firmness of the yarn. Some sent it in "hard twisted",
others "soft twisted", and it was very difficult to reduce the yarn to
one standard.' And he quotes from the reminiscences of an octogen-
arian, J.N. Hall, recorded by James, adding: 'To express it in technical terms, some spun to 16 hanks per pound, others to 24 hanks.
When the manufacturer got his yarn back it had to be sorted and the
hard yarn used for warp, the soft for weft. There were two troubles,
one of size and the second of twist. These differences combined with
the delays the weavers endured accounted for the welcome the new
spinning machines received.'[24]

In weaving, the only development had been John Kay's flying
shuttle, patented in 1733. Previously the weaver had thrown the
shuttle through the shed by hand. Kay's invention replaced the hands
of the weavers by pickers, which hit the shuttle across, the momen-
tum coming from cords controlled by the weaver who sat upright at
the loom. The invention was particularly important when weaving
broadcloth as the assistant weaver was no longer needed. It is impossible to say how widely the new shuttle was used but it does appear
that, despite the fact that it was originally intended for the broad-
loom, narrow loom weavers, particularly in the West Riding, found it
advantageous and adopted it first. Two technical and a social reason
would appear to account for this. The flying shuttle made weaving a
more comfortable job and if, as appears likely, Kay also introduced
the idea of mounting the shuttle on wheels, this would have increased

the speed of weaving. From the evidence given to the 1806 inquiry it seems clear that the decade of the 1770s marked the general adoption of the flying shuttle in the West Riding. The West of England manufacturers were much slower to use it for broadcloth although they did introduce it on their narrow looms for making cassimeres.

The majority of the products of the wool textile trade went into the manufacture of apparel fabrics, but there has been a tendency to underestimate the amount of cloth that was used for other purposes, for furnishing fabrics for example. Some of the output of Norwich worsteds was used for this purpose in the more fashionable establishments. Most important, however, in the non-apparel field was the raw material used in carpet making. Carpets were originally knotted, although this type need not concern us here. The woven carpet was a common product of the hand loom but it was possible to use either woven or felted carpets in place of the traditional knotted type. Machine-woven carpets became the major section of the industry in the nineteenth century but in the previous century it is probable that many floor coverings, where they were used, were made of felts. The proper felt is made without any spinning or weaving. Layers of raw wool are obtained by taking carded material and treating it with pressure, while wet. It should be born in mind that felts have never been as widely used in Western Europe as they were, and are, in the Middle East or, to be more exact, in the vast area that lies south of the Caucasus. It is probable that the number of genuine felts made in the West was comparatively small. It became much more common to obtain a felt by first weaving the material and then so heavily fulling it that a cloth indistinguishable from felt was obtained. Many of the lower priced broadcloths were really fabrics of this type. They may well have had a much wider use for non-apparel purposes in the eighteenth century than is generally appreciated.

2 The Coming of the Factory System, 1770–1835

The Development of Mills and Factories in Yorkshire

Recent studies of Yorkshire and the West of England have documented in considerable detail the emergence of mill and factory production.[1] The beginnings of the movement away from domestic organisation have, however, received somewhat less attention in respect of the other textile districts. It was in the West Riding of Yorkshire that the first phase of the new mill system was established but its emergence came about in quite varied ways. Entrepreneurs from a broad range of backgrounds, mill premises both large and small and distinct differences in the organisation of business produced this variety.

The opportunities provided by new technical inventions and soaring demand throughout most of the 1780s and 1790s were an encouragement to change. Pressures built up in the domestic system causing bottlenecks and frustration. A particular pressure was on the fulling mills. The increasing demand for their services in the late 1760s and then again in the 1780s and 1790s caused problems for clothiers. They were forced to look further afield for mills available to do work for them and even then the work was often subject to long delay. Clothiers from south of Leeds, for example, had sometimes to travel to mills on the Wharfe, outside the woollen manufacturing area, to get cloth fulled.[2] Expansion in the number and size of fulling mills was taking place but not at the rate demanded by the trade. In 1780 there were approximately 104 fulling mills at work in the West Riding. By 1800 there were about 197.[3] In that same period the amount of broad cloth fulled rose threefold and narrow cloth by almost 100 per cent.

By 1800 very few of the Yorkshire fulling mills did not house the new scribbling and carding machinery. It is difficult to believe the small, pre-1770 fulling mills would have had the space for scribbling engines. It therefore seems likely that many of them were enlarged or rebuilt on a larger scale. The new mills were, of course, purpose built to contain new machinery and, in some instances, room for hand processes as well. The main wave of new building in the woollen industry in Yorkshire came between 1790 and 1801. In that period the number of steam or water powered scribbling mills increased from 36 to 243. And besides these there were an unknown number of hand, horse and wind powered mills. The majority, but not all, of the new scribbling mills also housed fulling stocks. The mills varied substantially in size. Some would have had just one or two scribbling machines, others 20 or more. Gott, at Bean Ing, Leeds, by the late 1790s had 38 scribbling and carding machines in his factory; but the average number of machines per mill was probably nearer six to eight.[4]

Contemporary commentators attempted to make a distinction between a mill and a factory in the West Riding woollen trade, describing a mill as a place where the miller did work for others on commission and not for himself, whereas a factory was a place where the occupier worked on his own account. But this distinction is far from satisfactory because it is apparent that many scribbling millers did some work for themselves and many factory occupiers would also do commission work.

The first of the new scribbling mills was at work in West Yorkshire by the mid-1770s. Initial development was hesitant. By 1785 there appear to have been less than 20, by 1789 only 36. But in the following ten years their numbers increased six-fold and their capacity improved, especially with the building of much larger mills from 1792 onwards. No particular pattern seems to emerge from the geographical location of the mills in the first ten years of their existence. The early ones were dotted about the West Riding in most of the parishes. There is little to suggest that the earliest development took place on the western fringes of the county closer to the source, in Lancashire, of new technology. In the 1790s, however, perhaps the most rapid growth was in the broadcloth area south and southwest of Leeds, including the Calder Valley from Wakefield upstream to Brighouse. In Leeds itself the building of the large factories of Messrs. Wormald, Fountain and Gott, Fisher and Nixon, and others in the 1790s brought a new dimension to the industry.

Unlike in the West of England, there is not a great deal of evidence to suggest the widespread existence of large pre-machinery or machinery workshops. There is the occasional reference to quite large buildings housing hand processes but few clothiers seem to have been large enough to consider such investment necessary. The different scale of organisation between Yorkshire and the West of England undoubtedly explains their absence from Yorkshire. However, the building of new mills for scribbling did, in many instances, provide the opportunity to bring domestic labour and hand processes into the mill premises with, so it has often been argued, the benefit of control over the quantity and quality of labour, the saving of time and money previously needed to transport materials and finished products to and from outworkers and the reduction of fraud in the use of wool and yarn. The other side of the coin, the fact that the workers had to walk a long way to factories and thereby lost time they could profitably have been using for producing cloth at home, seems to have been somewhat ignored. There are, incidentally, many examples of jennies and hand looms being used in Yorkshire mills before the spinning and weaving processes were mechanised.[5]

The growth of mills in the Yorkshire worsted industry came very much more slowly and only 22 were in operation by 1800. The problems involved in operating Arkwright's water frame meant that it was some years after its initial trials that worsted manufacturers were convinced of its usefulness. The first attempts were made just over the Yorkshire boundary in Lancashire where, at Dolphineholme in 1784, three partners, Thomas Edmondson, a Mr Addison and a Mr Satterthwaite built a mill, to be powered by horses and water, 'intending to carry out in worsted that which had been accomplished in cotton by the aid of machinery'. Technical difficulties were slow to be overcome, the partners quarrelled and in 1791 the mill closed. It was re-opened four years later with larger and improved frames and with much more success.[6] The first recorded spinning of worsted by water power in Yorkshire was at Low Mill, Addingham in 1787 in a building which had originally been intended for cotton spinning. Within a few years other mills had been opened in the Calder Valley, the Worth Valley and in Leeds. Perhaps a reason for the slow development of worsted mills before the end of the eighteenth century was that the industry was substantially centred on Bradford but that town was very ill supplied with water for power and also had to face labour opposition to the new factory system. Bradford township's first mill was not built until 1800.[7]

The beginnings of the factory system did have some implications for the location of the various branches of the wool textile industry. Many of the outlying worsted districts declined, Masham for example. For a while there was a greater growth of the worsted industry around Halifax as a result of the lack of water power and the problems of labour opposition in Bradford. The worsted industry had, however, to compete for mill sites with both the cotton and woollen industries in much of Halifax parish and there is evidence of considerable substitution of use of mill buildings in that area, presumably as a result of fluctuations in activity in the various textile trades.

From the building boom of the 1790s to the end of the Napoleonic War seems to have been a difficult period for mill owners and tenants. Although between 1801 and 1815 the amount of broad cloth milled did rise from 264,000 pieces to 330,000 pieces, narrow cloth production remained fairly static. Many new woollen mills were brought into use during the period. Some 71 have been accounted for but in spite of this there were about 19 fewer mills at work in 1815 compared with 1801. Even making some allowance for the problems of identification of mills and the dating of their entry to and exit from the industry, it still seems most likely that many mills failed, went out of use or were converted to other processes in this period. Some woollen mills were converted to worsted manufacture, for example Laister Dyke Mill at Bradford in 1809. Other mills were changed to flax or cotton manufacturing or for other uses such as corn milling or wire drawing. The broadcloth accounts suggest that the years 1807 to 1809 and 1811 were years of mill closures. In those four years eight fulling mills in the Aire Valley and two in the Calder Valley closed and closures may have been more common in the narrow cloth areas where trade was even less satisfactory.[8]

The situation was rather different in the worsted branch of the industry. Very little worsted spinning was being carried out in mills by 1800 but in the next 15 years the number of mills increased from about 22 to about 54. Much of this expansion was in the parish of Bradford and particularly in the township itself. There were six worsted mills in Bradford parish by 1800 but 39 by 1820. The number of worsted mills also increased in Halifax parish and at Bingley and Keighley. The latter town saw considerable mill building and from about 1810 the widespread conversion of its earlier cotton mills to worsted spinning. The worsted mills built in this period were larger and their location was rather more concentrated. Some of the remoter mills were converted to other uses. Addingham Mills, for example, were changed to flax spinning.[9]

Although there may have been a burst of woollen mill building activity in 1815 and 1816 it was not until 1819 that widespread mill development recommenced. Between that year and 1835 about 160 new mills came into operation with busy periods of building for much of the 1820s, less activity in 1831 and 1832 and then renewed growth from 1833. This was also a period of increased size of mills. By the late 1820s powered spinning was beginning to be carried out in woollen mills using the mule, although it was not until the 1830s that the mule began to compete seriously with the jenny in the woollen industry. The incorporation of powered spinning in mills stimulated the increase in their size and also perhaps persuaded manufacturers to more fully integrate their processes, by bringing more of their hand labour under the mill roof. Large scale mill building progressed, particularly in Huddersfield and the Colne Valley and in the Leeds district in the 1820s. Starkey's Mill at Longroyde Bridge, Huddersfield, built in 1819, was one of the first of the large mills in this new phase of development. By 1835 its insurance policies show the impressive range of new machinery it was housing including 96 pairs of power looms, and 16 pairs of narrow hand looms, 26 scribbling and carding engines, many mules, cutting machines, hydraulic presses, powered and hand billeys, jennies and gigs. Starkey's Mill was undoubtedly far better equipped than most. It was also substantially larger, with insured fixed capital of about £24,000, probably more than six times the average for mills in the West Riding woollen industry as a whole. In 1833–4 Starkey's were employing 521 workers and using 84 steam horse power, whereas the average for the West Riding woollen industry as a whole in 1835 was 58 workers and 20 horse power per mill.[10]

A profile of the distribution of size of woollen mills by employment is available for Yorkshire for 1833 from the *Report from the Commissioners on the Employment of Children in Factories*.[11] Very few woollen mills employed more than 75 workers, the majority having a workforce of under 50. The commissioners did not, however, receive replies to their enquiries from even the majority of mill owners and a comparison of the employment figures for 1833 with those in the Factory Returns in 1835 suggests that a preponderance of larger mills are included in the former statistics.

The growth of the number of worsted mills in the Yorkshire industry progressed fairly steadily between 1815 and 1835. In general there seem to have been somewhat fewer fluctuations in the rate of mill development in the worsted trade. The number of worsted mills increased from 54 to 204. The beginnings of the incorporation of power loom weaving in mills from the 1820s probably meant an increase in the average size of mills. In 1835 the 204 mills had an average of 82 workers and used an average of 19 horse power.[12] In terms of employment they were therefore substantially larger than their woollen counterparts. Estimates of replacement value of fixed capital for both woollen and worsted mills also suggest a substantial increase in size between 1815 and 1835, particularly when falling building and machinery costs are taken into account.[13]

Factory Growth and Investment

Detailed estimates have been produced of fixed capital formation in the Yorkshire woollen and worsted industry from 1770 to 1835. The estimates were arrived at by an attempt to trace all mills working in the period and by the use of insurance policies to calculate the replacement cost of fixed capital, adjustments being made to allow for non-insured capital and the predominance of larger mills amongst post-1820 insurance policies issued by the large London fire insurance companies, notably the Sun Fire Office. The figures shown in Table 2 suggest that the fixed capital stock of the Yorkshire

Table 2   Fixed capital stock and formation in the West Riding wool textile industry, 1780–1835

Date	No. of mills working	Total value of fixed capital (£ thousand)	Annual average net fixed capital formation over previous 5 years (£ thousand)
1780	5	5	–
1785	19	19	2.8
1790	50	50	6.2
1795	126	167	23.4
1800	243	401	46.8
1805	268	556	31.0
1810	258	645	17.8
1815	278	751	21.1
1820	327	948	39.5
1825	404	1273	64.9
1830	493	1676	80.7
1835	610	2227	110.1

SOURCE: D. T. Jenkins, *The West Riding Wool Textile Industry, 1770–1835*, 1975, Ch. 5.

industry, valued at current prices, was approximately £2.25 million in 1835. This figure takes no account of fixed capital in domestic workshops, finishing shops or in fulling mills not used for any other mechanised process. Moreover it excludes warehousing not on mill sites and all other fixed capital not directly associated with the factory industry. The estimates suggest the peak periods of investment were in the 1790s and from the end of the Napoleonic War period.[14]

The compact geographical confines of the Yorkshire textile district and the volume of insurance policies, parliamentary reports and topographical literature enable mills to be identified and counted with relative ease. The identification of mills scattered through most other counties of Britain is far more complex. It is conceivable that an accumulation of detailed local studies will in time enable a jigsaw to be pieced together. At present only some preliminary assessment of fixed capital investment in the industry is possible. By using the Yorkshire estimates for 1835 and relating them to power and labour employed the resultant Yorkshire capital:power and capital:labour ratios can then be applied nationally, using the factory inspectors' estimates of labour employed and of power, the latter being adjusted to allow for those counties where horse power was not recorded. Thus on the basis of employment of 40,376 workers in Yorkshire, average fixed capital per head was about £55. Equating this to national employment produces a fixed capital stock estimate of almost £4 million. The similar calculation based on horse power produces a figure of about £4.6 million.

To convert the 1835 capital stock estimates to capital formation figures requires some estimate of the growth in number and size of mills in the different regions. Rough calculations are more easy for some areas than others as a result of the local studies available and the varying comprehensiveness of the coverage of the data in the *Supplementary Reports of the Central Board of His Majesty's Commissioners Appointed to Collect Information in the Manufacturing Districts, as to the Employment of Children in Factories, and also the Propriety and Means of Curtailing the Hours of the Labour* in 1834. Estimates of the growth of mill numbers are shown in Table 3. This indicates for each area the number of mills in use at the end of each five year period, the number of new mills that had come into use during the previous five years and the number of mills that had gone out of use.

The estimate for Scotland takes as its starting point the 90 mills recorded in 1835.[15] It is, of course, possible that this figure is on the low side because of the isolated situation of some mills and the possible lack of knowledge by the factory inspector of their existence. The same closure rate of mills in the industry is assumed as for Yorkshire. Dates of establishment of 24 mills are provided by the

Table 3   Estimated development of wool textile mills in Britain, 1780–1835

		1780	1785	1790	1795	1800	1805	1810	1815	1820	1825	1830	1835
Yorkshire	A	5	19	50	16	23	268	258	278	327	404	493	610
	B	5	14	33	81	124	58	41	33	57	92	98	117
	C	—	—	2	5	7	33	51	13	8	15	9	—
Lancashire and Cheshire	A	1	4	10	25	48	54	52	56	65	81	99	122
	B	1	3	6	16	25	13	8	7	11	19	20	23
	C	—	—	—	1	2	7	10	3	2	3	2	—
Gloucestershire and Hereford	A	—	1	2	12	24	37	50	70	99	109	119	120
	B	—	1	1	12	15	16	16	25	36	12	12	1
	C	—	—	2	2	3	3	3	5	7	2	2	—
S.W., S. and Eastern Counties	A	—	—	5	36	82	100	149	175	189	193	198	202
	B	—	—	6	38	57	22	61	32	17	5	6	5
	C	—	—	1	7	11	4	12	6	3	1	1	1
Midlands	A	—	3	5	9	10	10	10	10	12	13	16	19
	B	—	3	3	5	1	—	—	—	2	1	4	4
	C	—	—	1	—	—	—	—	—	2	—	1	1
Northern Counties	A	—	1	3	8	15	17	16	17	20	25	31	37
	B	—	1	2	5	8	4	2	2	4	6	6	8
	C	—	—	—	—	1	2	3	1	1	1	—	1
Wales	A	—	—	2	4	18	29	53	71	82	90	95	97
	B	—	—	2	2	18	14	30	22	14	10	6	3
	C	—	—	—	—	4	3	6	4	3	2	1	1
Scotland	A	—	—	—	4	8	19	42	53	57	73	85	90
	B	—	—	—	5	5	14	31	14	5	19	15	6
	C	—	—	—	1	1	3	8	3	1	3	3	1
Totals	A	6	28	77	224	448	534	630	730	851	988	1136	1297
	B	6	23	53	164	253	141	189	135	146	164	167	166
	C	—	1	4	17	29	55	93	35	25	27	19	5

A = mills in use.   B = new mills per quinquennium.   C = mills out of use per quinquennium.

1834 Supplementary Reports. It is assumed in order to produce the estimate that these 24 mills were representative of all and thus numbers of mills in use every five years were calculated on a proportionate basis.

For the four northern counties, where 37 mills were counted in 1835, the same closure rate is assumed and definite or approximate dates of establishment have been determined for 17. The rest are presumed to have been estimated at dates proportionate to the 17. Very little information is available about Lancashire and Cheshire mills. In 1835 there was one mill there for every five in Yorkshire. This relationship has been assumed to have been constant since the 1780s. For the Midland counties, consisting of part of Derbyshire, Nottinghamshire, part of Staffordshire, Leicestershire, Warwickshire and Lincolnshire, there is reason to believe that the factory returns are incomplete. From the 1834 Supplementary Reports and work by Dr S.D. Chapman, the date of establishment for 13 mills can be gauged.[16] A closure rate similar to that in Yorkshire is assumed and rate of establishment of the other mills is based on the 13 for which information is available.

Trends in the establishment of the 97 Welsh mills, again probably not a complete count, are based on 61 identified in J.G. Jenkins' detailed study of the Welsh industry. Calculations for the southern and south western counties rely heavily on K. Rogers' study of Wiltshire and the Frome district of Somerset and on the 1834 Supplementary Reports. These two sources enable 111 mills to be identified. There was a higher exit rate than in Yorkshire as one might expect, bearing in mind the state of the West Country woollen industry. Trends in eastern and south-eastern England, London, the South Midlands and Oxfordshire are assumed to have followed those identified for Somerset and Wiltshire. The evidence for Gloucestershire and Herefordshire where 120 mills were identified in 1835 is based on Dr J. Tann's study of the former county, which allows the history of about 100 mills to be traced.[17]

With so many assumptions necessary the results cannot be taken as more than a very rough estimate but arguably they give some indication of the development of the factory industry in Britain. They suggest that mill development in Yorkshire was substantially ahead of other areas in the 1780s and 1790s. In 1790 almost two-thirds of the new mills were in Yorkshire. But more rapid mill development elsewhere in the early years of the next century resulted in only about two-fifths of mills working being in Yorkshire immediately after the end of the Napoleonic Wars. During the 1820s mill development

Table 4 *Estimated fixed capital stock in wool textile mills, 1780–1835 (£ thousand at current prices)*

	1780	1785	1790	1795	1800	1805	1810	1815	1820	1825	1830	1835
Yorkshire	5	19	50	167	401	556	645	751	948	1273	1676	2227
Lancashire and Cheshire	1	3	7	24	58	81	94	112	137	186	248	329
Gloucestershire and Hereford	—	1	2	16	41	78	125	189	287	349	405	444
S.W., S. and Eastern Counties	—	—	3	32	95	143	253	322	372	419	457	509
Midlands	—	1	2	5	7	8	10	11	13	17	21	27
Northern Counties	—	—	1	4	11	15	18	20	22	33	43	59
Wales	—	—	—	1	4	7	16	23	29	34	39	43
Scotland	—	—	—	3	8	23	50	85	97	139	170	198
Totals	6	24	65	252	625	911	1211	1513	1905	2450	3059	3836
Annual average net fixed capital formation per quinquennium	—	4	8	37	75	57	60	60	78	109	122	155
Gross formation	—	5	11	47	103	109	132	153	185	158	320	407

again occurred more rapidly in Yorkshire to the extent that by 1835 almost half of the mills then operating were based in the county. When one takes into account mill size as measured by employment, Yorkshire predominated, accounting for 57 per cent of mill workers in 1835.

To convert mill numbers into estimates of fixed capital stock it was necessary to assume that the variance in size in 1835, as measured by employment, was proportionately constant going back in time. Thus, for example, whereas average employment in Yorkshire mills in 1835 was 66, the number was only 8 in Wales and 39 in Scotland. Thus, by taking average fixed capital every fifth year for Yorkshire mills and by adjusting the figure for each region according to the proportionate difference in size in 1835, the regional average value was converted into a fixed capital stock total for each period. Annual average net fixed capital formation was then calculable for each five year period. The results are shown in Table 4.

The conversion of the net figures to gross investment depends on the extent to which one should assume that capital was depreciating. Early contemporary estimates are not available but there is a range of examples of practices used later in the nineteenth century for various types of mills. One of the earliest is for Marshall's flax mill at Leeds. Between 1829 and 1841 machinery there was written down at 7.5 per cent annually. The allowance was increased to 10 per cent between 1842 and 1857 but a revaluation of machinery in the latter year indicated that 7.5 per cent was more realistic.[18] At Black Dyke Mills buildings were depreciated at 2.5 per cent annually in the 1840s, machinery at an annual average of 12.2 per cent in the 1840s and 12.3 per cent in the 1850s, and the engine and shafting at very variable rates in the 1840s, but averaging at 2 per cent.[19] In the 1860s Messrs. Wormalds and Walker wrote down machinery at 7.5 or 10 per cent and, after that date, there are many other examples available of the value of buildings being depreciated by 2.5 per cent and machinery by 7.5 per cent to 15 per cent.[20] Income tax officials allowed 2.5 per cent on buildings and 7.5 per cent on machinery for the 'Oldham Limiteds', although elsewhere they would sometimes allow as much as 10 per cent on machinery.[21] The worsted spinning firm of Oates Brothers of Halifax depreciated their mill buildings at 2.5 per cent and their engine at 5 per cent in the 1880s.[22] The woollen firm of W. & E. Crowther of Slaithwaite allowed 2.5 per cent on buildings and 12.5 per cent on machinery in the 1870s.[23] Other similar practices are also recorded. An early accounting text book for textile manufacturers recommended a series of rates 'compiled from the author's experience'; the recommendation for buildings was from 2.5 per cent and for plant and machinery from 5 to 10 per cent. Motive plant was rated as 5 to 7.5 per cent.[24]

Considering the nature of early machinery it would seem appropriate to take somewhat higher figures for depreciation in this earlier period. It is therefore assumed that realistic allowances might be 2.5 per cent for buildings, 10 per cent for machinery and 5 per cent for power plant. Insurance valuations suggest that these items accounted for roughly 27, 9 and 59 per cent of capital respectively, allowing 5 per cent for site preparation.[25] Thus an annual rate of 7 per cent for depreciation of fixed capital in the industry would seem to be the appropriate figure to use to convert the net investment figures to gross estimates.

Regrettably, for the period before the 1830s, it is very difficult to make progress in the calculation of total capital formation in the industry. The size of the domestic sector is unknown, the relationship between fixed and circulating capital in the factory industry is only known for a very few firms for occasional years. Figures worked out by one of the authors for the West of England and by Dr Gulvin for Scotland do reach reasonable agreement.[26] They suggest that fixed capital represented about 20 to 25 per cent of the total capital. There were obviously great differences between individual firms. In addition, assessments of circulating capital are complicated by some manufacturing firms engaged in merchanting and thus possibly having disproportionately high assets in circulating capital. This was the case with Gotts of Leeds, whose co-partnership accounts are available. Other entrepreneurial activities are sometimes inseparable in available accounts.

A firm for which some information is available is Messrs Fosters of Black Dyke Mills, Queensbury. Between 1837 and 1852 fixed capital varied between 19 and 41 per cent of their total assets, averaging 29 per cent.[27] But Fosters were a somewhat exceptional firm. They engaged in merchanting and their integrated nature and high degree of mechanisation presumably affected their capital stock. It seems likely that in the smaller mill, the scribbling mill of the woollen industry, for example, fixed capital was of more significance, and it is also probable that in the industry as a whole, fixed capital was progressively becoming more and more important as factory production developed.

There are several overall contemporary estimates for the value of the total capital stock in the industry in about 1800. Christopher Rawden of Halifax, using his own works as a basis, considered the total national capital stock was £6.5 million. Gott of Leeds estimated £5.1 million, again based on the experience of his own works. He and Rawden believed that capital stock was one-third the value of output. John Ratcliffe of Saddleworth agreed with this ratio and Joseph Lewis of Stroud estimated a somewhat similar value of capital stock of £6.1 million. These estimates formed the basis of Edward Law's speech in the House of Lords on 1 May 1800, where he stated: 'The property computed to be engaged in this trade is one-third of the total value of the goods made in the course of a year, and assuming that to be £18,600,000, the total of that capital may be fairly estimated at £6 million sterling.'[28] A comparison of these contemporary estimates for total capital with the estimates of fixed capital in Table 4 suggests that the fixed capital of the factory industry did not amount to much more than 10 per cent of total capital in the industry at that date.

Entrepreneurship and Capital Supply

Generalisation about the sources of supply of entrepreneurship and capital is far from easy. But research in progress will, hopefully, before long produce a much clearer picture.[29] In both Yorkshire and the West of England the majority of the new factory entrepreneurs had had previous connections with the industry, generally through involvement in its domestic organisation. Many of them were able to bring with them financial resources previously gained in the industry. The scale and methods of organisation of domestic manufacture were undoubtedly an influence on the scale and sources of supply of capital for factory development.

For example in the Yorkshire woollen industry where domestic organisation was on a relatively small scale, the joint stock or company mill developed a particular importance:

> From the first introduction of machinery the clothiers united to build mills in shares. At first a few and on a small scale as experiments by the more enterprising, then more extensively as the success of their neighbours, and the increase of trade, naturally and gradually led to the extension of the system up to the present time. The numerous woollen mills scattered throughout the populous clothing villages of the West Riding are principally owned and occupied by the clothiers.[30]

Although there is no way of determining the number of company mills they were of substantial importance within Yorkshire from the 1790s. They did not emerge in other areas. One of the earliest, the Ossett Mill Company founded in 1785 is well documented. It was established by a number of local clothiers who subscribed to the building of the mill; 35 persons purchased 44 shares at £50 each to provide capital. Further money was raised through loans and mortgages and at various times the mill, which was used for fulling, scribbling and, later, spinning and weaving, was operated by the shareholders or let to tenants. The Ossett Mill Company survived until the 1890s.[31]

Such company mills were operated in a variety of ways. Some were built or rented to provide fulling and powered scribbling and carding for their shareholders. They would also take in the work of others. Some companies included shareholders who did not need the services of the mill personally, some let their mill to be worked by others. It was said in 1844 that the company mill was not the exception but the rule, and that many small clothiers had shares in mills. Some clothiers had shares in more than one mill. A detailed description of how they were established was given to the Committee on Joint Stock Companies in 1844:

> When the shareholders are numerous, say forty (they seldom exceed but often amount to that number) they subscribe £50 per share in the first instance; they then buy the land and proceed with the building; they next borrow on mortgage the largest amount they can gain credit for, which will generally pay for the building and steam engine; the machinery is obtained on credit. If the times are good they will generally succeed not only in working off their incumbrances, but in raising the condition of the clothiers themselves. But when the speculation is soon followed by bad harvests and consequent bad times, they not infrequently get into great difficulties.
>
> When smaller numbers unite to build, larger sums are subscribed. Similar companies are also formed to rent and occupy mills already built. Sometimes the parties are reduced in number by death, by retiring from business, and other causes when the shares are bought in or sold to other clothiers and sometimes these mills are under these circumstances let to newly formed companies.[32]

The company mills were run by the shareholders or a Committee of them. The Gill Royds Mill Company at Morley met regularly at a local inn and fined non-attenders. The company mill committees determined prices, employed someone to run the mill and decided on operating methods.[33] Their legal position was difficult; common law did not recognise them and there were regular problems of fraud which at times made their survival precarious.

The joint stock company allowed the small clothiers to gain a foothold in the new industrial system. Larger clothiers were able to own or rent their own mills to do their own work or they would enter into partnership with someone else as, for example, Rogerson and Lord of Bramley, the former of whom kept a detailed diary of their activities from 1808 to 1814.[34] They, like many others, were wholly or mainly dependent on commission work, scribbling, carding, fulling and dyeing for others. They did not consider themselves manufacturers initially, although many of them in due course added jennies, mules and then looms to their machinery and began to work more and more for themselves as the small clothiers on whom they relied (and who relied on them) gradually declined in number.

Besides the money that clothiers were able to generate themselves, initial capital for mill development in the woollen industry arrived in a multitude of ways. Landowners on occasion played a major role. Lord Dartmouth, for example, was responsible for the building of 23 textile mills on his estates in Yorkshire by 1805, making good use of building materials from his land and power from his streams.[35] Some other landowners were similarly involved in speculative mill building. Many of the worsted mills in Bradford were built as speculations by industrialists and others not immediately connected with the worsted trade.[36]

There is more debate about the role of mercantile capital. Dr Wilson has shown that, with the notable exception of the firm of Wormald, Fountaine and Gott, Leeds merchants were loath to enter manufacturing, although they did of course provide the capital for the finishing branch of the industry.[37] Many instances exist of merchants owning mills and letting them to manufacturers rather than becoming merchant manufacturers themselves. But they were in the minority. It was much more common perhaps for manufacturers to enter merchanting than for merchants to become involved with manufacturing.

Merchants from other trades also entered the wool textile industry. Corn and seed merchants, stone merchants and linen merchants sometimes became involved. Fixed capital finance was also provided by other industrial interests. There are cases of millwrights, engineers and manufacturers in other trades, corn millers and wire drawers for example, joining the industry. Fixed capital was transferred in and out by mill owners and entrepreneurs regularly changing the use of the premises. Advertisements for partners with capital were not infrequent in the newspapers.

It is becoming clearer that the banks played a greater role in the provision of fixed capital than has hitherto been supposed.[38] By, for example, allowing short term loans to be regularly renewed as a matter of course manufacturers were able to use bank loans for longer term investment and not just for circulating capital. There were many other ways by which money for investment in mills and machinery could be raised. Credit on the purchase of building materials, machinery and steam engines could enable some return from the investment to be made before payment. Entrepreneurs often called on friends, relatives, business, social and church contacts. The mortgage of land and property was undoubtedly an important source of funds, as the volumes in the West Riding Registry of Deeds bear witness.

The extent to which the new factory entrepreneurs looked to outside sources for their initial fixed capital is unknown. It may well be that only those who had established business connections and reputations were able to call on a wide range of outside sources and that, bearing in mind the small size of the early mills, the majority of the entrepreneurs had to depend largely on the resources of themselves and their families. Certainly there is the impression that later manufacturers, as a matter of course, attempted to rely on their own resources for further investment in mill extensions or the installation of new machinery.

The provision of circulating capital was a greater problem for manufacturers and they almost inevitably had to depend on outside funds. Fixed and circulating capital needs and supply cannot be completely separated. The ease with which finance for one could be obtained would affect the allocation of other financial resources. By early in the nineteenth century the banks were undoubtedly performing a major role. The evidence from bank records, the balance sheets of individual firms and the consequences of bank failures clearly indicate this.[39] But the key to the provision of circulating capital was credit, and the relative lengths of credit in each stage of the process from the purchase of raw materials to the final sale of the finished product determined the adequacy of supply of circulating capital to manufacturers. As was to be shown later in the nineteenth century, in times of great business activity manufacturers were able to depend entirely on credit to finance their manufacturing activity. When credit supply tightened or when raw material values or finished product prices suddenly fell they were often faced with disaster. The prudent, responsible manufacturer therefore built up and used his own resources for a proportion of his circulating capital needs.

Lengths and methods of credit are a recurrent theme in the contemporary discussion of the progress and problems of the industry throughout the nineteenth century. The amount and extent of credit a woolstapler could and would grant must have been a major influence on manufacturing activity. As is discussed later, the length and price of credit that manufacturers had to give to buyers would be crucial to their business prosperity. At different periods and in different branches customary credit arrangements developed which at times weighed down manufacturers with an insurmountable burden.

Raw Material Supply

Between 1775 and 1830, the great dispersion of the merino sheep, which in the nineteenth century brought wide changes to the raw material supply of the industry, was the major development and one which considerably changed the wool textile trade of the nineteenth and twentieth centuries.

After the successful protectionist policy lasting for several centuries, merino sheep from Spain were exported and the first major dispersion took place in 1765 when the King of Spain gave three hundred merino sheep to his relative, Prince Xavier, Elector of Saxony. They were placed at a stud farm, carefully guarded, developed by selection and before long they were producing wool that was considerably finer than the Spanish. These Saxony wools were superfine merinos of 70s quality and upwards and some indication of their excellence is shown by the fact that superfine woollen suitings have ever since been known as Saxony suitings. These wools were ideal for heavily milled woollen cloths and, as finally developed with their very distinctive crimp, have never been surpassed for this purpose. Later Australian wools, although as fine in quality, had slightly different properties which made them ideally suited for combing, but this was a mid-nineteenth century development. During the period covered here, the development of the merino in Saxony and nearby countries, was important because it increased, though at first only slightly, the supply of merino wool available and produced after some years of careful breeding, a much finer wool extending, as already indicated, the fineness range available to 80s and beyond. Ultimately and most valuable of all, it provided the merino sheep for the newly discovered wool lands of Australia, thereby increasing the quality of merino wool available to the manufacturer. The age-long problem of having an adequate supply of fine wool was solved.

Something should also be said about the dispersion of the Spanish merino in so far as it affected the availability of specific types of fine wools. In central Europe, the Elector of Saxony's move was followed by many others. Frederick II of Prussia imported some and thereby started the Silesian fine merino wool growing trade. Maria Theresia, in one of her several attempts to bring the production of fine wool cloth to the Austrian Empire, introduced them into Hungary which became an important centre of merino wool growing and one where it lasted considerably longer than elsewhere in Central Europe. All these wools were very similar in type but had distinctive differences and manufacturers certainly had their preferences, perhaps influenced mostly by what they were used to. It is also necessary to emphasise how many there were.[40] By 1802 there were said to be four million pure merino sheep east of the Rhine. The effect of this on merino wool production can easily be seen. Meanwhile France obtained 383 sheep and established a merino stud at Rambouillet, where the descendants of these sheep can still be seen, but this move had little or no effect on the British supply, the wool going mainly to French manufacturers. The same point applied even more strongly to exports of the merino sheep further afield, for example, to Sweden and later to Russia. America also introduced the merino sheep and the United States was a leading centre for many years but most of the wool produced was, of course, used there. The French Rambouillet was a rather larger animal than the Saxony or Silesian merino and produced somewhat coarser wool. This wool was also longer and possibly this could have had some effect on the more successful early development of the combing of merino wools in France than in England, although the main reason for this lay in the different types of combs and spinning methods that were introduced.

As far as Britain was concerned the merino's arrival here was thought to be important and in one respect it was, as many of the sheep that came were transferred to Australia, but the large import of Spanish merinos had surprisingly little basic effect on the native wool supply. During the first decades of the nineteenth century, the British manufacturer when he wanted merino wool still used Spanish for the 60–64s range of qualities and the Saxony or Silesian for the finer 70–80s.

Although as yet the effect on the wool supply position was negligible, it was during these years that the great movement of the merino sheep to Australia began. In 1797 Captain Waterhouse was sent to Cape Town to obtain provisions for the penal settlement; he also purchased 32 merinos and they formed the first flocks, particularly those which Captain MacArthur bought. MacArthur was the key figure in the early history of the sheep there and he made further purchases from George III's flock at Kew.[41] Despite many obstacles, mostly official, these sheep prospered and by the end of the period considered here, were beginning to have their first effect on the wool supply position of the British industry. This great development was financed entirely by British capital and the main people who led the move came from this country. And, once the nineteenth century was reached, the moves into Australia were increasingly financed by banks and by wealthy English landowners who saw the opportunities that lay ahead.

German wool first came into the country around the turn of the century. Henry Hughes stated at the House of Lords inquiry of 1828:

> I believe the first wool which was imported to this country was in 1800 or 1801. I was in Germany myself in 1803 and recollect sending some wool from Leipzig to London at that period but there had been some shipped before I shipped any myself. It was a new trade to this country: and the manufacturers for some years refused to use any of them at all because they were dirty, and they had to that period of time been accustomed to use only Spanish wools which were imported into this country washed and cleaned at different places in Spain ... but latterly the importation of German wools has been double or treble that of Spanish wools.[42]

As might be expected with a new trade, several different methods of importing were possible. In some cases manufacturers bought direct; William Playne, a West Country clothier, went himself to the sales at Dresden and Breslau and clearly enjoyed his visits.[43] Hughes was a merchant and it seems likely that the main quantities of German wool were purchased through merchants, as was Spanish wool. Later the wool sales at Hamburg took on considerable importance.

The methods of home supply of wool continued as before. The influence of Bakewell and Ellman spread ever wider and supply continued to rise. The expanding industry was still able to get by far the largest proportion of its supplies of raw material from the home grower. The wool reached the user in one of three ways. It was purchased either direct from·the grower, through the English wool sales or through a wool merchant or stapler, the last method being the most common. The main disadvantage of the manufacturer buying direct from the farmer was that the average grower would want to sell his whole clip at one time for cash and this clip would not have been sorted, often not even classed, and contained a number of different types of wool, many of which would be quite unsuitable for the purposes the manufacturer had in mind. It would, therefore, seem likely that only a comparatively small part of the farmer's wools were

Table 5 Wool imports, 1775–1834 (million lbs.)

Annual averages	Total	From Spain and Portugal	From Germany	From Australasia
1775–9	1.5	1.5	—	—
1780–4	1.9	1.9	—	—
1785–9	3.2	3.2	—	—
1790–4	3.4	3.4	—	—
1795–9	4.1	3.8	—	—
1800–4	7.5	6.5	0.4	—
1805–9	7.4	6.2	0.4	—
1810–4	9.6	7.5	1.8	—
1815–9	16.1	7.2	5.8	0.1
1820–4	18.1	5.6	15.9	0.3
1825–9	28.1	4.7	20.0	1.1
1830–4	35.3	3.4	24.0	2.8

NOTES: England and Wales, 1775–91; Great Britain, 1792–1816; United Kingdom, 1816–34.
Spain and Portugal includes Gibraltar, Azores, Madeira and Canaries. Tiny quantities from Australia are recorded from 1806.
Germany includes Prussia and Netherlands.

SOURCES:B. R. Mitchell with P. Deane, *Abstract of British Historical Statistics*, 1962, pp. 191–2; *Report from the S.C. of the House of Lords on the State of the British Wool Trade*, 1828, *BPP.*, 1828 (H.L. 515) VIII, Appendix Table I.

sold direct to the manufacturer. The wool staplers and merchants were therefore the main original purchasers.

The English wool sales had long been a distinctive feature of the trade. They were normally used by the wool staplers and merchants but when clips came from large farmers, who had done some kind of classing, manufacturers could, and would, purchase. Indeed, the wider range offered made it more practical for a manufacturer or comber to buy at these sales than from individual farmers. He also had less travelling to do. However, more important to a manufacturer were the supplies he obtained from the wool staplers, whose importance to the trade in the period considered here cannot be over-estimated. They were a knowledgeable group of men and the evidence they gave at the various parliamentary inquiries gives a good picture of their work. Heaton quotes Hustler, one of the most famous Bradford staplers, who, in his evidence in 1800, said that he was accustomed to buy wool in 19 different counties while his partners and agents bought in at least another 14.[44] Wool staplers tended to be fairly substantial businessmen and through their ability and willingness to extend credit to purchasers of wool, provided perhaps the most important source of working capital for manufacturers.

These three main sources of supply accounted for most of the wool used, but there were other methods. As Heaton pointed out, every manufacturing town had its market where the small clothier could buy a hundred or so fleeces, but only small amounts of wool were sold in this way.[45] Buying English wool in the late eighteenth century appears to have been the more pleasant side of wool textile manufacturing. Contemporary comments and poetry illustrate the enjoyment manufacturers experienced in setting out to buy wool.

As the work done by the agricultural improvers was largely aimed at producing better mutton, it naturally followed that more and more of this British wool was essentially a by-product of this meat-producing industry. These wools were usually known as skin wools. They tended to cover all the types previously indicated. In quality they were similar to fleece wools but tended to be shorter. Sheep being bred for mutton would be killed when the meat was at its best. The length of the wool was a secondary consideration. It could be anything from three to twelve months' growth and would often be lambs' wool which would also mean short wool. Very little skin wool was therefore of use for worsteds but it certainly added a valuable extra source of supply for the woollen section. All skin wool was supplied through wool staplers. An additional source of raw material was wool waste. Here the great expansion occurred later in the nineteenth century but noils, the short fibres removed during combing, were known and were used for the lower priced types of woollen cloths.

The major extension in the use of other animal fibres – alpaca, mohair, camel hair and cashmere – came in the nineteenth century but already there was a certain amount of interest in some of these fibres, with camel hair probably the best known. The original camlet, made on the Continent, would appear to have been made from camel hair but when this cloth was made in England it does seem that other material, as well as camel hair, was used.

The wool textile trade had always used a range of other fibres. The late eighteenth century was no exception, but as yet comparatively little other fibre was mixed with wool before spinning. Cotton, or for that matter any other fibre, can be mixed with wool in two basic ways. It can be blended before spinning, this is true blending, or it can be used as a quite separate yarn, for a cotton warp and wool weft fabric, for example. If not in quantity, then certainly in value, the most important mixing at this period was done with silk. For many years silk, almost always as a separate yarn, was used in the Norfolk worsted trade, which turned more and more to this type of expensive and beautifully designed fabric. At one time linen, again almost always in the form of yarn, had been mixed with wool. The fabric, known as linsey woolsey, was such a product but its manufacture declined, perhaps due to the increased availability of long wools.

Technological Developments
The great changes of the years between 1775 and 1835 occurred mainly in yarn-making but a few power looms were introduced and there were important developments in finishing. The preparatory processes, the scouring and the picking, remained little altered. Bourn's circular card, improved by Arkwright, was brought into the scribbling mill which became such an important feature of the trade.[46] As far as the worsted trade was concerned, combing remained a hand operation; Cartwright's early inventions had little effect and for most of the period the combers remained the aristocracy of labour in the trade, earning high wages and well organised in a union which had an almost national constituency. They were the typical tramping artisans, the only group of workers of this type in the wool textile trade.

Turning to the spinning developments and dealing first with the problem of converting the web of wool from the card into a slubbing, there appears to be no record of the origin of the idea of placing the card wire on the last roller in the form of strips, so that the doffing comb knocked off strips of raw material which were rolled together to form pieces that looked very similar to the rolags obtained by the hand carder. These were pieced together on the slubbing billy, which is said to have been used in the cotton trade by 1788 and was quickly introduced to the woollen trade. It was obviously derived from the jenny and could, like the jenny, be used in the home. It first appears in the West Riding about 1780 possibly even before it was used for cotton, but until the 1790s the bulk of the yarn for the woollen trade was still prepared on the spinning wheel. After 1790, however, the change-over took place quickly.

The jenny had been invented by James Hargreaves in 1767. Owing to the fact that he had made a few spinning jennies before he attempted to obtain a patent, he was not successful in maintaining any patent rights. Although originally intended for cotton it was quickly adopted for woollen spinning. Copying the simple wheel method of drafting with twist, it produced good level yarn from short material. The relative simplicity of the jenny, added to the fact that there were no patent rights, meant that it could be and was widely used in the cottages – there was no need for power and it could be easily driven by hand by turning a large wheel at the side of the machine.

But as indicated above, the carding machine was the key to the early factory and in most cases the roving or slubbing made thereon were taken to the cottages to be hand spun on the jenny. The billy described above and based on the jenny rather changed this pattern. Once continuous rovings were produced there were advantages, mainly because of better controlled working conditions, to have jennies in the factory as well, and the larger West of England clothiers appear to have adopted this pattern, but in Yorkshire the small master clothiers still collected the continuous slubbings and spun them in jennies in their own houses.

Many of the jennies there were still hand driven but power, either water or steam, was gradually applied to them, and they were increased in size to up to 120 spindles or more; the early ones had as few as 12. There has been considerable discussion as to when the jenny moved into the factory and when it became steam driven and it is difficult to decide when exactly the move took place. Doubtlessly it differed in the various areas but this question is not of great importance in the overall concept of the development of the spinning factory. The carders and the slubbing billies were the key machines of the early factory and the complete spinning factory (i.e. producing spun yarn and not just the slubbing) was not finally achieved, particularly in the West Riding, till the coming of the mule.

With worsted spinning the problem was greater. The crucial machine was Arkwright's water frame but it was difficult to adapt this to the worsted sequence with complete satisfaction, not only for the drawing-out of the top but also for the final spinning. No machine was really satisfactory until the early 1800s. The first power looms appeared in the worsted trade in the 1820s but the woollen trade had none as early as that.[47] Weaving there remained a task for the hand loom, mainly because of the weakness of the woollen yarn which could not be woven with any speed of passage of the shuttle. This was particularly noticeable when broadlooms were being used and even when power looms did come they did not run much faster than hand looms.

In the finishing trade considerable changes took place, mostly in gigging and shearing and, of course, occasioned many of the notable riots. Gig mills were a different problem; they had been known for several centuries but little used except, apparently, in Gloucestershire. Shearing frames on the other hand were a complete innovation. The first, which caused most of the riots, were not satisfactory, consisting of two hand shears fitted into a frame and operated by a lever; nevertheless, they were used. Towards the end of the period the rotary machine, which was to solve the problem, came into the picture. This machine was one of the most interesting introduced during these years. The idea of using a spiral blade, first appears in a patent of an American, Samuel Dorr.[48] The idea reached Europe shortly after 1800 and a number of textile inventors, particularly on the Continent, tried their hand at improving it. The real break-through came in Gloucestershire and seems to have been mainly the work of Lewis of Brimscombe, near Stroud. He did not claim that the idea was his, only that he made it work and there is no doubt that he did so. The basic idea of the machine was so good that it was adopted elsewhere, most notably when one of Lewis' work-people, realising what an excellent idea it would make as a lawn-mower, proceeded to patent it and sell it to the famous Norfolk firm of Ransome. One small point of interest is that these early circular shearing machines often worked across the width of the cloth. This was in one way unsatis-factory, as it meant that the machine had to be re-set after each width had been done. On the other hand, on certain weaves, notably twills, a finer cut was possible. More generally, however, the perpetual cutter, as it was called, came when the blade was made the full width of the cloth. The cloth then moved under it and the whole process became continuous.

To sum up, at the end of the period discussed here many machine problems remained to be solved and even under the best conditions production between the yarn making and weaving was not yet in a proper balance. Even when spinning had been speeded up by the coming of hand jennies, one weaver still needed four or five spinners to keep him fully occupied. Dyeing still remained unchanged with the necessity of a clean water supply more important than anything else, especially as the trade increased in volume and more and more effluent was emptied into the streams and rivers of the clothmaking areas.

Developments in Power
The range of experimentation with new machinery, particularly for the scribbling and spinning processes in woollen production and for spinning in worsted manufacture, stimulated a wide variety of attempts to use different sources of power. Hand, horse, wind, water and steam power were all being carefully investigated by wool textile

manufacturers in the last three decades of the eighteenth century. Although water and steam rapidly came to supply the power for the new machinery, the role of more primitive means of power in the early transition to mechanisation and factory production should not be overlooked or underestimated, despite our fragmentary knowledge of the employment of manual and wind power. While it has been suggested that there was no great advantage from the factory system over cottage industry until power was available to work machinery at high speed,[49] there does appear to be considerable evidence of a transference of some elements of the wool textile industry from domestic manufacture to specifically constructed or converted buildings before the application of mechanical power.

Concern about the viability of new machinery and the worth of investment in new buildings and power plant encouraged some entrepreneurs to experiment initially with more traditional power sources, often in converted sheds and workshops, barns and warehouses. For the last two decades of the eighteenth century insurance policies survive for a number of mills specifically described as hand-operated.[50] Some can be traced as having later started to use horses, and in more than one instance, a steam engine. The new scribbling and carding machinery was occasionally being worked by hand in the West Riding and one of the early attempts to use new spinning machinery, possibly a form of mule, in the worsted industry was at the Paper Hall in Bradford where James Garnett employed ten or twelve workers to turn machines by hand in the early 1790s.[51] In the West of England new carding machines were being made in Frome in 1791, that were advertised as being 'on such improved mechanical principles that a boy may constantly work them'.[52] And the Clarks of Trowbridge at one time in the early years of the nineteenth century used two blind brothers to turn carding engines.[53] These hand operated mills using new machinery should, of course, be distinguished from pre-machinery workshops using older hand implements.

The horse wheel had been in use in a variety of trades before the 1780s. Its adaptation to power textile machinery appears to have been quite common in the closing years of the eighteenth century. In the West Riding of Yorkshire many premises were converted or purpose-built to house horse wheels. They appear to have been particularly common in the Leeds area where insurance policies record them in the 1790s at Farnley, Rawden, Bramley, Armley and elsewhere. They were used to turn scribbling and carding machinery and, although perhaps typically worked by single horses, some were substantially larger. One, worked by four horses and powering six machines, was advertised for sale in 1799.[54] Horse mills were likewise in regular use in the West of England where some survived until the second decade of the nineteenth century.[55] No examples have come to light of their use in the worsted industry for powering spinning machinery but at Dolphinholme Mill near Lancaster, possibly the earliest worsted spinning mill, built in 1784, there is evidence that it was originally intended to use horses as well as water.[56] Arkwright's spinning frame was initially designed to be driven by a horse gin before it was adapted to water power and became known as the water frame. References to horse driven textile machinery cease soon after 1810.

The relatively early arrival of steam power in the West Riding wool textile industry is now well documented although not adequately explained. More detailed evidence has also been produced of the comparatively late and, except in special cases, slow development of steam power in the West of England. Elsewhere, including Scotland, little is at present known about the application of steam power to textile machinery until 1838, when the factory inspectors incorporated power statistics in their Factory Returns.

In Yorkshire steam was used so soon after the introduction of the new mills that it is perhaps doubtful to suggest that it was substituted for water power as, the development of steam and water power was to a great extent, taking place side by side. There is an unconfirmed use of a steam engine in a woollen mill in the Spen Valley before 1780 but more definite evidence does not appear until 1790, in which year engines were at work at Holbeck near Leeds and at Birkenshaw near Gomersal.[57] From 1792 the installation of steam engines in woollen mills progressed rapidly but their use in worsted mills came rather more slowly. By 1800 about a third of all wool textile mills in the county were employing steam power, with over 80 engines in operation. Undoubtedly the majority of them were pumping engines of the Savery and Newcomen designs. There are a number of references to engines being used to pump water back above a wheel.[58]

Those engines that were not used to pump back water were often intended to augment water power in times of water shortage. On the Dartmouth Estate at least four mills were using steam engines to compensate for poor water supply in the 1790s. But there are also many examples of mills being built in the West Riding before 1800 to use only steam power. Its use allowed the industry to develop away from often inaccessible riverside sites which imposed restrictions on the size and construction of mills. In the area south and south west of Leeds, and where substantial mill development was taking place, sites with adequate water power were scarce. Thus, in that area, steam powered mills were established in the mid-1790s at Gomersal, Heckmondwike, Holbeck, Gildersome and Birstall. Most of the engines were probably of local manufacture. Only nine or ten emanated from Boulton and Watt's Soho foundry.[59] Watt had been initially suspicious about supplying engines to textile mills in Northern England 'because there are so many mills erecting on powerful streams in the North of England that the trade must soon be overdone and consequently our labour may be lost.'[60] But in 1792 the firm did supply two large engines to Leeds firms. One went to Wormald, Fountain and Gott for Park Mills at Bean Ing and the other to Markland, Cookson and Fawcett's cotton and worsted mill. They received a few more orders from local wool textile firms in the next few years but they never gained a substantial foothold in West Yorkshire. There was local competition to contend with, particularly from the Leeds firm of Fenton, Murray and Wood, in spite of their patent rights which did not expire until 1800. Fenton, Murray and Wood were building engines by 1797 as were the Low Moor Ironworks near Bradford. Late in 1797 John Rennie advised Matthew Boulton of the potential competition of Fenton, Murray and Wood and, in due course, Watt reacted by purchasing land adjoining the Leeds foundry to prevent its expansion, although it has also been suggested that Watt intended to open a factory to supply the growing demand for steam engines in the north.[61]

The reasons for this relatively early and arguably rapid growth of steam power in the Yorkshire industry are not altogether clear. Yorkshire was well supplied with water power. Although many of the prime sites were already occupied by corn and fulling mills there does not appear to have been a shortage of sites with water power available in most parts of the textile districts, although certainly in some areas, for example the upper Calder Valley, there was strong competition for suitable locations before 1800. Elsewhere new water powered sites were being developed later. However, adequate and reliable water supply for power was not uniform throughout the area. South of Leeds between the Aire and the Calder few streams were strong and constant. But on the other hand this was the area of the developing coal field and the lowest coal costs and some mills even mined their own coal. As steam power became more efficient the incentive to use the more costly but more reliable steam engine increased and it was very much in this area of the county that the early use of steam power occurred. However, in the western part, where the Pennine streams flowed fast, adequate falls could be created and water could, if necessary, be stored in quite large quantities, steam power was a much later innovation. This helps explain the later development of steam power in the worsted industry which being located mainly in the north-west of the district was generally further from the coalfields and closer to good waterside locations. The exception was the short-lived branch of the worsted industry in Leeds which was dependent on steam power.

In the West Country the advent of steam power was considerably slower. Gloucestershire and Wiltshire could boast only one engine each in 1805 and ten years later Gloucestershire still had only four.[62] Boulton and Watt did receive enquiries from West Country manufacturers. The first was in 1791 from Henry Wansey of Salisbury, who wanted to drive carding engines, but nothing came of this, nor was there any immediate result from the later enquiries from Warminster, Trowbridge and Bradford-on-Avon.[63] Slightly later, after 1810, the remarkable growth of Trowbridge, making mainly cassimeres, was based almost entirely on steam power and the sale of engines there was so good that George Haden, who had been a foreman of Boulton and Watt, settled in the area and started what was to become a very successful business, although not in the end supplying the wool textile trade. The firm came to specialise, and lead the way, in the introduction of central heating.

As far as the area was more generally concerned, the details that the clothiers received of coal consumption, together with the initial cost, appear to have been off-putting. Coal costs were three or four times as much as in the Leeds district and in many parts of the area water power was reasonably reliable. Coal at the pithead in the Mendip coalfield in the 1790s was about 6s.3d. a ton, not very much different from pithead prices in the West Riding, but there were considerable carriage costs which, it is said, quadrupled the price by the time the coal reached Trowbridge and Bradford-on-Avon. In Gloucestershire at the same period coal was about £1 per ton.[64] In the first decade of the nineteenth century engines were, however, installed in woollen mills throughout the area and the opening of the Somerset Coal Canal in 1811 which reduced coal prices in the Trowbridge and Bradford area, had some effect on stimulating steam power installed in that area, but canal charges were relatively high, particularly in the area further east, such as Chippenham and Calne. Later, there was a scheme to cut a canal to Frome in Somerset but nothing came of it and it is noticeable that Frome stayed largely dependent on water.[65]

It is suggested elsewhere that the effect of higher coal prices on the

Table 6   *Steam and water power in Yorkshire wool textile mills in 1835*

Woollen Mills

Power of wheel or engine h.p.	Water power		Steam power	
	Total h.p.	No. of wheels	Total h.p.	No. of engines
50+	210	4	280	4
49–40	160	4	683	17
39–30	125	4	1527	48
29–20	306	14	1815	80
19–10	1242	101	1677	125
Under 10	629	114	236	34
TOTALS	2672	241	6218	308

Worsted mills

Power of wheel or engine h.p.	Water power		Steam power	
	Total h.p.	No. of wheels	total h.p.	No. of engines
50+	—	—	420	7
49–40	—	—	485	12
39–30	60	2	716	23
29–20	84	4	707	33
19–10	400	32	462	50
Under 10	329½	64	216	34
TOTALS	873½	102	3186	159

SOURCE: *Factory Returns*, 1835.

ultimate cloth price, and therefore the selling price, was very marginal but uncertainties over supplies as well as fear of much higher prices did dissuade manufacturers from installing engines. Trowbridge, which did go over almost entirely to steam, became the success centre of the West of England.

Although in some West of England districts coal costs were noticeably falling in the first three decades of the nineteenth century and problems in the use of water power were being aggravated by the penning back of water, the development of steam power did, outside of Trowbridge, remain slow. K.H. Rogers has traced in Wiltshire and the Frome district of Somerset about nine engines in woollen mills by 1810, another 17 by 1820 and four more in the 1820s.[66] It is only in

1838, however, that one can make a relatively satisfactory assessment of the rise in the use of steam power in the West of England and its importance relative to water power. In that year in Gloucestershire 66 per cent of power was produced by water, with corresponding percentages of 32 and 59 in Wiltshire and Somerset respectively.[67]

In Scotland the remoteness of the main wool textile districts, and in particular the border area, from the coalfields held back the development of steam power. It was almost unknown in Wales and the border counties of Northern England. The Devon trade was dependent on water power.

But the use of steam power progressed quite rapidly in Yorkshire and in Lancashire, particularly in the central parts of the textile districts. A detailed view becomes available for 1835, when the newly-appointed factory inspector, I.R. Rickards, calculated the number of engines and their power, parish by parish. His figures perhaps overestimate the actual amount of power being used because in some mills power was also being directed to other purposes and, moreover, occasionally the full amount of power an engine was capable of producing was not required. The results of Rickards' calculations are shown in Table 6. The figures illustrate that by the mid-1830s steam power was relatively far more important than water power. In most of the county this was the case but water power still predominated in the parishes of Almondbury, Mirfield, Halifax, Saddleworth, Otley, Keighley, Addingham, Skipton and Gargrave, most of which were Pennine parishes. In the Yorkshire woollen industry 70 per cent of power was being generated by steam; in the worsted industry 78 per cent.

3 Trade, Markets and Products, 1770–1835

The State of Trade 1770–1805

Around the turn of the eighteenth century a range of somewhat similar contemporary estimates exist for the value of output of the wool textile industry. Christopher Rawden of Halifax, a central figure in the Yorkshire trade, suggested that in 1800 national output was around £19.5 million. In that year, because of the concern about the potential repeal of wool export restrictions, other attempts were made to value the trade. There was, of course, more reason to overestimate than underestimate its value and the number of people dependent on it; and many of the estimates are perhaps interdependent. A general rule of thumb which seems to have been used was to assume that output was roughly three times the value of wool input, a ratio that was still applied much later in the nineteenth century. On this basis, Edward Law in his House of Lords speech, valued output at £18.6 million. He estimated also that there were more than one and a half million persons who were 'immediately concerned in the operative branches of this vast manufacture'. William Hustler, the major Bradford wool-stapler, suggested a similar figure for output, but reported that his father had calculated that in 1782 three million people were 'dependent upon' the industry.[1]

A rather more independent, and perhaps more reliable, estimate for wool output is available for 1805. In that year John Luccock, in his important treatise on wool, examined previous estimates and attempted to assess home wool output county by county. He concluded that the value of output of English wool was just over £5.5 million.[2] To this figure Phyllis Deane has added £300,000 for the value of Scottish wool, based on Sir John Sinclair's possibly conservative estimates and £1.8 million as the value of the 8 million pounds of foreign wool imports. Using the often accepted contemporary multipliers of four for long wool and two for short wool, she concluded that the value of output of the industry was about £18.5 million.[3] Because of the high wool prices for that year the figure suggests a considerably lower total for the late 1790s than other estimates. In view of the state of the industry and changes in wool prices, there must be some doubt, however, that it is appropriate to use the same multipliers for the 1790s and 1805. It may be that the gap between Phyllis Deane's estimate of £13.8 million as the value of the final product in 1799 and her figure of £18.5 million in 1805, is too great.

More confident calculations seem a forlorn hope but if we accept the 1805 figures as a rough approximation they suggest that the value of the output of the industry had increased by around 80 per cent in the previous 35 years. As there is little evidence of major growth in the Yorkshire worsted trade in the period, it was the woollen industry that was mainly responsible for the increase. Benjamin Gott, in 1800 valued the output of Yorkshire woollens as £6.5 million.[4] If Hustler's estimate of £1.4 million for the output of worsteds, the same figure as for 1772, is included the conclusion is that between 50 and 60 per cent of wool textile output emanated from Yorkshire by around the end of the century, compared with a third in 1770, and that the increase in the value of Yorkshire output was as great as, if not greater than, the rise in national output. Bearing in mind the cheaper nature of Yorkshire cloth, perhaps over 60 per cent of the volume of output was of Yorkshire origin.

The statistical sources and the interpretation of them do not permit great confidence in these findings but the trends would seem to agree with other evidence of the state of the industry in the various regions in the last quarter of the century. The returns of cloth milled show clearly the development of the Yorkshire woollen trade. Output of narrow cloth pieces doubled between 1770–4 and 1800–4. As average piece length increased by almost 40 per cent, the length of narrow cloth produced rose by 130 per cent. Output of broadcloth pieces rose two and three-quarter fold. With lengths similarly increasing, yardage milled increased 300 per cent. In addition to these cloths there was an increase in other woollens, the production of which was not included in the cloth milled returns. The main phase of this expansion was between 1782 and 1796, with a further boost in the last two years of the century. What then explains Yorkshire's amazing success in the manufacture of broadcloth?

An explanation must strike a balance between the advantages and successes of Yorkshire and the problems faced by West of England

Table 7   *British wool textile exports to the United States*

	£ thousand	% of total British wool textile exports
1784–6	739	19
1794–6	2016	35
1804–6	2726	40
1814–6	2471	29
1824–6	1651	24
1834–6	2506	37

SOURCE: R. Davis, *op. cit.*, Table 45. The figures quoted are Davis's revised valuations.

manufacturers. Traditional explanations based on factor endowments and relative factor costs are, on the whole, irrelevant to the eighteenth century situation. Access to waterpower, coal for steam power and iron for machinery may have had some significance in the next century but Yorkshire's progress was well under way before new mills and new methods were of any consequence. Dr Wilson places Yorkshire's success squarely in terms of its relationship with foreign markets.[5] Its growth was highly dependent on its export success particularly in the United States. Between 1770 and 1800 the proportion of wool textile exports going to the United States rose from 25 per cent to 40 per cent, the growth of the American market being almost entirely gained by Yorkshire manufacturers. After 1782 Yorkshire merchants flocked across the Atlantic disposing of vast quantities of goods to the geographically enlarged market, as the interior frontier extended. In the 1790s an average of almost £2 million worth of wool textiles were sent annually from Britain, compared with less than £0.75 million in the early 1770s. Exports in 1799 were almost four times the level of 1772.[6]

Wilson has rightly argued that the vast majority of West Country cloth passed through the hands of London merchants whose interests were very varied and who had neither the specialist knowledge nor inclination to involve themselves fully in the complexities of the American market.[7] There was, in any case, only a very limited potential market in the United States for the high quality West of England product. As Heaton pointed out in great detail, however, Yorkshire merchants were very active in cultivating American connections. Many of them made frequent transatlantic crossings. A large colony of West Riding exiles became well established in the East Coast ports.[8] Of the 53 cloth merchant houses operating in Leeds in 1782 at least a score had partners who spent all or some of their time abroad.[9]

Wilson is persuaded to separate entrepreneurial dynamism from merchanting success and is not convinced of any entrepreneurial superiority in Yorkshire.[10] But isolated comparisons of the timing of the introduction of new machines and methods, which he argues show little distinction, are perhaps not a sufficient indicator. The close relationship between merchants and manufacturers in the West Riding, including the latter sometimes undertaking some of their own merchanting, suggests that dynamism in merchanting cannot be entirely separated from entrepreneurial activity. Manufacturers were in a better position to respond rapidly to changes in market needs and appear to have done so. And one has to admit that contemporary comment suggests an enthusiasm and interest amongst West Riding entrepreneurs unmatched by their West of England counterparts. Not unnaturally this is the result of the trade expansion but optimism should not be underestimated as a factor in further trade promotion. Much weight then may be placed on the marketing methods of the Yorkshire trade. But its success in foreign markets has also to be explained by the difference in the quality of its cloth being outstripped by its lower prices in the eyes of the purchasers of its product. The transition to broadcloth manufacture was the result primarily of the belated introduction of the flying shuttle and perhaps a relative cost advantage. Broadcloths were more easily tailored.

The problems of the West of England and Norwich trades are examined below. It would be wrong, however, to think that the expansion of the Yorkshire trade from the 1770s was all plain sailing. The greater dependence on foreign markets increased the potential severity of demand fluctuations. The cloth milled returns suggest annual fluctuations of output of 20 per cent or more were not uncommon. Output of broad and narrow cloth rose from 1774 to 1778, but then followed three years of quite deep depression as access to American markets was made exceedingly difficult during the War of Independence. Peace in 1782 allowed the expansion of American sales to get under way. They tripled in the next ten years. The worsted trade did go through short periods of great activity. James described the interval between the close of the American war and the commencement of the French Revolutionary War in 1792 as one of the most flourishing periods the trade had ever known.[11] In addition to the United States, wool textiles also found increasing markets in Northern Europe, the West Indies, Latin America, Canada and Asia.

The quantity of broad and narrow cloth milled doubled in the decade. Home demand is difficult to assess but with stable, or even falling, food prices and good employment levels, it does not seem unreasonable to suggest that it was rising.

The outbreak of the French Wars led to a sudden contraction in demand. Although Yorkshire clothed the French army, trading links, particularly to Southern Europe, were severely restricted. However, the fall in output from 1792 to 1794 was more than made up for by the 25 per cent increase in cloth milled in Yorkshire in 1795, leading to much new mill building.[12] Output remained high for the rest of the decade and into the first few years of the nineteenth century.

The Continental War and the American Embargo

From about 1805, for ten years, the rapid expansion of the Yorkshire trade largely subsided. The dependence which Yorkshire had developed on trade with Europe and the United States left the local industry more susceptible than in other areas of the country to the political problems in Europe and the long drawn out arguments with the United States. Output of broadcloth did continue to rise, but at a much slower rate and narrow cloth output reached a peak. Investment in new mills was outstripped by other mills going out of use or being converted for other purposes. Home demand was more buoyant but the decade did witness quite severe harvest fluctuations and thus periods of stagnant orders for cloth.

1805 to 1808 were years of depression. The Berlin Decrees and the Orders in Council led to a dislocation of the European trade and the need to reorganise it through Scandinavian and Mediterranean ports, thus bypassing the major areas of conflict. The export of stuffs to Germany was halted, except for those got in by backdoor methods. Access to the Baltic ports was impeded and trade with Russia largely inhibited.[13] That Continental trade which did survive was precarious and costly. Leeds firms were badly affected; some failed. Rogerson records in some detail the local uncertainties, the difficulties of selling cloth and of getting payment, although he seems to have fared reasonably well himself.[14]

In 1808 Spain's successful revolt from Napoleonic rule and the flight of the Portuguese royal family to Brazil disrupted business with the Iberian peninsular, but provided on the other hand a boost through the improved access to South and Central America, where British traders scored notable successes. Heaton's description of the adventures of John Luccock admirably shows the exertions which the capture of this market required.[15] Luccock had married into the

Lupton family, one of the most influential mercantile concerns in the West Riding and heavily engaged in trade in Portugal and the United States. The French takeover of Lisbon and the Non-Importation Act in the United States curtailed these traditional markets. Direct trade with Brazil seemed to the firm to be a means of maintaining business and in 1808 Luccock was sent to Rio where he remained, except for two visits home, for ten years. He arrived to much confusion as the reorganisation and extension of the Brazilian trade put pressure on local port and mercantile facilities. If others matched his entrepreneurial zeal in trading through Rio and Buenos Aires, of dealing with transport delays, payment problems, speculations and dumping, and promoting wool textiles, then British merchants exhibited much energy and ingenuity in developing this new market.

The initial mercantile excursions to South America in 1808 led to much overstocking and unremunerative trading. West Riding mills were active in sending goods. James argued that some of the cloth found its way via South America into the United States.[16] However, the market gradually settled down and a healthy demand for wool textiles emerged amongst the small but rich middle and upper class. Trade expanded sixfold in the 20 years from 1807 but demand had found a maximum level by the mid-1820s. The widespread emergence of protectionism impeded further expansion for some time. The crisis of 1825 and consequent payment problems made traders more wary of further trade promotion in the area.

The on-off nature of the American trade embargo and the difficulties created by the uncertainties of the enforcement of the restrictions have been described in vivid detail by Heaton.[17] Such was the importance of trade with America that the violent year by year fluctuations which resulted were sufficient to influence the whole

Table 8   British wool textile exports to Latin America

	£ thousand	% of total wool textile exports
1795–6	15	0.3
1804–6	115	1.7
1814–6	426	4.9
1824–6	750	11.1
1834–6	720	10.7

SOURCE: R. Davis, op. cit., Table 45. The figures quoted are Davis's revised valuations.

state of trade. A very wide variety of fabrics were shipped to the United States. Negro blankets, 'plains' and lower grades of woollen cloth were in demand in the Southern States, and to the North went large quantities of broadcloth, cassimeres, kerseymeres, flannels and other medium quality worsteds and woollens. There was an active Yorkshire mercantile colony in East Coast ports. Some British manufacturers, Gott for example, appointed agents who solicited and sent orders, collected accounts and remitted money in return for a commission.[18] Commission merchants also sent orders for cloth direct to manufacturers or via agents in British ports. After the restoration of free trade manufacturers at times sent speculative consignments, if necessary disposing of goods through auction sales.

The original Non-Importation Act of April 1806 was very slow to be implemented. But from the time it was first put into operation in November of that year until June 1812 when war broke out, trade was restricted, except for three periods totalling 19 months in all. Initially it operated for only five weeks and then was suspended for most of 1807.[19] In that year trade carried on more or less as normal. Lupton wrote to an American customer in May 1807:

> Such of our merchants who have resident partners on the other side, or from their connections may be supposed to have the best information, are relaxing very little in sending out goods above the price limited by the Non-Importation Act, under the idea that it will certainly not be acted upon.[20]

The postponement of the embargo, in 1807, enabled trade and stocks to be built up to a great extent. The total was somewhat inflated by some goods for the West Indies being sent via American ports. But in 1808 United States imports of British wool textiles fell to only £2 million, less than a half of the previous year's level. Volume of sales fell less than their value, however, as the Act, and then the embargo, exempted some types of cheap woollen cloth, valued at less than five shillings per yard. This made it possible for traders to bypass the restrictions by falsely invoicing more valuable cloth to get it through the customs. Whilst trade continued, the volume depending upon the extent of enforcement of restrictions, added difficulties arose in British merchants obtaining payments. The receipt of an American payment was greeted with much relief.[21]

Late in 1808 and at the beginning of the following year there was renewed optimism on the receipt of news that the embargo was being lifted. Joseph Rogerson greeted the news very happily.[22] Trade did pick up for a while but in early August news arrived of the Non-

Intercourse Bill. Rogerson wrote: 'I hope it is not true'.[23] Some trade continued but in a very hesitant way. Sudden orders would be received for very quick delivery, with precise instructions about how the goods were to be sent. Orders could suddenly disappear when delivery seemed impossible. Goods were sent to ports in Nova Scotia, New Brunswick and elsewhere, to be smuggled in.[24]

The short war broke out in the summer of 1812, exacerbating the difficulties. Resumption of peace led to a flood of goods. £4.2 million of British wool textiles were imported to the United States in 1815 but high prices exaggerate the volume. Merchants were accused of dumping goods, but Lord Brougham, in Parliament, praised the action: 'It is worthwhile to incur a loss upon the first exportation, in order, by the glut to stifle in the cradle those rising manufacturers in the United States, which the war has forced into existence, contrary to the natural course of things.'[25] Overstocking and the rise in United States home production reduced average trade to £2.7 million in the next three years. As prices fell adventurers in the market found themselves having to cut their losses by auctioning goods. Although prices were uncertain this method of sale had the advantage of immediate cash payment.[26] The glut of goods quickly gave rise to pleas for protection. Existing duties were raised in 1816 to a level of about 25 per cent *ad valorem*.

As for the general state of the industry, after two years of reasonable business 1811 proved disastrous. Less cloth was milled in Yorkshire than in any of the previous seven years. United States markets were more firmly closed, Napoleon's blockade was pursued vigorously, bankruptcies and unemployment were commonplace; two banks failed in Leeds.[27] Manufacturers were pleading for money and, to top it all, they were faced with labour disputes and the threats of the Luddites.

But then, with the assistance of the repeal of the Orders in Council and the restoration of trade to Spain and Portugal, business began to recover. Rogerson was able to write of 1812: 'This year taking it altogether has been a very lucky one for us (tho' it has been in the midst of wars) and I think I may say that it has been a very good one for the country at large – Thank God for it!'[28] He made a handsome profit on his year's business; a record amount of Yorkshire broadcloth was milled and wool prices were high, stimulating attempts to use shoddy.

Recovery continued in the following year. Broadcloth milled in 1813 was 20 per cent above the 1812 record. European markets were picking up in anticipation of peace. German ports were re-opening following the disastrous retreat from Moscow, benefiting the worsted industry in particular. Fancy worsteds were coming into vogue and James tells of several innovations in the Yorkshire worsted trade including plainbacks, which were twilled on the face and plain on the back. These cloths figure regularly and in large quantities in manufacturers' sales books for several decades.[29]

Peace in Europe and with the United States led to immense speculation and a rapid overstocking of many markets. English and Scottish mills producing for the export trade were extraordinarily busy.[30] Some, however, suffered from the collapse of demand for uniform cloth and the high expectations of many manufacturers were not fulfilled. Markets could not soak up the goods sent, prices fell and heavy losses were incurred.[31] There were also more specific problems; for instance West of England, particularly Devon and Somerset, trade with India suffered heavily from the loss of the East India Company's monopoly.[32] Even those manufacturers producing for the more stable home market suffered from great competition as exporters attempted to transfer into the home market.

With the exception of 1818, foreign trade fell for the five years following peace. Markets to a great extent were overstocked and worries about Continental competition were rife. Depression and low prices in the home wool trade led to a successful campaign for a tax on foreign wool, but also to a lifting of the restriction on the export of British wool. Wool imports peaked in 1818 to beat the 6*d.* a pound tax.[33]

The aggregate trade figures conceal, for this period, a considerable shift in the type of cloth demanded by foreign markets. The volume of exports of woollen fabrics fell by more than half to 1820 and then only recovered slightly in the early years of the next decade. Stuffs, however, were much more in demand; exports of them increased by almost two-thirds in the same period, overtaking woollens in importance. The increase in the drawback from the tax on soap used for washing long wool – the figure for 1820 was more than double that for 1810 – reflects the rise in Yorkshire.[34] The most notable trade expansion in stuffs was to Russia, Germany and the United States. Russian trade was assisted by the Government agreeing to pay Russia in British woollens, although within a few years Russia's preferential treatment to Prussian goods reduced trade somewhat.[35]

Thus the worsted trade was much more optimistic than the woollen trade in the years following peace, but the latter's difficulties in foreign markets did not drain it of all confidence. Export prices did not fall disastrously low and there was some new investment in larger

Table 9   Composition of wool textile exports, 1815–25 (annual averages)

	1815–19	1820–4
Cloth of all sorts (thousand pieces)	474.2	369.2
Napped coatings, duffels, etc. (thousand pieces)	82.3	60.6
Kerseymeres (thousand pieces)	88.7	93.7
Baizes of all sorts (thousand pieces)	55.9	42.2
Stuffs, woollen and worsted (thousand pieces)	703.6	1064.1
Flannel (thousand yards)	4341.5	3598.0
Blankets (thousand yards)	2424.4	1751.1
Carpets and carpeting (thousand yards)	804.3	760.3
Woollens mixed with cotton (thousand yards)	772.6	893.5

SOURCE: *Report on the State of the Wool Trade*, 1828, *loc. cit.*

mills. Home market demand maintained the West of England trade, although production was not at full capacity.[36] But the Devon trade, however, sank to almost nothing following the loss of East India Company business and the widespread sale of mills in 1817. Rochdale suffered badly in her Continental markets but America absorbed an increased proportion of the town's output.[37]

The State of Trade in the 1820s
The cessation, in 1820, of the returns of cloth milled in Yorkshire means that the annual fluctuations in the Yorkshire woollen trade have to be identified thereafter from more fragmentary evidence. The final year of the returns suggests a continued fall in the production of narrow cloth and little recovery from the previous year's low level of broadcloth output. This coincides with low wool imports in 1820, but a somewhat false impression is given because of the exceptionally high wool imports in the previous two years in anticipation of the tax on foreign wool. Six pence per pound was levied from 1820 but this high rate survived only four years, as in 1824 the duty was reduced to a penny a pound.[38] Exports of woollen cloth were very low in 1820. Most classes of goods suffered a fall with markets contracting particularly in Spain, Italy and North America. A major problem was the overstocked markets through over-trading in the previous two years. The continued fall in food prices should, however, have sustained the home market. Trade began to pick up in 1821 with the recovery of the North American market and increasing trade in South America. The Spanish market, however, sank disas-

Table 10   *Exports of yarn and wool textiles, 1815–34*

Annual averages	Declared value £ millions	Annual averages	Declared value £ million
1815–9	7.7	1825–9	5.3
1820–4	6.0	1830–4	5.7

NOTES: 1815–29: Great Britain
1830–4: United Kingdom

trously and European trade was generally stagnant. Contemporary opinion was sure that the wool tax put British manufacturers at a disadvantage but the later reduction of the tax had little noticeable reverse effect.[39]

Although many markets continued to improve over the next three years the post-war high levels were not reattained. Manufacturers producing for North America were happy but markets were lost in Russia, Portugal and Spain. In spite of the increasing difficulties of trade to the East, exports on the whole were maintained, but colonial demand noticeably declined.

Various sources suggest, however, a general rise of confidence in the woollen trade as a whole in the first half of the 1820s.[40] The trade was less stable, risk of failure was high but optimism, particularly in Yorkshire, remained evident. Confidence was even more noticeable in the worsted trade. The transfer of export demand towards worsteds continued, the level of trade avoiding substantial annual variations. Worsted exports, including some woollen stuffs, had almost doubled in value between 1816 and 1826, even though long wool prices had fallen in the intervening period. The success of worsteds may be partly explained by increasing ingenuity in the range of cloth available. European trade was maintained, increasing to some major countries, but the greatest market gains were in the Americas.

By early 1825 boom conditions existed in many parts of the industry. Demand for labour led to pressure for higher wages and strikes resulted in Yorkshire and the West of England.[41] Although demand for cloth was being boosted by speculation, a series of events late in the year caused a sudden reversal of circumstances. The collapse of the South American market as the result of the ending of loans to the new Republican Governments caused the loss of £$\frac{1}{2}$ million of trade;[42] the increase in the United States tariff contributed to the loss of £$\frac{3}{4}$ million of trade in that market.[43] The only redeeming feature was the

Table 11   *Direction of wool textile exports, 1824*

	% of declared value		% of declared value
Russia	1.5	East Indies and China	14.5
Germany, Prussia and		United States	29.2
Netherlands	14.5	South America	13.0
Spain, Portugal and		West Indies	3.4
Gibraltar	11.9	British Colonies in	
Italy	3.9	North America	5.8
Europe	32.2	Africa	0.7

rise in demand for the East Indies and China. The *Leeds Mercury* placed the blame for the crisis squarely on speculation at home: 'Within the last 12 months one portion of the British public has exhibited a degree of knavery and another a degree of gullibility altogether unparalleled even in the disastrous period of the South Sea mania.'[44] The depression led to bank failures, bankruptcies in both the North and the West, and unemployment. Hirst in Leeds suffered badly through, he claimed, the sudden substantial drop in the value of his cloth in, or on its way to, America and because of the reduction of the value of his wool stock.[45] Wool prices had risen in the speculation earlier in the year.

The panic was very short-lived; by March 1826 the *Leeds Mercury* was writing of symptoms of returning prosperity,[46] and until 1829 contemporary reports show a recovery of optimism. Foreign sales of Scottish woollens, although still small, were rising.[47] Worsted manufacture continued to follow the trend of the first half of the decade, with a huge increase in exports to the United States and South America, and successes in Italian and Spanish markets. The German market expanded massively. It would seem that the speculation and overstocking of 1825 in the short term taught merchants and manufacturers a lesson as manufacture was geared more to specific orders. The West of England was busy again by 1827 but complaints of Yorkshire competition continued to gain strength.[48]

Various witnesses to the 1828 Commission reported increasingly prosperous trade. Brooke specifically mentioned the rising demand for blankets and carpets. Varley reported that the 'stuff trade has increased prodigously since the low price of English wool'.[49] The *ad valorem* United States tariff of that year had a short term effect and

perhaps stimulated the sending of cheaper goods across the Atlantic.[50] However in late summer of 1829 sudden depression descended
once again. Woollen manufacturers were hurt more than worsted
producers, the West of England more than Yorkshire, perhaps ex-
plicable by the loss of cassimere business in the United States after
the tariff.

Trade gradually began to pick up again in 1830. German and
American demand for yarn boosted exports; large United States
orders for blankets encouraged the manufacturers concerned and
there was an improvement in trade to South America, Italy, Turkey
and Canada.[51] In general, however, European trade remained low.
The worsted trade benefited from the large transatlantic orders;
stocks began to reduce and business was brisk.[52] For the next six years
overseas trade witnessed steady expansion. Yarn sales abroad progressed almost year by year. In 1831 stuff exports to the United
States were more than double the average for the previous few years
and James was able to describe 1832 to 1836 as being 'among the
most prosperous periods in the history of the West Riding stuff
trade', as a result of high levels of both home and foreign demand.[53]
The result was a wave of new mill building and a general high level of
capital investment. The woollen industry shared in the prosperity.
West of England manufacturers encountered improving demand,
boosted in 1832 by exceptional East India Company exports of over
two million yards of cloth to China. With the expiry of the Company's
monopoly, trade fell in 1833. China business then improved again,
although Gloucestershire mills suffered from the reduction of East
India Company orders.[54]

The 20 years following peace in 1815 were undoubtedly very good
ones for the worsted industry. Investment was encouraged and the
volume of stuff exports more than doubled. Drawback on soap used
for washing long wool in Yorkshire more than trebled, reflecting both
increasing home demand and a continuing relocation of the worsted
industry to Yorkshire.[55] The value of woollen goods exported fell
considerably and only a part of that fall can be explained through
falling prices as there was a decline also in the weight of woollen cloth
exported. The carpet trade improved but exports of flannels and
blankets fell during the 1820s. The problems for the woollen industry
were in most markets. Comparing the post war years with the end of
the 1820s the only major markets which had increased their imports
of British woollens were Germany and Holland, Italy and South
America. The markets of North America, the Colonies and most
other European countries declined over the period as a whole.

It seems likely from what one knows of the progress of the Yorkshire woollen industry in this period that the losses in export markets were felt most severely by the West of England and by the less important woollen areas. Contemporary comment in Yorkshire does not portray a picture of steadily declining output. It seems likely, however, that improvements in home demand may have compensated somewhat for falling exports.

For the wool textile industry as a whole generalisation in this period is difficult. Wool imports rose very substantially. Estimates of home wool used are not accurate enough to identify short term trends but the considerable fall in wool prices and the difficulties discussed at length in the 1828 Report suggest a relative decline in the use of English wool. The export figures overall, measured by volume, show a decline and the magnitude of that fall is such that it seems unrealistic to believe that it could all have been compensated for by increasing home demand.

The Fortunes of the West of England
The more one follows the fortunes of the West of England broadcloth trade at the end of the eighteenth century, the clearer it becomes that it was no longer a growth industry. Two themes dominated the years between 1775 and 1800: The introduction of the cassimere and, towards the end of the period, the coming of machine spinning. The former was temporarily the more important. The invention is always attributed to the Bradford-on-Avon clothier Francis Yerbury. There is much that is obscure about his patent, not least in the technical language; indeed, few patents are so ambiguous and one wonders if this was deliberate. Yerbury was not the first clothier to make the twilled cloths in the West, as he tried to claim.[56] Did he perhaps only give them a name?

The great point about the cassimere was the fineness and consequent light weight. Austen, the assistant commissioner, investigating the condition of the hand loom weavers of Trowbridge in 1839 gives comparative settings.[57] The broadcloth had from 3230 to 3800 ends in the warp and would have been about 100 inches wide in loom, giving approximately 36 ends per inch. The cassimere had 2280 ends with 42 inches which is approximately 54 ends per inch. The technical changes involved in turning from broadcloth to the cassimere have not always been appreciated. Yarn for the cassimere was about three times as fine as for broadcloth. Obviously good wool was used for the best broadcloth but it had been spun well within its spinning limits; consequently yarn would have been strong and there would also have been opportunities for the skilled blender to mix in other types of wool. With the cassimere trade this was not the case and there were continual complaints that the yarn used in these cloths broke frequently during weaving. However, despite the obscure nature of the patent, it can be taken as establishing the beginning of the popularity of the cassimere which did a great deal to maintain the high class trade of the West of England in the period under review.

In 1800 the West of England's reputation for the highest quality broadcloths and for the new cassimeres remained firmly established even if, as far as broadcloths were concerned, it was beginning to be challenged by the West Riding.[58] But there was as yet little or no sign that the century-old supremacy of woollens over worsteds for men's wear, was to be completely reversed during the next one hundred years. The country squire still wore Uley Blue on Sunday and Stroudwater Scarlet on Monday. However, the popularity of the cassimere might have suggested an increasing demand for the finer, thinner fabrics which worsteds would ultimately be best able to meet. The fine cassimeres that we have examined and of which a very large number of patterns still remain,[59] are the finest woollen cloth known to us and the nearest woollen cloth to the superfine worsted of the late nineteenth century that was ever manufactured.

During the eighteenth century the West of England trade had tended to split into two main groups, the first and more important centred around Stroud in Gloucestershire, and the second, slightly less important, around Trowbridge and Bradford-on-Avon on the Somerset/Wiltshire borders. The area between these two concentrations, notably around Malmesbury, which had once been a major cloth making centre, was no longer of great importance but it is interesting that a little later a Bradford-on-Avon clothier named Hill moved to Malmesbury because, it was said, he thought he would meet less opposition there to the introduction of machinery.[60] Overall it would seem that the Gloucestershire trade around Stroud was still expanding a little, but in the Trowbridge and Bradford-on-Avon area the expansion in cassimeres about balanced the falling demand for that area's broadcloths.

During the first years of the nineteenth century the most notable change was the increase in the twill, single width cassimeres already mentioned. New firms such as Salters, Stancombe and Clark in the Trowbridge/Bradford-on-Avon area entered the trade, devoting most of their production to these narrow fabrics.[61] Trowbridge, Westbury and Frome were well known for them but rather strangely, not Bradford, the home of the inventor. As the demand for cassimeres declined manufacturers of them were more successful in making other changes, this time to fancier cloths. Clark's records for the early years of the century show a large proportion of cassimeres early on, but after 1807 other fabrics such as wool dyed drabbed mills, etc., become the main product.[62]

Statistical evidence of the size of the industry at this time is very scarce, thus making the figures given in the *Minutes of Evidence taken before the Select Committee on the State of Children Employed in the Manufactories of the United Kingdom* in 1816, important.[63] The list was sent up by John Bush of Bradford-on-Avon, a solicitor, who wished to draw attention to the excellent way in which the children were treated and to emphasise that there was no need for any government legislation. There has been a tendency to regard this return as incomplete but a detailed analysis has shown that John Bush did include by far the majority of the mills in his area. A comparison of the 1816 figures and the 1835 Factory Returns suggests that the number of factory workers in Bradford-on-Avon declined by more than half in the intervening period, when factory employment was rapidly expanding elsewhere. In Trowbridge employment almost doubled. As indicated above, Bradford-on-Avon continued to make broadcloths, whereas Trowbridge turned to cassimeres. The importance of responding quickly to consumer demand for a new cloth is clearly indicated. But it may also be of some significance that, as the 1838 Factory Returns show,[64] Trowbridge converted almost entirely to steam power, perhaps giving rise to the contemporary description of the town:

> Trowbridge steeple, long and leetle,
> Dirty town, and nasty people.[65]

Further west the old Devon/Somerset trade was declining fast. Its greatest days had been during the seventeenth century when Devon or Exeter serges were one of the country's leading, perhaps indeed the leading, export. This trade had been greatly damaged by the French wars of the early years of the eighteenth century but later faced increased competition from Norwich. Further French wars at the end of the century would have given the final blow if it had not been for the orders for Long Ells placed by the East India Company for the China trade which lasted until that Company's monopoly was broken in 1833. According to the Factory Returns of 1838 there were still more than 3000 hand looms in Devon. The returns also showed 39 woollen mills, but the question of what constituted a mill was perhaps even more uncertain in Devon than elsewhere in the country. Exeter, which in the seventeenth and early eighteenth century had been the finishing and selling centre for the trade, had quite lost this position with the rise of the East India Company trade. Cloths bought by the Company were sent undyed to London. At Wellington, Fox Brothers were a well-known firm which, after the decline of the East India Company business, turned successfully to making a wide range of fine woollen and worsted cloths.

These years saw the establishment of the Scottish woollen trade on a sound basis which enabled it during the rest of the period covered by this study to replace the West of England as the main manufacturing area for fine woollens.[66] Its early history has been briefly summarised. There were several sections of the Scottish trade, the most important being in the Border country with Galashiels the chief centre. Further north around Alloa – the Hillfoots area as it was called – was closely linked to Glasgow as its main selling centre and specialised in tartans. Finally in the north at Aberdeen, Crombies, destined during the later decades of the century to become one of the famous woollen manufacturing firms in the world, was already established.

The Problems of the Norfolk Trade
The prosperous decades of the 1740s and 1760s do not seem to have been repeated for the Norfolk trade in the last quarter of the eighteenth century. And it may be that this previous expansion which was based at least partly on the extension of foreign trade, was in the longer run to be a cause of decline. Contemporary estimates of the size of the industry at the end of the century do not inspire confidence but Dr Corfield has probably rightly argued that modest expansion was still continuing in the 1770s and 1780s, particularly as a result of broader overseas sales and the regular annual order for camblets from the East India Company.[67] However, the 1770s was a difficult decade with depression for several years and high unemployment. All was not well also in the following three decades. General depression in the worsted trade for much of the 1790s created unemployment and the trading problems early in the new century further exacerbated the difficulties. Peace in 1815 restored some markets and Norwich responded with new cloths. But there is strong evidence of further decline from the mid-1820s and in the 1830s, particularly in the country districts.[68]

A careful distinction needs to be made, of course, between relative and absolute decline. In the face of the rise of the Yorkshire worsted trade, Norwich and Norfolk's contribution to total worsted cloth output was relatively declining from the mid-eighteenth century or earlier. It may not, however, have been until the second half of the 1820s that a consistent downward trend in absolute output emerged, although in the previous three decades trade depression and market difficulties resulted in short periods of contraction.

How far did Norwich suffer from West Riding competition? It was not necessarily the case that the rise of the Yorkshire industry was at the expense of Norfolk production, although it is easy to see how Yorkshire's success could so easily give rise to contemporary comment about the decadence of the Norfolk industry, and to concern and pessimism within that industry.[69] There is evidence that during the middle decades of the century Yorkshire did make inroads into Norfolk's trade in medium quality worsteds, but the latter industry was still expansionary and this competition gave little cause for concern.[70]

What must be remembered however is that, on the whole, Norfolk and the West Riding were producing very different cloths for very different markets. The camblets of John Sutcliffe of Halifax in 1775 were priced at 21s. to 23s., while those made in Norwich of the same dimensions and at roughly the same period, were valued at 47s. to 68s., and sometimes as high as 115s.[71] The latter prices are supported by the Bridewell Museum pattern books. Whilst the development of the West Riding worsted trade was based very much on plain worsteds, later with cotton warps, the speciality of the Norwich trade was fancy cloths, often with a considerable silk content. It is difficult, therefore, to be convinced that the rise of the plain Yorkshire worsteds stole from Norwich its major customers. Moreover, as Dr Edwards has pointed out, local explanations for the problems of Norwich, although making comparisons with Yorkshire, only rarely specifically blame Yorkshire competition for Norwich's difficulties.[72]

What then were the problems which Norwich and the Norfolk trade faced? It seems probable that explanations for decline lie more in market changes than in production problems. A succession of difficulties in overseas markets are apparent. Those foreign markets developed in the middle of the previous century were notoriously unreliable. The first blows came with the wars against France, resulting in the loss of both important French demand and markets in Southern Europe, including, in particular, Spain and Portugal. The European difficulties were soon added to by the disruptions to American trade. With these problems resolved only a few years of recovery were possible before yet more difficulties. French competition, both at home and abroad, produced more of an impact perhaps than Yorkshire's growth. The lowering of protection against French textiles in the home market led to a sudden rise from 1826 in the imports of French woollens, worsteds and silks. It seems very likely that the Norwich trade bore the brunt of these imports and was affected in the same way as the silk industry.

What then of the traditional explanations of locational difficulties, technological backwardness, labour resistance, entrepreneurial conservatism, inadequacies of water power and shortages of coal and iron? Are all these factors irrelevant? To a very great extent they must be. They all tend to boil down to the suggestion that Norwich was much more poorly equipped to undertake changes in her production methods, to reduce costs and to compete more with Yorkshire. But the initial divergence of growth trends was taking place before new technology played any role in the Yorkshire trade. Moreover we have suggested that competition from Yorkshire was of little relevance. The nature of Yorkshire's product could have meant only slight nibbling at the margins of Norfolk's markets. In any case the new technology, requiring power, that in due course became available, was at first largely inappropriate to the fancy, high quality, high labour-skill products of Norwich.

Instead we need to ask why markets for Norwich's goods did not rise so rapidly and why in due course they declined. The answer to the first question would seem straightforward. The general expansion at the very top end of the textile market was inevitably less than for more standard goods. The second question is more complex. Was there an absolute decline in demand from the 1820s or was Norwich losing out to Continental competitors? Rising real incomes in the upper echelons of society at home make the former suggestion unlikely. But it may be that fashion was moving against Norwich goods. In the 1820s in the high class ladies' trade there is evidence from costumes that taste was moving from the heavily glazed worsted which Norwich certainly made to very fine woollen merino fabrics with silk decorations and occasionally overprinted. Many of these latter cloths were almost certainly of French origin. Likewise in the non-apparel trade there is an impression that, in the early decades of the nineteenth century, glazed worsteds went out of favour for curtains and furnishing fabrics and, increasingly, chintzes came into popularity.

Thus it seems to us likely that both at home and abroad French competition, not unconnected with fashion changes, reduced Norwich's hold over markets. The reaction was to turn more and more to higher quality silk and worsted mixtures in order to compete. Perhaps the rise in the quality of the market was also Norwich's downfall although it should be remembered that a small section of the trade survived through the 1840s and 1850s servicing a mainly London market for exceptionally high quality and expensive goods.

There were perhaps other problems as well. Norwich came to rely on Yorkshire yarn and, at times, found difficulty in obtaining supplies. High quality cloth was more susceptible to sudden and severe fashion changes, with the implication perhaps that small manufacturers with little capital could suddenly find themselves encumbered with stocks of expensive goods that were no longer in demand or specialist yarn that was no longer of use. But the Norwich trade produced to merchants' orders and thus this seems of minor relevance.

This discussion, of course, still begs the question why Norwich did not attempt to move more towards the Yorkshire type of trade. But is this a realistic question to ask? Until the 1790s the Norfolk trade was still expansionary. There was little reason to follow the path pursued by Yorkshire; indeed, the gulf between the types of products of the two industries was increasingly widening. When decline did set in, in the 1820s, the nature of markets, methods and labour skills were so different that the extent of transition required must, rightly, have seemed impossible.

4 Capacity and Location, 1835–1870

The Relocation of the Industry

The Worsted Industry

An analysis of the extension of the capacity of the wool textile industry, in terms of mills, employment and capital is shown in Tables 12, 14 and 18. Trends are clearly recognisable although the figures take no account of domestic activity and the various doubts about the factory returns mean that the detailed statistics have to be interpreted with care.[1] Moreover they are not a satisfactory indicator of changes in the productive capacity of the industry because of the improving productivity of labour, power and machinery and because the factory returns do not always distinguish between plant standing and that actually in use.

For most of the nineteenth century the development of the United Kingdom worsted industry is really the history of the Yorkshire industry. The decline of the Norwich trade left Yorkshire manufacturers with little home competition by the 1830s. At no time subsequent to 1835 were more than 19 per cent of factory employees in the industry located outside Yorkshire. In 1850 the only other counties with more than 1000 factory worsted workers were Norfolk, Lancashire and Leicestershire. There were almost 71,000 in Yorkshire. In terms of mill numbers the major periods of growth in mid-century for the worsted industry were from 1835 to 1850 and in the early 1860s. The total for 1871 is substantially out of line with previous and later figures and with what one would have expected from the state of trade, possibly as a result of under-registration by the factory inspectorate.

The number of worsted mills in Norfolk increased in the 1840s to 11 employing 1400 workers by 1850, but no further growth took

Table 12   Mills and employment in the worsted industry, 1835–74

| | Yorkshire | | United Kingdom | |
	Mills	Employees	Mills	Employees
1835	204	16740	212	17816
1850	418	70905	501	79737
1857	445	78994	525	87794
1862	443	76483	532	86063
1867–8	626	121117	703	131896
1871	516	92398	630	109557
1874	520	114388	692	142097

SOURCE: *Factory Returns*

Table 13   The Norfolk worsted industry

	Mills	Employees		Mills	Employees
1838	3	385	1861	11	1283
1850	11	1400	1867	4	445
1857	10	1187	1871	10	880

SOURCE: *Factory Returns*

place. There were still 10 mills in 1871, although by that date only 880 workers were employed. The figures do, however, suggest that the Norfolk factory industry did survive at a low level through the middle of the century. Shawls made from various exotic combinations, notably fine spun worsted with much silk introduced, had become the main product of the Norwich trade. But competition from the cheaper Paisley and other cotton shawls was making this business precarious, although the final blow was not to come until the end of the century when shawls ceased to be a fashion article.[2]

Increased concentration of worsteds in Yorkshire was accompanied by a tightening of the boundaries of the industry within the county. In the early decades of the century manufacturing declined relatively in many of the outlying villages of the textile district and further afield in the Pennines. Masham, Ripon, Hawes, Kildwick, Selby and York all lost their worsted industry between 1810 and 1830. Another very noticeable change was the decline in the industry in Leeds, where an extensive worsted trade had developed in the second half of the eighteenth century. Local firms specialised in camblets and, from the 1780s, also in wildbores. The camblet trade, which provided cloth for clothing poorer women and for export to Northern Europe and North and South America, was susceptible to substantial variations in activity and the Leeds worsted trade fluctuated in the early decades of the nineteenth century.[3] Domestic manufacture was gradually transferred to mills from the 1790s and by 1835 there were ten in Leeds parish, most of which were close to the town itself. At this time, the majority of the Yorkshire worsted merchants were based in Leeds and dyeing and finishing facilities had developed there. The Leeds worsted merchants attempted unsuccessfully to establish a stuff market at Leeds in 1829. Unfortunately they chose a bad year for in May 1830 the *Leeds Mercury* reported that the Leeds worsted trade had been so depressed the previous winter that it had almost become extinct.[4] But it revived and survived. In 1850 there were eight mills still working, employing almost 1000 workers. The industry contracted in the mid-1850s but the census figures show that it continued on a small scale through the rest of the century.[5] It did not, however, participate in the growth of the worsted industry elsewhere in Yorkshire.

A number of reasons seem possible for its apparent stagnation. The transfer of worsted merchants to Bradford during the 1840s left the Leeds trade without the advantages from which it had previously benefited. The failure of the large firm of Hindes and Dereham in 1839, with huge losses, adversely affected others financially.[6] The closure of their extensive combing shops in Meadow Lane reduced combing capacity in Leeds. The large number of other failures in the Leeds worsted trade in the late 1830s and early 1840s might suggest that the local firms were backward in the innovation of cotton warps.

The transfer of worsted merchanting to Bradford was very rapid in the 1840s. Sigsworth shows, on the basis of trade directories, that the number of Leeds worsted merchants declined from 52 in 1837 to 28 in 1853 and 17 in 1861, whereas over the same period the number in Bradford rose from 25 to 157. Merchants transferred also to Bradford from Halifax, Manchester and elsewhere.[7] The cause of this sudden and substantial movement again seems to have been the introduction of cotton warps which gave such a boost to the Bradford trade and increased its prosperity when the industry elsewhere was in the doldrums. One of the earliest merchants to make the move was Jacob Behrens. After many frustrations in dealing with Leeds merchants he set up his own warehouse in the town in 1834. He expanded rapidly and moved to Bradford in 1838, explaining that that was where nine-tenths of his goods were made. He considered the move inevitable and claimed to have set the example for the general movement. Certainly other English and foreign merchants followed close behind him.[8]

The Woollen Industry

In the woollen industry the expansion of mill numbers was rapid from 1835 to 1850 and again in the 1860s. Yorkshire's position, as measured by factory employment, rose steadily to the 1860s and then fluctuated between 55 per cent and 65 per cent of the United Kingdom total. Employment also expanded in Scotland and Lancashire and a few less important counties but the middle decades of the century witnessed overall a further concentration of the industry into the major centres and a continuing decline in the west and south-west of England. At mid-century, besides Yorkshire and Scotland, only Lancashire, Gloucestershire, Wiltshire and Somerset had more than 1000 factory woollen workers.

Scotland's increasing role in factory employment from this time on is partially explained by its backwardness in factory development

Table 14   The United Kingdom woollen industry

	1835	1850	1856	1861	1867	1874
Mills						
U.K.	1121	1497*	1505	1679	1762	1925
England and Wales	995	1306*	1282	1456	1524	1606
Scotland	90	182	196	184	193	259
Yorkshire	406	880	806	924	899	998
West of England**	205	147	114	107	116	n.a.
Employment (thousands)						
U.K.	52.9	74.4	79.1	87.0	130.4	138.8
England and Wales	47.8	64.4	69.1	76.3	105.1	108.8
Scotland	3.5	9.5	9.3	9.8	14.8	27.7
Yorkshire	23.6	40.6	43.0	50.5	62.3	76.8
West of England**	12.6	11.1	10.0	10.1	12.1	n.a.

SOURCE: *Factory Returns*
NOTES: *Excludes a figure (about 100?) for spinning and weaving mills in Lancashire.
          **Wiltshire, Somerset and Gloucester. Totals for 1835 are not complete.

previously. The number of its factory workers more than doubled to 23,000 in the decade of the 1860s. This increase was attained more through a growth in the size of the mills than the number of them. The period from 1835 to 1870 witnessed the major expansion of the Scottish industry into home and foreign markets. As a supplier of high quality goods it was largely to supplant the West of England. One of the main reasons for success was the variety of fabrics produced and the excellence of design and production of the various regional specialities. There was a widespread geographical distribution of the trade. By the 1830s the border counties of Berwick, Roxburgh, Selkirk, Peebles and Dumfries were moving ahead as the main centre. A third of factory workers were located there in 1850. Important mills were developed at Galashiels and along the River Tweed at Walkerburn, Innerleithen, and Peebles. Cloth was woven at Hawick but the town developed a greater reputation for knitted fabrics.

The second most important area for the weaving trade was that situated to the north of the Firth of Forth around Tillicoultry, Alloa and Alva, in what is known as the Hillfoots district. There, in the counties of Clackmannan, Fife and Kinross, 25 per cent of Scottish factory workers were located in 1850. This area also had a number of large spinning mills concentrating on producing high quality woollen yarns for hand knitting. Patons of Alloa was to become a household name. Kinross specialised in the spinning of cashmere.

The third main area of woven woollen production was situated at Aberdeen and at a few other seaside towns on the North-East coast. In importance and interest this area was dominated by the firm of Crombies, who became perhaps the most famous woollen cloth producer in the whole of Britain.[9] The firm specialised in high quality overcoatings with a fine raised finish. One or two other firms in the area, notably Harrisons of Elgin, became the only ones outside Yorkshire to specialise in fabrics made from rare fibres.

There were also a number of producers of woollen cloth in the Glasgow area. The 1851 Exhibition reports show that tartans were their main production.[10] Other developments were taking place in this period. The reputation of Harris for tweed was emerging, although production was tiny.[11] The knitting trade in Shetland likewise was beginning to become better known. Within Scotland at mid-century the factory inspectors recorded woollen mills in three-quarters of the counties. Although as the century progressed expansion was concentrated in the major centres, the industry survived in almost all the counties where it had previously existed, although

Table 15   The Lancashire wool textile industry

| | Woollen | | Worsted | |
	Mills	Employment	Mills	Employment
1835	99	4575	8	1076
1838	101	4947	12	924
1856	99	9409	9	2087
1861	101	9227	3	840
1867	125	11 338	10	1979
1874	98	11 822	46	5317
1879	104	11 564	34	3735
1884	94	11 781	19	3817
1889	88	10 306	10	1974
1895	112	9412	8	1698

SOURCE: *Factory Returns*
NOTE: The Returns for 1850 and 1871 contain obvious inaccuracies.

often this was the result of a few individual, successful firms developing specialities and well known trade names.

Such was the pre-eminence of Lancashire in the manufacture of cotton and the importance of that industry in the economy, little attention has been focused previously on the wool textile industry within the county. Yet throughout the nineteenth century the industry was of considerable significance employing in the peak years of the early 1870s over 17,000 factory workers. Although this figure does not compare with the 352,000 factory cotton workers within the county in 1874, it still amounted to an important trade.

Rochdale escaped the flurry of cotton mill development from the 1770s and remained quite firmly based on wool until at least the middle of the nineteenth century.[12] Its first woollen factories were established in the 1790s and it maintained a quite separate identity from the Yorkshire trade just a few miles away. In 1812 it was reported that 'the trade of our country is flannels and baize – broad baize called Lisbon baize, flannels and light baize . . . none of our description are manufactured in Yorkshire'.[13] Some of the baize had worsted warp, some was made entirely of woollen yarn. There was a large export trade in baize and shalloons, particularly to Flanders and Portugal, but also to Spain, Holland and Russia. This trade was adversely affected by Napoleon's embargo but exports to North America developed to replace it and around 1812 absorbed two-thirds of the town's production.[14] The restoration of peace enabled the town to re-open the old markets and retain the new, so a period of prosperity was entered with the number of woollen manufacturers in the town rising from about 128 in 1818 to 205 in 1824.[15] In 1821 baize was being exported to the United States to be worn by slaves and to Holland where it was used for petticoats. In that year a local manufacturer commented on the amazing weight of wool used in the neighbourhood, most being used for baizes but a large quantity of finer wools also being manufactured into flannels.[16]

A more detailed profile of the district's woollen manufacturing activities emerged in 1828. Baizes were being manufactured with cotton warps, using Southdown wool for wefts, and an export trade had developed in them to South America. A local flannel and baize manufacturer complained of great competition from cotton goods, particularly from calicoes and fustians. Cotton was introduced presumably to counteract this competition and a new type of baize was developed: 'We have latterly introduced a great deal of cotton with the woollen, making an article called Dometts, and another article called Domett Baize that has almost superceded woollen baizes.'[17] But from the mid-1820s there is a suggestion of a decline in the number of local woollen manufacturers.[18] Rather more detail on the size and location of the Lancashire factory industry is available for 1838. Rochdale was clearly the major centre accounting for over half the employment and number of mills. The huge parish of Whalley, which incorporated many of the isolated Rossendale mills, was second in importance, and was the centre for the manufacture of bockings. In 1838 the Lancashire worsted trade appears to have been of little significance but it did develop quite substantially in the 1870s, only to decline again thereafter.

The Lancashire woollen industry progressed steadily until about 1871. It consisted of mills much larger than the national average; in 1856 the Lancashire mills employed on average 95 workers whereas in Yorkshire and England and Wales the numbers were 66 and 54 respectively and the Lancashire mills remained substantially larger in terms of employment for the rest of the century. After 1871 the Lancashire industry encountered problems; mills and workers declined as the flannel industry was faced with a number of problems. In the previous decade the industry had been given a boost by the cotton famine. A greater use of flannel for underclothing had come into vogue,[19] but in 1880 a trade journal reported that the woollen manufacture in Rochdale had dwindled rapidly in the previous 10 or 15 years, and that it was then little more than a quarter of its former dimensions.[20] In the following few years various reasons were given for the decline. There were complaints of lack of enterprise, tariff problems, difficulties arising from heavy local rates, high railway charges, the failure of a local bank and the vagaries of fashion.[21] There were many local failures in 1881 but the trade was picking up again in 1884.[22] It was reported as being brisk in 1886, but then in 1888 the introduction of flannelette, consisting only or mainly of cotton, caused concern. Flannelette was a modification of the 'Harvard' striped or checked shirting by Potters and Taylor of Manchester who marketed it as imitation flannel. There was much opposition to it in Rochdale where it was described as 'rubbish' and as a 'fraudulent article'. The Lancashire flannel manufacturers challenged the use of the word 'flannelette' unsuccessfully in the courts in 1895.[23] At this time also the fancy flannel trade was in decline through Scottish competition;[24] the figures for mills show a substantial decline in the ten years after 1879 and by 1895 employment had fallen still further.[25]

A scattered wool textile industry survived in the four northern counties of Durham, Northumberland, Cumberland and Westmorland throughout the nineteenth century. County Durham maintained a small but important carpet weaving trade, the major centre of which was Barnard Castle, which had five factories in 1827 and more later, and employed at one stage over 600 workers. The remnants of this local activity survived until the 1880s.[26] It was said that the waters of the River Tees were ideal for producing brilliant colours in dyeing. Carpets were also produced at various times in Darlington and Durham City. In 1814 the County Justices put up a loan of £400 to encourage the re-establishment of carpet weaving in Durham. The firm that emerged gained success in the American markets and survived until 1903 when Crossleys of Halifax bought the goodwill, the buildings being let out to another firm.[27] In the 1860s it was a major local employer, with 500 workers, manufacturing £100,000 value of goods annually.[28] In Bishop Auckland, Chester-le-Street and Sunderland there were small local industries, possibly mainly dependent on the demand for yarn from the carpet weavers.[29]

In Darlington the Pease family, who had originated in West Yorkshire in the early eighteenth century, were instrumental in establishing an important local worsted spinning industry which supplied yarn to the Devon serge trade, as well as to the South of Scotland, Lancaster, Nottingham, Yorkshire and the Continent. Large factories were established at an early date but labour shortages hampered growth. By 1838 there were three mills employing 400 workers. In 1866 Henry Pease and Company's 550 hands, employed in three mills, were producing 400,000 pounds of worsted yarn annually, as well as 110,000 pounds of woven cloth; 600 or more were still employed in 1905.[30]

In Northumberland, Hexham, Morpeth and Berwick-on-Tweed developed small worsted spinning works early in the nineteenth century. At one stage there were two firms making flannel at Morpeth and small isolated country mills provided work for local communities and yarn for country weavers. Two small mills in Hexham, run by Messrs W. and H. Hart, were using steam power for wool carding early in the nineteenth century; they worked on both a commission and freelance basis.[31] The industry in Cumbria was mainly centred on the Kendal district where woollen, worsted and carpet manufacturers were still active in the 1860s, using mainly water power. At that time several of the firms employed over 200 workers and two were manufacturing 400,000 pounds of goods annually.[32] The tweed and hosiery yarn mills at Alston were built to provide employment for local women in the mining community.[33]

The Irish wool textile industry in the nineteenth century was of very little significance in terms of United Kingdom production. It was widely scattered throughout the country. Domestic manufacture survived on a widespread local basis and the few factories were mainly very small. The 141 factories in Ireland in 1885 employed only 3136 workers, an average of 22 compared with an average of 77 in other United Kingdom mills. After very little progress through the middle of the century the industry increased in vitality in the 1880s. The report of the Cork Exhibition of 1883 said the Irish manufacturers were giving up 'old and hackneyed designs . . . honest enough in fibre, but coarse, unfinished and intolerably ugly, and were beginning to pay attention to numerous novelties, skilfully and tastefully produced, with good design and finish.'[34] Most of Irish production was for domestic consumption but a small export trade did emerge, particularly from the late 1890s, to the United States and elsewhere, as a result of active promotion on the part of some major Irish manufacturers.

The main product development in this period was Donegal tweed made from coarse local wool in the plain weave with contrasting colours in warp and weft, and with the novelty of little lumps of uncarded wool spun into the yarn to give a distinctive effect. Donegal tweeds became a fashion garment but, as they were so distinctive the vogue for them could undergo rapid short-term changes. Increasingly, cheap imitations of them were made, particularly in Yorkshire.

By 1871 very little survived of the Devon industry. In 1838 there had been 39 mills and almost 2000 factory workers; by 1871 the number had fallen to nine mills and 350 employees. The decline was most substantial in the 1840s when capacity fell by more than half and the last few years of the 1860s also appear to have been disastrous. The census returns suggest that total wool textile employment in the county fell by two-thirds in the 1850s and 1860s. The surviving Devon industry was a scattered miscellany of mills making a variety of cloth. Some firms sought military orders and some attempts were made by more far-sighted entrepreneurs to compete with the finer Yorkshire worsted trade. These included firms in Somerset – Fox of Wellington for example.[35]

The years from 1835 to 1870 also witnessed real decline in the West of England. The traditional cloth making town of Bradford-on-Avon suffered greatly. In 1841 the banking house of Hobhouse of Bath went bankrupt, mainly because of the way in which they had been supporting Saunders and Company of Bradford-on-Avon and Cooper's of Staverton.[36] As Piggott's Directory of 1842 wrote: 'Perhaps few places in England have felt the vicissitudes and migrations of trade more than Bradford, there being at present but three or four clothing establishments in full employ.'[37] The broadcloth trade was indeed nearing its end. The number of people employed in the mills did not greatly change but this disguises the disappearance of the domestic industry. There were occasional periods of trade recovery which were sufficient to encourage short bouts of new investment. In the early 1850s for example, there was resumed industrial activity in Bradford-on-Avon, but in the three counties of Wiltshire, Somerset and Gloucestershire factory employment in 1871 was only two-thirds the level of 1835 and, in the meantime, domestic industry had all but disappeared. Trowbridge and Stroud increasingly stood out as the main manufacturing centres.

The all new wool products of the West of England trade may be divided into flannels, coatings and overcoatings, and speciality cloths such as Bedford cords and riding tweeds. The word 'flannel' covers a great variety of cloths. At the top end of the trade there were West of England flannels made from the best wools that could be obtained. They were used for trouserings and also for suitings. Usually, but not necessarily made in grey, they were normally manufactured in the West of England in the prunelle 2/1 twill, as opposed to the 2/2 or plain weave that was used elsewhere. Occasionally there was a fashion run for striped flannels but generally it was the plain cloth that was sought. The best West of England flannels were excellent fabrics, their only fault as suiting cloths arose from the fact that

Table 16   *The wool textile industry in Devon*

| | Woollen | | Worsted | |
	Mills	Employment	Mills	Employment
1838	39	1810	—	—
1850	14	767	7	306
1856	17	1250	2	20
1861	16	753	5	130
1867	17	939	2	137
1871	9	353	2	119
1895	16	1077	*	163

SOURCE: *Factory Returns*
NOTE: *less than 5

woollen cloths, however well made, tend to stretch, which meant the flannels bagged at the knees. It was for this reason that there would occasionally be fashion demands for worsted flannels but these lacked the warm soft handle of the best woollen flannel. Few flannels were made from cross-bred wools and the other two main groups not made in the West of England were the comparatively small amount made by the Yorkshire low woollen trade and the large amount of considerably cheaper Rochdale and Welsh flannels made for entirely different purposes, largely for underclothes.

The mid-decades of the century produced quite good demand for West of England lightweight coatings which were worn during the late spring, summer and autumn, not for warmth purposes but for protection against rain. Some form of waterproofing was therefore essential. This was achieved to some extent by the use of the 2/1 twill which gave a warp surface from which rain was more likely to run off and by various rather unsatisfactory forms of waterproofing. The problem with waterproofing has always been that if sufficient chemical is used to be effective, the handle of the wool is lost. At the period being discussed here no satisfactory method existed. Later the coming of rubber-proofed garments, such as mackintoshes, were to have a severe effect on this trade. West of England high quality overcoatings in this period suffered, more perhaps than any other cloth, from competition from Yorkshire low woollens.

The smallest section of the West of England trade was that making traditional cloths such as Bedford cords, riding tweeds, buckskins and beavers, many of them the remnants of the old traditional broadcloths, surviving because of the specialist purposes for which they were used.

On the fringe of the West of England area was the Witney blanket trade. Witney blankets were the best and most famous produced, but considerable quantities were also manufactured in the West Riding.[38] Naturally heavy in weight, they used considerable quantities of wool. Witney concentrated mainly on merino blankets, Yorkshire tended to use the coarser cross-bred wools. Welsh flannel scored reasonable success during this period. It was made in several ways but usually in the plain weave and from coarse Welsh wool. Its main use was for shirts and other undergarments. The mills were small and very scattered. Only in Montgomery were more than 500 employed in the factory industry; Newtown and Welshpool were the main centres.[39]

Aggregate employment in the wool textile industry may be deduced from both factory returns and the censuses of population. The former take no account of domestic textile occupations nor do they include certain groups of factory employees, such as overseers and managers. The latter are difficult to interpret because of uncertainty over classifications. In some years there are, for example, unspecified categories for 'weaver', 'factory textile worker', 'fancy goods manufacturer' and others.

The two sources clearly show the changing balance between domestic and factory employment. The censuses show little change in total employment between 1851 and 1871; according to them, the labour force in the industry amounted to just over a quarter of a million. In the same period however, factory employment rose from 154,000 to 234,000, and the latter figure may be an underestimate. These various figures are unsatisfactory not solely because of doubts about their reliability and interpretation, but also because they give no indication of the effect on labour productivity, of changes in the number of hours worked, in the composition of the labour force and in the type and amount of machinery tended. In particular the faster speeds at which machinery was being worked throughout the period after the 1850s suggests that labour productivity rose rapidly. The greater use of broader looms later in the century caused a similar effect. Attempts to introduce the two-loom system in Bradford and district from the late 1850s helped the productivity of worsted weavers but not of the loom and likewise, in the same period, the introduction of the power comb had an immense effect on the productivity of combers.

Table 17   Employment in the woollen and worsted industry from the Census of Population* (thousands)

1851	254	1891	275
1861	235	1901	235
1871	263	1911	248/261
1881	252		

SOURCE: *Committee on Industry and Trade: Survey of Textile Industries, loc. sit.*, p. 164.
NOTE: *excludes carpets and rugs.

Investment 1835–1914

The estimate of the fixed capital stock of the factory industry in 1835 (see Chapter 2) was just under £4 million. If a constant relationship between employment and capital is assumed for the following decades, the fixed capital stock might be as shown in Table 18. The calculations in this section are carried through to 1912 because of the uniformity of the method used. The adjustment to current prices is made on the basis of the Rousseaux price index of principal industrial products.[40] Net investment per annum is converted to gross investment on the basis of an annual depreciation rate of 2.5 per cent for buildings, 8 per cent for machinery and 5 per cent for motive plant, which, using the same weights as in Chapter 2, give an annual rate of depreciation of 5.3 per cent. This is no more than a very rough estimate. Relative importance of various items of fixed capital may have changed during the course of the century particularly with increasing efficiency of motive power. Of more significance is the probability of an improvement in the capital/labour ratio through technological development and the reduction of hand workers in factories.

It was more common at the time for estimates of capital stock values to be calculated on the basis of machinery. There are many such estimates for the cotton industry but fewer for wool textiles. However, in 1886 Jacob Behrens quoted a Bradford architect as estimating that a local mill of 500 broad and 500 narrow looms, including the necessary combing, carding, preparing and spinning machinery, and also including the buildings, engines, boilers, shafting and accessories and the land, would not cost less at current prices than £70,000 or £71,000![41] Behrens prided himself on being well informed and it may therefore be that a figure of £70 per loom fixed capital value in an integrated wool textile mill was not unrealistic. Contemporary estimates based on spindles are available for the cotton industry but not for wool textiles. Feinstein has argued that a figure twice the 24*s*. per spindle often quoted for the cotton industry would seem appropriate, given the additional machinery and power required in wool textiles.[42] This may be rather high, as it would appear unlikely, even taking into account the extra machinery, that the additional capital requirements per spindle would have been double. However, if Behrens' figure of £70 per loom in integrated mills and £2.10*s*. per spindle in spinning mills is applied to the amount of machinery in wool textile mills in 1885, the replacement value of fixed capital amounts to £11.3 million. To this must be added the fixed capital in weaving-only mills and the extra capital in integrated mills with extra spinning capacity. A figure of about £1.5 million might be appropriate. These figures are no more than a very rough guess but interestingly are not substantially more than the calculations based on employment.

The figures may perhaps be taken as a rough estimate of fixed capital stock and trends bearing in mind the reservations above and that, in some periods of bad trade, labour would be laid off although capital stock would remain fairly constant. With the decline in the domestic industry, these figures come closer to the total fixed capital stock of the industry.

Estimates of circulating capital, and thus of total capital, are, as for the earlier period, more difficult to generate. There are diverse contemporary suggestions. In 1884 Henry Mitchell believed that fixed capital formed between one-third and one-half of total capital in the worsted trade but his estimate of total capital in the Yorkshire worsted industry of £30 to £40 million was far in excess of Behrens' assessment.[43] Early this century in the West of England firms aimed to turn over their capital twice in a year, and their fixed capital was typically a quarter of their total capital. But contemporary comment for many areas of the industry also suggests a considerable diversity of experience between different firms and vague generalisations such as these are not very helpful.

The estimates for fixed capital formation stress the periods of investment activity in the mid-1830s, the first half of the 1850s, the 1860s and the decade before 1912.

Table 18   Fixed capital stock and formation in the wool textile industry, 1835–1912 (£ million)

	Stock at 1835 prices	Stock at current prices	Net formation per annum over previous period at current prices	Gross formation per annum over previous period at current prices
1835	3.84	3.84	—	—
1838	4.79	4.79	0.33	0.56
1847	6.93	6.80	0.22	0.53
1850	8.47	7.39	0.20	0.58
1856	9.19	10.35	0.49	0.97
1861	9.52	10.21	−0.03	0.51
1867	14.41	15.46	0.88	1.58
1874	15.40	16.80	0.19	1.05
1878	14.03	12.24	−1.14	−0.40
1885	14.85	11.88	−0.05	0.59
1890	15.95	12.47	0.12	0.77
1895	15.13	10.12	−0.47	0.12
1901	14.08	11.26	0.19	0.76
1907	14.14	13.88	0.44	1.12
1912	15.62	15.90	0.40	1.20

NOTES: Two half-timers are counted as one employee.
See text for methods of derivation of figures.

5 Raw Materials, Technology and Power, 1835–70

Raw Materials: Home and Foreign Wools

Home grown wools still provided the main raw material for the industry in 1835. The 1828 evidence in the House of Lords' report gave an excellent picture of the state of the wool trade. There seems to have been an admirable lack of prejudice. The importance of the German merino wool for fine cloths was rightly emphasised and the first sign of the coming of the great Australian sheep farms commented upon with remarkable prescience, but there is no doubting the fact that the industry still depended for its bulk supplies upon the home grown product. It was the so-called deterioration in the quality of this wool and the question of falling prices that dominated the proceedings. It is perhaps a little strange that no one understood that the deterioration in quality had caused the fall in prices and that without the rise in quantity, consequent on the switch to mutton rather than wool sheep, shortage of wool would have been an even worse problem. It is, of course, clear that the report, as valuable as it was, represented very much the agricultural point of view, but it remains a little surprising that those clothiers and wool merchants who gave evidence did not have a somewhat clearer understanding of what was happening, although Arthur Young made the point in his *Northern Tour* and it was further commented upon by Banks in his *Qualified Export*.[1]

As late as 1851 the worsted industry used an estimated 15 million pounds of imported wool and 65 million pounds of English wool. By 1857 the gap had widened to 85 million pounds of English wool against 15 million pounds of foreign. The position in the woollen trade was rather different and in 1858 it used about 76 million pounds of imported wool and 80 million pounds of English, as well as perhaps 45 million pounds of shoddy and mungo. By 1858 Australian merino wool had had little effect on the English worsted trade. As Barnard points out, 'the woollen trade utilised 83 per cent of the retained imports of wool from all foreign and colonial sources and indeed, until the end of the sixties, it remained the only substantial consumer of Australian wool'.[2]

The fact that the worsted trade was mainly using British wool meant that there was a steady demand for this commodity. Nevertheless, meat had become the dominant factor in British sheep farming. It followed that the consumers of wool did not have complete control of the supply in the sense that their wishes and demands would ultimately be reflected in the price and type of the product produced. It is also worth remembering that the main product of the English worsted trade at the time had a cotton warp with a British wool/worsted weft. The price of this yarn depended on demand for cotton in the cotton trade and was therefore likely to move somewhat independently of the demand from the worsted manufacturer. The effect of this was clear during the American Civil War.

The woollen industry was more fortunate in that the Australian grower at this time existed only to supply it. Most of the Australian wool was exported washed, and every attempt was made to meet special demands. One of MacArthur's sons was in England in 1825 and attended the London sales, listening to what his customers had to say about his product.[3] There are other examples of Australian wool growers' efforts to keep closely in touch with the market.[4] As a result of all this, the fine woollen manufacturer was excellently catered for but unfortunately his business was declining. The manufacturer of cheaper woollens was not quite so well provided for. He had only the shorter and poorer sections of the Australian clip to choose from. This comparative shortage of poorer, cheaper wool for the woollen trade undoubtedly played a part in the growth of the waste industry which was so important in providing a steady supply of cheap material for this expanding section of the trade.

The merino wool served the woollen industry entirely. In the 1830s the fine woollen manufacturer, still centred mainly in the West of England but with several important firms in the West Riding competing, used largely fine merino. In 1840 German imports at 22 million pounds which, however, would not have been all merino still exceeded Australian at 10 million pounds, but ten years later there had been a complete reversal; 9 million pounds from Germany as compared with 39 million pounds from Australasia.[5] The first settlers and the first merino sheep farms in Australia were in New South Wales. In the case of Sydney, the Camden Park type of merino as developed by MacArthur was based on the Spanish merino but, particularly in areas developed a little later, it was common to introduce sheep from Saxony. This early Sydney wool was only 2–3 inches long, and quite fine, mainly about a 64s quality. Other areas of Australia soon began to produce wools of slightly varying types but this is hardly the place to go into the minutiæ of merino wool growing, only to emphasise the large variety offered within the range of 60s quality upwards.

Table 19   Wool imports, 1830–69 (million lbs.)

Annual averages	Total	From Australasia	Re-exports
1830–4	35.3	2.8	0.7
1835–9	53.0	6.8	2.0
1840–4	53.3	14.0	2.4
1845–9	70.5	27.6	5.9
1850–4	95.4	43.7	15.1
1855–9	121.1	51.1	29.7
1860–4	167.2	75.0	50.6
1865–9	236.3	134.2	92.3

Australia was not the only area to make contributions to the widening range of fine merino wools available to the English manufacturer. South Africa was the other leading producer for the United Kingdom, and it grew wools with rather different qualities to the Australian. These wools felted more quickly but were not quite so good for making heavily fulled cloth; they usually carried more dust and sand, which gave them a lower yield than the Australian. They did however scour to a good white. They appear to have been sent over in the grease almost from the start. Most distinctive, however, with these wools was the custom there, not practised in Australia, of shearing at less than a year's interval, every 6 to 8 months for example, which had the advantage of giving a wider range of length in each quality. This practice, therefore, further added to the range of new materials becoming available to the British manufacturer. The widening range and increasing quantity of British wool becoming available has been dealt with in some detail in Chapter 2. There were no major new developments in the period covered here. Any areas which had not, by 1830, made the change to the type of sheep developed by Bakewell and Ellman realised that they must do so and consequently the supply increased still further.

During these years the wool textile industry became to an increasing extent a consumer of material other than new wool. The worsted branch used cotton and the woollen used cotton and wool waste. Obviously the reasons were quite different. Both were widely used and the wool textile trade was to become almost as large a consumer of other materials as it was of new wool. The industry's growth and development during the period covered by this volume and particularly after about 1850, cannot be understood unless this widespread use of other raw materials is appreciated.

Cotton was used in both the worsted and woollen sections but for rather different reasons. As far as worsteds were concerned, cotton yarn was used in the warp. There was a specialised business supplying cotton yarns on warp beams to the worsted trade and reasons for the growth of this product will be discussed later. With woollens the cotton could be used as a warp or it could be mixed, i.e. blended, before spinning with the other components of the cloth. This widespread use of cotton in the woollen trade will be better understood when the many complexities of the wool waste raw material trade have been explained. Of the other fibres, flax and silk were also used. Flax, once important, had shrunk to relative insignificance. Silk had a limited importance in East Anglia; in addition, comparatively small amounts of silk were also used in the West Riding, mainly in the Huddersfield fancy waistcoat trade. Most of this silk was used in thread form; it was unusual to blend raw silk with raw wool before spinning.

From about 1850 the great growth of woollen production and the reason why, even after 1870, and right up to 1914, it was able to remain a growth industry rested on the ever-increasing use of various forms of wool waste. As the worsted trade did not use waste – it made waste which the woollen trade used – and as the total amount of waste used came to equal half the total raw material consumed by the whole trade, its importance is very clear. For this reason it is necessary to give a description of the various types of waste that were available; the best breakdown would be:

(1) those obtained from the actual processing
(2) those obtained from tearing up the yarn
(3) those obtained from tearing up cloth.

The division is not entirely satisfactory. For example, there were materials that should really be described as waste that came from earlier processes such as when the shorter wool from the sheep skin was removed – 'pie' pieces as they were sometimes called. This was certainly one of the poorest types of raw material offered to the woollen manufacturer, but quantities were not large and it can be omitted here.

Wool reclaimed from actual processing included the best of all waste, namely noils. Noils were so good, in fact, that it can be argued that they should hardly be considered as waste. It has become traditional in the woollen trade to allow the phrase 'new' or virgin wool to be applied to cloths containing noils. However, many noils, especially those that had been carbonised, were more akin to waste fibres. In any case, noils were essentially waste from the manufacture of worsted yarns.[6] Then there was the waste in the worsted yarn-making processes such as laps, essentially the waste part of tops; consequently the wool was long and good but might be heavily contaminated with oil. Laps probably did not become available in any quantity until the final development of machine combing. The woollen trade also used what was known as broken tops; these were worsted tops that had been broken into small handfuls, so that they could be re-processed in the woollen trade. They were expensive and only used in certain speciality fabrics, notably for the white part of grey mixtures, and should certainly not be considered as waste.

There was also the waste made by the woollen manufacturer as he processed his material. The main part of this was called soft waste and came entirely from carding. It was normal for the manufacturer to re-use this himself. If possible, he put it straight back in the blend being processed but this was not always possible as the carding of any batch would be completed before the spinning. Other types of waste from woollen yarn manufacturing processes, such as the fettlings from the carding, were usually too poor to be used again for cloth manufacturing.[7] Waste yarn could be torn up and re-used; and garnetted worsted yarn was much sought after by the woollen trade. Torn up woollen yarns, having originally been made from shorter material, were considerably less desirable than the product of torn up worsted yarns.

The third group of waste was by far the most important and contained the main quantities and qualities of reclaimed material. It came from torn up cloth and torn up knitwear and was, of course, the material that over the years came to be known as shoddy, mungo and extract. Fibres from new worsteds were the best of all. These were from all-wool worsted cloths that had not been worn; 'tailor's clippings' was perhaps a better name. The yarn in these fabrics was made from long wool and the cloth would not have been fulled, consequently less severe treatment was needed when tearing. Indeed, these torn up worsted wastes could be better than some of the poorer types of wool. They were often longer than many noils, which in some ways they slightly resembled. They were frequently sorted to shade and could then be used without re-dyeing. If they had to be re-dyed, obviously it had to be to a darker shade than the original waste. For this reason considerable quantities of so-called new black worsteds were available. The full development of this excellent waste did not, however, come until the manufacture of 100 per cent merino worsteds was established in the latter decades of the nineteenth century.

Old worsteds were rags obtained from worn fabrics and naturally during wearing some deterioration would have taken place. They represented an important source of raw material for the woollen trade. As with new worsteds, the full range of possibilities available with these wastes did not become clear until cotton warps were largely a thing of the past. Because the wool used in woollen yarns was shorter and because woollen cloths had usually been fulled, rags from woollen goods tended to be put together without differentiating between the old and the new. This raw material was short but useful, and was the main source of supply for shoddy and mungo in the middle decades of the nineteenth century.

Union material was the poorest form of cloth that could be torn and re-used. It derived originally from the great quantity of mixed wool and cotton cloth that was made by the worsted trade. It was possible to remove the cotton by carbonising, a treatment using sulphuric acid, which destroyed the cotton but left the wool material more or less intact. Because of this treatment the recovered material was short and the poorest available to the manufacturer of shoddy and mungo goods; it was usually called extract.

One general point should be emphasised. As, in the middle of the nineteenth century, so many worsted cloths were made with cotton warps, this meant that until the coming of carbonising, such fabrics could not be torn up and re-used. Cotton was too strong a fibre to be treated in the tearing machines or 'devils'. Most of the waste, during these early years, must therefore have come from the woollen trade.

Finally, however, another important group of waste material remains to be considered, namely hosiery clippings; that is, knitwear that had been torn up. Generally speaking, hosiery was rather better than torn up cloth. The knitting of yarn did not produce as tight a fabric as weaving, consequently the tearing up did not call for such drastic action and could, in fact, be done on a garnet machine which was considerably less severe and, therefore, less damaging to the fibre, than the devil. This material often retained its felting property better and was of a reasonable length of between one and two inches. Once again there was a division between the new hosiery clips from material that had not been worn, and waste from old hosiery, usually described as Berlins. Why this type of waste should have been given that name has never been properly elucidated. As with woven cloth, some hosiery material contained cotton and in this case carbonising was necessary if the waste was to be re-used.

We turn now to the supply position of these wastes. The market in noils was important and long-established and specialised marketing arrangements were developed for it. By the 1890s, in addition to supplying the home trade, over 10 million pounds per annum were exported to Germany, Russia and Belgium. It was, however, the material recovered from rags that took on particularly adverse connotations in the minds of the general public, because the word shoddy found its way into the language to mean something of inferior standard. More sensibly, the French called it 'Renaissance' wool.[8] For the production of many types of cloth, reclaimed wool, blended with new or with other fibres, especially cotton, was an invaluable raw material. This section of the trade has received little attention in published works. Until recently we have been dependent for much of our knowledge on Jubb's little volume published as early as 1860.[9] However, a recent very detailed examination, particularly of the supply side, has provided a major and comprehensive analysis of the growth of this part of the wool textile industry.[10]

The meaning of the two terms shoddy and mungo rather changed over the years. Shoddy was originally wool reclaimed from soft rags, particularly from knitted garments such as stockings, but later the word tended to be more confined to torn up worsted cloth. Knitted waste then formed a category of its own. Mungo was recovered wool from 'hard' rags such as thickly woven or heavily milled cloth. Spinning properties were thus reduced but blended with other fibres, mungo was of importance for heavy, well-milled low woollens.

Extract was the poorest of all. The acid used damaged the wool and made this waste of rather limited use. Poor rags, reclaimed wool of poor standard or insufficient staple length to be re-spun, and wool fibres obtained during the finishing processes were often called flocks and sometimes 'fud' and were used as furniture stuffing. Even poorer wool waste, such as dust and other similar material, was made use of as manure as long as it contained a sufficient amount of oil, and was particularly popular in the Kent hop-fields.

Cotton and linen rags had for centuries been used for the manufacture of paper, both in Britain and on the Continent, but it was not until the second decade of the nineteenth century, as far as is known, that the wool recovered from woollen and worsted rags began to be re-used commercially in the textile industry. Initially only the softer, so-called shoddy rags were reprocessed. This development took place in what was to become known as the Heavy or Low Woollen district of Yorkshire, and has usually been attributed to Benjamin Law of Batley.[11]

At first progress in the use of shoddy was slow, although it was said in 1818 that a large trade in woollen rags between London and Yorkshire had emerged.[12] Evidence given by the various Yorkshire merchants and manufacturers to the House of Lords committee on the State of the Wool Trade in 1828 makes it clear that by that date shoddy was well established. John Varley, a woollen manufacturer of Stanningley, acknowledged its substantial use in the manufacture of duffels for the home market and for export to Germany, Flanders, India and to the North American Indians. Shoddy duffels also were apparently in demand for workhouse clothing. J. Sutcliffe, a Huddersfield wool stapler, was prepared to acknowledge that goods were not necessarily spoilt by using shoddy, as rags could be well worked and Thomas Cook, the important Dewsbury manufacturer, reported using imported rags for some cloth. At that stage he believed that one-seventh or one-eighth of the rags used in the industry were imported, a proportion which Nussey, a woollen manufacturer from Birstall, agreed with. He roughly estimated on the basis of rag imports, and presumably on the rag-grinding machinery in use, that over two million pounds of shoddy were being consumed annually at that time.[13] In terms of total wool consumption that was still an insignificant proportion, but it was to grow very rapidly in later decades.

Additional stimulus was given in the mid-1830s by the success attained in the grinding of harder rags to produce mungo. The innovation was the result of the efforts of Benjamin Parr of Batley who, it was said, provided the name for the new material through his insistence that it 'mun go' through the carding machine.[14] Mungo was not suitable for use in soft, loosely woven cloths but could be blended with shoddy and wool for use in thicker, heavily milled fabrics or blankets, carriage cloths, overcoats, uniform cloths, etc. During the course of the nineteenth century the relative use of shoddy and mungo came to depend on fashion in the market place.

The expansion of the use of recovered wool was dependent on adequate supplies and gave rise to an intricate rag collecting, sorting

and marketing operation, both at home and abroad. Initially domestic rags formed the bulk of those used, with London being the main
source. The rags were collected, as Mayhew vividly illustrated, by a
host of small individual collectors, who in turn sold them to dealers.[15]
Supplies reached Yorkshire through direct purchases or, more normally from the 1850s, from sales by auction. The initiative appears to
have come from the rag dealers and merchants themselves as Dr
Malin could find little evidence of West Riding manufacturers actually seeking out supplies before the 1850s.[16]

In due course the rag collecting system extended beyond London
and reached all parts of the United Kingdom. Rags from Manchester,
Glasgow and Ireland had a poor reputation for worn and wretched
quality and those from the heavy industrial districts were very dirty.
Better rags came from London and the agricultural areas but it was
said in the 1880s that the best rags came from the seaports, where
'thick and unpatched stockings, Guernseys and flannel shirts, and
indigo jackets and trousers' were collected as clean 'as if washed
before selling to the rag collector'.[17]

If imported rags only accounted for one-seventh or one-eighth of
those consumed in 1828, by later in the century they attained almost
as much importance as domestic rags. Unfortunately, Board of Trade
classifications do not enable imports to be accurately tracked
throughout the period. Up to 1836 imported rags for re-manufacture
were grouped with woollen cloth. Then rags were separately identified but no division was made in terms of their intended purpose –
manure, flocks, shoddy or mungo. Later changes created further
confusion. The first import of rags for re-manufacture occurred
around 1820 but supplies from abroad developed only very slowly.[18]
Falling wool prices in the 1840s acted as a decelerator, but from 1849
wool prices rose sharply and demand for reclaimed wool followed.
Germany was the main external source, but from the 1830s small
quantities were arriving from various Baltic and Mediterranean
ports, and from further afield. Russia, Sweden, Denmark, Portugal
and the United States exported irregular supplies. Other countries
desirous of protecting supplies of rags for their home paper industries
put embargoes or high duties on exports and thus precluded supplies
to Britain.[19]

France was one country from which supplies were at first
unobtainable, but the Anglo-French Treaty of Commerce, which
permitted exclusive and duty free access to large supplies of rags of
exceptional quality, provided a major new source for the West
Riding. Rapid railway development in France in the 1850s aided

collection. The exclusive access to supplies only lasted a few years, as French trade policy became more liberal with other countries. Reuss, a Dewsbury German-born rag merchant and auctioneer, summed up the importance of the treaty, thus:

> What this district owes to Cobden for procuring under the Commercial Treaty free egress for woollen rags from France into England no man can tell; the quantity of rags, some of the very best to be got, which have been sent to us by France during the last twenty years are simply stupendous.[20]

France soon became the major supplier of imports but during the middle of the century sources had become wider, thus improving the range and quality of rags available, supply of course reflecting the type of cloth consumed in the various markets. Baines wrote of a 'thorough ransacking of every country where woollen rags are to be found'.[21] Mungo imports began to arrive from the United States in significant amounts. Rags, often of a very poor quality, found their way to Britain from many remote corners of the world. Supply improvements were assisted by a number of factors. Carbonising methods improved and gradually allowed more cotton warp rags to be used; the auction system, which developed in Batley and Dewsbury during the 1850s, guaranteed suppliers a fairer sale and perhaps better prices for their rags and, thirdly, the beginnings of the ready-made clothing industry began to produce additional quantities of tailors' clippings.

Supply problems did emerge from time to time. Embargoes on some rag wool imports as a result of cholera epidemics in Europe curtailed supplies for short periods in the 1880s and 1890s, particularly in 1892, when it was reported that the prohibition of import of foreign rags was hurting trade in 'shoddyopolis'.[22] Manufacturers were also facing increasing demand for rags from the competing wool textile industries in Germany, where it was reported that shoddy was becoming a large industry, particularly in Berlin,[23] and from the United States, which led to a re-export trade in rags and an export of the higher qualities of British shoddy and rags for shoddy. The Wilson tariff in 1895 quadrupled imports of rags and shoddy to the United States and demand rose in many other European countries, and Japan by 1905. Britain exported shoddy and mungo also to Russia, Scandinavia and Germany.

However, Dr Malin shows that the supply of rags from home and abroad on the whole managed to keep up with the needs of the industry. To the 1850s supply of domestic rags responded to requirements. Later rag supplies were affected by changes in wool prices. As wool prices rose in some periods and manufacturers attempted to reduce the amount of new wool in their blends, so supplies generally responded well to the resultant increases in shoddy prices. On the other hand with falling prices, adequate recovered wool supplies were maintained until the difference between price and transport costs was too low to allow a return to rag collectors and merchants. Thus in spite of the almost continuous fall in wool prices from the 1870s to 1903, imports and domestic supplies of rags remained fairly stable. The improvement in the prosperity of the woollen industry in the decade before the First World War resulted in a greater demand for rags and supplies, as usual, responded. Japanese army demand for cloth and blankets provided a particular boost for the use of shoddy and mungo.[24]

Throughout the century the provision of rags much depended on the rag merchants who based themselves in the heavy woollen district, and merchants elsewhere in London, Liverpool and on the Continent. The first specialist merchants had emerged by the 1830s, mainly from amongst manufacturers with surplus supply.[25] By the 1850s there were several hundred at work[26] including a group of Germans who maintained close contact with supplies from their home country. They bought rags either through private dealers or more frequently, from the 1860s, through auctions, sorted them according to type and colour into many hundreds of classes, often building up sufficient stocks of a particular type or colour over several years. The manufacturers depended on the skill of the rag merchants' sorters to grade types and colours, good colour matches often enabling the manufacturer to avoid the expense of dyeing. At the end of the 1860s an exchange was operating in Dewsbury for dealers to buy and sell rags.[27]

Rags were being pulled on the Continent by the late 1820s. Gradually Continental dealers built up the experience to sort and grind rags themselves, realising that better prices were available in Britain as a result. Thus gradually through the middle decades of the century the supply of rags from the Continent declined, but shoddy and mungo imports more than took their place.

Technical Developments 1835–70

These years saw two main developments; first the establishment of the power loom in both the woollen and worsted sections of the trade and then the successful application of machine combing. They also witnessed the completion of the mechanisation of all the other processes, none of outstanding importance but all of which played their part in the technical growth of the trade.

The processes are dealt with in the usual order. First, for the scouring of the wool and, for that matter, the drying, machines appeared about 1850. The wool was conveyed by rakes through tanks containing water with some kind of alkali added, stale urine still being the usual ingredient. This machine essentially reproduced the effect of raking the wool in a basket in a stream. It carried out the operation faster but probably caused more felting and, therefore, more fibre breakage than the hand process. Wool–drying machines, to replace the old open-air methods, came at the same time. The material carried on a moving surface went through a hot air chamber. Like the wool scouring apparatus this was a simple but effective machine which was, however, somewhat wasteful of steam heat. The first picking machines appeared at the same time; in the West of England at least they were known as 'bumbles' probably because of the noise they made – a not unpleasant humming sound. Basically they consisted of a main cylinder with spikes which tossed the wool about and both opened it and also removed a part of the spile, which was a rather generic name covering most types of vegetable fault.[28]

The problem arising from the presence of vegetable matter was made worse during the period under review because of the increased use of Australian and, to some extent, River Plate wool, both of which contained large quantities of an obnoxious burr which could not be shaken out. Some burrs, if left in, would unwind, leading to a large number of small pieces of vegetable spile. It was so bad that new machines were especially designed, without complete success, to remove them. Usually the wool was presented to a series of small rollers in the form of a web and the theory was that the burrs stood out and were knocked out of the web. The trouble was that either the machine removed too much wool with the burrs or, if set less close, left too many burrs in. Until the coming of carbonising, essentially a chemical process, these burrs presented an unsolved problem.

The blending, where the laying out of the various colours and qualities as well as the oiling usually with a watering-can took place, remained entirely a hand process. But the last mixing before carding was done in a willey (sometimes called a tucking machine) which was mechanised in the 1830s. This machine consisted of a centre roller with smaller rollers placed around, fed by a feed sheet, and depositing the wool either on the floor or into a bale or sheet. All these machines used in the preparatory processes had a rather Heath-Robinson look but represented mechanisation of a sort. The problems were not all that difficult, given the technology of the time, and the answers that were produced were not very startling, but they worked; indeed, scouring and drying machines installed around 1870, when owing to good trading conditions there was a considerable amount of re-equipping, were working well into the twentieth century.

During this period carding developed considerably and although the basic principles remained the same – a main circular roller (the swift) with smaller rollers (workers and strippers) around it – there were a number of improvements which turned carding into a reasonably satisfactory, if somewhat complicated, process. To start at the beginning, the feed sheet remained as Arkwright had left it and the first main improvements were in the intermediate feed that linked the three parts (that was the usual number) of cards together. The first card, called the scribbler, had rollers, which were set relatively far apart from each other, and in the final card (the carder) they were set sufficiently near to remove small entanglements. A third card placed between the scribbler and the carder was called the intermediate, not to be confused with the intermediate feed. This was the early practice but later there was a tendency to have a scribbler comprised of two parts and a carder, also of two parts. In any case, the problem was the linking together. Several types of intermediate feeds were tried during the period, the Apperly feed invented in the West of England, and the Scotch feed invented in Galashiels, were good examples. Incidentally, one might well ask: why not feed the material straight through? The reason was that by taking it off after each part one made the fibre less parallel and also obtained increased mixing.[29]

But it was at the end of the carding machine that the main developments took place. Previously the doffing comb, working against the doffer (i.e. the name of the last roller) on the carder, knocked off pieces of slubbing which closely resembled the rolags that the old hand carder had produced. The resemblance was not, of course, accidental. These slubbings were joined together by billy boys on the slubbing billy, one of the distinctive names in the woollen trade until 1850 and even after. Considerable ingenuity was exerted in inventing machines that would do away with these laborious hand piecings of the slubbings. None of them appears to have been completely successful, certainly none was widely adopted. The only piecing machine the authors have seen in a working condition was on the island of Islay; if that one example is sufficient to judge, then trouble lay in the difficulty of forming the join. This machine clearly could not do it as well as the trained slubber using his or her fingers.

Meanwhile, in the U.S.A., due mainly to the work of John Goulding, a satisfactory solution was found by placing the bands of card wire around the doffer, not across, and the doffing comb thereby knocked off continuous lengths of fibre. The basic idea, as is often the case, was simple; the application was more difficult. One problem was the tendency of the wool to build up on the swift, where it was not removed by the card wire on the doffer and with the single ring doffer, as it was called, this had to be overcome by giving the doffer a slight undulating movement which was not entirely satisfactory. A better and more generally adopted method was to have two ring doffers, one above the other, and then the rings on the top doffer were placed opposite the blank spaces on the lower and in this way the swift was completely cleared. The trouble here was that the top doffer would tend to take rather more than its fair share of the material. This was usually overcome by making the rings of the bottom doffer a little wider, but the problem was to decide how much wider. These difficulties having been overcome the next problem was how to rub the removed tape-like strips of material into a sliver or roller. Eventually rubbers with both a forward and a sideways motion were developed which made the new system, usually called the condenser, a satisfactory answer to the problem that had been puzzling the industry for so long.

John Goulding, who finally found the solution of the problem, himself began experimenting in 1820 and his efforts were aided by inventions pertaining to special portions of the process. One such invention, covering the important ring doffers, he purchased from Ezekial Hale of Haverhill, Massachusetts; and another, for a method of winding the ropings, from one Edward Winslow who subsequently co-operated with Goulding in perfecting the new device. Indeed, Goulding in the specifications of his patent, which he in fact received in 1826 stated:

> I do not claim the construction of the individual parts of the machinery used in the processes before described, but the combination and arrangement by which they are made to produce thread from wool, or other fibrous material, by a continuous operation.[30]

Britain was remarkably slow in adopting the idea, perhaps because of prejudice in that it came from the U.S.A., and possibly because the condensing system produced a rather different type of roller (or continuous rolag) than that coming from the old slubbing method. The fibres, it was said, lay straighter, more parallel, less circular (less like a coiled spring) and this meant that the cloth made from a condenser would not full so well. There was something in this argument, much publicised at the time by Vickermann, but it was completely outweighed by the fact that the consuming public no longer wanted the heavily fulled cloths. The long-delayed acceptance of the condenser by the British woollen textile trade was one of the first examples of a tendency for technological backwardness to appear in the industry.

The successful mechanisation of combing was, with the coming of the power loom, the most important advance made between 1835 and 1870. It had certainly taken a long time. The first attempts to introduce machine combing had been made by Edmund Cartwright of power loom fame, and in some ways his invention in combing was the more original of his two innovations, but it worked even less successfully than his loom. His earliest combing patent was dated 1789. The contrivance therein specified was quite different from his later machines and there was never any chance that it would operate satisfactorily. The patent of 1790 was more important because it did introduce the principal of the circular comb which in the end developed into Noble's comb of 1853. A further patent of 1792 improved this comb and it was this machine that, because of a crank-lasher copying the motion of the human arm, received the name of Big Ben, a famous prize fighter of the time. Cartwright had attempted to copy the action of hand combing and he evolved an interesting machine, but it was never widely adopted in practice because of the excessive fibre breakage it caused.

James, in his book on the worsted trade, has an interesting paragraph which admirably summarised the problems of machine combing at this early period. Quoting, he says, from a 'gentleman thoroughly conversant with the industry', he writes:

> The first combing machine introduced into Bradford, which was about this time [1794] must have been either Cartwright's or Hawksley's improvement; it was set to work by the late Robert Ramsbotham, on the premises behind his house in Kirkgate . . . The machine, which was worked by a horse running in a gin, does not seem to have answered the expectations of its purchaser, for after working for some time it was taken down and sent away; indeed, it would appear to have been a source of loss and annoyance, as the old gentleman is said to have taken off his hat to it as it left the yard; no doubt at the same time expressing the charitable hope that 'Big Ben' as it was called, might prove a better servant to its new master.[31]

The reference to Big Ben would suggest it was based on Cartwright's third patent. Incidentally, many manufacturers when first using new machines must have felt like this old gentleman.

Further combing inventions followed, the best being that of Platt and Collier in 1827, but patented in Platt's name only. Collier was an enterprising English engineer; he lived in France and also influenced the course of the development of shearing frames. The 1827 advance was important and it represented a further development, some might say the introduction, of the principle of combing between two circular combs, which is usually considered Noble's idea. It was he who brought it successfully to completion but the idea was perhaps derived from a French invention made by Goddard of Amiens in 1816 in conjunction with Collier. Donnisthorpe in 1842 patented an unsuccessful machine, but Heilmann's work in France was the next important development. Heilmann was a Frenchman, born in Alsace, and the idea was brilliantly conceived and although planned for cotton was equally suitable for the shorter types of wool. It was this invention that led to the French combing shorter wools than was common in England; this fitted in well with their practice of mule spinning and played a part in the successful manufacture of all wool merino worsteds in France before they were equally well processed in the West Riding.

Meanwhile in Britain after 1843 Lister came to dominate the whole picture of combing inventions. James Burnley's attempt to write a book about the history of combing, which incidentally was financed by Holden, met with an unfortunate fate, well illustrating the position in the industry. He was sued by Lister for attributing to Isaac Holden an idea which Lister claimed to have had himself. This comb used the new nip principle combined with a circular comb, and a screw gill which had been adapted from an important invention made by Lawson and Wesley in about 1833 for the flax trade. The whole position of combing inventions is very complicated, but by the 1850s development had passed under the control of Lister, who admittedly did once say that Donnisthorpe, who had worked with him, had departed and he thought that full justice should be done to him:

> I took out a patent for the nip machine but though I did so I feel that I am not the inventor, really and truly Mr. Donnisthorpe was the first to have the idea of combing the nip with a screw gill.[32]

Actually Heilmann invented the nip principle and Lawson and Wesley the screw gill. There is no need to detail here the many and complicated legal struggles that followed and the manner in which Lister proved an outstanding entrepreneur. He normally bought up any patent that might conceivably have challenged his position; James well summarised what happened when he wrote that in his patent of 1851:

> Lister had fully perfected his machine; and though he took out many patents in the following years, he has not, it is generally considered, thereby added in the slightest degree to the efficiency of that machine. His object has been to anticipate every possible modification or contrivance whether by mechanical equivalent or otherwise whereby the principles of his patent might be interpreted and yet evaded.[33]

It is a pity that James' excellent survey, which was published in 1857, ended at this point and therefore does not go on to describe the final work.

The perfecting of the circular comb by Noble came in 1853 and that of Holden's square comb in 1856. The Noble comb was the best answer and it is strange that we know so little about the inventor himself. A leading figure in the worsted trade in the twentieth century has even suggested that he never existed,[34] being merely a name used by Lister in his complicated and involved business endeavours of keeping wool combing in his own hands. Whether this be the case or not cannot be decided here. These inventions had, as a group, mechanised the combing process and the days of hand combing were over; all the major processes of the wool textile trade had been mechanised.

Table 20   Combing machines in factories

| | No. of combing machines | | |
	1867	1874	1904
Yorkshire	997	1174	2636
United Kingdom	1038	1276	2823

SOURCE: *Factory Returns*

This final successful mechanisation of wool combing gave great impetus to the worsted section of the trade. As so often in the wool textile industry it is difficult to separate cause from effect. This is particularly the case with combing; the final successful mechanisation coincided with the arrival of merino wools from Australia that were long enough to comb. These two factors combined over the following years to change the West Riding worsted trade from being an industry that largely made cloths with cotton warps and coarse worsted wefts to one using largely fine merino wools. The two leading names are without doubt Lister and Holden and the exact contribution of both has not been worked out with complete satisfaction. Perhaps neither of them were quite as important as inventors as has sometimes been thought. Lister's genius arose in the way in which he could utilise other men's ideas and keep control of the whole patent position. Holden's square comb was a good machine but it must be remembered that it has not lasted as well as Noble's. Holden should be considered as a great business entrepreneur rather than as a great inventor.

An important difference between the woollen and worsted systems of yarn production should now be noticed. As far as the woollen trade was concerned the sliver coming from the condenser on the carding machine could go straight to the spinning mule. With the worsted, however, a number of drawing processes were necessary to reduce the thick top to a fine roller from which the ultimate yarn could be made. Therefore it is appropriate to discuss these worsted drawing processes before proceeding to the spinning of woollen and worsted yarn.

It is well known that Arkwright, in addition to inventing the water frame for spinning, also introduced the lantern frame for drawing. The principle of roller drafting was the same in both. It is usually considered that the lantern frame came after the water frame but it is difficult to see how one could have been used without the other. Be that as it may, it is clear that Arkwright's lantern frame was the beginning of a series of inventions made mainly for the cotton industry but taken up quickly by the worsted. Their object, as indicated above, was to convert the top into a fine sliver that could go to the spinning machine. Dr Ure, in his *Philosophy of Manufactures* in 1835, has an interesting quote that seems to indicate that Arkwright rightly recognised the importance of good drawing. He is quoted as saying that:

> when bad yarn made its appearance in any of his mills, he swore a loud oath according to the vile fashion of the time and ordered his people to look to their drawings, convinced that if they were right, everything else would do well.[35]

The real key to the production of good yarn in the woollen trade is in the carding and in the worsted trade in the drawing. Arkwright's lantern frame, evolved as early as 1780 from the cotton trade, was used for worsted drawing until superseded by roving frames equipped with bobbins and flyers, but the basic roller drafting still remained.

We come now to the actual spinning and deal first with woollen yarns. Crompton's mule, as originally invented, combined spindle and roller drafting and was not suitable for woollen spinning. It did, however, have a number of features which could be combined with the spindle drafting of Hargreave's jenny to make a good woollen spinning mule. It was perhaps wrong to have called the machine a mule; the name 'jack' was applied to it in America. During the first part of this period a number of variations were made to the mule, the later improvements to it coming mainly from Robert Roberts for the cotton trade. As a result by 1870 a woollen mule, which in principle more nearly resembled the jenny but in appearance looked more like a mule, was admirably fulfilling the essentials of the operation. One of the authors can remember many such mules still being used 60 years later. The workmanship, notably of those made by Platt Brothers of Oldham, was greatly to be admired.

To turn to worsted yarn two major systems were in existence: frame spinning (derived from Arkwright) and mule spinning (derived from Crompton). The English worsted spinner favoured the former, the French the latter. Two points call for comment: first the tenacity with which the English worsted spinners stuck to Arkwright's ideas and, after much criticism in the nineteenth century, their complete vindication in the twentieth century, when the French gave up the mule; secondly the important developments in worsted spinning using the roller principles which were introduced: first the so-called cap-spinning and second, the ring-spinning. These new inventions were concerned entirely with the way the twist was introduced and the winding-on of the spun yarn effected. Both still used the basic roller drafting principle for the attenuation of the sliver. Both used the basic flier and spindle idea, which first appeared in the fourteenth century and was used on the flax or Saxony hand spinning wheel and which Arkwright took over without any real alteration for his first water frame. However, in both the cap spinning and the ring spinning the basic conception of twisting and winding-on was so changed as to look quite different and instead of having to drive a heavy flier round there was only the stationary cap in the cap spinning and the small traveller in the ring spinning. Consequently, much higher spindle speeds could be obtained and the rate of production greatly increased.

The second great development of the period was the final successful adaptation of power loom weaving to the industry, first to worsteds and then to woollens. Fortunately we have detailed figures and can see what happened as far as the introduction of looms was concerned, but the most interesting problem of the kinds of looms and how opinions about their value changed is much less clear. Although there was some experimentation with power loom weaving in the West of England in the 1820s,[36] it was in Yorkshire that the power loom was first brought into use in the worsted industry. The wool textile industry was, of course, somewhat behind the cotton industry in the innovation. The first definite reference in the wool textile industry to its use comes from Bradford, where the Horsfalls were using steam-powered looms in 1824. Two years earlier a James Warbrick had attempted to use a power loom at a Shipley mill but it was destroyed by local hand loom weavers. There is also the suggestion of power looms being used in James Akroyd's mill in Old Lane, Halifax, by 1822.[37]

By 1830 several firms are known to have been using power looms including Stansfield and Briggs of Burley Mill and the Marshalls of Bradford. A woollen and worsted mill in the East Riding had power looms in 1828,[38] and there are woollen mills known to have had power looms by the early 1830s, including Joseph Arundel of Rothwell and Joshua Lockwood of Huddersfield.[39] The far from complete 1835 survey of power looms in factories lists 3336 power looms in Yorkshire factories, 89 per cent of which were in worsted mills and another 7 per cent in mills which were used for weaving both woollen and worsted cloth.[40] Elsewhere in the 1830s power looms were being brought into use. There were several near Norwich in 1840.[41] At Hawick they were in use as early as 1830.[42] In Wales there was an attempt to use them in the Newtown flannel trade in 1835 but they were not successfully introduced until the 1850s.[43] More progress was made in the West of England, particularly in Gloucestershire, where 101 power looms were in use by 1838; the first may have been brought into use in 1836. Manufacturers in Wiltshire and Somerset waited a few more years.[44]

By 1850 the growth in the use of the power loom may be followed in rather more detail. There are some figures for the 1840s in the reports of the inspectors of factories but they do not enable a comprehensive picture to be produced. For example, in Saunders' district within the West Riding of Yorkshire, recorded power looms for worsted manufacturers were as follows:[45]

1836	2768
1841	11 458
1843	16 870
1845	19 121
1850	29 539

The factory inspector's returns show that in 1850 there were more than three times as many in the worsted industry as in the woollen industry.

Yorkshire possessed 95 per cent of the power looms in the worsted industry, with the additional few in Lancashire and Norfolk. The factory inspector did not record any power looms in Scotland which was presumably an oversight. By 1867 the figures suggest the transition to the power loom was all but over. There was a large increase in their numbers in the early 1860s which, of course, corresponded to the very large increase in the number of mills in this period. In 1850 there were 428 power looms in Norfolk. Their numbers declined thereafter to only 276 in 1871.

The figures for 1850 show clearly what little headway the power

Table 21   The innovation of power loom weaving

Power looms in the woollen industry (inc. shoddy)

Year	England	Scotland	Wales	Yorks.	Lancs.	South-West	Gloucester
1850	9168	247	2	3849	4839	225	224
1856	13 463	665	263	6275	5933	623	421
1861	19 889	1303	455	11 405	6377	1241	618
1867	43 177	3418	389	20 713	7891	1807	1033
1871	35 494	9708	693	21 681	11 107	1441	852
1874	45 878	11 758	584	30 917	10 227	2586	*
1878	51 903	6284	456	36 721	9550	3042	*
1885	50 385	7958	865	36 396	8722	2630	*
1889	52 414	9836	940	37 626	9797	2582	*
1904	42 222	7300	1076	31 429	6378	1616	953

Power looms in the worsted industry

Year	England & Wales	Scotland	Yorkshire
1850	32 617	0	30 856
1856	38 819	135	35 298
1861	42 968	80	40 577
1867	71 556	110	69 212
1871	54 908	1145	48 905
1874	75 591	6156	65 789
1878	76 149	11 244	68 701
1885	78 477	1432	70 406
1889	66 630	761	61 376
1904	51 510	1203	48 930

NOTE: *There are no separate figures available for the county of Gloucester from 1874 to 1889.

loom had made in the woollen industry. The big phase in the transition to it came between 1856 and 1867 in which period the number of looms in Great Britain increased from 14,391 to 46,984. From then on the numbers increased steadily until 1889. Table 21 also shows the slower development of the use of the looms in Scotland where the big changeover may have taken place in the late 1860s. In the Lancashire woollen industry, on the other hand, the major growth seems to have been before 1850. By that year Lancashire had substantially more power looms at work than Yorkshire. The largest increase in any one period in the south-western district of Devon, Cornwall, Wiltshire, Somerset and Dorset, if one discounts the dubious figures for 1871, was between 1856 and 1861 but there were twice as many looms by 1874 and over 3000 by 1878.

The later innovation in the woollen industry may be explained by a range of factors, the major of which is perhaps best summed up by Baines:

> In order to produce these two principal characteristics of woollen cloth, the *felting* and the *nap*, it will easily be seen that woollen yarn must not be spun so tight and hard as worsted, cotton or linen yarn. The fibres must be left as loose as possible, first that they may felt and afterwards that they may constitute a nap. Hence woollen yarn, both for the warp and weft, is spun into a much softer, i.e. feebler, looser and less twisted thread, than other kinds of yarn. But the feebleness of the yarn constitutes a principal difficulty in applying the power-loom to the woollen manufacture. The threads are more liable to break by the passing of the shuttle through them, and the weaving is consequently more difficult. This difficulty is increased by the great width of the web, which in broad cloth, before it is milled, is 108″. Owing to these combined causes, the power loom in the woollen manufacture works much more slowly than in the worsted; in the latter, on the average, the shuttle flies at the rate of 160 picks per minute, whilst the power-loom in weaving broad cloth only makes 40 to 48 picks per minute – that is, just the same as the hand-loom.[46]

In the woollen manufacture, therefore, for a long time the lack of greater productivity from the power loom persuaded manufacturers that it was not worth their while going to the expense of installing the new, more costly looms and using mechanical power. The incentives to do so only gradually increased as the cost of steam power was reduced during the 1850s and 1860s, and as some wage rates increased during the same period. An important part of the cost of weaving was the setting up of the loom which had to be done by hand. Thus the value of the power loom was further reduced. And there were other problems: water power, which remained in substantial use in many areas, was irregular and at times meant that looms had to be left standing; hand loom weavers could work more continuously. It was also suggested in 1850 that the power loom was unpopular because it 'does not work with the tenderness of a skilful human hand – damage may be instantly done and take the weaver two hours to repair'.[47] There were also complaints that, due to more oil being used to keep the loom going, the pieces came off the loom more dirty.

The innovation of power looms in woollen manufacture came first, therefore, in the production of lower quality cloths. They were being used in the low woollen trade in the 1850s. Their use spread as technical change allowed them to work at greater speed. The number of picks per minute they were capable of weaving doubled between the 1870s and 1904 for some types of cloth.[48] It was reported that in the fancy woollen trade new fast looms were being introduced in the 1880s.[49] The gradual disappearance of broadcloth manufacture also tended to encourage their adoption.

In worsted manufacture the advantages of the power loom were very much clearer. Although they could not work as fast as in the cotton trade, by the 1850s they were being worked at 160 picks per minute, the rate rising to 180 in 1866 and perhaps over 200 by 1890.[50] This showed a substantial advantage over manual operation. The difference in the power utilisation in woollen and worsted power loom weaving was quite substantial. In 1861 in the worsted industry the 17,154 looms in weaving-only mills were worked by 2505 horse-power, an average of 6.8 looms per horsepower. In the woollen branch of the industry the 1067 power looms in weaving-only mills required 294 horsepower, an average of 3.6 looms per horsepower.[51]

The productivity of power for weaving was clearly substantially greater in the worsted industry. At Black Dyke Mills in 1849 power looms were each weaving between two and three more pieces than hand looms, although this may not take into account the intricacy and quality of the cloth.[52]

As the quoted statistics make clear, we are well informed regarding the coming of the power loom and the demise of the hand loom, but information about the changing development of the type of loom is much less well documented. The problem will only be understood if the difference between the plain and the fancy loom is appreciated. The distinction had always existed, the broad loom produced plain cloth, the draw loom fancy cloth. Early power looms only produced plain or near plain cloth and the wool textile trade of Britain never much cared for the Jacquard loom, that is, the mechanical development of the draw loom. This gap in machine type was probably as much a reason for the survival of the hand loom weaver as the oft quoted tenderness of the woollen yarn. The development of semi-fancy looms was crucial and this was another mainly American conception. Cole is correct when he writes 'the invention of the Crompton fancy loom was an advance greater than any single improvement achieved' during these years.[53] The Crompton loom was soon copied in England and the development of the Dobcross loom at Dobcross on the Lancashire border and the Hattersley loom at Keighley depended upon it.

In the worsted trade the disappearance of the hand loom was therefore quite rapid. The productivity advantage of the power loom over the hand loom gave the latter little chance of survival. In 1838 there were about 1400 hand looms at work in the Bradford worsted weaving districts including Bingley and Keighley. By 1857 James could report that 'comparatively few pieces are now woven by hand in Bradford parish'.[54] A few worsted hand loom weavers hung on until the 1870s but they were of little importance.[55] The Fosters of Black Dyke Mills ceased employing hand loom weavers in 1869 although they had been of little significance to the firm for the previous twenty years. They were perhaps simply kept on until they had fulfilled their working lives or had found other employment.[56] A detailed study of Oxenhope, within the Bradford worsted district, shows a decline of hand loom weavers there from 249 to 1851 to 113 in 1861.[57]

In the woollen branch of the industry, however, the disappearance of the hand loom was very much slower. The initial lack of advantage of the power loom over it allowed almost a generation of hand loom weavers to be employed after the first use of the power loom for woollen weaving. The main period of transition was the 1850s or even the 1860s. At Galashiels in 1863 there were 600 hand looms and 295 power looms. In 1886, 402 hand looms survived although 1085 power looms were working. The Ballantynes of Galashiels and Walkerburn introduced power looms in 1859 and replaced their hand loom weavers by 1868, but hand looms were still in use in some parts of Scotland at the end of the century for more intricate work and in the Harris tweed trade.[58] In Wales, although the power loom was brought into use about 1850, hand loom weavers continued in existence, particularly in the western counties, into the twentieth century. Even in 1947 6 per cent of looms in Wales were worked by hand.[59] A particular reason for the power loom making slow progress in Wales was that its marginal advantage over the hand loom was reduced by the irregularity of water power.

In Lancashire hand looms were still being used in Rochdale after the 1870s.[60] In the West of England the quite early introduction of the power loom spelt doom for the hand loom weaver rather more rapidly. The failure of many firms and the habit, which also existed in Yorkshire, of only giving weaving to outworkers in times of brisk trade, gave the hand loom weaver little scope for survival. In 1863 in Trowbridge, it was said that the hand loom weaver was almost forgotten but some did survive until the 1880s, weaving fancy narrow cloth for manufacturers who were too afraid of fashion changes to install power machinery.[61]

In Yorkshire the demise of the hand loom weaver may have been slower. The range of cloth produced gave him an important position in some parts of the industry until late in the nineteenth century. In 1862 although the making of blankets by hand loom was gradually disappearing in the heavy woollen district, the Children's Employment Commission reported that the hand loom trade in the local carpet industry was still improving.[62] There were still, at that date, a few hand loom blanket shops around Dewsbury with some 500 looms. At Leeds in 1858 some 200 hand loom weavers were still at work but they did not survive long.[63] But elsewhere they existed until much later. In the Huddersfield fancy woollen trade one-quarter of the looms were still worked by hand in 1866.[64] And 20 years later, hand loom weaving, although described as a declining trade, was still reported as being very active around Skelmanthorpe, Shelley and Scissett. It was still the major occupation of the inhabitants and had, for the previous few years, been quite remunerative, one firm (Norton Bros) having increased wages and paid bonuses. About this time, hand loom weavers were being encouraged to come from Scotland. Described as 'these sturdy champions of a diminished industry', the hand loom weavers south-east of Huddersfield owed their survival to the demand for 'novelties'.[65] They wove very intricate shawls and other fancy woollens of above average quality. There was still a hand loom manufacturer at Huddersfield in 1875.[66] But at the same time elsewhere in the county hand loom weaving was described as an 'old man's trade' carried out by 'the martyrs of the moors'.[67] Its extinction had been hastened by the United States tariff increases, the United States having been a major market for hand woven goods. A few hand weavers survived as pattern and sample makers. They appeared as a tiny group in the 1901 Census and Clapham described the 200 or 300 who survived in 1907, still working at home, as making 'a queer assortment of things, including fancy waistcoats, flannels and what not'.[68] In so far as they had any importance it was in the pattern and sample-making section, where it usually proved more economic to weave by hand rather than go to the trouble of setting up a power loom just to weave a short length of cloth.

The period saw few major changes in finishing machinery, the wet processes of scouring and milling were already being done in simple machines by 1835 and there were few new inventions. The rotary fulling or milling machine continued to replace the old stocks. Probably the most notable change came from the drying. The old out-of-door tenter had to some extent been replaced by indoor tenter houses but the process remained entirely hand-performed in 1835. Then a tentering machine was introduced in which the famous, even notorious, tenter hooks for holding and sometimes stretching the cloth were fitted onto a travelling lattice and the whole placed inside a chamber which was steam heated. The saving in time and labour was large, as a report on the machine shown in the 1862 Exhibition clearly indicates:

> Whitely or Nortons' patent tentering and drying machine makes it possible for one man and a boy to dry two thousand five hundred yards of cloth a day, irrespective of weather; whereas by the old system of large drying houses, heated stoves and outdoor drying, it would take eight to ten persons to do the same quantity. Seventy-five per cent saving in the cost but the machine costs £600 and is therefore out of real reach of small manufacturers.[69]

It is noticeable in many inventories and sales of about 1850–1870 that tentering machines are the highest priced items in the mill.

The dry processes were little changed; the rotary shearing machines by 1835 had replaced the old hand shears in almost all mills and were usually of the broad width type but Lewis's cross cutter, which cut from list to list and was therefore intermittent in action, was still favoured particularly in the West of England because twills could be cut cleaner with them. Other processes were unchanged and the next main developments came after 1870 and were essentially chemical rather than mechanical.

The finishing machines that had been produced by 1870 had increased production but had left the basic craft skills of the workers in the finishing departments of the woollen and worsted mills – particularly the woollen – unchanged. The scourer and miller (or fuller as he was often still called) had to watch the changes that were occurring in the appearance of the cloth as closely as ever, the rotary shearing machine needed constant watching, gigging by machine called for as much skill as gigging by hand and, in total, the skill of the finishing foremen played a major part in the success of the factory.

Baines, in a well known passage, lists the 34 processes that made up woollen cloth manufacturing. Sixteen of them came after weaving and a list of them with additional comments will perhaps indicate how much did depend on these workers. They have been much less discussed than the weavers and others, partly because they appear less in the parliamentary papers and other accounts of the industry, but there is no doubt that they were more skilled and more important.[70]

Baines began his finishing sequence with No.19, 'Scouring the cloth with fuller's earth, to remove the oil and size' and followed with No.20 'Dyeing, when piece-dyed'. Next came No.21 'Burling, to pick out irregular threads, hairs, or dirt' and a number of women workers were employed in this section. Baines should here also have included knotting, as the same group of workers usually picked off the knots that remained from repairs done to the yarn in the weaving process. No.22, 'Milling or fulling, with soap and warm water, either in the fulling-stocks or in the improved milling machine, where it is squeezed between rollers' came next and was followed by No.23, 'Scouring, to remove the soap'. This process was done in the same machine as his No.19 and it was often more difficult to remove the soap that had been added to assist the fulling than it had been to remove the earlier dirt. Slightly faulty pieces, particularly those that smelt, were usually caused by a failure to remove this residual soap. No.24, 'Drying and stretching on tenters' and No.25, 'Raising the nap of the cloth, by brushing it strongly on the gig with teazles fixed upon cylinders' followed. No.26, 'Cutting or shearing off the nap in two cutting-machines, one cutting lengthwise of the piece and the other across' came next. This description indicates the high quality finishing that Baines was describing and suggests that many manufacturers used both types of rotary shearing machines mentioned above. No.27 was 'Boiling the cloth, to give it a permanent face'. This process was only just coming into favour and its development will be discussed in the next section. No.28, 'Brushing, in a brushing machine' and No.29, 'Pressing in hydraulic presses, sometimes with heat', followed and, rather surprisingly, No.30, 'Cutting the nap a second time'. No.31 was 'Burling and drawing, to remove defects, and marking with the manufacturer's name'. These two processes should not have been listed together. True burling was done earlier (see No.21 above) but pieces of spile that had been missed then could be removed at this late stage although the surface of the cloth was likely to suffer. Drawing, or dress mending as it is better called, was really a separate process and one that needed carrying out with great skill. To put the manufacturer's name on was not difficult. No.32 was 'Pressing a second time', essential because of the damage done to the surface of the cloth in Baines' earlier second cutting – No.30. No.33 was 'Steaming, to take away the liability to spot'. This process was often done before the pressing and finally, No.34 'Folding or cutting for the warehouse' completed the routine. Here the word 'cutting' is misleading, as it has nothing to do with the shearing mentioned above and simply refers to the fact that sometimes the manufacturer did not sell complete pieces but had to cut them into lengths.

The worsted finishing routine was much simpler. First there was the scouring and then the drying; because there was no fulling there was nothing to correspond with the difficult second scouring in the woollen routine. Tentering, cutting and pressing followed and completed the process. Worsted cloth was essentially made in the weaving; the traditional woollen cloth had always been made in the finishing. This was their great difference and accounts for much of the difference in the development of the two sections of the trade. It is rather strange that Baines does not mention the mending that took place immediately after the weaving or occasionally after the first scouring. Presumably it was still done by the weaver.

Power: Steam Versus Water
Up to 1856 the factory inspectors recorded nominal horsepower but they were becoming aware that their figure substantially underestimated the power actually used, as improvements in boilers and engines and better gearing and lubricating oil were allowing engines to do more work. There were various contemporary estimates that steam engines could produce between 20 and 50 per cent more power than their nominal horsepower. The two large 100 nominal horsepower engines at Saltaire were working at 228 and 235 indicated horsepower in the early 1860s.[71] In the autumn of 1856 the factory inspectors decided that 'the nominal power of a modern manufacturing steam engine cannot be considered more than an index from which its real capabilities may be calculated' and they decided that for subsequent returns they would attempt to record power employed (indicated horsepower) by engines and wheels. As a result of this change the pre-1856 power statistics are not strictly comparable with those of 1861 and later.[72]

The use of steam power through the middle of the nineteenth century was stimulated by the increasing efficiency of steam engines

and mill gearing. The more widespread introduction of belting transmission systems created added advantage. The gains may have been
greatest in the woollen industry, which needed more power in
relation to labour. In 1861 in England and Wales the worsted industry employed 3.1 workers per horsepower. The woollen industry
needed 2.3 workers for each horsepower. More efficient and cheaper
steam power was particularly beneficial in the weaving branch of the
industry where more power was required to give power looms the
edge over hand looms. It is no coincidence that the development of
power loom weaving in woollens coincided with steam power improvements. Moreover, in the spinning branch of both worsted and
woollen manufacture, more efficient steam power was beneficial.
The throstle needed substantial power and the mule was given a
greater advantage over the jenny as power costs were reduced,
although the latter was of less relevance by the 1850s.

Further improvements in the generating and use of steam power
were made in the 1860s and 1870s. Steam pressures were raised,
there were improvements to the design of engines and boilers, and
standardisation of parts reduced maintenance costs.[73] The application of power to combing, to a wider range of finishing processes and
particularly to woollen weaving, further stimulated the use of steam.

The use of water for power survived for many decades, particularly
in the industry away from the main centres, and can be traced without
difficulty from the Factory Returns until 1871. But from the 1874
Factory Returns onwards details of power were no longer recorded.
In 1850 in England and Wales 35 per cent of the nominal horsepower
recorded was produced by water, but this figure no doubt overstates
the importance of water as the nominal horsepower measurement
was becoming increasingly unrealistic, especially for steam engines.
But in that year, according to the recorded figures, water was producing the majority of power for the woollen industry in the counties
of Gloucester, Somerset, Cumberland, Oxford and a number of
others. In Devon, Westmorland, Shropshire, Herefordshire and
Dorset, waterwheels were still providing all the power for the local
industry and in Wales steam power had made very little progress. In
Scotland 65 per cent of nominal horsepower was generated by water.

In the worsted manufacture, water power was of much less significance in 1850 In English worsted factories only 13 per cent of
nominal horsepower came from water. In Scotland, where the worsted industry had made little progress, 42 per cent of nominal power
was derived from water. In the main wool textile district, Yorkshire,
water power by 1850 had substantially declined in importance, pro-

ducing only just over 10 per cent of nominal horsepower in the worsted branch of the industry and 23 per cent in the woollen branch. But with the exception of the counties of Lancashire and Wiltshire, water power still predominated in other woollen manufacturing areas. Only a few worsted manufacturing counties were, however, so dependent on water and the industry in a number of counties including Norfolk and Leicester used little or no water power.

A more accurate assessment of the relative importance of the two sources of power becomes possible in 1861 when the factory inspectors decided to substitute the measurement of indicated horsepower for nominal horsepower. Although there may be some reason to suspect that some millowners were unable to accurately assess the exact capabilities of their engines and wheels, the figures undoubtedly give a rough indication of the situation. In the woollen industry in England and Wales 21 per cent of total power was being derived from water and of the 6675 indicated water horsepower recorded, 1075 h.p. related to the Welsh industry where the steam engine was still making no significant contribution. In the West of England counties of Gloucester, Somerset, Wiltshire, Devon and Cornwall, 2386 indicated steam horsepower compared with 1748 water horse power were recorded. In the Scottish woollen industry in 1861 water still provided 65 per cent of power.

In 1871, the last year in which detailed measurement is possible, in the woollen industry in England and Wales water provided 13 per cent of the power, in Scotland 27 per cent.[74] Changes in the relative importance of water power for different parts of the country are indicated in Table 22 which suggests that although the relative role of water was steadily declining from 1838 to 1871, the absolute amount of power generated by water changed little. This is rather what one would expect. Any manufacturer who had a reasonable supply of water power tended to keep it even if he did add steam power as well. The more rapid disappearance of the use of water power in the worsted industry resulted from the industry being quite heavily concentrated into a few areas, most of which were close to coalfields, and also because of the substantially larger average size of worsted mills, with consequently greater power needs. In 1871 the average woollen mill in England and Wales used 32 horsepower. The equivalent figure for worsted mills was 82 horsepower.

Water power continued to be used in most areas of the British wool textile industry until the twentieth century. But with the exception of the very rural parts of Wales, Scotland and the Border Counties of England, few mills relied entirely on water. Some of those that had

Table 22   *The decline in the use of water power in the wool textile industry*

Woollen industry (including shoddy)

Year	England A. h.p.	England B. h.p.	England C. %	Wales A. h.p.	Wales B. h.p.	Wales C. %	Scotland A. h.p.	Scotland B. h.p.	Scotland C. %
1850	12 528	6247	33.3	39	560	93.5	850	1653	65.3
1861	25 141	5600	18.2	92	1075	92.1	1578	2328	59.6
1871	44 930	5870	11.6	218	815	78.9	6829	2476	26.6

Year	Yorkshire A. h.p.	Yorkshire B. h.p.	Yorkshire C. %	Wiltshire and Somerset A. h.p.	Wiltshire and Somerset B. h.p.	Wiltshire and Somerset C. %	Gloucestershire A. h.p.	Gloucestershire B. h.p.	Gloucestershire C. %
1850	9347	2806	23.1	850	487	36.4	806	1485	36.4
1861	19 634	2816	12.5	1264	430	25.4	1079	1045	49.2
1871	37 697	3143	7.7	1136	148	11.5	1022	591	36.6

Worsted industry

Year	England A. h.p.	England B. h.p.	England C. %	Scotland A. h.p.	Scotland B. h.p.	Scotland C. %	Yorkshire A. h.p.	Yorkshire B. h.p.	Yorkshire C. %
1850	9769	1501	13.3	121	88	42.1	8397	992	10.6
1861	25 426	1667	6.2	808	226	21.9	23 029	1455	5.9
1871	47 140	1682	3.4	1830	364	16.6	43 960	1528	3.4

A. Steam horsepower
B. Water horsepower
C. Water horsepower as a proportion of total horsepower

NOTES: Figures for 1850 represent nominal horsepower. Those for 1861 and 1871 represent indicated horsepower. The statistics for the two periods are therefore not strictly comparable.

been initially located, decades earlier, close to a good supply of water for power, continued to use that water but supplemented the power it provided with a steam engine, which also enabled the mill to continue production in times of excess or dearth of water. Thomas Laycock of Aireworth near Keighley provides an example: his combing, spinning and weaving mill on the River Worth used water for power for five months of the year and steam for the other seven in 1868. And a number of his neighbours likewise employed both steam and water.

The mills in the rural districts around Keighley in Yorkshire were on the fringes of the textile area on higher reaches of the county's streams and rivers. The mills were below average size, were often of very early construction and could still make use of water power. Elsewhere high up on the Yorkshire Pennines water power was still being used for wool textile manufacture. In the basin of the River Tame at Saddleworth many mills continued with water. And in the valleys of the Holme, Colne and Upper Calder rivers and their tributaries, many water mills were recorded in 1868 but few of them were totally dependent on their wheels. The woollen industry in the Kendal district of Cumbria was still heavily dependent on water power and in the West of England, in the Stroud district, at Witney in Oxfordshire and Frome in Somerset, water power was still of some significance.[75]

In the major industrial centres, however, the incentive to continue using water power had slowly declined through the middle of the century. The gradually reducing price of coal and the increasing efficiency and durability of steam engines made the initial, and perhaps reducing, capital cost of purchase seem less daunting. The incentive to increase the size and capacity of mills, and in the woollen industry to install power looms, meant that often power needs extended far beyond the original water power capabilities of the site. The desire to work capital for as many hours as possible as the industry became more capital-intensive, made mill owners, dependent on water power, more and more frustrated when they faced lack or surfeit of water. This was aggravated by the restrictions on the working hours of labour. The Border woollen industry in 1850, faced with the problem or irregular water supply, complained about not being able to work their labour when water was available and the factory inspector acknowledged that the area had 'strong claims to separate considerations' on the question of relay working but for insuperable administrative problems. The problem arose again as a result of the 1874 Factory Act, which further limited hours. There were complaints from Scotland and suggestions that the Act would prove fatal to small mills dependent on water.[76]

In the main industrial centres the increasing pollution of, and debris in, the rivers created a nuisance for water power users. But above all the transition from water to steam power was encouraged by the occasional severe period of drought such as that of the late summer of 1864 which threatened the output of some firms in Yorkshire, as did the drought in the autumn of 1884.[77]

One final point deserves mentioning. The manufacturing processes as they developed in the early factories, called for increasing amounts of steam. This meant that anything approaching a modern factory had to have steam available. If power was obtained from steam the position was straightforward. Part of the steam could be taken direct from the boiler and used for this purpose. Steam heating was needed in both types of drying machines, those for the wool and those for the yarn. Traditionally the dye vats had been heated by fires underneath them but the more modern machines that came into use after 1850 were heated by steam pipes. Heating was also needed for other finishing processes, notably the roll boiling and the pressing. In addition, as rather more attention began to be paid to the welfare of the workers, steam heating during winter was introduced. This wide use of steam which could amount to as much as 20 per cent of the total steam produced in the factory was an obvious encouragement to switch from water power to coal.

6 The State of Trade, 1835–70

The Course of Trade 1835–1843
The mid-1830s are an appropriate point to continue our examination of the progress of the industry. The problems encountered in the 1820s and earlier had by no means all disappeared. Seasonal, structural and cyclical fluctuations continued to present difficulties to manufacturers. The uncertainties of export markets did likewise. But in a number of respects the 1830s produced optimistic features. The technological changes discussed in the previous chapter helped reduce costs and expand factory output. Developments in wool supply, the use of reclaimed fibres and of cotton and hair provided the industry with more versatility and enabled a variety of important developments in products. The outstanding features of the middle decades of the nineteenth century were the success of cotton warped worsted cloth and of low woollens, the extension of the range of products of the industry and the domination of world markets by those products. However, although the vast majority of contemporary comment and report eulogised the efficiency and successes of the industry as a whole, there were undoubtedly areas which were less worthy of praise and which were perhaps indicative of the difficulties that were to arise in the last third of the century.

From the 1830s it becomes possible to follow the experiences and problems of the industry in much closer detail. The regular reports of the factory inspectors and the commencement of market surveys in local and national newspapers enable the diversity of factors influencing different parts of the industry, sometimes in contradictory directions, to be identified. The survey that follows, based largely on these market reports, is intended to illustrate the complex influences under which the industry had to organise its production and trade. The annual values of exports of cloth and yarn are shown in Table 23.

Following the slight down turn in trade experienced in some areas in 1834 exports rose rapidly in 1835 and 1836. Fine worsted yarns and fine stuff fabrics were much traded at home and abroad. James reported that 'spinners and manufacturers were fully and lucratively occupied'.[1] Wool supplies coped with demand although prices rose to their highest level for 15 years. The *Leeds Mercury* reported complaints that prices were bad for the cloth trade but reasoned that such comments were 'as old as the trade and as incurable as the unreasonableness of human expectations'.[2] Profits were reduced but return on capital remained adequate to further stimulate mill building. American demand for British cloth boomed in 1836; two-fifths of British exports of wool textiles were channelled to the United States that year.[3] The trade boom was mainly in response to specific orders. Cook of Dewsbury Mills reported 'inordinate demand' from across the Atlantic and complained: 'We cannot put up goods of quality in these times of swollen orders. There is not a loom in the trade in Yorkshire unemployed at this time and a monstrous quantity of blankets is being produced.'[4]

But by the second half of 1836 speculative trade was becoming more evident. 'Adventurers were pouring consignments across the Atlantic' and there is evidence of manufacturers producing more for stock.[5] Brisk trading conditions expired late in the year and gloom descended very quickly. 1837 was a dismal year for manufacturers. Dewsbury Mills' trade to the United States was halved and they saw no prospects of quick revival, particularly as some competitors were selling at below cost. Exports of blankets fell from their all-time peak of 4.3 million yards in 1836 to 2.4 million yards in 1837. Exports of flannels, baizes, kerseymeres and mixed cloths all fell. The home trade gave no relief. The year 1837 was described as 'the most unfortunate in the modern annals of [the] worsted industry . . . a year of extraordinary depression'.[6]

Prospects looked somewhat better at the beginning of 1838. There was some recovery in the American market and some signs of an export revival but home demand was poor and the *Leeds Mercury* was not encouraging: 'In the economy of providence occasional dearth and sterility are part of a plan the wisdom of which we can no more dispute than we can alter the plan itself.'[7] The paper forecast further poor harvests and was right. The worsted trade fared better than the woollen trade, and, although its home demand remained stagnant for the following three years, its export business was buoyant and soared rapidly to unexpected heights with the overwhelming demand for its new cotton warped lighter and fancier cloths. Wool-

Table 23   *Exports of wool textiles and yarn, 1835–59*

	£m		£m
1835	7.2	1848	6.5
1836	8.0	1849	8.4
1837	5.0	1850	10.0
1838	6.2	1851	9.9
1839	6.7	1852	10.2
1840	5.8	1853	11.6
1841	6.3	1854	11.7
1842	5.8	1855	9.7
1843	7.5	1856	12.4
1844	9.2	1857	13.5
1845	8.8	1858	12.5
1846	7.2	1859	14.9
1847	7.9		

lens remained depressed. Occasional signs of revival quickly disappeared. In June 1839 the Leeds paper was still despondent, anticipating 'a period of embarrassment of some duration, ruinous to many individuals in the mercantile classes and very trying to the operative population'.[8] The failures came; 13 of them in the West Riding woollen trade in 1839 and 17 the following year.[9] Jowett listed 130 failures connected with the wool textile trade as a whole, including dyers, merchants, warehousemen, woolstaplers, woolbrokers and drysalters. Some of the major losses were in the stuff trade; the largest failure, with debts of almost £¼ million, was the famous firm of Hindes and Dereham of Leeds and Dolphineholme. Its collapse brought down Thos Legg and Sons, the London woolstaplers, and a number of fancy manufacturers and warp sellers at Huddersfield, Thurlstone and Kirkheaton. Presumably the consequences reached even further.

The *Leeds Mercury* predicted that the trough had been reached in December 1839 and by August 1840 reported: 'alarm is subsiding, men are no longer enquiring with anxious trepidation who is to go next, nor trembling alive as to their own danger. We believe that the tide has fully turned'.[10] It was wrong as far as the woollen trade was concerned. Although there were some orders, exports continued to decline. Some antedated government blanket purchases to take advantage of lower prices benefited Witney and the heavy woollen district but those engaged in government contract work were few and, with them having little other business, there was little work subcontracted to other firms.[11] Failures continued, including the major Leeds woollen merchants and manufacturers, Obadiah Willans and Sons. Jowett recorded 73 connected with the trade during 1841. In Gloucestershire the number of manufacturers was just under half the total of 1832 as a result of 50 failures in the intervening period.[12]

Failures were fewer in 1842. The *Leeds Mercury* continued to make encouraging prophecies. It was sure, in March, that 'this year will witness the first heavings of a tide which will conduct the country to a state of commercial and manufacturing prosperity more palmy and prosperous than it has ever before witnessed'.[13] But woollen manufacturers saw no respite. In January Reuben Gaunt of Farsley was doing little work in one mill and none in his other.[14] The factory inspectors reported in June that 'great and general depression continues unabated' with 'no well grounded hopes for speedy revival'. In December they recorded that 'the deplorable state of affairs continues'.[15]

The worsted trade was happier, profits were being made. The Marriners of Keighley and the Bairstows of Sutton traded successfully.[16] Although in 1840 there were complaints of low prices and uncertainty caused by money market difficulties and Chartist disturbances, exports continued to rise. Trade with China was good. Mousseline-de-laine and Orleans cloth were in much demand. The following year uncertainties continued. The failure of the United States bank created worries for American traders but prices were maintained. There was extensive United States and German export demand. The ups and downs continued in 1842. Plug riots and other disturbances depressed trade. Merino cloth continued to lose favour but mixed fibre fancy goods were in demand.[17]

By the autumn of 1843 the *Leeds Mercury* was able to report accurately that 'the fury of the hurricane of 1837–41 has spent itself', and it was wondering when the next depression would come.[18] The factory inspectors had reported the improvements in June,[19] Reuben Gaunt's Top Mill had started running again in February. Dewsbury Mills were less sure. Thomas Cook wrote to Philadelphia, begging for orders: 'Things are bad with us and we have great misery and destruction of property. Many of our neighbours have been carried away . . . and the general distress is painful.'[20] But by the end of the year there was general agreement that the bad times had passed. Exports were beginning to rise noticeably including flannels, blankets, kerseymeres and other cloth. What had caused the depression? The regularity of the business cycle was recognised but the events of 1837 to 1843 cannot be explained just in those terms for this was a period of seven years of unsatisfactory trade for much of the wool textile industry. The initial problems arose from the events of 1836. Buoyant home demand and large overseas orders, both for immediate sale and for speculation, had encouraged widespread investment in the wool textile industries and had forced up the price of wool. Rapid changes in wool prices made the trade very nervous: 'Unequal and irregular vibrations in the price of wool and woollens makes the balance of profit and loss almost a matter of accurate calculation as the throw of a dicer's box'.[21]

The *Leeds Mercury* explained in July 1838 that cloth prices followed upward movement in wool prices only slowly and with difficulty; but they fell with wool and often in a greater ratio than the fall in the wool prices warranted. Of particular concern was the possibility that high prices of wool would suddenly fall encouraging merchants to force down prices or delay their deliveries or orders.[22] With wool supply short in periods of peak demand, some manufacturers had to turn to inferior wools and produce lower quality cloth. With rising demand they could sell but they were the most vulnerable when times changed, so manufacturers were becoming nervous by mid-1836. In June the *Leeds Mercury* pointed out that the time had not yet come when the United States would cease 'to exhibit those extreme points of excitement and depression to which it seems more liable than any other nation with which we have dealings'.[23] The depression arrived within a few months; American merchants, early in 1837, began to have difficulties meeting 'the enormous, the extravagant extent of their engagements'.[24] Financial problems started in February leading to failures by May, 'but the grand convulsion was witnessed at the commencement of June, when several of these great American houses went down with a crash, and involved in ruin a multitude of manufacturers, especially those of Bradford'.[25] Panic followed, stock values were reduced; joint stock banks, which had been generous with their credit in 1835–6, tightened. Although the *Leeds Mercury* believed that manufacturers had been cautious and denied there had been much speculation and overtrading, markets at home and abroad were overstocked. Thomas Cook wrote to Philadelphia: 'It is now clear that last year's fever of speculation has resulted in much overstocking and we do not expect a quick recovery . . .'.[26] There were signs of improvement in the spring of 1838 with the American revival but then unfortuitous other factors appeared. Some were insignificant but, with the nervous state of the trade, were magnified. Others were much more serious. The harvest was poor, food prices were rising. The home trade seemed in jeopardy. The

Leeds Mercury summed up the situation:

> It cannot too often or too strongly be impressed on the minds of our merchants and our operative population that the amount of employment for capital and labour is inseparably connected with the amount of food, and in the direct ratio of the amount of one will be the amount of the other.[27]

Throughout the nineteenth century manufacturers and merchants followed the harvest prospects very closely. The home winter trade of 1838 was ruined and the spring trade of 1839 was no better. The rapid expansion of food imports led to an outflow of bullion, an increase in Bank Rate, restriction on commercial discounts and a curtailing of circulation. Manufacturers and merchants faced yet further financial difficulties. The panic in the United States in October aggravated the situation by hurting the American trade. Harvests remained poor and food prices high until summer 1842, but subsequent falling prices and the prospect of better home demand did not for long restore confidence as increased United States duties on the importation of wool textiles promised to affect the export trade.[28]

The brightest spot in these seven years of depression was the worsted industry's success with new cotton-warp cloths. It has been suggested that in the woollen industry the depression held back the use of cotton[29], but this does not appear to have been the case with worsteds where development was rapid and trade expansion in foreign markets very successful.

The Use of Cotton

The period dealt with in this chapter saw the widespread use of cotton in the wool textile trade. The number of technical problems involved in manufacturing cloths of two fibres as different as wool and cotton is not always appreciated. In almost every way they react differently. For example, acid has comparatively little effect on wool. It is, in fact, possible to boil wool in sulphuric acid without doing any great harm and it actually gives wool certain new properties; on the other hand, sulphuric acid, even in relatively dilute quantities, destroys cotton. Conversely it is possible to treat cotton with quite a concentrated solution of alkali and do no harm and, rather as with acid on wool, get new properties (mercerisation, for example), while treatment by even dilute alkaline solutions does great harm to wool. In addition, many dyes only colour one or other fibre. If attempts are made to use the same dye for both fibres, then frequently quite different methods of application have to be employed so much so that it is just as difficult as if two separate dyes were used.

The problem may be illustrated with indigo. This most important of all dyes needs to be processed in a relatively strong alkaline bath. The early chemicals used for this were far too strong for wool and it was in fact for this reason that the wool dyers went on using urine or alternatively the woad vat long after the cotton trade had adopted newer and, relatively speaking, more scientific methods.

For this reason it has been thought best to indicate separately something of the use of cotton warps in the trade and how these problems were overcome. The widespread introduction of cotton warps to the Bradford worsted trade from the late 1830s set it on a wave of prosperity which lasted, with few serious fluctuations, for almost 40 years. The joint use of cotton and wool fibres in wool textile manufacture was not new in the 1830s. Cotton, like silk, had previously been used on a widespread basis but in relatively small quantities in various branches of the trade. Benjamin Gott was manufacturing cotton warped woollen cloths, swandowns and toilinets, in Leeds in the early nineteenth century.[30] In the 1820s flannel and baize manufacturers at Rochdale were using cotton in cloths called Dometts and Domett baize and Henry Hughes, the Blackwell Hall factor, recorded that much cotton was being used in the manufacture of woollen cord for breeches.[31] In the worsted trade some cotton had also been used from early in the century. The Clays of Rastrick were obtaining cotton warp and weft and bleached cotton regularly from Oldham. In the 1820s fancy goods manufacturers in the Huddersfield district were producing cloth with cotton warps and worsted wefts.[32] The trade statistics show that small quantities of woollen cloth mixed with cotton were being exported. The statistics do not, of course, enable the type of cloth to be identified and there may be doubts, in any case, about classifications. However, the figures suggest an average annual export of 833,000 yards between 1815 and 1824. In the following year exports soared to over twice that amount, this boom coinciding with additional efforts to combine cotton warps and worsted weft satisfactorily. Joseph Barratt received enquiries from America for what was called 'summer cloth' suitable for men's summer coats. Barratt made enquiries and discovered that a Manchester worsted manufacturer had attempted to make this but had been unable to overcome the problem of dyeing the mixed animal and vegetable fibre. Barratt claims to have been more success-ful and to have built up an export trade in mixed cloths of reasonable quality. Others apparently also entered the trade and somewhat debased it by selling defective goods. It is by no means certain that

Barratt's claim can be taken too seriously.[33] From 1826 to the early 1830s the export figures do not suggest much increase in business.

But much more progress in the manufacture of cotton warp worsted goods was made in the mid-1830s. Messrs Wood of Denby Dale near Huddersfield and Robert Milligan of Bingley were amongst the pioneers by 1837. Milligan wrote:

> We claim to be among the earliest manufacturers who successfully used cotton warps in Bradford goods for women's wear. Our first goods were cotton warp double twills, but there was much difficulty in dyeing these satisfactorily, and it was not until September, 1838, that we made a fair start with cotton warps in goods designated by the name of 'Orleans cloth'.[34]

The two main problems for the innovation were the acquisition of satisfactory cotton warps and the solving of the dyeing difficulties. Although manufacturers initially claimed that warps were difficult to obtain the response of cotton spinners appears to have been quite quick as from 1837 mixed cloth output rose rapidly and complaints subsided. In the longer term the Yorkshire cotton industry adapted itself to serve the spinning and doubling needs of worsted manufacturers.[35] The dyeing difficulty was initially faced by dyeing the cotton warp before it was woven, the worsted weft being matched with it. This limited the number of colours that could be used. The great step forward came when bichromate of potash was substituted for copperas as a mordant. Baines explained that bichromate of potash was

> perhaps the finest mordant in existence for receiving vegetable colouring matter, and its adoption completely revolutionised the trade, not only because it largely increased the number of colours obtained, but because of the great rapidity of its action. Before the use of bichrome a black dyed piece took one day to prepare and another to dye; the whole process can now be accomplished in two hours.[36]

From 1837 the Bradford worsted trade commenced a rapid conversion to cotton warped goods; fourteen firms in Keighley were producing them by 1844.[37] By September 1838 the Bradford newspaper was reporting that they had 'displaced a very considerable quantity of machinery previously employed on merinos' and that through their elegance and beauty and reduced costs were creating competition for goods exclusively of cotton. By mid-1843 the same paper could write about 'a new era in the history of the Bradford trade'.[38] And by 1857, when the vast majority of worsted cloth was

being made with cotton warps, James was able to look back and say
that the cotton warp

> has imparted a new character to the worsted industry, enabled the
> manufacturer to suit the requirements of the age by producing
> light and elegant stuff goods, rivalling in cheapness articles from
> cotton and in brilliancy and delicacy those from silk. Hencefor-
> ward the trade assumes a new and broader aspect and exhibits a
> power of adaptation of all classes of goods, and a capability of
> expansion which, a few years previous to this, could not be con-
> ceived.[39]

Also from the late 1830s cotton was beginning to be more widely
used elsewhere in the wool textile trade. The Lancashire worsted
trade around Colne, having experienced for a long time a decline in
demand for its serges, was given a boost when it started manufacturing cotton-warped mousselines-de laine, which were 'particularly
adapted for printing colours upon' and 'have added much to the
ornamental character of worsted'. In 1857 James described the
Colne mousseline-de-laine manufacture as 'extensive and rapidly
increasing'.[40] In the woollen branch of the industry the union cloth
trade based on Morley was created and cotton warps were coming
into use in blanket manufacture. Hagues and Cook of Dewsbury
Mills found they were able to reduce their production costs by 10 per
cent as a result.[41]

Wool textiles manufactured with cotton were therefore the major
growth point of the wool textile trade from the late 1830s. Exports of
them increased from little over 1 million yards in 1837 to 5 million
yards in 1841, 20 million yards in 1844, and over 50 million yards by
1854. The reasons for the success and rapid expansion of the innovation are complex, as is the timing. Technological change was the
permissive factor, and, through the improvements in quality it
allowed, undoubtedly gave a considerable boost to the trade, but
technological change itself only came about when sufficient incentive
persuaded manufacturers to experiment.

Over the long term tariffs, fashion and changing relative prices of
wool and cotton were the significant reasons. Tariff increases in the
United States after 1824 and a 'stepped' tariff system encouraged
those woollen manufacturers dependent on the United States to
attempt to reduce costs by using cheaper fibres and more efficient
production methods. Heavy tariffs imposed on worsted goods in
1842 and 1846 may have had a similar effect but the United States
worsted industry had made little progress by then and Bradford

manufacturers had little to fear from home competition.[42] The tariffs in the Zollverein countries did however affect the worsted trade. The 1834 tariff on cotton had hurt British cotton exporters, but some of the trade was replaced by cotton warped worsteds, which through their cheaper price and lower weights were better able to compete with the German home produced cotton goods than all-wool worsted would have been.[43]

The relationship of fashion to the change is debatable. James argues that a taste was developing for 'light, elegant and cheap articles of dress, which lacking the wearing qualities of former stuffs, yet were more showy and attractive' but does not explain the causes of the rising demand for 'beauty' in dress.[44] The cheapening of worsted fabrics through cotton warps brought them into the range of more pockets. The resultant innovation of more fancy stuffs encouraged a change in dress styles but can one also argue that fashion was changing earlier and causing an initial stimulus to innovation in the worsted industry? Perhaps it was. By September 1837 the Leeds newspaper was commenting that fashion changes were occurring, persuading 'the gentlemen who lead the town in Bond Street and other fashionable parts of the metropolis' to turn from costly fabrics to new types of cloth, with the macintosh displacing the heavy, double milled overcoat, and lighter weight 'fancies' with printed or woven patterns coming into vogue.[45] Two years earlier the Bradford newspaper had reported a considerable demand for 'fabrics of a new description . . . of varied, rich and elegant patterns'.[46] The speed of the transition to mixed worsteds also suggests that fashion was ready to demand them.

A further reason, and perhaps the most important, is convincingly argued by E.M. Sigsworth. As he points out the relative prices of long wool and cotton widened, particularly after 1830. The substitutability of cotton for many other textiles in both home and foreign markets required a response from wool textile manufacturers. This response came through experiments with new technology and the use of cotton. The *Bradford Observer* explained the change in these terms: 'The present low price of cotton and the taste for low priced fancy goods have induced manufacturers to substitute the former for wool in the warp which has very materially diminished the consumption of wool in stuffs.'[47]

Explanations of tariffs, fashion and changing relative prices of textile fibres may explain the transition in the long run, but what of the actual and sudden timing of the change? The trade figures, if they are reliable, clearly date the innovation to 1837–38 before the dyeing difficulties had been conquered. Perhaps a short term explanation is through a rapid response to the sudden downturn in trade from late 1836 which lasted throughout 1837. These difficulties after a period of flourishing trade caused manufacturers to seek rapidly for new fabrics and their successful innovation of cotton warps coincided with a revival in the American market.

The Course of Trade 1843–50

Recovery in 1843 led to a short period of intense activity throughout most of the wool textile industry. The Saddleworth fine woollen trade was more prosperous than it had been for years. The West of England trade was 'active and profitable', with much new investment taking place.[48] Profits were also good in the worsted trade; the Fosters of Black Dyke Mills almost doubled theirs, compared with the previous year, and the Marriners and Bairstows did likewise.[49] There were large spring orders from America and manufacturers were receiving higher prices. Home demand for worsted goods was buoyant.[50] The Leeds woollen trade, however, was less happy. Fine woollen broad cloths 'felt but very little of the effects of the revival of trade'.[51] Exports of yarn and manufactured wool textiles rose noticeably in 1844, and 1845 started well. But the *Leeds Mercury* prophecy of November 1843 came true. The paper had written: 'We can get a tolerably correct idea how soon another period of deficient harvests will overtake us. We have had two fair crops. Should 1844 be good, the probabilities are that 1845 and 1846 will be bad, one or both. It is against all probability that we shall reach 1847 without a bad, a really bad, harvest'.[52] 1845 was poor, 1846 was terrible. The home market difficulties which were becoming apparent by late summer in 1845 were aggravated by disturbing political news from America, fears of German tariff increases which in due course turned to reality and difficulties in the money market resulting from railway speculation. The Bradford worsted trade was adversely affected. Machinery was stopped and the factory inspectors suggested that difficulties had been 'much aggravated by the great increased production of goods in the market within the last few years'. They, like others, hoped for severe weather.[53] Confidence was again quickly sapped as the memories of the previous lengthy depression in some of the trade were revived. A manufacturer described the *Leeds Mercury* of 18 October 1845 as being 'filled this day with the most doleful apprehensions for the prosperity of the country'.[54]

Exports from the wool textile industry as a whole fell slightly in 1845 and much more substantially in 1846. The worsted trade to the

United States and Germany accounted for much of the decline. The factory inspector reported much distress and suffering in Bradford although James was less pessimistic. He thought 1846 could 'be classed among the better years of the worsted manufacture'. There were bright spots. The repeal of the Corn Laws, for which Baines and some manufacturers had for long been campaigning, was welcomed. The Walker tariff in the United States provided for easier trading relationships[55] but profits for the two years were low. The Bairstows had their worst years of the decade with a return of only 2.3 per cent on their capital in 1846. The Fosters did rather better but the Mar-riners fared badly with a loss in 1845 and a profit of just a few pounds in 1846.

The year 1847 started with little confidence and extreme caution. This caution enabled the worst of the commercial distress to be avoided. It was said to the Commission on Commercial Distress that Yorkshire almost entirely escaped it, but there were bankruptcies including the woollen firm of S. and S. Smith of Luddenden Foot, which brought down Jos. Thornton, the Gomersall woolstapler, and Pringle of Haddington in Scotland, his father-in-law. They absconded owing £100,000 to three Scottish banks.[56] Reuben Gaunt recorded 'failures to an enormous extent have taken place. This has been a dreadful year for the mercantile world. Most of those who have not failed have lost a great deal of money'.[57] But the evidence suggests that failures were not too widespread or too damaging. However, the wool textile industry was badly depressed. Robert Baker, the Leeds and Bradford factory inspector, wrote in October: 'I have never known the state of the manufacturing districts so bad as at present within my recollection . . . In the worsted districts things have been bad for 16 months, but excepting in the manufacture of goat's hair, they are far worse now than ever.'[58] Besides financial difficulties the particular problems of the year were the worry of the potential consequences of the Ten Hour Bill, a reduction in trade with Italy and railway speculation by some millowners which 'injured their means to sustain their trade'. French protectionism was also a cause for great concern in Bradford.[59] However, 1847 did produce rising worsted exports to the United States and elsewhere.

Trade revival became apparent in the spring of 1848, but recovery was not uniform. The European political upsets affected trade to the countries involved. Activity remained poor in Scotland.[60] There were fears that goods intended for European markets would be forced on to the British market but, although in the short term fears were realised, markets soon revived.[61] In the worsted industry production was adversely affected in the summer with only one third of the capacity of machinery being utilised but by July greater activity was apparent and the 'autumn was a season of great activity in the stuff market'.[62] Profits were made although exports to most of the major markets fell, including Russia, Germany, France and Spain. Trade with Scandinavia, Portugal, Mexico and some South American countries showed some improvement.

For most of the next three years trade was, in general, good. Home demand revived, exports expanded and substantial new investment was undertaken. The plain and fancy woollen trade, although varying with the seasons, was very satisfactory; the worsted trade most active. Demand for heavy woollens was good. Thomas Cook had a very full order book and admitted that the quality of his product was suffering from his attempts to fulfill orders. He commented that he had never seen so many new customers.[63] There was demand for railway covers, for worsted yarn to export, camblets for the East Indies and Orleans and coburg cloths for the United States.[64] Wool prices rose in response to demand but manufacturers were able to obtain good prices and profits were excellent. For many areas of the wool textile trade the bad years outnumbered the good in the 1840s. However, the volume of complaint in difficult times should not be allowed to mask the substantial progress that was made. The capacity of the worsted industry extended substantially. Over the decade the volume of yarn exports tripled and that of wool textile manufactures more than doubled.

Another factor which gave some relief to the worsted trade during the difficult period of the late 1830s and early 1840s was the increasing yarn export trade. In 1824 the Government had lifted the ban on the export of yarn and it had subsequently risen considerably.[65] Exports were mainly to Germany and the United States although small quantities were going, by 1832, to a range of other countries including Russia, Italy and the British colonies in North America. In terms of value the trade was not great. It amounted to 4 per cent of the total declared value of wool textile yarns and manufactures exports in 1832, 11 per cent in 1842 and 14 per cent in 1850. The steadiness and prosperity of the export trade for Bradford spinners was however mitigated by problems in the home trade, particularly the gradual disappearance of Norwich demand. The latter still existed however in the late 1830s as the *Bradford Observer* reported uncompleted yarn contracts for Norwich.[66] But markets also existed in the Midlands hosiery trade, the Huddersfield fine worsted trade and in Lancashire and Scotland from mousseline-de-laine manufacturers.

The yarn trade which had provided a stable growth element to the wool textile industry in the 1830s, continued to expand rapidly throughout the 1840s and 1850s. The quantity exported more than trebled during the 1840s and from 1850 to 1860 doubled. The periods of major expansion were the first half of the 1840s and, particularly the years 1854 to 1856. In the latter period supply was inadequate to service the huge increase in overseas demand which came mainly from Germany and Belgium. Yarn exports to Russia had also been substantial before the war and recovered subsequently. There was a small yarn export to the United States, but it declined somewhat in the 1850s. Mohair yarn was also being increasingly demanded by France.[67]

Table 24   Exports of woollen and worsted yarn

Annual averages	thousand lbs	Annual averages	thousand lbs
1825–9	298	1850–4	14 477
1830–4	1775	1855–9	23 864
1835–9	2765	1860–4	29 447
1840–4	6069	1865–9	35 788
1845–9	9661		

Manufacturers and merchants, perhaps more than their counterparts in any other industry, had to pay very close attention to all news emanating from their foreign markets. The state of export demand could fundamentally change in the space of a few days through war, political problems, harvest failure, tariff changes, financial failures and many other influences. Home demand was by no means exempt from such factors. Orders for many types of cloth were seasonal. Fashion changes and demand levels for the following season had to be continually judged. Production for the spring and summer markets started in January and manufacturers keenly awaited a change from winter weather to see whether their market expectations were realised. A change in fashion, amongst other factors, could create a sudden stimulus to demand and a spurt of activity in the mills in the spring. Production for winter demand was underway by August, by which time some assessment was possible of the harvest and thus of food prices for the following year. Although the influence of the harvest on home textile demand declined during the course of the century food prices still substantially affected the spending margin of many of the consumers of textiles.

The winter trade was particularly susceptible to the weather. A mild winter could do great damage to demand. Orders for blankets, over-coatings and suitings would soar immediately a spell of very cold weather set in. The later snow and frost was arriving, the more despondent manufacturers became and it was generally agreed that the non-appearance of hard weather until the new year would con-siderably reduce overall winter orders and leave manufacturers hold-ing stocks.

The Course of Trade in the 1850s

A number of features stand out in the decade of the 1850s. There was a further significant rise in productive capacity. Technological prog-ress stimulated a further transfer from domestic to factory production and brought about the rapid disappearance of hand combing. The industry became aware that wool textile manufacture on the conti-nent of Europe was progressing in leaps and bounds. The increasing capacity of manufacture at home and abroad put pressure on wool supplies which, although increasing, for much of the decade could not meet demand, thus leading to unprecedented price increases with consequent effects on manufacturing levels and confidence. The decade opened brightly. Trade revival was sustained with export demand for worsteds particularly good from Germany, Italy, Turkey and the Levant, the British North American colonies and the United States. The woollen trade was likewise very active and both branches were given an additional boost in the second half of 1850 when a good harvest suggested encouraging prospects for the home trade.

However by the autumn of 1850 warnings were being sounded. *The Economist* noted that wool prices were beginning to rise and suggested that there could not 'fail to be a considerable anxiety, both on the part of the producer and consumer, in order to ascertain whether such an advance is justified by the facts connected with the trade, and whether therefore it is likely to be continued'.[68] But wool imports did respond: they rose by over 10 per cent in 1851, and exports and re-exports somewhat fell. However, rising prices were not abated in spite of the more hesitant trade that they occasioned. The industry did not work to full capacity in 1851, demand for many woollen goods was lower than expected. Fine worsted experienced poor trade although cotton warped worsteds did a little better.[69] Fear about wool supply and wool prices continued. Gold discoveries in Australia and the Kaffir war gave rise to rumours of labour shortages and some manufacturers attempted to persuade the Colonial Office to send sufficient labour to Australia to secure the 1852 wool clip.[70] A partially successful attempt to 'get up' a speculation in wool by cornering the import market further aggravated fears. Manufacturers were worried also about European demand following a poor harvest.[71] But the home harvest was good and trade in 1852 was reasonably prosperous at home and abroad.

In 1853 wool imports rose by 27 per cent above the level of the previous year, with a fall in re-exports and exports combined. There is no reason to believe there was a fall in home wool supplies. The home industry continued therefore to see an expansion in the supply of its raw materials, but demand went on outstripping supply and price rises increased. Cotton warp prices were also increasing.[72] But in spite of the resultant caution and fears of what the consequences of a sudden price fall would be, 1853 was a year of great activity. In the Scottish border woollen industry demand for hosiery, tweed and shawls was unprecedentedly great. All parts of Yorkshire reported prosperity. There were complaints of insufficient labour. The worsted trade received good orders from Australia and the United States and, as a result of the rise in wool prices, extended its range of mixed fabrics.[73]

In the second half of 1853 the state of trade began to alter and by the autumn activity in both the woollen and worsted industries was much reduced and further difficulties were being anticipated. American demand was falling off. German demand was less satisfactory. Fear of war between Turkey and Russia was sapping confidence and to cap it all, the harvest was bad.[74] A year that had been described as 'beyond all dispute, the most prosperous one ever recorded in the annals of British commerce' ended on a sour note and was followed by a year of difficulties.[75] Wool imports fell, prices remained high. Exports fell, partly as a result of the speculative demand of the previous year. In particular exports to the United States and Australia were adversely affected.[76] Demand from some European countries held up better, but prices of goods for both home and overseas markets were forced down, leading to financial difficulties and, in both the woollen and worsted trades, to failures. The worsted trade was the most depressed. Six Bradford firms stopped payment in the first half of the year and the Bradford newspaper described 1854 as a year 'full of disaster'.[77] It was most affected by export problems and a very slight fall in the price of English long combing wool adversely hit those manufacturers who had been producing on very narrow margins and were unable to easily respond to demands for lower product prices. Depression was less severe in the woollen trade. Activity in Scotland was described as decidedly flourishing in April with almost every mill in full operation. In Yorkshire the Leeds area woollen

Table 25   Exports of wool textiles, 1854–69 (£ millions)

	Cloths and coatings	Flannels and blankets	Worsted stuffs mixed & unmixed	All wool textiles
1854	3.1	0.7	4.4	9.1
1855	2.4	0.5	4.0	7.7
1856	2.8	0.8	4.7	9.5
1857	3.0	0.9	5.6	10.7
1858	2.5	0.7	5.6	9.8
1859	2.9	1.0	6.9	12.1
1860	3.0	0.8	7.0	12.2
1861	3.0	1.0	6.1	11.1
1862	4.4	1.4	5.9	13.2
1863	4.0	1.4	8.3	15.5
1864	4.5	1.5	10.8	18.6
1865	4.0	1.2	13.4	20.1
1866	5.3	1.2	13.3	21.8
1867	5.3	0.9	12.1	20.2
1868	3.8	1.0	13.1	19.6
1869	4.3	1.1	15.1	22.7

trade factories were fairly busy and the heavy woollen district received some respite from Government army and navy orders and from its ability to some extent to substitute shoddy for wool. A 'tolerable demand' was maintained for Rochdale flannels and the Huddersfield fancy trade maintained reasonable activity for much of the year. The West of England trade was reported as having done likewise.[78] A good harvest and forecasts that the difficulties would only be short-lived restored some confidence. One trade journal commented that there was 'no reason to despair for a continuation of our manufacturing and mercantile prosperity'.[79]

Contemporary comment and business records suggest that the slight downturn did not lead to a build up of stocks. Thus trade was able to pick up quite rapidly in 1855, with the woollen trade in particular having an active year. Although in January the *Bradford Observer* described the trade as 'dull as can be, not a transaction passing . . .'[80] and although wool prices remained high and exports to Canada, United States and Australia were still depressed, James could still describe the year as one of 'good demand and fair profit.'[81] and the *Bradford Observer* noted at the end of the year that 'there is not a textile manufacture in the United Kingdom which can boast a healthier, a sounder or a more legitimate trade during the past year than the worsted trade of the Bradford district.'[82] This satisfactory state of affairs was explained through both a large and steady home trade and better remuneration from exports, in spite of the difficulties in major markets, arising, so it was suggested, from the trade being on a surer footing following the failures of the previous year. Much of the woollen trade experienced brisk activity. Government military orders were flooding in and there were complaints that insufficient yarn was creating difficulties in the supplying of large orders making the Government purchase furs instead. Yarn shortages enabled The *Economist* to complain bitterly, yet again, about the factory hours legislation and the activities of the factory inspectors:

> Whilst all classes have been voluntarily to the utmost of their means to assist our gallant soldiers, some factory hands, by the Factory Act, have been deprived of the power of easy good wages in their service. Would furs have been purchased abroad, could woollens sufficient have been produced at home?[83]

The Yorkshire heavy woollen district also received substantial Government military orders from France and Turkey. The Scottish trade was described as generally satisfactory with great activity in the border district and the Leeds trade was referred to at the end of the year as being sound and healthy, with particular mention being made of a sudden revival in the demand for tweed from the manufacturers of Guiseley, Yeadon and Rawdon and of a steady business in broad cloth at the same time.[84] However at the end of the year rising food prices following the harvest and the tightening of money with the rising bank rate was creating a suspicion of further difficulties. Wool imports, which had previously fallen slightly, were beginning to rise but so were prices, again leading to renewed fears about profit margins. However, 1856 was an uneventful year with low stocks, steady trade and quite full employment, encouraging yet a further extension in productive capacity throughout the industry. The harvest was fair but war demand was easing off, and late in the year money problems arose again, damaging those manufacturers with extended credit and large stocks.[85]

1857 commenced quite well however. The woollen trade did steady business during the spring and summer although the dissolution of Parliament created a slight setback. Scottish trade was satisfactory.[86] But then commercial and monetary crisis had its impact. The crisis was severe but quite short in duration. The extended credit that had been given in previous years to firms expanding their capacity to reap the rewards of the buoyant demand led to these firms encountering severe financial difficulties as their obligations matured. The downturn in trade prevented manufacturers selling their goods and stocks; the fall in wool prices reduced the value of their stocks. The failure of some remittances from abroad further aggravated the manufacturers' financial difficulties.[87] The situation that arose in Leeds was described by John Smith, partner in the local bank of Becketts and Co. He discussed the difficulties manufacturers faced in raising finance and the great state of alarm that existed in Leeds, where manufactured goods became 'perfectly unsaleable' and financial obligations could not be met. A treasury letter provided relief, confidence was restored and within a few weeks business was resuming. He suggests that there had been no great excess of credit in the West Riding except perhaps at Bradford where there had been some speculation in wool, financed by a system of bill discounting. Although there were no failures of any consequence in Leeds, there were about a dozen very large ones in Bradford, including the firms of Cheeseborough, and Lister and Haigh.[88] In December the factory inspectors reported that many mills were closed, others were working only short time. Scottish manufacturing was depressed. But on the brighter side changes in the United States tariff were further easing trade across the north Atlantic.[89] At the end of the year the commercial reports in the press strongly admonished the wool textile trade for what was described as its commercial immorality. The *Leeds Mercury* was particularly forceful in its condemnations describing how, as a result, many prudent tradesmen had been crippled in business and how 'many a one will lose the hard earned accumulations of years of toil, and penury and want be carried to the poor man's cottage'.[90]

By January 1858 there were reports that trade was beginning to recover. Commercial depression had led to a reduction in capacity in the industry which perhaps rapidly eased the way to a steady and more profitable trade.[91] In April, although Yorkshire was described as still generally depressed, there were symptoms of improvement in the woollen trade in Scotland and by October the factory inspectors were able to report that considerable recovery was occurring in most branches of trade including Scotland, and concern was again being shown for the adequacy of supply of raw wool. Prices had fallen after the depression but were again beginning to rise. Is it 'not high time we were bestirring ourselves to find places, countries and soils where the growth of wool can be augmented', commented Robert Baker.[92]

The two following years of 1859 and 1860 were prosperous. Scottish tweeds were much in demand and the woollen trade in Scotland was described as 'never in a more flourishing state than at present . . . particularly in the manufacture of tweeds, which is now beyond question the staple trade of the South of Scotland'. In Yorkshire the woollen trade had 'seldom been so brisk' with 'machinery standing idle for want of labour'. The adequacy of supply of labour was again causing acute difficulties, particularly in the worsted trade, and agents were being sent to the South and West to attempt to persuade people to migrate north.[93] Thus the decade ended, as it had begun, with a state of great activity in the industry, and the ten years before the Anglo-French Treaty, the United States Morrill tariff, and the Civil War and consequent cotton famine can be summed up as a period of great extension of trade and expansion in the industry, in spite of the difficulties of 1857.

This review of the decade has, however, indicated some particular features, the major one of which is undoubtedly the adequacy of supply of wool. The inability of supply, which of course was inelastic in the short term, to keep up with the booming demand forced up prices and put pressure on both manufacturing financial resources and confidence. As explained above, product prices did not necessarily respond rapidly to increases in raw material prices which led therefore to reductions in profit margins, although not necessarily in absolute profits, because of the high level of manufacturing activity. It is doubtful whether detailed estimates of changes in home supply of wool during the decade will ever be calculable with any degree of confidence. Such estimates as do exist suggest a slow increase in the size of the domestic clip. Certainly there seems to be no reason to believe it was declining.

Up to 1853 wool imports rose quite steadily, the total in that year being 68 per cent above the 1848 level. The increase was obtained mainly from Australia but additional supplies were also forthcoming from the East, South Africa and South America. Exports and re-exports also rose in the period. Their quantities varied but they only made a small proportionate difference to the amount of wool remaining for consumption in Britain. But the rapidly increasing foreign supplies could not keep up with demand. Although long wool prices were described as reasonable in 1849–50, they rose rapidly thereafter.[94] *The Economist* in November 1850 remarked on the recent, considerable increase in price of wool and forecasted shortages 'as consumption is rising faster than supply and stocks are depleting'. It forecast that production in the Colonies would be stimulated and was able, a year later, to remark on a large increase in supply of colonial wool.[95]

Difficulties became more apparent in 1853. In that year poor supplies from Australia, particularly from New South Wales, slowed down the rate of growth of supply to Britain. There were also complaints about quality and worry about future supplies because of the reported scarcity of labour in Australia, the spread of scab and the increasing value of the carcase for meat.[96] The slight downturn in trade in 1854 temporarily halted the price increases but there was a very noticeable and quite sudden change in Continental demand for wool. Supplies from Europe to Britain began to decline. Re-exports more than doubled in 12 months. Exports of British wool increased. The clamouring European demand for wool instigated attempts to by-pass the London wool market by establishing an auction house for Australian wool at Rouen in 1854–5, but this had only a short life.[97] Direct imports of South American wool to Europe through the port of Antwerp increased.

From 1855 total gross and net imports rose again and remained at a high level. Prices soared. Complaints about the inadequacy of supplies resumed. The response from the wool exporting countries was insufficient. The causes of the supply difficulties in Britain clearly arose from the rapidly increasing demand as capacity of both woollen and worsted manufacturing was extended in response to rising home and foreign demand for cloth and yarn, and from rising demand for wool in Europe and the United States as their domestic wool textile industries expanded. The consequences of inadequate supply and rising prices were manifold. The use of shoddy as a substitute for virgin wool increased, rag imports rose and more use was made of cotton. At Galashiels some woollen manufacturers started using some cotton in trouserings and shawls. The local press stated that: 'This step has been resorted to solely from the enormous price of wool'.[98] Union cloth manufacture in the Yorkshire heavy woollen district was stimulated. In worsted manufacture yet fewer all-wool goods were made 'in consequence of the high prices of the material'. Some Lancashire worsted manufacturers converted to cotton manufacturing although many reverted to worsted in the following decade as cotton and wool price relatives were reversed.[99]

The consequence of rising wool prices on the profits of wool textile manufacturers is less easily determined. It has been argued that by 1856–57 a point had been reached where raw material prices made continued output unprofitable, which depressed new investment, and contributed to the commercial difficulties.[100] Contemporary comment would suggest that profit margins were being squeezed. Such was the complaint in the worsted industry. But the evidence of the

Bairstows, Marriners and Fosters is somewhat contradictory. The Fosters' return on capital declined after the peak years of 1849 and 1850 but remained at a very healthy level throughout the decade, with an average return on capital of between 9 and 18 per cent. Their profit as a proportion of the value of their sales was very high in 1849 and 1850, fell in 1851 but then rose and remained high for the rest of the decade with the exception of 1853 and 1857. It was a very successful period for them. The Bairstows' experience was less healthy. They made losses in 1854 and 1857 and very low profits in 1855. The following year however was a very successful one and they managed a return of over 18 per cent on their capital. The Marriners had bad years, with losses in 1852 and 1853, and their accounts show their bank borrowing rose steadily from 1854 to 1858, but it was higher at the beginning of the decade when they had large stocks. It may be that these firms were not typical of the trade as a whole but their experience does not suggest that very high wool prices inevitably led to lower profits. They do not provide clear evidence of declining profits in 1856, but the experience of a west country firm, J. & T. Clark of Trowbridge does support the hypothesis.[101]

Continental Competition 1840–60
The rising export of yarn to Continental manufacturers and the displays of foreign manufacturers at the London Exhibition of 1851 and the Paris Exhibition of 1855 were increasing the awareness of British manufacturers of the growth of foreign competition. The important United States market was becoming particularly competitive. In the early 1820s Britain had supplied 95 per cent of United States imports of wool textiles. By 1830 the proportion had fallen to under 85 per cent, mainly as a result of German competition. Britain remained dominant in the transatlantic trade in worsted cloth and blankets. In the 1850s about 70 per cent of the United States import of worsted goods came from Britain and no other country was important in the supply of blankets.[102] The trade in flannel, woollen cloth and cassimeres was, however, much less successful. Flannel exports to the United States which at one stage in the 1820s reached over 3 million yards a year, had by the early 1830s fallen to less than 100,000 yards and remained very small, except for a brief period during the Civil War. This reduction was the result of the success of United States domestic producers rather than European competition. The blanket trade was given a boost by the low duties of 1846 and exports soared during most of the 1850s reaching over 6.5 million yards in four years during the decade and an annual average

of over 5 million yards. But the Morrill Tariff Act of 1861 raised duties and gave domestic producers sufficient protection to oust British blankets so that by late in the 1860s exports hardly exceeded 100,000 yards.[103]

European competition in the American wool textile market was strongest in woollen cloth. Up to 1844 95 per cent of the woollen cloth and cassimeres imported into the United States were of British manufacture but in the following years British exports fell whereas those from Germany, Belgium and France rose to the extent that by 1849 Britain's share of the total had declined to little over 40 per cent.[104] Britain's poor export performance was the subject of much contemporary debate. A letter to the *Leeds Mercury* in June 1853 suggested that Belgian and German fine woollen cloths had to a great extent supplanted British cloths in the American markets through better dyeing and the declining quality of the latter. Also there was criticism of the British standards of cleansing cloth which, so it was said, obscured the 'richness of colours' and a suggestion that British concentration on cheapness had led to adulteration in dyeing and also in the quality of fibre used,[105] but evidence from patterns seems to disprove this. A later correspondent argued that foreign success was

> not because they can make better cloths or make them cheaper in proportion to quality than the Yorkshire or West of England manufacturers, but it is chiefly because the cloths which are made by the French, Germans and Belgians, for the consumption of their own countries, are just the style of goods which suit the taste of the people of the United States.

The letter writer argued that British manufacturers could not sell the bright shining-faced goods the Americans liked, in the London market 'within 25 per cent of their cost'. It was said that English manufacturers could scour, dye black and mill their cloth as well as anyone and were fully capable of making goods of all qualities. Blame for Britain's poor performance was placed instead on American merchants:

> Are we then to continue allowing the French, Germans and Belgians to hold their position? Unless the American merchants make efforts to acquaint manufacturers as to the precise finish style required, in contrast to the cloths required for the English market, or unless manufacturers of ample means will go over to the United States, make themselves thoroughly acquainted with the style of cloth required, then come back to England, determine to accomplish their object and consign their goods to some of the New York commission merchants – unless one or other of these plans be

Table 26 *Imports of cloths and cassimeres into the United States (thousand yards)*

	Germany	Belgium	France	England	Total
1840	17	93	90	4500	4697
1842	16	203	296	3475	3996
1844	44	360	595	3784	4778
1847	274	338	1704	2208	4528
1849	810	297	1173	2113	4996

SOURCE: *Wool, Worsted and Cotton Journal*, May 1853

taken, the foreign superfine cloth trade will never find its way to England again . . .[106]

Whichever view is correct, either would appear to have been a poor indictment of British woollen manufacturers and provided a bad omen for the future. There was probably substance in both arguments. An article in *The Times* claimed that the Germans attributed their success to their better dyeing and finishing and to their providing a 'firm, close woven body of cloth, mellow and with a short nap, bearing a natural gloss, not due to too much dressing and devilling'.[107] With an average of over 30 per cent of the value of British exports of wool textile manufacturers going to the United States in late 1840s including over 2 million yards of woollen cloth and cassimeres it seems most dubious that British manufacturers were unable to properly service American fashion. Germany also gained considerable success in supplying woolien and worsted yarns to the United States, providing by the early 1860s some 70 per cent of United States imports whereas Britain made only minor headway in that market.[108] French success was aided by the bounty paid by the Government after 1848 but when that ceased French exports of woollen goods fell again and were of only very minor importance in the United States market by the mid 1860s. The trade in all-wool worsted remained of more significance.

The International Exhibitions of 1851 and 1855
The Crystal Palace exhibition gave many British wool textile manufacturers their first view of the capabilities of their foreign competitors. The exhibition was reassuring for many but worrying for some, although the distinct impression is gained from the contemporary reports and discussions that the exhibition did not have a great deal of

impact in persuading British manufacturers to examine their products and business methods.

Bradford manufacturers made particular efforts in showing their wares at the Great Exhibition of the Works of All Nations. They had initially welcomed the idea and the Bradford newspaper in the previous year had expressed hope that Bradford exhibits would 'be of such a character as fully to sustain our increasing reputation as an enterprising and enlightening manufacturing community, perfectly alive to the advantage derivable from this opportunity of an exposition of our products to the world's inspection'.[109] The people of Bradford gave more per head to the exhibition funds than any other town in Britain and the efforts manufacturers made in displaying their goods rose above those of their neighbours.[110] The *Leeds Mercury* commented, when criticising the plain Leeds display, that 'Bradford had taken prodigious pains . . . with brilliant effect, to give their goods every advantage of handsome fitting and tasteful display.' The handsome fittings included large quantities of plate glass and solid mahogany cases. Leeds exhibits, on the other hand, were described as 'more like a woollen draper's shop, or a woollen merchant's counter, than a department of a showy bazaar'.[111]

The French examined the wool textile displays at the Exhibition very closely and a lengthy and detailed report was produced which gives a useful insight into the relative positions of the two countries, particularly as regards worsted spinning and manufacture.[112] It was pointed out, however, that 1851 was not a good year for France to exhibit because it was coming out of a violent political crisis. Therefore it was suggested that those French exhibitors who 'upheld with dignity the honour of the flag' gave a very imperfect idea of the resources and value of French wool textile manufacture. There was also a hint of reticence on the part of French manufacturers to exhibit for fear of their ideas and designs being poached.[113] These comments were perhaps most relevant to woollen exhibits; France was reasonably well represented in the worsted classes by firms from Reims, Amiens, Roubaix and Paris although there were only about 18 of them.[114]

The French report acknowledged the English superiority in the spinning of English long wool which, as a result of machine combing and other technical improvements and consequent economies in the use of labour, meant that the cheaper yarn produced could be manufactured into a cotton warped mousseline-de-laine selling at 30 centimes a metre, a third cheaper than the price at which they themselves could produce a similar quality. They were impressed also by the alpaca and mohair yarns which were hardly produced in France and had to be imported to Amiens from Norwich and Bradford.[115] In the production of yarn of combed merino wool, however, the French could claim superiority. Little progress had been made in the use of this wool in the British worsted industry where in 1851 only 50,000 spindles, out of some 200,000, were being used for spinning it, but it was acknowledged that England was beginning to make remarkable progress and threatened to become very competitive to French manufacturers, particularly as the power weaving of merino yarns expanded. However, at that time, the French *rapporteur* concluded that English worsted merino spinners 'have not yet attained the same degree of perfection as the French industry' which was able to produce a superior and more regular yarn.[116]

Both the English and French reports clearly indicated the gulf that existed between Britain and France, the two main worsted producers, in the production of their different specialities, mixed cloth and all wool worsteds respectively, a gap which, when fashion changed in later decades, was to have severe implications for the Bradford trade. The prize medals for worsted yarns and stuffs were mainly divided between French and English manufacturers but there was also recognition for the products of some manufacturers in Saxony, Austria, Belgium, Russia and Prussia.[117]

There was a reasonable representation of Leeds firms but only four exhibitors from the heavy woollen district presumably because it was believed there that its low qualities would be out of place. Huddersfield, however, was well represented, showing a remarkable range of cloth, which gained them 11 medals.[118] The local manufacturers had seen the exhibition as a means of avoiding 'the dangers of an insensible decay' to their trade and of endorsing their 'pre-eminence in certain branches of manufacture'.[119] West of England cloth was exhibited by London merchants and a few of the local manufacturers. The representation of the West of England trade is not easy to calculate for this reason but only four firms from Somerset, six from Wiltshire and ten from Gloucestershire had their own displays. The Scottish border trade was well in evidence. The remnants of the Norwich trade made an effort but few flannel manufacturers from Wales and Rochdale provided displays and the Saddleworth district had little representation.[120]

The British woollen manufacturers ranked well in the medal lists. Those from Leeds, who gained 15, were encouraged. West of England manufacturers did well in relation to their numbers in spite of it being suggested that they 'had not precisely comprehended the exact object of the Exhibition, which they imagine to be for goods of a pre-eminent character rather than for variety of production'.[121] In terms of numbers of exhibitors Britain completely outstripped other nations and her number of medals perhaps reflected this but other countries made a substantial showing in the medal lists, particularly the Zollverein States and Saxony, and France, which the *Leeds Mercury* suggested would make home manufacturers wake up to 'the skill and energy of our foreign competitors'.[122]

British wool textile manufacturers were able to gain some satisfaction from their showing but were they taken in by the small numbers of foreign exhibitors? Four years after the London exhibition another opportunity arose for them to view the progress of their foreign counterparts. The Paris Exhibition of 1855 was not altogether welcomed by many British wool textile manufacturers. With French tariffs shutting out a great deal of trade to that country they wondered if the result of it would only be to make the French aware of their ideas. Moreover their trade was active and there was a reluctance to give the time and energy that exhibiting in Paris required. Jacob Behrens, who had exhibited in London with 'gratifying pecuniary results', took a rather different view seeing the Paris Exhibition as a means of getting goods to France and obtaining 'good profit from the permission to sell one's exhibits, if one could get plenty of them there' – in other words it was a method of legal smuggling. And, arguably, those who did make the effort to go may have been able to reap their rewards when the 1861 Treaty eased trade.[123] The British reports of the Exhibition hoped that it would have the effect of relaxing the strict protective system of France.

The Leeds, Huddersfield and Bradford Chambers of Commerce all sent representatives to Paris who reported in some detail on the exhibits.[124] The report to the Huddersfield Chamber is by far the most revealing and shows a perceptive view of the competitive dangers of growing European manufacturing activity. It made particular mention of the developing mechanical skill and the increasing continental trade with America, suggesting that:

the reason for the success of the continental manufacturers . . . is the especial pains they have taken to adapt their goods (to foreign markets) . . . and that any loss we have sustained thereby, is not attributable to our inability to compete with our Continental neighbours, but to the absence of well sustained efforts to produce a style of goods suitable for those markets, and to the fact that the attention of our manufacturers is principally confined to the manufacture of goods adapted to the home market, which are

quite a different class from those suited to the markets just mentioned.[125]

The ever increasing home trade, and preference home producers
gave to it, it was suggested, was allowing continental manufacturers
easy entry into neutral markets and manufacturers were warned not
'to underrate the policy or advantages of studying the wants of the
best foreign markets . . .', although the Council of the Huddersfield
Chamber somewhat contradicted the point by saying that they had
'no reason to fear but that British capital, industry and enterprise may
still maintain for us the pre-eminence which we have hitherto enjoyed for producing goods adapted to the varied wants of the
world'.[126]

The Leeds deputation were very critical of the display efforts made
by their local manufacturers: 'Generally the goods from foreign
countries were beautifully put up, and contrasted in this respect
favourably with the Leeds stall which had every disadvantage of
situation, deprivation of light, and want of taste and judgment in the
method of exhibiting.' They acknowledged that tasteful arrangement
and display made goods from other countries take on a better character than they inherently possessed and that there was evidence also of
a spirit of enterprise amongst their continental competitors. However, they concluded that in the finer class of fabrics France, Austria,
Prussia and Belgium showed 'great excellence of make and beauty of
finish and colour' but in the useful common qualities of woollen
goods, price for price, Leeds was far superior.[127]

British woollen manufacturers gained few medals. They were, they
argued, adversely affected by the jury's decision to take no notice of
goods displayed by merchants. There was a comment that 'there is
little novelty of design in goods' from the West of England.[128] The
Bradford deputation was impressed with the further superiority of
the French in all-wool worsteds, and cloth of wool and silk mixed, but
concluded that Bradford 'had nothing to learn from other countries
as far as the manufacture of mixed wool and cotton fabrics'. In view of
the problems over wool supply it paid particular attention to the
wools on display and drew attention to French and Canadian combing wools. Few all-wool worsteds were exhibited by Bradford manufacturers and they were clearly outshone by the French and Saxon
merinos. However, the deputation felt that there were 'no insuperable difficulties' to Bradford success in that area. It was pointed out
that the French bounty on exports was to a great extent mitigated by
the taxes they paid on the import of wool for weft, and that there was
only a tiny tax on the export of French wool that British manufacturers could use.[129]

The reports on the Paris Exhibition reiterated the findings of four years previously. There was an indication that even in that short space of time great progress was being made on the Continent, and although the visitors to the exhibition indicated their awareness of this, their reports did not suggest there was cause for great concern. This complacency was added to by the small number of firms who decided to exhibit and the lack of effort they put into their displays. Alexander Redgrave, a factory inspector, was very critical of the 'absence of preparation', the lack of adequate efforts 'to produce greater effects'.[130]

The British Wool Textile Industry in the 1860s: Trade and Tariffs

A multitude of influences on the British wool textile industry in the 1860s permitted most of the trade to experience a prosperous, though turbulent, decade. The influences were complex and their inter-relationship is far from easy for the historian to unravel. Moreover, the prosperity that the industry encountered was accompanied by the need to adapt to some adverse circumstances, notably severe United States tariffs. Perhaps the major feature of the decade was the American Civil War and the resultant cotton famine which had immediate implications for both the woollen and worsted industries in the period 1862 to 1865 through changing price relationships between cotton and wool, with consequent effects on demand, and through market disruption. There were longer term implications also. Peace in 1865 brought need for readjustment. Alterations in prices and shortages of some cloths had created or speeded up fashion changes which were not to be reversed for a long time.

The decade started brightly, continuing the high level of activity and prosperity which had been a feature of the closing years of the 1850s. Complaints of labour shortage continued and there were reports of migration to the textile districts from Norfolk and other rural counties.[131] But through the summer of 1860, as wool prices maintained their high levels, manufacturers appear to have become increasingly concerned about the potential consequences of a sudden fall in prices. The worsted trade was particularly jittery. Although it was managing to maintain exports at the record level of 1859, manufacturers complained of declining profit margins and held back on wool purchases. The price of combing wool was very high, with lustre wool used for the manufacture of Orleans and coburgs, which had become the great staple of much of the trade, in particularly short supply partly as a result of a loss of sheep in the drought of 1859.[132] The cool, wet summer of 1860 reduced demand for summer cloths and late in the year both branches of the industry began to show

concern about the future of their American markets following the
disturbing news about the Morrill tariff and a growing awareness of
the possibility of civil war. Merchants were holding back orders until
the market situation became clearer and risk of falling wool prices
diminished.[133]

But if the future of American trade looked uncertain in 1860, the
trade treaty with France, being negotiated by Cobden, was greeted
with high expectations. Throughout the 1850s manufacturers had
been exasperated by the difficulties of trading with France, where a
rapidly rising home industry and high import duties effectively excluded many British manufacturers. Exports to France from Britain
had been increasing during the 1850s but the value of imports from
France had been rising rapidly and considerably exceeded the value
of exports. The negotiations for a treaty with France were followed
very closely by the wool textile industry. The Huddersfield Chamber
of Commerce claimed that the commercial treaty would be most
advantageous to the trade of the woollen district and in a letter of
thanks to Cobden recorded that local manufacturers were 'sanguine
that by the best use of the means at our command, we shall be able to
produce a class of goods suited to the needs of a large mass of the
industrial population of France'. The Chamber was quickly asking for
a French Consular Representative in Huddersfield in order to promote 'commercial intercourse' with France.[134]

The Bradford Chamber of Commerce gave assistance in the negotiations. A deputation from Leeds and Bradford went to Paris and
Jacob Behrens, a member of the group, was particularly active in
safeguarding the interests of the Bradford mixed worsted trade and
Cobden acknowledged that as a result of Bradford's support and
assistance low *ad valorem* duties were negotiated for stuff instead of
the 'by weight' duties which had been expected.[135] The 1860 Treaty
lowered duties across the range of wool textile manufactures and for
some classes of goods effectively opened the French market for the
first time.[136] The initial consequence of it was a boom in trade. For the
five year period from 1856 to 1860 the average annual value of
exports of tissues was £224,000. For the five years 1861–6 the
equivalent average export total was £1,806,000. The gains were
greatest to the manufacturers of mixed worsted stuffs but woollen
broad and narrow cloth manufacturers saw a massive expansion in
their cross channel trade and blanket manufacturers who had previously been able to do little business in France were able to develop
an export trade.

The initial reactions to the consequences of the treaty were very

Table 27 *British trade in wool textiles with France, 1855–74*

Annual averages	Imports from France of wool textile manufactures (£ thousand computed real values)	Exports to France of woollen and worsted yarn (£ thousand declared real values)	Exports to France of woollen and worsted cloth (£ thousand declared real values)
1855–9	582	173	237
1860–4	1184	310	1178
1867–9	1385	546	2337
1870–4	2793	351	3386

favourable. The Batley Chamber of Commerce expressed relief that the expansion of trade with France helped mitigate the effects of the American tariff.[137] The Huddersfield Chamber in 1862 recorded that the treaty was being carried out to the entire satisfaction of the local traders.[138] But within a year or two it was being claimed that the industry had been over-optimistic about the benefits the treaty would bring and complaints were revived about the level of French tariffs. The *Leeds Mercury* recorded in 1864: 'The trade with France has been in a languishing state throughout the year and the buoyant expectations which many people entertained of a large and extensive trade with that country have not, up to the present, been realized'.[139]

The trade statistics show lower cloth export figures to France in 1863–5 compared with the total for 1862 but trade in that year was undoubtedly boosted by exceptional initial demand. As the manager of the *Magasin du Louvre* in Paris later explained, there was, immediately following the tariff reductions, a rush to buy English cloths.[140] This gave rise to very high long term expectations amongst British manufacturers who were perhaps disappointed when in 1863 the peak level was not maintained. But even so exports continued in the next three years at five or six times the level of the late 1850s. What is true is that there were some successful rapid adjustments in the French wool textile industry to challenge British imports. Roubaix manufacturers successfully competed with Bradford lustre cloth exports and French wool textile manufacture generally managed to expand in spite of lower protective barriers. The 1860s in the French industry was a period of rapid movement to mechanisation, increasing output and rising exports particularly to Britain whose imports of French wool textile manufactures more than doubled between the late 1850s and the mid-1860s. The French industry was helped by the abolition of wool import duties in the 1860s, by the remaining tariffs and by fashion changes to its advantage including the rising demand for all-wool worsteds.[141]

The 1860s was a chaotic period in the history of United States protectionism and the wool textile industry in Britain was substantially affected by the complications which arose. In 1846, and again in 1857, tariffs had been reduced. In 1857 the reduction of the *ad valorem* duty on wool textiles from 30 per cent to 24 per cent had the effect, so it has been argued by an historian of the American industry, of substantially increasing the competitiveness of British and other European manufacturers in the American market.[142] British trade in wool textiles of the United States clearly benefited. The reimposition of fierce protectionism from 1861 quickly negated the gains that British manufacturers had made in the United States in the previous two decades. The Morrill Tariff Act, passed in March 1861, supposedly attempted to compensate American manufacturers for the advantages foreign manufacturers had in United States markets as a result of the former having to pay duty on wool imports. The tariff was framed on the basis of a dual system. A specific duty was levied to compensate for the wool import duty and an *ad valorem* duty was charged as a purely protective measure. On cloths and dress goods the specific duty was levied at 12 cents per pound weight and it would seem that this figure was arrived at on the basis that wool valued at 18 to 24 cents a pound was taxed on import at three cents a pound and on the assumption that four pounds of wool went into one pound of cloth. This highly optimistic ratio together with the 25 per cent *ad valorem* tax provided considerably increased protection to United States manufacturers. British manufacturers of low woollens were hurt most as the effective duty on their products was the highest and it was in their type of goods that United States manufacturers were best able to service home demand. The British worsted industry was least affected because of the embryonic nature of its American counterpart.[143]

Further tariff acts in 1862 and 1864 increased levels of protection and broadened the consequences for British manufacturers to the extent that by the mid-1860s only British manufacturers of relatively high quality goods, with a high degree of price inelasticity, had any real chance of maintaining their American markets. Although the 1861 Tariff had less effect on worsteds, by 1864 the worsted trade was suffering. The *Bradford Observer* described the tariff charges of 1864 as 'oppressive', as they reduced exports of lower worsted goods to the United States, although in due course the problem was some-

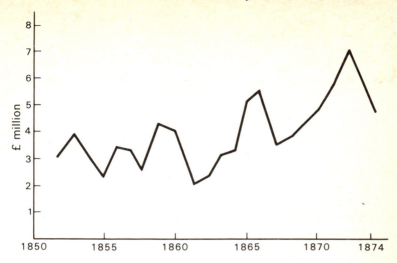

Fig. 2 Exports of wool textiles, including yarn, to the United States (declared real values)

what mitigated by the termination in 1866 of the treaty between the United States and Canada which brought to an end the import of duty free combing wool from Canada.[144]

The value of British exports of wool textiles to the United States was roughly halved between 1860 and 1861 but the fall cannot be entirely explained in terms of increased protectionism. From early 1861 markets were being disrupted by the threat of civil war. The Federal attempt to blockade the South from March 1861, although hardly enforced, disrupted some trading links, although wool textile business in the Southern States was not of great importance. Some trade was re-routed through Nassau in the Bahamas. The *Huddersfield Examiner* reported several times in 1863 that blankets and woollen clothing were being sent to the Southern States through Nassau and the trade returns clearly indicate that this was the case. Blanket exports to Nassau increased seven fold between 1861 and 1863.[145]

The Repercussions of the Civil War
Generalisation about the overall impact of the Civil War and the

cotton famine on wool textile manufacturers is dangerous, such was the range of repercussions. A direct and immediate effect was felt in the Yorkshire heavy woollen district. A sudden demand for adequate supplies of uniform cloth, blankets and other heavy cloth forced the Federal War Department to look to Britain and France for supplies and substantial exports followed but the American woollen manufacturing industry in due course adapted to supply home needs and demand for imports was not maintained at the high level for long.[146] But whereas one area of West Yorkshire benefited in the short term from the American situation other areas immediately suffered. As already indicated, worsted manufacturers' markets in the United States were curtailed and yarn exporters saw a sudden drop in demand for their products as their German customers cut back on manufacturing when the American markets shrank. Yarn exports to Germany decreased in 1861 but soon more than recovered. One area of the worsted trade was sustained. In 1862 there were reports of large consignments of low priced 'mournings' being sent to the United States.[147]

The Civil War and associated tariff policy had specific direct effects on the transatlantic wool textile trade but far reaching consequences arose from the soaring price of cotton worldwide as shortages began to bite from 1862. Prices of American Upland cotton had remained fairly constant through the 1850s although a slight rise in prices was evident towards the end of the decade. But in 1862 prices soared and for the following three years the average price was over three times that of the 1850s. Wool prices were not static; in the same period, long wool prices rose by about 50 per cent. Short wool prices showed much less upward movement. The result of this was that the price differential between cotton and wool, which had been widening gradually for much of the previous 30 years, to wool's disadvantage, was suddenly narrowed, making wool textile prices on world markets seem more favourable.

Early in 1861 it was being anticipated that changing price relativities and the shortage of cotton would lead to wool being substituted, and to prosperity in the wool textile industry.[148] But initially the effects were slow to take place. Cotton imports were at record levels from 1859 to 1861 and stocks at Liverpool and Manchester were good. There was some speculation in cotton but caution was being shown for fear of a quick solution to the American problems.[149] However, in 1862 the cotton shortage began to bite and prices soared. The price of American Upland cotton doubled within a year and continued to rise. Wool textile manufacturers who used cotton

Table 28   *Price changes in cotton and wool, and cotton imports, 1850–70*

	Wool	Cotton	Cotton
	Lincoln half hog (pence per lb.)	American Upland (pence per lb.)	Net imports (million lbs.)
1850–2	12	6	675
1853–5	15	5½	759
1856–8	17	7	866
1859	18⅝	6¾	1051
1860	20⅛	6¼	1141
1861	19½	8½	959
1862	20½	17¼	309
1863	22⅝	23¼	429
1864	27⅜	27½	648
1865	25¾	19	675
1866	23½	15½	988
1867	18⅞	11	912
1868–70	17½	11	1018

SOURCE: B. R. Mitchell with P. Deane, *Abstract of British Historical Statistics*

warps were faced with sudden increases in their warp prices. Some substituted wool and contemporary comment suggests that the proportion of cotton warped cloth in total wool textile output fell but as production and exports were rising rapidly it was believed that the total quantity of cotton used in the industry did not significantly change. This was the view of the local factory inspector in 1864. He suggested that although the total cotton input to the industry was constant, the proportion of cotton used in the total output fell by as much as 60 per cent.[150] It was said that the use of cotton in the Yorkshire heavy woollen district decreased.[151] In worsted manufacture there may have been attempts to reduce the amount of cotton in mixed cloths but this is by no means clear. The trade statistics are difficult to interpret because of changes in methods of measurement in the 1860s, but they would seem to show that the proportion of mixed worsted to all-wool worsted exports continued to rise with the quantity of all wool worsted exports remaining fairly static, whereas mixed exports more than doubled between the late 1850s and the mid 1860s. This would suggest that the narrowing of the price differential between the two types of worsted cloth did not lead, as far as the British industry was concerned, to a substitution of supply towards the all-wool fabric. Nor is there any clear evidence of this happening in the home market.

Table 29   Exports of all-wool and mixed worsted cloth

Annual averages	Total million yards	Mixed %	All wool %
1858–61	133	50	50
1864–6	213	79	21

Mixed worsteds, however, were undoubtedly substituted for cotton goods in both the home and overseas markets. The Bradford newspaper observed in 1866:

> Fortunately for the worsted trade the very high price of cotton goods has pushed into general demand amongst a new class of consumers the mixed fabrics of this district; and they are likely to continue in extensive consumption should ever the prices of the two fabrics assimilate very much nearer in price.[152]

The factory inspector's comment that as much cotton as previously was being used in the wool textile trade may even have been an underestimate. The export figures for mixed worsteds and comments about home demand for them would suggest that even if the proportion of cotton in mixed goods was reduced quite substantially the absolute amount of cotton consumed would still have risen. The worsted trade seems to have been able to obtain adequate supplies of cotton warps. The factory inspector commented in 1864 that this was the case and newspapers reported that cotton warp manufacturers in Manchester and the West Riding spinning for the worsted trade remained active.[153] The *Leeds Mercury* commented in December 1864: 'Those Yorkshire spinners of cotton who make for the Manchester market have suffered equally with the Lancashire mill-owners, while those who do for the Bradford market have been much better off.' But some concern was expressed in the summer of 1862 about curtailed supplies of warp.[154]

The increased activity in wool textile manufacture further exacerbated labour supply problems. It had been anticipated that the wool textile industry would have absorbed 'a considerable number of hands thrown out of work in the cotton trade' thus mitigating the unemployment problem in Lancashire and the difficulties of labour shortage in Yorkshire.[155] There is evidence of a movement of labour eastwards across the Pennines. The 1871 census records that the Yorkshire population included some 30,000 more people born in Lancashire and Cheshire than in 1861.[156] By that stage some may have returned home, but other evidence suggests few cotton workers found jobs in the wool textile industry. Skills were different, demand for male labour relatively lower than in cotton and there seems to have been little enthusiasm amongst Yorkshire manufacturers to employ Lancashire labour even though the manufacturers continued to complain of labour shortages. An editorial in the *Bradford Observer* early in 1862 discussed the situation:

Bradford the Goschen of Lancashire
From across the border of the county the cotton manufacturers look to this happy district with envy, and the starving operatives, with admiration and desire. Some time ago a letter appeared in our columns from a Lancashire gentleman who having heard that Bradford could give labour to unemployed hands was naturally anxious to promote an immigration from his district where the operatives were in a bad condition. . . . The spinners and manufacturers of this district, however, gave no sign and we must take their silence for evidence of their opinion that there was no permanent or even large temporary want of operatives in the district. Meantime numbers of Lancashire operatives are found begging for the means of existence in this and the neighbouring towns, but we hear of no master in want of hands supplying himself from their ranks. . . . We warn the Lancashire operatives that they are but invited to jump out of the frying pan into the fire . . .[157]

The factory inspectors watched the position closely. In April 1863 they reported an influx of Lancastrians to Yorkshire but indicated that few gained employment. Mr Allbut, the certifying surgeon at Batley, suggested that 'not understanding the woollen trade they could not obtain employment and returned home'. On the other hand, it was also stated that in spite of worsted factories around Halifax being in want of some descriptions of hands and the worsted trade being a better prospect for cotton operatives than the woollen trade 'few cotton workers applied to worsted firms for jobs'.[158]

The uncertainty created by the Civil War and the United States tariffs led to two years of relatively poor trade for the British wool textile industry in 1861 and 1862, in spite of the upsurge in exports to France. Short time was worked in much of the industry in 1861 but good harvests in the autumn helped revive home demand until the Trent affair in November sapped confidence.[159] The factory inspectors reported that in 1862 the woollen and worsted trades were in a satisfactory and profitable state all year but the export trade statistics do not altogether bear this out. Heavy woollens were in demand at home and abroad but worsted exports were the lowest for six years. Some woollen firms which had previously had markets in Lancashire missed the demand from that area.[160]

Late in 1862 there were reports of general revival of demand with stocks falling and yarn and some cloths became scarce. The factory inspectors were predicting a rosy future for the worsted trade. They wrote that the trade

> wants for the supply of raw material; but with a large supply it seems likely to be very greatly extended; and though somewhat dependent upon fashion and fancy for the absorption of its goods, it is yet a manufacture for the many, and for most, if not all climates, whereby it will always command success'.[161]

The extension of its trade came rapidly. The quantity of its exports was 40 per cent higher in 1863 than in 1862; the increase in value was 42 per cent as prices rose. The woollen export trade was much less expansionary. A good harvest again helped the home trade of both branches. The worsted trade was working to full capacity and was giving out some weaving on commission to Lancashire factories.[162] Rapid improvement continued in 1864 although there were minor hiccups. The war in Schleswig-Holstein affected some fancy goods manufacturers. A drought in the late summer curtailed production of some Calder Valley mills still dependent on water power.[163] Financial crisis late in the year and the stoppage of the Leeds Banking Company brought down some local firms, giving rise to complaints that the woollen trade was allowing credit to run riot. The *Leeds Mercury* accused some manufacturers of being reckless and of building on 'a rotten framework of artificial credit'.[164] Although throughout 1864 there were rumours that the American war was at an end, there were no great impediments to trade. The German-Danish war brought some demand for heavy woollens but also curtailed some general Continental demand.[165]

The following year the Civil War came to an end. The consequence was a further boost in demand for the worsted trade but little benefit to woollen manufacturers. The worsted trade was initially worried by the news of peace; orders ceased, prices fell, but fears were ill-founded. Cotton supplies did not recover rapidly and a huge restocking demand resulted in the United States for worsted. There were reports that buyers 'bought not by bales and cargoes but took at one stroke the contents of entire warehouses' and the Bradford newspaper observed that 'commerce took a fresh leap, buyers flocked over to this market, all our manufacturers were filled with orders.[166] Volume of exports of worsted cloth rose in 1865 to 24 per cent above the level of the previous year and to almost 100 per cent above the 1862 level.

The post-war boom continued for over a year and overseas demand for worsted goods remained high for the rest of the decade. The immediate post-war boom came to an end with the financial crisis of the summer of 1866 and its repercussions created some despondency which was not quickly alleviated. The failure of the respected house of Overend, Gurney and Co. in particular shook the trade. Before confidence could be restored further severe changes in the U.S. tariff in 1867 yet again reduced the United States market. There were reports of goods being returned unsold, and of stocks building up in manufacturers' hands,[167] but there were few failures and the Huddersfield newspaper commented in 1868 that in spite of 'dull and dragging depression' the trade was quite optimistic and remained on a sound financial footing.[168] Various sources late in the year reported that more business was being done but overall the period from 1867 to 1869 was a relatively quiet one in the woollen trade. Glutted markets in the East, high food prices at home and the threat of disturbances in Europe all combined to affect business. Experience within the industry was very diverse. Some cloths suffered as cotton prices fell. Wincy, a light cotton cloth with a wool filling which had been made with all wool during the cotton famine, reverted to its former nature, and the cotton industry regained some of its former trade that wool textiles had captured, but the events of the 1860s had created some fundamental long term changes to the wool textile industry in terms of markets, fashion and level of business. The use of shoddy and mungo had been given a boost.[169] New markets had emerged for British manufacturers.

A comparison of the direction of trade between 1856 and 1866 is revealing. European markets took on greater importance whereas

Table 30   Direction of exports of woollen and worsted cloth, 1856 and 1866
(proportion by value)

	Worsteds		Woollens	
	1856 %	1866 %	1856 %	1866 %
Europe	40	43	13	19
United States	34	27	35	24
Colonies	15	12	23	25
Latin America	9	4	21	16
Far East etc.	2	14	8	17
Total exports (£ m)	4.7	13.2	4.8	8.5

the proportion of trade in the United States fell. A distinctive feature
was the increase of trade to the Far East. Its development in the early
1860s was a matter of some contemporary comment, particularly
after the disappointment that had been expressed about its poor
growth up to that time. The trade was subject to quite substantial
annual variations. All-wool worsteds formed the major part of it but
little was known about it even at the time as it was controlled by a few
merchants. The *Leeds Mercury* commented in 1866:

> information as regards this trade [the China trade] is exceedingly
> difficult to obtain; it is in a few hands and therefore to some extent
> is a monopoly and apparently the partners engaged in it perpetu-
> ally endeavour to surround themselves with a cloud of mystery.[170]

The China trade was somewhat immune from fashion changes but
those changes were becoming very noticeable in many other markets
in the 1860s. Broadcloths had gradually been going out of favour and
a worsted coatings trade had been developing for men's wear. The
Huddersfield Examiner reported in 1870 that 'the better class coating
trade goes on increasing year to year' and by that time the broadcloth
trade of the Leeds district had declined to a shadow of its former
self.[171] In the worsted trade the introduction of the crinoline permitted women to dispense with costly petticoats and consequently increased demand for worsted dress fabrics from a wider market. 'A
harder and less flexible cloth was . . . required to comport with the
metallic contrivance with which women now delight to surround
themselves.'[172] Cotton warped worsteds made with lustre wool were
most suitable but the supply of the latter could not keep up with
demand, prices rose, narrowing the gap with all-wool worsteds made
from softer merino wools the prices of which were more stable and,
perhaps encouraged by the cotton famine, in some markets demand
for all-wool worsteds gradually began to replace that for mixed
worsteds. The French in due course were to benefit from the change
as a result of their expertise in the manufacture of the all-wool
product.[173]

The yarn trade for much of the 1860s was fairly stable. It suffered
early in the decade from the effect of the American tariffs on imports
from Europe but soon recovered. It expanded in the last three years
of the decade as a result of good demand from Russia, Germany and
France. If one assumes, as was undoubtedly the case, that most of the
yarn exports to Holland were destined for Germany then over three-
quarters of British woollen and worsted yarn exports found their way
to that market.

Perhaps the most notable overall feature of the 1860s was the

changing balance in British wool textile manufacture exports between woollen and worsted goods. As explained elsewhere the statistics do not permit a totally accurate assessment but whereas in
1859–61 worsted cloth formed an average of 57 per cent of the value
of exports of wool textile manufactured goods, in the last three years
of the decade the proportion had increased to 65 per cent. It is likely
that a similar but lesser trend was taking place in the home market.
The statistics for capacity of the industry bear out the movement.
Fashion changes and foreign tariff policies particularly in the United
States, together with the woollen industry developing more rapidly
than the worsted industry in many foreign countries, provide the
explanation.

7 Capacity and Organisation, 1870–1914

Capacity and Relocation

The location of the factory industry in 1874 as measured by concentration of employment is shown in Table 31. The figures for 1874 are used in preference to those of 1871 because of doubts about the accuracy of the latter.[1] Overall 68 per cent of factory employment was in Yorkshire, another 14 per cent in Scotland, 7 per cent in Lancashire and 3 per cent in the West and South West. Although factories were to be found in the majority of other counties they were mainly surviving individual firms, rather than important centres of production. There were a few yarn spinning factories based on Leicester, mainly supplying the local hosiery trade and in Kidderminster producing carpet yarn. Although there were 70 mills in Ireland, employment only amounted to 1500 workers. Eleven worsted mills were still working in East Anglia employing 1000 workers and scattered mills continued to survive in the four Northern Counties.

The last quarter of the century witnessed a continuation of previous trends. Yorkshire's predominance rose to over 72 per cent of factory employment. The size of the industry in East Anglia and the South West declined further. Peak employment had been reached in Scotland in 1874 and a gradual decline followed; the same situation occurred in Lancashire. On the other hand, as already indicated in Chapter 4, there was an expansion of manufacturing in Ireland and the growth of the hosiery industry in the Midlands was providing work for a larger workforce by the end of the century.

Total factory employment in 1895 was at very much the same level as 20 years earlier but whereas the workforce of the woollen and shoddy industry had increased by 17 per cent, that of the worsted industry had fallen by 16 per cent; the fall occurred mainly in the early 1890s and continued into the middle of the next decade.[2] However between the two Censuses of Production of 1907 and 1912 there was some slight recovery. In the wool textile industry as a whole in these five years employment rose by 7.5 per cent.[3]

The decline of the wool textile industry in many of its traditional areas is amply illustrated in the 1904 factory returns which record no mills in Norfolk and only 5 in Devon, 14 in Wiltshire and 10 in Somerset.

The amount of machinery in United Kingdom wool textile factories between 1867 and 1904 is shown in Table 33. The figures would suggest a substantial decline in machinery capacity but they miss two important factors. The first of these is that in the closing decades of the nineteenth century looms were becoming wider. Comparative figures are unavailable but the factory returns for 1904 make it very clear that the vast majority – 75 per cent – had a reed space in excess of 60 inches. Secondly, and of more importance, was the extent to which machinery was being run at faster speeds. Baines, writing in 1858, recorded that the average speed of worsted looms had increased from 96 picks per minute to 160 in ten years, and that whereas in the old fly frame spindles made 2800 revolutions per minute, in the new bell (cap) frame they made 6000.[4] Baines was, of

Table 31 *Location of United Kingdom wool textile industry in 1874 and 1895*

	Employment in woollen and shoddy mills		Employment in worsted mills	
	1874 % of U.K. total	1895 % of U.K. total	1874 % of U.K. total	1895 % of U.K. total
England	77	79	93	96
Scotland	20	17	7	4
Wales	1	2	—	—
Ireland	1	2	—	—
Yorkshire	55	63	81	86
Lancashire	9	7	4	2
Wiltshire, Dorset, Devon, Cornwall and Somerset	6	4	1	—
West Midlands*	1	3	5	5

SOURCE: *Factory Returns*

NOTE: *included Gloucester, Hereford, Salop, Stafford, Worcester and Warwickshire

Table 32   Mills and employment, 1874–1904

	U.K.		ENGLAND & WALES		SCOTLAND		YORKSHIRE	
	Mills	Employment (thousands)	Mills	Employment (thousands)	Mills	Employment (thousands)	Mills	Employment (thousands)
Woollen and shoddy industry								
1874	1925	138.8	1606	108.8	259	27.7	998	76.8
1885	2026	144.0	1610	113.3	274	27.5	988	83.6
1895	2260	162.9	1834	131.4	309	27.5	1115	102.2
1904	1538	—	1195	—	244	—	725	—
Worsted industry								
1874	692	142.1	648	131.8	43	10.3	520	114.4
1885	725	138.2	697	132.5	24	5.5	593	116.0
1895	725	119.5	701	115.1	22	4.3	637	102.4
1904	841	—	818	—	22	—	746	—

SOURCE: *Factory Returns*

course, referring to the plain Bradford loom; the dobby loom, used for fancier cloths, was much slower: it never attained speeds of more than 100 picks a minute.

Dorothy Hunter, writing in 1910, produced some comparative figures for the West of England. One manufacturer stated that a woollen spinner could at that time spin twice as much yarn as 30 years earlier and a worsted spinner six times as much. A weaver of serges was said to have been able, 30 years previously, to take charge of two narrow looms weaving 70 picks a minute; in 1910 two wide looms running at 131 picks a minute could be tended by one person. 'This increase of 85 per cent in the pace of the loom, plus 80 per cent in the width of the stuff means, practically speaking, that one weaver can do the work formerly done by three'.[5] These figures refer to a serge weaver who would have been using the plain loom, but few West of England cloths could be made on this loom. In any case there was the worry in going over to it that fashion trends would dictate against its use and require expensive re-equipping with the dobby loom. In general the increase in speed of looms was less substantial in the woollen industry than in the worsted industry.

Table 33   *Machinery in wool textile factories, U.K. 1867–1904*

| | Spinning spindles (in millions) | | | Power looms (in thousands) | | |
	Wool and shoddy	Worsted	Total	Wool and shoddy	Worsted	Total
1867	4.3	2.2	6.5	47.1	71.7	118.8
1874	3.3	2.2	5.5	58.5	81.7	140.2
1885	3.2	2.2	5.4	60.0	79.9	139.9
1889	3.2	2.4	5.6	64.1	67.4	131.5
1904	2.7	2.9	5.6	51.8	52.7	104.5

SOURCE: *Factory Returns*

There are very many other contemporary examples of increasing speeds of machinery. The speed at which the machinery could be run depended on the raw material being used and on the final product. For this reason it is unrealistic to generalise about increasing machinery speeds for the industry as a whole. Moreover figures for the quantity of machinery available give no indication of the amount of time it was being worked. Overtime was common when trade was good, short time equally so when it was bad; shift working was rare.

The gradual disappearance of the manufacture of traditional cloths in Yorkshire and the emergence of new specialities led to local concentrations of production in particular fabrics, although the divisions were far from absolute. The low woollen trade, using shoddy and mungo, was concentrated in Dewsbury, Batley and Ossett and the neighbouring villages, with other major centres at Elland and in the Colne Valley above Huddersfield. Blankets were produced widely, but firms between Dewsbury and Mirfield, at Gomersal and around Mytholmroyd formed the bulk of the trade. Liversedge and Halifax were centres for carpet and rug production. The majority of the Yorkshire mills producing flannel were situated around Saddleworth. Bradford maintained its pre-eminence in wool dealing, top making, worsted weaving and merchanting. Major firms in the alpaca and mohair spinning trade were located in the Aire Valley above Shipley. Halifax and the upper Calder valley remained the important centre for the Yorkshire cotton industry but there were many wool textile mills producing such a variety of woollen and worsted cloth that there is little point in indicating any particular local specialism. Huddersfield likewise had a wide-ranging trade, but perhaps developed a reputation in particular for good quality worsted coatings. Most people who knew the wool textile trade well, if asked to say what was its finest product, would have referred to the superfine 70s quality worsteds of Huddersfield. The district was also a centre for cotton doubling and for packing; the villages to the south of the town maintained the production of fancy woollens of intricate weave.

Yarn spinning for the hosiery trade was the recognised specialism of Wakefield. The area around Yeadon and Guiseley gained a reputation for Yorkshire tweeds. The district was hurt by high foreign tariffs on cheaper cloth but it gained also from the movement of some demand away from cloth made from shoddy as real incomes rose. These tweeds were made from the coarser types of new wool, many coming in increasing quantities from New Zealand, including both shorn and slipe wools. The big development in the woollen branch of the Yorkshire trade in this period was the continued success of low woollens, but there were few new major innovations. The increased size of the industry did call for new sources of raw material and the development of the extract trade. The result was that the ever shorter material needed yet more skilful processing to produce a satisfactory fabric. This the Yorkshire manufacturer achieved and, considering the raw material he started with, the cloths produced by this section of the trade were indeed remarkable.

Through the middle of the nineteenth century, Leeds gradually gave up its pre-eminence in the woollen industry and broadened its industrial spectrum.[6] By the last third of the century there were fewer woollen cloth manufacturers in the town, although the industry survived quite strongly in many of the outlying villages. Leeds did however develop some new specialisms. Some local firms specialised in unshrinkable flannels for sports and underwear; other firms maintained close contact with the needs of clothing manufacturers. Ready-made clothing manufacture was introduced to Leeds by John Barran in the 1840s. With mainly Jewish entrepreneurship and labour the industry developed to employ 23,000 people in Leeds before the First World War, amounting to about 10 per cent of those working in the national clothing and tailoring trades, although it made up a much higher proportion of the woollen and worsted clothing industry.[7]

The success of the ready-made clothing industry developed largely out of rising real incomes for the mass of the population and the emergence of new attitudes to clothes buying, including the average person desiring a larger wardrobe. Initially supplying the home market and making some contribution to the supply of civil and military uniforms, the clothing trade gradually extended its outlets and developed, in the closing decades of the century, a major export trade particularly to the Colonies. The value of clothing exports from Britain rose from £3.7 million in 1881 to over £8 million in 1912 and 1913. Hooper believed that between one-third and one-half of this trade was in woollen and worsted apparel.[8] Thus in the period from 1870 to 1914 clothing exports made an important contribution to the prosperity of the woollen and worsted trade. Clothing firms developed elsewhere in Yorkshire, notably in the upper reaches of the Calder valley and in Huddersfield. London remained, however, the major centre of the industry, because of the concentration of the ladies' trade there.

In Leicestershire a woollen and worsted spinning trade survived to service the local hosiery industry although the latter bought the vast majority of its yarn from further afield, both at home and abroad. The spinning firms were not large: 29 of them employed just over 3000 persons in 1895; ten years later only 16 factories survived. Worsted spinning firms in Kidderminster serviced the important local carpet weaving trade. The decline of the West England trade between 1870 and 1914 was substantial: in 1904 only 40 relatively small woollen mills survived, producing a wide range of fabrics. The region was unable, or unwilling, to respond to the great changes occurring in consumer demand, particularly the switch from woollens to worsteds in the better class men's section of the trade. Increasingly the West of England industry was pushed, as it were, to the fringes. As the century progressed cloths made were specialities, almost always fancy and particularly difficult to manufacture. Vestings were a case in point: they were much in vogue in Victorian times and were difficult to weave. Fancy designs meant much time spent in setting up the loom; and long runs were rare. Trouserings were also made, particularly for the winter season. They were a better production job because they were used in, and therefore manufactured in, greater quantities than the vestings. The loss of what was left of the woollen trouserings trade to the Scottish manufacturers was a major blow to the West Country around 1870. Coatings, usually manufactured in the prunelle twill or the Venetian weave, provided the best trade and there were also other speciality markets, notably the cloths used for riding usually made in the cavalry twill weave and notoriously difficult to manufacture. Also, in the Stroud area certain non-apparel cloths, notably those for covering billiard tables and, towards the end of the century, for covering tennis balls, helped a great deal.

Changing consumer demand was therefore the fundamental reason for the decline of the West Country trade. Little weight can be placed on technological problems and failures, although the impossibility of using the fast Bradford loom for fancy cloths kept costs higher. There may have been the disadvantage of high coal prices but the cost of coal was only a very marginal expense for manufacturers. The records of a mill in which one of the authors worked in the 1930s show that against a total turnover of around £100,000 a year the coal bill came to a little over £1000. The cost of raw materials was about £36,000.

Perhaps an additional problem in the second half of the century was lack of proximity to the tailoring and clothing trade markets, and the continuation of traditional marketing methods. West of England manufacturers sold most of their cloth to London merchants and business proceeded in a very formal way well typified in the annual spring and autumn showings of new ranges followed by the production of card samples, lengths and finally, one hoped, pieces. Only occasionally was the long-established routine varied. A leading manufacturer of the period, whose memories went back to around 1900 once told one of the authors how he had been showing in London and his customers had asked to see a new pattern very urgently. 'When will it be ready?' 'Monday.' 'Could it not be sooner?' 'Saturday?' 'Yes!' The head of the marketing firm would come in specially to see it. The manufacturer pondered long and anxiously what he should wear. The traditional morning coat and trousers seemed wrong, perhaps a very discreet Shepherd Check. He was greeted with the words 'Well, my boy! Off to the races?' Born into this tradition it is, perhaps, not surprising that the West Country did not sell to the new multiple clothiers exemplified by Burtons and later, in a rather different way, by Marks and Spencer.

To some extent there was also isolation in the field of technical education. Local courses were held but were not always well attended, although in due course the local textile schools that were established had a number of excellent principals, notably T.E. Ashenhurst who wrote standard books on textile designs.[9] It is, perhaps, a little surprising that his work did not have more effect in raising the standard of design which certainly did not respond to the new demands made upon it. Good designers played a major part in the success of the Scottish woollen tweed trade as has repeatedly been emphasised. The same sense of isolation also appears in the technological field in the second half of the century when West of England manufacturers had to look to North Country machine makers. Previously there had been several good ones in the West but they disappeared as trade declined, so this technological gap was an effect of the trade's decline, not a cause.

One final question remains. Why did the owners of West of England mills not respond to these new challenges as their ancestors had done before? Perhaps the main reason was that the decline was so slow. There were few major failures after the period around 1840 when, in addition to the two large mills in the Wiltshire/Somerset area, Shepherds of Uley near Stroud went bankrupt. The main manufacturers had a real care for the welfare of their workers. They themselves lived well in pleasant houses. They enjoyed sport, playing a large part in both the town and the county cricket teams. Several had their own bands; at least one had a pack of beagles. Many played their part in local affairs. Several, notably Laverton in the Wiltshire/Somerset area and Winterbotham in the Gloucester area, were Members of Parliament. When they did decide to give up business they, as the local newspaper put it, 'declined business'. They were far more concerned with the way of life rather than with any entrepreneurial adventuring. They were, in Professor Coleman's words, 'gentlemen, not players'. Perhaps this account may conclude with another personal story. The father of one of the authors, then manager of a mill, was pulling a slightly damaged piece over the perch with a stock-buyer. The buyer stopped and said 'You seem rather more interested than . . . down the road. I was pulling a piece over with him before I called on you and he turned to me and said "Oh! What an occupation for a gentleman".'

The years from 1870–1914 saw relative prosperity in many parts of the Scottish trades, with the exception of the industry around Glasgow. In particular the Lowland tweed trade was very successful. There were, of course, periods of depression, periods of intense pessimism. Markets were lost abroad through protectionism; competition at home particularly from Yorkshire caused problems but on the whole capacity was maintained in the long term.[10] Fashion gradually dictated that it was essential for any well-dressed man to have a Scottish tweed suit. The varieties were numerous, ranging from the Harris type right through to the twist suiting and the single yarn tweed often decorated with complicated silk stripes, for which the border areas were famous. In the two decades before the First World War improved organisation and better marketing really brought the name of Harris Tweed to public attention.[11] The Hawick knitwear trade moved to a position of pre-eminence in the high-class knitwear industry. Individual specialist firms throughout Scotland maintained, or increased, their reputation for high-class woollen cloth.

Why then did Scotland succeed in the high class woollen trade where the West of England had, to a great extent, failed? Most people inside the trade in Britain would have given as the main reason the quality of Scottish design. It was indeed noticeable that other areas that felt they were falling behind in this section of manufacturing, turned increasingly to getting Scottish designers to their own mills. The pages of the valuable journal *Scotch Tweed*, published in Galashiels between the Wars, gave lists of places where Scottish designers had gone. They certainly covered the world but it would not be unfair to argue that, having left Scotland, they did not usually manage to do very much to change traditional habits elsewhere. As far as the West of England was concerned, the only successful attempt to compete in this new, high quality tweed trade came from one firm, William Bliss of Chipping Norton.

The Scottish designers were most effective in their own country and produced some of the most attractive woollen fabrics ever made. Without denigrating their skill, it is reasonable to argue, however, that some of their success was due to the wide range of new materials that this industry used. One of the coarsest of wools, that from the Blackface sheep, was used on the island of Harris to produce one of the best of all coarse woollen tweeds. On the Shetlands the quite unique Shetland sheep, relatively coarse in fibre diameter but with remarkably soft handling, was used to produce the finest and best of knitwear, including the Shetland shawls. The typical Scottish tweed was made from the best of the native Cheviot wool blended with a proportion of Southdown and New Zealand Half-Bred. All three were outstanding wools. When finer qualities were needed the industry bought the best of the Australian clips. When even more exclusive fabrics were sought, Scotland was able to produce yarns and fabrics made from the more rare, expensive fibres such as cashmere and vicuña. The comparison with the West of England which concentrated almost entirely on Australian merino wool stands out.

One general point may also be made; the fact that Scotland was successful in developing a knitting trade, running almost parallel to its woven trade, meant that as knitting began, in the later years of the period covered in this volume, to challenge the long held supremacy of weaving, then the Scottish textile trade as a whole did not suffer as did the traditional wool textile weaving areas of Britain which did not have a similar parallel development. In the later twentieth century when knitting moved even further ahead, this remained an important reason for Scotland's success in maintaining its wool textile trade.

Integration and Specialisation

The course of development in the organisational structure of the two main branches of the industry, woollen manufacture and worsted manufacture, differed substantially. Whereas the woollen branch pursued a general trend throughout the second half of the nineteenth century towards the integration of its manufacturing processes into single factories, the factories of the worsted branch became more and more specialised with integrated mills accounting for a much lower proportion of employment than in the woollen industry.

Table 34 analyses the changing structure of the two industries both in terms of number of firms and of employees. With only a small amount of power loom weaving in woollen mills until the 1850s the specialist spinning mill inevitably accounted for the majority of firms and employment in 1850. But thenceforth change was rapid: the specialist spinning mills made up 62 per cent of all mills and 47 per cent of employment in 1850; by 1874 the proportions were 30 per cent and 9 per cent respectively and further reduced to 25 per cent and 7 per cent in 1889.[12] Their decline was most rapid in Yorkshire and the West of England but they survived relatively more strongly in Scotland and in Wales and Leicestershire. Their disappearance was quickest in the period from 1856 to 1867, which coincided with the major phase of the introduction of power loom weaving. But specialist weaving mills were of really insignificant importance to the woollen industry; at no time did they account for more than 4 per cent of the employment in English and Welsh factories. They were hardly known in Yorkshire where in 1889 there were only 52 employing 3127 workers, out of 945 mills with almost 90,000 employees. Wales and Lancashire had only four specialist weaving mills each in 1885. The five south-western counties also only had four. In Scotland, as might be expected, they had a more important role. The development of the tweed trade, using much yarn from England, gave rise to specialist weaving firms. In 1871 20 per cent of mills and 30 per cent of workers were in the specialist weaving branch of the factory industry. However, this was a peak year and the proportions declined thereafter.

The development of integrated firms in the woollen trade was most rapid from 1850 to 1874 by which date, in England and Wales, they accounted for 48 per cent of the total and 79 per cent of employment. These proportions then remained fairly constant for the rest of the century. They were of less importance in Wales where, in 1885, they accounted for 16 per cent of all firms and 53 of employment. Likewise in the same year in Scotland they formed 43 per cent of mills and 66 per cent of employment. They were of above average importance in Lancashire and the South West.

In the mainly Yorkshire-based worsted industry there was, from 1856, a gradual movement away from the integrated organisation which had started to appear with the innovation of power-loom weaving. But this movement should, perhaps, not be overestimated. In 1856, the peak year, 58 per cent of the factory workers were in integrated firms which accounted for 29 per cent of total firms. By 1889 the proportions were still 40 per cent and 17 per cent. In other words at no time were there more workers in either specialist spinning mills or in specialist weaving mills than in the integrated ones. Although the greatest proportional rise in firms was in the specialist weaving sector, the increasing size of the spinning mill maintained their greater importance in terms of employment. Their numbers increased significantly in the 1880s and 1890s. The disintegration process was further hastened in the late 1890s by specialist combinations, when many combing departments were hived off to the Woolcombers' Association. In 1904, 68 specialist top-making establishments were recorded by the factory inspectors all but one of them in Yorkshire.

What then were the reasons for these rather different trends? Various explanations have been suggested, some rather contradictory. The reasons would appear to be partly historical, partly technical and partly commercial. Arguably the smaller size and generally later innovation of new technology to manufacturing processes might

Table 34   *The organisation of the wool textile industry, 1850–89*

	Spinning mills		Weaving mills		Spinning and weaving mills	
	% of all mills	% of employment	% of all mills	% of employment	% of all mills	% of employment
The woollen industry						
England and Wales						
1850	62	47	I	I	22	41
1861	50	25	2	2	30	61
1874	30	9	3	2	48	79
1889	25	7	5	4	47	77
Scotland						
1850	91	73	—	I	9	25
1861	67	30	3	6	29	64
1874	39	13	15	23	41	63
1889	30	13	17	22	41	62
Yorkshire						
1850	60	50	I	I	20	34
1861	46	27	3	2	30	55
1874	18	9	3	2	56	78
1889	12	7	6	3	55	77
The worsted industry						
Yorkshire						
1850	39	24	22	21	36	53
1861	37	24	31	14	28	61
1874	39	30	34	15	25	55
1889	36	33	38	20	19	44

NOTE: There was also a category 'other mills' in the factory returns

have increased specialisation in the woollen branch but the reverse was the case. Clapham argued that integration in the woollen industry arose out of the traditional practice through which the master clothier or master manufacturer of the late eighteenth and early nineteenth centuries habitually supervised all the processes of manufacture.[13] One must, however, suspect that Clapham over-emphasises the role of the master manufacturer in the Yorkshire woollen trade. The point may have relevance for some other parts of the country but in Yorkshire would seem to be more relevant to the worsted branch particularly as the larger scale organisation of domestic worsted manufacture gave potential factory entrepreneurs greater resources on which to start their manufacturing activity.

There are more specific reasons for the survival and growth of

integrated firms in the woollen industry. The preparatory processes
were less complex and costly compared with worsteds. Moreover
manufacturers liked to manage their own yarn production to ensure
satisfactory quality for the weaving and finishing processes. As Clapham put it:

> His success depended so largely on the skilful composition of his
> yarn, that it must as a rule be made under his own eye and not
> bought from a neighbour. He is perhaps scribbling new wool and
> rag wool, or wool and cotton together, in proportion nicely calcu-
> lated so as to produce the maximum of effect in the finished cloth
> at the minimum cost. Or maybe he is twisting a tender coating of
> shoddy about a core of cotton yarn that will stand the tension of
> the loom and subsequent wear. These are tasks which a York-
> shireman, least of all, would care to trust as a regular thing to an
> outside spinner.[14]

He supported his argument by pointing out that most woollen and
worsted weaving yarns that were sold and bought in were made of
pure wool. The survival of relatively rather more specialist spinning
firms in Scotland and parts of the Midlands arose from the demands
of the hosiery and shawl trades. Specialist spinners around Huddersfield supplied the Scottish trade; there was also, of course, a reverse
trade of the export of Scottish woollen yarns to Yorkshire as well as
some internal yarn trading in Yorkshire: Huddersfield spinners, for
example, supplying some of the yarn needs of Bradford coating mills.
There was specialist spinning also for the carpet trade, but on the
other hand there was not a large export of woollen yarn to stimulate
specialist spinning in the main woollen districts.

In the worsted industry, however, the yarn trade became of increasing importance during the second half of the nineteenth century.
As the value of exports of worsted tissues declined between the late
1860s and the end of the century, the export trade in tops and
worsted yarns steadily rose. The growing uncertainty of the cloth trade
and the range of yarns required for different cloths and to keep up
with fashion changes stimulated the specialist production of them and
the unwillingness of weaving firms to take the risk of making and
stocking their own. Moreover, the widespread use of cotton warp in
worsted goods meant that manufacturers were forced to buy some of
their yarn and therefore became accustomed to do so. Clapham also
suggests that specialist weavers could rapidly adapt the use of their
looms to different cloths in changing market situations.[15]

There may have been other financial reasons for a lack of integration in worsteds. The capital needed to start a specialist firm was

presumably less than that needed for a combined business although the consequence of this is contradicted by Sigworth's argument that easier access to capital 'paved the way to division in the industry'.[16] But capital problems would arguably have created division. As Clapham again suggested, combinations would have tended

> to throw a good deal of machinery idle periodically and to lock up too much of the circulating capital of the business, in the form of wool waiting to be spun or yarn waiting to be woven – for heavy stocks would have to be kept on hand to meet the varying needs of the weaving department.[17]

Connected with this was the constant worry of downward fluctuations in the price of wool. In a period of falling prices, long periods between the purchase of wool and the sale of cloth would adversely affect profit margins. Quick turnover through specialist activity reduced risk as well as circulating capital needs. This problem may have been less in the woollen branch of the industry through the manufacture of smaller batches of cloth at one time, and possibly through consequent lower stock holding.

The statistics for the organisation of the trades conceal some features. Although the integrated sector remained significant in the worsted trade the figures do not tell us a great deal about the meaning of an integrated firm. Some, perhaps many, may have been operating their spinning and weaving departments as almost separate businesses. As, for example, with John Foster's quite fully integrated worsted firm, spinning departments did not necessarily direct all their output to their weaving department nor did their weaving department obtain all their yarn requirements from the spinning department. John Foster's were major yarn exporters to the extent of maintaining a yarn warehouse at Amiens from 1853 to the Second World War.[18]

Doubts about the factory inspector's classifications make a separate analysis of the organisation of the shoddy industry uncertain. But the factory returns for Yorkshire for 1871, the first year in which the parts of industry were separately identified, show more spinning and weaving firms than specialist spinning firms. The same was the case in 1889 but most firms are not identified and shoddy-producing and shoddy-using firms are not separately classified.

Manufacturer's Combinations
In the 1890s a movement began to occur in the Yorkshire wool textile industry towards the combination of firms in some parts of the trade,

particularly in those areas of the worsted industry which worked wholly or mainly on commission. The move was heralded in 1883 by a combination amongst Bradford dyers to fix prices at a remunerative level.[19] The dyers had been receiving criticism for many years about the standard of their work and their inability to compete with the French. These complaints became particularly fierce in the 1870s with verbal attacks on dyers at the Bradford Chamber of Commerce. The dyers replied that the quality of their work was held down by the poor payments they received.[20] As Sigsworth points out, the cartel the dyers organised did appear to lead to an improvement in dyeing standards and was welcomed in particular by the major local newspaper:

> We feel sure it is a wise and right step and one for which they are commended. Now that they have fixed their prices at what they believe to be fairly remunerative, let them be paid cheerfully . . . and give the trade sound and honest work . . . that dyeing prices have been too low in the past is clearly demonstrated by the large percentage of dyers and finishers who have passed through the Bankruptcy Court.[21]

The newspaper's comments may well be considered as fair but the dyers' agreement on prices was opposed by their customers who persuaded the Bradford Chamber of Commerce to disapprove of it.

The combination was given formal and much firmer strength in 1898 with the establishment of the Bradford Dyers' Association which combined 22 firms, comprising 90 per cent of the Bradford piece dyeing trade. The amalgamation included all the major firms in the trade. The price paid for them was £2,839,640 and the Association was floated with a capital of £3 million in preference and ordinary shares and £500,000 worth of debenture stock. Its intentions were

> to enable the various firms unitedly to meet the more severe trading conditions which were appearing, by effecting economies and improvements in production through the pooling of technical skill and experience and the centralisation of administration, purchasing, distribution and accountancy.[22]

The Association subsequently bought in other firms including some in Lancashire and Scotland, acquired an interest in the British Cotton and Wool Dyers' Association which was sold again in 1905, and re-organised the trade through some closures and the concentration of specialist work. It paid particular attention to markets in the Far East, where it appointed a resident representative in 1901 and opened a Shanghai office in 1902, and in the United States, where it established a factory in 1911 at Bradford, Rhode Island. Although all was not plain sailing, the Association succeeded in paying an average annual dividend on Ordinary Stock of 6.6 per cent between 1900 and 1913.

The Bradford Dyers' Association was perhaps the most successful of the combinations. Its example was followed, but with disastrous consequences, by the formation in 1899 of the Yorkshire Wool-combers' Association, which comprised 38 firms with a nominal capital of £2.5 million. It rapidly encountered problems, and by 1902 was in the hands of a receiver. Little detail is known of its inception but it failed to bring in some strong existing commission combers and, when it started to get into difficulties, could not raise sufficient bank loans. After problems involving a court case and a suicide, a new organisation, Woolcombers Ltd, was formed in 1904 to acquire it.[23]

Other combinations included the British Cotton and Wool Dyers' Association, formed in 1900 through the amalgamation of 46 companies involved in dyeing, bleaching, printing and sizing cotton yarn, wool, and woollen and worsted yarns. There were also the Leeds and District Worsted Dyers' and Finishers' Association and the Yorkshire Indigo, Scarlet and Colour Dyers Ltd.[24] Attempts were also made to form a combination of fine spinners and another of fancy manufacturers but neither was successful.[25] Price fixing was arranged in wool carbonising through the Wool Carbonisers' Federation.[26] All the combinations seem to have been Yorkshire based. The reasons for their formation are mainly obscure; nor is a great deal known about their early operations. J.H. Clapham, who joined Leeds University as a lecturer and was writing on the industry in the early years of the twentieth century, took a small shareholding in a textile combine to attempt to keep in touch with what was going on.[27] As one writer has put it, 'the more successful a combine, the less the public learnt about it'.[28] Clapham concluded that there was no single compelling reason for amalgamation but suggested that the problems that the worsted trade in particular had faced in the last three decades of the nineteenth century had sapped vigour and interest amongst second and third generation families.[29] The firms that combined were mainly family businesses, but included a few partnerships and private limited companies. An examination of the constituents of the Bradford Dyers' Association suggests, however, that only six of the original 22 firms had been in existence before 1871.[30] The last few years of the 1890s were not very good for Bradford, particularly for the piece trade. Weak firms may have seen takeover as a means of escaping bankruptcy. *The Economist* suggested that the ill fortunes of the Woolcombers' Association resulted from some members of the com- bine being in a poor way,[31] and there were 'stories of men with oil cans standing behind the over-driven machines upon whose output was to be based the valuation of their mill for sale to "t'combine" '.[32] But the Woolcombers' Association problem arose particularly through its lack of monopoly whereas the Bradford Dyers' Associ- ation success arose through its localised situation, the size of its combination and, apparently, through 'early and effective centrali- sation of authority'.[33]

Limited Liability

Public and private limited liability companies were not very common in the British wool textile industry before the end of the nineteenth century. Compared with the cotton industry and many other manu- facturing industries wool textile manufacturers appear to have been very loathe to take advantage of the company legislation of the 1850s. Limited companies were steadfastly resisted in the West of England.[34] Jacob Behrens reported in 1886 'We have none in our district. I cannot remember one.'[35] There was some limited liability company promotion in the 1890s including the notable firms of J.T. and J. Taylor of Batley, John Foster's of Queensbury and Blenkhorn Richards of Hawick,[36] but in spite of these and a wave of others around the turn of the century Clapham was still able to complain in 1907:

> But a few years ago – in the early nineties of the last century – companies that issued reports and balance sheets, whose shares were regularly bought and sold, were rare in all branches of the woollen and worsted and associated industries; though private companies of course existed. Even now, after the outbreak of company promotion in the late 1890s, the number of spinning and manufacturing companies, whose shares are quoted on the West Riding Stock Exchanges, is comparatively small. It is never pos- sible, for example, to gauge the general prosperity of worsted spinning by comparing the balance sheets and dividends of scores of limited mills, whereas this is regularly done in the case of Lancashire cotton spinning.[37]

Between 1856 and 1883 in the wool textile industry, there were 64 public and 14 private 'effective' formations of companies registered in London under the limited liability acts. In the cotton industry the numbers were 464 and 86 respectively. In 1885 there were totals of 2606 factories/firms enumerated by the factory inspectors in the wool textile industry and 2628 in the cotton industry.[38]

A wave of new company promotion did come around the end of the first decade of this century and by 1926 some 44 per cent of firms in the wool textile industry were limited liability. They tended to be the larger firms, including 56 per cent of firms with more than 100 workers.[39] But this was a much smaller proportion than had existed, for example, in the associated carpet industry in 1913.[40] One can only speculate about the reasons for the slow growth of this new form of business organisation. With so many family businesses in an industry which had always been somewhat secretive about its activities there was perhaps opposition to publishing accounts and to bringing in outside partners. But although this might have worked against the establishment of public companies, even private limited companies were slow to get off the ground.

8 Raw Materials and Processes, 1870–1914

Changes in Wool Supply 1870–1914

Compared with the earlier periods this was one more of consolidation than novelty. In the merino field there was nothing to equal the dispersion of the merino breed, thereby solving the problem of fine wool supply and the development in Australia of rather longer merino wools which, combined with new machine developments, led to a wide use of these wools for worsteds. As far as the merino was concerned, consolidation was definitely the key word with Australia remaining the main supplier to Britain. In Australia new areas were brought into use, notably the very dry districts of Queensland and, as the merino thrives in this kind of country, good wools were produced. The only problem was the tendency of these areas to have severe droughts which could be sufficient to kill the sheep and drive the farmers off the land. These droughts did have the effect of increasing the fluctuations in wool prices. More generally, the years 1870–1914 were the heyday of the merino. Earlier problems had been overcome and the threats of the twentieth century, such as the coming of synthetic fibres, were not thought of. Naturally wool prices fluctuated and tended to fall over the whole decade but with increasing consumption, and production rising continually, the wool grower appears to have done reasonably well. Freight costs from Australia to England fell.

It was, in fact, in the non-merino field that the main changes occurred, chiefly as the result of the successful adoption of refrigeration. Consequently, New Zealand which had previously been little more than an adjunct to the great merino-growing area of Australia, came very much into the picture in its own right. The merino flocks there were reduced and eventually almost disappeared, to be replaced by British breeds, primarily brought in for their meat producing properties but increasingly giving some of the best non-merino wools in the world. The best New Zealand crossbred wools – the word itself is a little misleading as they were mainly from Romney Marsh flocks – had many qualities which enabled the cloth manufacturer to produce goods that appealed to the consumer and they certainly increased the types of fabrics that could be made. New Zealand wools covered a wider range than those from any other country, from the coarsest (36s) to the finest (super 70s). But the most distinctive feature of this clip was the skin wools, known in the trade as slipes. They became of increasing interest to the West Riding trade, because their strength made them particularly suitable for mixing with waste. They could equally well be used on their own to manufacture good types of Cheviot suitings and excellent blankets. Owing to the cleaning process the skins had undergone, these slipes in yield came midway between the true greasy and the true scoured.

There were two methods of removing wool from sheep's skins, either by painting the back of the skin with lime or by hanging the skin in a warm, humid atmosphere. In both cases a loosening of the fibre on the skin took place and the wool could be pulled away. The first was the traditional English method and the usual one in New Zealand, but elsewhere, notably in Mazamet in France, the famous European centre for skin wools, the second method was followed.

The other major wool growing area, South America, followed much the same pattern as New Zealand, beginning as a merino area and then turning mainly to breeds based on the standard British breeds. Here also the period saw the development of a group of fine crossbreds (56/58s) with their own special qualities. These came from the extreme south – Patagonia – and from the Falkland Islands. The former were known as Puntas after the name of the port, Puntas Arenas, from which they were shipped. Both groups of wool were interesting because, mainly on account of transport difficulties, the sheep, unlike most other non-merino sheep, were grown with wool as their main object. This undoubtedly accounted for the care that was taken in preparing the clip for the market.

South American wool was interesting for another reason. The wools produced there with the exception of the Puntas and the Falklands went much more to North America and Continental European centres than to Britain. Rightly or wrongly, there does appear to have been a feeling in the British wool textile trade that these wools were inferior in some undefined way to those of Australia. It does appear that this was largely prejudice. The wool textile trade has always been rather traditional in its approach to the use of wool, although not of other raw materials, and having become accustomed to the Australian types stayed with them. The Puntas and Falkland wools were also sold in London. The growth of the Puntas market was largely the work of a long established firm of London wool brokers, Jacomb Hoare. Wools from the Falklands first appeared in England in 1871 and by 1908 there were 700,000 sheep there producing nearly five million pounds of wool a year. The original Falkland sheep came from Scotland – the Cheviot breed – but there was other blood introduced; the wool, however, still showed many signs of its Scottish ancestry. The Patagonian wool first appeared in the London saleroom about 1885; the original sheep had been brought over from the Falklands and the wools from the two areas have always had much in common. By 1914 approximately 100,000 bales were sold and as the bales from this area weighed double those from Australia they amounted to 70 million pounds, the produce of about 10 million sheep.

The often discussed difference between West Riding and Continental worsteds was frequently said to arise from the fact that the latter used so much South American wool. This would appear difficult to substantiate; in so far as the continent did produce certain varieties of worsteds not manufactured in England, this would seem to have been due much more to a difference in processing, namely the use of the mule instead of the frame in spinning. There can, however, be no doubt about the importance of the South American wool to the European manufacturer.

Two other major wool producing areas were South Africa, where the early development has already been briefly described, and the U.S.A. The former remained faithful to the merino and was a major exporter, especially to the U.K. market until 1914 and later, but the U.S.A. turned more to British mutton breeds and therefore to the production of crossbred wool rather than merino and in any case, increasingly consumed this wool in its own woollen and worsted mills that were being built there.

The manufacturer continued to obtain his wool in much the same manner as before, the main difference being the increasing amount of Australian wool that was sold in Australian sales. However, because of the rising production, large quantities were still sent to London which remained throughout the period covered here an important selling centre. Ultimately the Australian sales did become the more important and this growth had an effect on the buying methods of British manufacturers. Leading British top makers established Australian offices.

In the worsted trade the buyer would usually be a top maker, who was in many ways a wool merchant, and sometimes a spinner or manufacturer when they did their own combing. As far as Australia was concerned, and to a lesser extent South Africa and New Zealand, the buyers depended almost entirely on the auction system and there was little direct buying from the farms. Woollen manufacturers were different. Few had buying offices in Australia and New Zealand, some still bought in the London auctions but in this trade in woollen types a group of wool merchants established a distinctive place which they never held in the worsted industry. They set up scouring and, later, carbonising plants in Australia, and exported standard types of scoured wool. These merchants were usually of Australian extraction, their preparation of these types of wool often being a natural growth of their woolbroking and merchanting activities. Home-grown wools were now becoming less important but the manufacturers still bought from traditional staplers who, as before, bought direct from the farmers or at the local sales. Manufacturers also continued to buy direct but most used staplers to some extent.

There were, as stated, few major changes in sheep breeding but within the general pattern traced above certain developments, or attempted developments, do deserve a mention, particularly as quite small changes in wool qualities can have startling effects on cloth types. Without doubt the most notable attempted development was to produce a sheep combining the qualities of merino wool with the meat-providing ones from British breeds. The efforts never completely achieved the desired result. The most successful was the Corriedale; the most interesting, from the wool user's standpoint, was the so-called Half-Bred, a straight Lincoln/merino cross which gave a wool much nearer in fibre diameter to the merino.

One result of these experiments was to produce wools of the same fibre diameter but with quite different processing features. For example, the Southdown, the Corriedale and the New Zealand Half-Bred were all 56/58s, but there the resemblance ended. The Southdown was a tight stapled wool, ideal for making felts, particularly for the printing trade. The Corriedale had a much more open staple, lacking the felting properties of the New Zealand Southdown and, although longer, had less appeal for the woolman. The New Zealand Half-Bred rivalled the Southdown in its appeal to the user; in appearance it was less crimpy and tight stapled but an excellent white. Combined with the best Scottish Cheviot it produced the finest Cheviot suitings.

Two points can be made. First, none of these efforts to produce a dual purpose sheep really succeeded. If the farmer decided to aim for this he had better choose one of the British breeds that produced good meat and a relatively high quality wool. Two sheep perhaps stood out, the Southdown and the Dorset Horn. In almost every respect they were better all-rounders than the specialist crossings mentioned. Another alternative was the Cheviot, often more popular in its North Country version than in its traditional Border country form. Late in the twentieth century the Australian grower gave up the attempt to produce a new breed or cross and mainly used the British breeds instead.

The second point is that, for commercial reasons in many countries, notably in Britain in the twentieth century, most sheep were crosses. Not cross-bred in the sense of a merino cross but a combination of two or more British breeds. In this way high lambing rates were obtained which was the main object of almost all sheep breeders in Britain. The basis of these crosses was usually the Border Leicester, which had excellent fertility and was widely used in the Scottish Border country for crossing with the Cheviot, thereby producing the well-known Scottish Half-Bred. This was good from the meat producing point of view but from that of the woolman, the result was relatively large quantities of somewhat undistinguished wool.

These decades showed a considerable decline in the number of sheep in the British Isles, which was mainly due to the difficult period through which agriculture was going. This decline had little effect upon the wool textile trade for the simple reason that there had been such an expansion of sheep based on British breeds, and therefore producing similar wools in other parts of the world, that consequently the actual amounts available to the British wool textile trade continued to increase. In so far as this meant that the trade became ever more a user of imported rather than native raw material, it did have long term effects, placing the British wool textile trade in a somewhat similar position to the cotton trade but the ultimate effects of this were long delayed and did not play an important part until the early twentieth century.

Emphasis has been laid on the adaptability of the wool textile trade in using ever shorter types of material, including shoddy and mungo; naturally the same technical expertise led the trade to make increasing use of both shorter wools which previously had been neglected, and also of the so-called rare hairs. The first point was illustrated in the increased use of lambs' wool, the cloth made from which was characterised by its greater bulkiness and kindness of handle. These properties were noticeable in the raw wool stage and, if the right precautions were taken, particularly that the correct twist was used in the yarn and the weave and set was correct, they did come through in the finished product. Lambs' wool was not as good for fulling, which may have accounted for its unpopularity during earlier periods. However, in the nineteenth century its qualities became more generally recognised, partly because of its great suitability for high-class knitting yarn which was then an expanding market. The period covered here brought an increase in the amount of lambs' wool available, because of the new refrigerated meat trade. The standard product of this New Zealand trade was Canterbury lamb. The wool from it came in various lengths, beginning with the shortest, the so-called milk lamb, and extending to the full-grown hogget.

One section of the wool supply trade, that of East Indian wool, remains to be mentioned and it has been left to the last because, with one exception, it did not play a very important part in the wool textile trade of Great Britain. It really represented the third section of the wool trade as a whole, less important than the merino and the British-based trade because it was available in less quantity in the world market, but still of considerable importance. The name is unfortunate as the wool certainly did not come from East India, even if one knew exactly what geographical area was being described in these words. It was in fact the product of the large number of relatively unimproved sheep that, during the nineteenth century, inhabited the vast areas that lay between Asia Minor and India and even beyond. Being unimproved, the wools had the distinctive quality of possessing both the fine inner and coarse outer fleece typical of the primitive sheep and of many other animals. They were particularly suitable for making yarn for carpets, and indeed had long been used for making carpets in the areas where they were grown. With the development of machine-made carpets the demand for them increased and they were sold, partly through merchants and partly in Liverpool auctions, for processing on both the woollen and worsted systems for the important but specialised carpet trade. The woollen spinner making these yarns for the carpet trade or the woollen spinner producing for his own carpet section, used large weights as carpet yarns were thick. Buyers of other types tended to despise the wool, perhaps partly because of the risk of anthrax. Considering that the other branches of the wool textile trade were willing to use so many different types of raw material, the almost complete separation of the East Indian (Carpet) wool trade from the rest was strange and it continued well into the twentieth century.

The wool waste trade described in some detail in Chapter 5 continued to progress and was the main reason for the expansion of the woollen section of the industry. The coming of all wool merino worsteds and the increasing popularity of these cloths for men's wear meant that a better shoddy was available. Excellently prepared by the shoddy manufacturer, new worsteds or tailor's clippings, as they were called, were a better raw material than many of the shorter types of wool. At the other end the steady improvement in carbonising techniques considerably increased the amount of low waste available.

Rare Hairs

During the second half of the nineteenth century interest in the rarer hairs was at its peak and although the quantity consumed was only a small part of the raw material consumption of the whole industry, they nevertheless deserve a section of their own. The rapid rise of the worsted industry and its prosperity in the middle decades of the nineteenth century owed a very great deal, as has been made clear, to the development of the use of cotton warps but a part of the success of the industry was due to the use of alpaca and mohair in wefts which, with cotton warps, permitted the spinning of lustre fabrics of great softness and brilliance. Just as, in the end, the use of cotton warp disappeared in the worsted trade, so with rare fibres and by the end of the period dealt with in this volume, the use of alpaca and more particularly, mohair in both warp and weft to produce lightweight and very lovely fabrics was more important. The typical rare hair fabric of the twentieth century was 100 per cent mohair.

Although initially alpaca was of equal, perhaps greater, importance than mohair, over the decades this position changed, partly because the animal producing mohair proved much more adaptable to new areas. For this reason mohair is described first. Its successful use occurred at about the same time as that of alpaca with the three alpaca spinning firms being also major users of it. They were not able to dominate the trade to such an extent, partly because of the steady improvement in the availability of supplies. The existence of mohair had been known in Britain for several centuries, but it had not been available because of the prohibition of its export;[1] yarn was imported from the Levant, and used particularly for the manufacture of camblets.

Mohair and alpaca had similar properties. The fibre was fine, had good length and particularly good lustre, strength, durability and softness of a particular type. It had few serrations and a staple length of between six and nine inches, depending on how frequently the fleece was shorn. The whiteness of mohair was particularly important and meant that all kinds of colours could be made, which was not the case with other rare fibres. An important point about mohair, alpaca and cashmere arose from the fact that they had either few or no serrations on the surface of the fibre, which meant that the fibre would not full and did not shrink when washed.

The lifting of restrictions on exports from Turkey enabled small quantities of mohair fo find their way to Britain in the 1820s and by the following decade it was being spun in small quantities in Yorkshire, Norwich and Scotland.[2] Like alpaca it was initially not easy to spin so as to produce an even thread, but Titus Salt attained a success similar to that with alpaca, and with the development of cotton warps, the demand for mohair yarns increased. However, supplies of the fibre from Turkey were erratic, both in quantity and quality. They had to find their way across land to Constantinople and were then brought to Britain by London merchants. As with the alpaca, attempts were made to naturalise the angora goat in other countries. There was a lack of success in some, including Australia, but it was successfully introduced to South Africa in the mid-1850s and within a few years supplies from there were being sent to Britain. By the 1880s South African supplies were rivalling those from Turkey in quantity. The goats were also introduced successfully into the United States where, by 1896, about 500,000 pounds were being clipped each year. Overall supplies of mohair improved steadily for most of the nineteenth century; they grew particularly quickly in the 1870s and early 1880s, more as a result of increased availability than extra demand. Fashion was moving away from the lustre type of fabric; average price per pound according to the trade statistics, was 3*s*.2*d*. in 1865–69, but had fallen to 2*s*.3*d*. in 1875–79. As lustre fabrics became more in vogue in the 15 years before 1914, so the demand for mohair soared and there was in addition the new demand for 100 per cent mohair cloths already mentioned.

Mohair was always used in a wider variety of fabrics than alpaca. It was of particular importance in camblets and plushes but was also used for a variety of dress fabrics and for braids and trimmings. Mohair yarn was exported in quantity to France, little mohair actually being spun there. The worsted mule, so favoured by French spinners, would not have been suitable for this straight type of fibre.[3]

Alpaca wool was obtained from a species of goat, a member of the llama family found in the Andes of South America, particularly in Peru. Llama, vicuña and guanaco were other members of the same family.[4] Alpaca wool was long and fine and had a downy handle; it had smaller and smoother scales than wool and it has been suggested that, because it was straight and well formed, it had a more uniform quality but this would appear to depend on the kind of wool with which it was being compared. James summed up some of its properties well:

> There is also a transparency, a glittering brightness upon the surface giving it the glossiness of silk, which is enhanced on its passing through the dye vat. It is also distinguished by softness and elasticity, essential properties in the manufacture of fine goods, being exempt from spiral, curly and shaggy defects; and it spins, when treated properly according to the present improved method, easily, and yields an even, strong, and true thread.[5]

It may be felt that James slightly overrated alpaca in this paragraph. It was in fact an extremely difficult fibre to dye and was not improved by passing through the dye vat. This was clearly shown by the fact that over the years there has been an ever-increasing tendency to use alpaca in its natural colour.

Alpaca had been known in Britain since about 1807. In that year some was brought back by British soldiers returning from Buenos Aires, but no good use was made of it.[6] In the following three decades attempts were made to breed the animal and grow its wool in Britain but with very little success as a result, so it was thought, of the higher humidity of the British climate.[7] Later attempts were made to introduce the animal to Australia without much success, so it would seem that for once the British climate had been unfairly blamed.

James suggested that a reasonably successful attempt to spin alpaca was made by Benjamin Outran of Greetland, near Halifax, in 1830, the yarn being used for ladies' carriage shawls and cloakings. But the success was not sufficiently apparent for the manufacture to be maintained.[8] Perhaps it never amounted to very much. Messrs Horsfall of Bradford experimented with it in 1832 but there is no doubt that the generally held view that Titus Salt was the first to prove how successfully it could be spun is correct. Apparently in about 1836 he was informed that a quantity of bales of alpaca were lying unsold in a Liverpool warehouse. He bought it cheaply, experimented with it and proved its possibilities, his actions and success subsequently being immortalised by Charles Dickens in *Household Words*.

Titus Salt's success arose through the ability to overcome the difficulties of preparing the long fibres for spinning. Average staple was well over six inches, although length of imported alpaca fibres was later reduced as a result of the more frequent shearing of the Peruvian flocks.[9] Moreover Salt's recognition of the enhanced lustre effect that alpaca wefts woven with cotton warps would give was of importance. Woven with silk warps 'it was found that almost any perfection of finish and beauty can be attained'. Later the tendency was to use alpaca in both warp and weft.[10]

Supplies of alpaca were limited. The difficulties of obtaining it from inaccessible Peru before the building of the Panama Canal were considerable, but a number of merchant houses developed the trade and, partly as a result, improved general trade with Peru. Supplies throughout the nineteenth century only increased very slowly because of the difficulty of naturalising the animal in other parts of the world. The trade statistics show considerable fluctuations in supply at various times. For example, imports in 1868 were little more than one-half those of the previous year, and this perhaps helps to explain why firms doing a large trade held large stocks.[11]

Although the British worsted industry became renowned for its alpaca products, spinning for most of the nineteenth century remained mainly the province of the three firms – Titus Salt, G. & J. Turner of Great Horton, Bradford, and J. Foster and Son of Queensbury. The three firms bought the alpaca from Liverpool merchants, at times two, or all three, of them combining to obtain supplies and thus presumably to keep down prices.[12] Their position in the trade was so dominant that few other firms appear to have attempted to break into their activities, preferring, if they wished to use alpaca, to buy the yarn. Those that did attempt to do spinning had no great success, with the possible exception of the Scottish firm James Johnston, who certainly used it at an early date but was, it would appear likely, making quite different fabrics from it than the Yorkshire firms already mentioned.[13] A number of Huddersfield firms, for example, exhibited cloths containing alpaca in 1851.[14]

The dominance of the spinning of alpaca by just the three firms was not confined to Britain. It was very little used elsewhere. Small quantities were re-exported to various other European countries and to the U.S.A. but the more important trade was in the already spun yarns, for example in the American and Utrecht velvet trades. A French commentator in 1851 stated that alpaca had originally been successfully spun in France but that its combination with cotton warps in Bradford undercut the French product.[15]

Cashmere, the wool of the Tibetan goat, first arrived on the European scene in the nineteenth century in the form of the lovely handling and beautifully designed Kashmir shawls. Supplies, however, did not come from Kashmir. The animal was found in Tibet and other parts of China and supplies have always come through China.

The cashmere goat, like many other animals including the primitive sheep, has two hairs, a long coarse outer and a finer inner. It was the fine inner fibre that was so valuable. The two types of fibre were separated by passing the cashmere through a combing process but unlike the normal combing practice, it was the noil which was valuable. Being short, this cashmere had to be processed on the woollen principle. Its main use was in knitwear, either made from 100 per cent cashmere or mixed with very fine Australian lambs' wool. The coarse outer fibre was much less valuable and should probably not be described as cashmere. In addition to being a remarkably soft handle, cashmere does not felt and this is an advantage when manufacturing fine knitwear.

Camel hair is probably the oldest of all the rare fibres used for textiles; there are many early records of it. Camblets were probably originally made from camel hair rather than from other fibres. Like cashmere, there was a fine inner hair and coarse outer, but the latter was a more useful fibre than the coarse cashmere. It was, however, the fine inner soft hair that should really have been known as camel hair. It was difficult to dye and was usually sold in its natural shade, which indeed was so popular as to make dyeing normally quite unnecessary; wool was often dyed camel when the shade was fashionable. Like cashmere, camel hair could be manufactured into 100 per cent camel hair fabrics or could be mixed with wool to produce a cloth which could be described as camel but which could be sold at a cheaper price.

Angora is the hair of the angora rabbit which had a very soft handle and was used for making fabrics for children's wear and for dresses. It must be distinguished from mohair which, as stated, came from the angora goat and was, of course, a very different fibre. Angora rabbits' wool has always been subject to sudden turns of fashion, sometimes being popular, often not.

Vicuña was the rarest of all these fibres and consequently the most expensive. Although very soft handling, its higher price was due not to its superior quality but to its rarity, the difficulty being that the animal was never domesticated. It was usually used in its 100 per cent form and natural colour, by hatters, hosiers, and by worsted manufacturers. Sauerbeck wrote in 1887 that only one pound of 'very fine and valuable wool' was obtained from a fleece and that it sold in Britain at the highest price for any kind of wool – at that time 5*s*.6*d*. a pound, three times the price of alpaca. Later the Peruvian Government controlled supplies of vicuña and restricted them even further to prevent the extermination of the vicuña goat.[16]

Table 35   *Imports of alpaca, mohair and other hairs, 1840–1914 (million lbs)*

Annual average	Mohair from Turkey	Mohair from British South Africa	Mohair Total	Alpaca, vicuña and llama wool Total	Total hairs
1840–4	—	—	—	—	1.0
1844–9	1.2	—	1.2	2.0	3.2
1850–4	2.4	—	2.4	1.6	4.0
1855–9	2.8	—	2.8	2.4	5.2
1860–4	3.1	—	3.1	3.0	6.1
1865–9	4.5	0.1	4.6	3.0	7.5
1870–4	5.8	0.3	6.1	4.0	10.8
1875–9	5.4	1.5	6.9	3.9	11.7
1880–4	8.7	4.2	12.9	3.7	17.9
1885–9	8.2	7.8	16.0	4.5	22.9
1890–4	6.7	9.5	16.2	4.6	22.8
1895–9	10.0	11.1	21.6	5.0	28.5
1900–4	10.4	13.5	24.3	5.6	37.4
1905–9	10.6	16.9	27.9	5.1	41.9
1910–14	9.5	19.5	29.5	5.0	41.9

Table 35, based on the Board of Trade returns, shows the imports of mohair, alpaca and other minor wools and hairs from the 1840s. The figures can only be taken as approximate. There are several problems of interpreting the trade statistics, not least the difficulty of the classifications used, particularly for hair. The figures do not take into account the re-export trade but this was of little significance until towards the end of the century. They reflect the revival in popularity of lustre fabrics from the late 1890s and show both the slow progress in increase of supplies of alpaca and the rising role of South African mohair supplies. The trade statistics occasionally show an export of British alpaca. This was presumably hair that had been combed in Britain and then re-exported.

Recovered Wool
Developments in the supply and use of recovered wool during the middle decades of the century have been discussed in Chapter 5. It is doubtful that estimates of consumption of shoddy by the British woollen industry will ever be determined accurately. One has to place much dependence on the calculations of the Bradford Chamber of Commerce, the derivation of which are, on the whole, unknown. It is probable that its estimates are more reliable for later in the nine-teenth century than for the earlier decades. Dr Malin makes various adjustments downwards for the period 1820–34, and upwards for 1855–70, based on a variety of contemporary estimates.[17] This does seem realistic, as Hooper, the Chamber's original statistician, had detailed and first hand knowledge of the wool textile industry when he commenced his various statistical calculations in the 1890s.

The Chamber's figures show that consumption of recovered wool rose consistently from 1870 to 1914, except in the late 1880s (see Table 36). Consumption increased two to three times; as a proportion of total wool and hair used in Britain, recovered wool rose from 20 to 25 per cent over the period. As is shown in the next section, when increasing shrinkage of wool is taken into account as much as 35 per cent of total wool and hair consumption before the First World War was recovered wool. If one roughly assumes that one-third of all new wool used was directed to the worsted industry, and this may be a low estimate, then it would seem that by the years before the First World War reclaimed wool was of equal or more importance than new wool in the woollen industry.

The vast majority of the reclaimed wool was used in Yorkshire but it is undoubtedly true that some manufacturers in the West of England, Scotland and elsewhere used small quantities, although rarely would they have been prepared to admit it. Likewise it seems probable that even worsted manufacturers experimented with shoddy from time to time. In 1904 57 per cent of spinning spindles in the woollen industry were in Yorkshire. If one assumes that four-fifths of all shoddy and mungo was used in Yorkshire, and this may be an underestimate, and that raw material consumption was proportionate to spindles in use in each region, this would mean that about 70 per cent of wool spun in the Yorkshire woollen industry was reclaimed wool.

The aggregate consumption figures suggest very clearly that the periods of peak expansion in the use of reclaimed wool were the decades of the 1850s and 1860s and the 20 years before the First World War. Growth was slow in the 1840s, presumably because wool prices were low, but the soaring of the prices in 1849, created a rapid movement to an attempt to blend more recovered wool. In the 1880s and 1890s growth was again slower this time the result of low wool prices, fashion changes and supply problems. The interrelationship between price fluctuations and supply of new and recovered wool are discussed in detail by Dr Malin.[18] The ease of substitution and the skill of Yorkshire manufacturers in blending enabled rapid short run substitution of recovered wool for new wool in response to price rises and supply shortages of the latter.

Domestically collected rags produced the bulk of recovered wool until the early 1870s. Then for a few years home and foreign supply was roughly equal. Growing competition from European users of shoddy and a rising home supply then again increased the relative proportion of the domestic supply. Up to 1860 imported rags came primarily from Germany, with additional supplies in the 1850s from Italy, Belgium, Holland, Turkey and the Near East, and Australia. In the later years of the century Germany and France provided the bulk of imports of rags, shoddy and mungo with neighbouring European countries also contributing. Only after 1907 were there significant imports from the United States. In the same decade supplies from British possessions also rose, but in 1910 65 per cent of imports still emanated from Europe.

The extent to which shoddy and mungo could be reprocessed was aptly described in a trade journal in 1882:

> Woollen rags undergo many peculiar metamorphoses. They are successively converted into mungo, shoddy and devils' dust, then reappear as ladies' superfine cloths from which they degenerate into druggets and are then used for the manufacture of flock paper. Finally the agriculturalist uses them as manure on account

of the large amount of nitrogen they contain. The presence of nitrogen also makes them of value to the chemist who boils them down with pearl ash, horns and hoofs of cattle, old iron, blood and clippings of leather, and produces the beautiful yellow and red salts known as the prussiates of potash. From these again the valuable pigment Prussian blue is made. Thus do old rags enter upon a fresh career, and it seems as if there was no limit to the means by which this waste product may be utilised.[19]

Raw Material Consumption and Output

An assessment of the changes in the volume of the output and of the capacity of the industry is severely complicated by the fact that all the potentially useful indicators that are available are subject to considerable and often unknown degrees of error. The indicators which are of possible use include raw material consumption, mills and machinery in operation and employment. Little progress would appear possible in terms of more direct calculations of output because, although information on the volume and value of the export trade is available, little is known in any detail about the proportion of output which was going to the home market.

Wool imports

Potentially the most useful measurement of long term change in the industry is raw material consumption. Statistics for imports of wool, mohair, alpaca and reclaimed wool are available. There appears, for this period, to be reasonable contemporary agreement about the volume of the home clip, and the balance of home wool retained can therefore be calculated. There is less certainty, however, about the consumption of home produced reclaimed wool and very little evidence for changes in the use of other fibres, particularly cotton. And, as is shown below, there are also considerable problems in comparing the volume of wool imports over the period because of the increasing importation of unwashed and unscoured wool.

The basic figures, in terms of five yearly averages are shown in Table 36. Assuming that they are realistic and ignoring, for the time being, the problem of the use of other fibres and of the changing nature of the wool imports, they indicate quite clearly a very substantial increase in the raw material consumption of the wool textile industry in the period between 1870 and 1914. Indeed average wool consumption in 1910–14 was 86 per cent above the average level for 1870–4. It would also appear that there was a progressive improvement in wool consumption throughout the period, except for the first few years of the twentieth century. The rate of growth was quite slow

Table 36 *Raw material consumption in the wool textile industry, 1870–1914 (million lbs.)*

	Foreign and colonial wools				Home-grown wools			Estimated quantity of wool from sheepskins imported	Estimated quantity of recovered wool consumed in the U.K.	Total quantity of wool, hair recovered wool etc. consumed in the U.K.
	Sheep and lambs wool imported	Mohair, alpaca etc. imported and hair	Re-exports of wool of and hair	Balance retained	Estimated total clip	Exports	Balance retained			
Annual averages										
1870–4	307.0	10.8	126.6	191.2	159.6	9.2	150.4	23.0	89.0	453.7
1875–9	392.4	11.7	195.4	208.7	155.0	10.4	144.6	20.1	104.0	477.4
1880–4	481.3	17.9	264.4	234.8	135.4	16.5	118.9	20.0	123.0	496.6
1885–9	599.5	22.9	321.5	300.9	134.6	22.1	112.5	25.0	101.0	539.4
1890–4	691.3	22.8	371.3	342.8	146.4	16.6	129.8	32.2	118.0	622.8
1895–9	715.6	28.5	339.5	404.6	137.8	22.9	114.9	33.6	132.0	685.1
1900–4	607.7	37.4	265.4	379.7	136.0	31.2	104.8	29.6	145.0	659.1
1905–9	707.3	41.9	319.2	430.0	133.4	39.2	94.2	35.4	193.0	752.6
1910–14	782.3	41.9	318.6	505.6	131.8	36.3	95.5	35.0	206.4	842.6

SOURCE: Bradford Chamber of Commerce, *Statistics relating to the Woollen and Worsted Trades*, 1917

in the 1870s but much more substantial from the mid-1880s to the end of the century, and again after 1905.

It is, however, necessary to reduce these figures substantially to obtain realistic wool consumption estimates. The majority of the wool consumed was imported and throughout the period an increasing proportion of that wool was entering unwashed and unscoured, for two reasons: firstly more and more Australasian wool was being sent in that state and, secondly, a greater proportion of wool was being obtained from other sources, which traditionally sent wool in an unwashed condition. The increased import of unwashed wools from Australia resulted from two factors in particular: more rapid transport facilities reduced the risk of fermentation in dirty wool and, secondly, Bradford manufacturers preferred their wools in the grease, as that enabled them to be better sorted to their own standards.

In order to adjust the figures to obtain estimates of clean wool consumption it is necessary to calculate changes in the proportion of wool imported unwashed or unscoured and the clean yield of that wool. Sauerbeck noted that in 1869 about 70 per cent of Australian wool was washed before shearing; in 1887 he believed that the proportion had fallen to 30 per cent[20] and it continued to fall, to as little as 10 per cent by the 1920s. But the washed or scoured wool imported still had more impurities to be removed before it could be processed; one estimate in the 1880s suggested that washing alone, before shearing, only removed between one-half and one-third of the grease.[21] However improvements in washing and scouring in Australia, using machinery imported from Britain, substantially increased the yield of Australian washed/scoured wool in the decades before the First World War.[22] In the calculations that follow (see Table 37) it has been assumed that the proportion of washed wool imported from Australia declined from 70 per cent in 1870 to 20 per cent by 1914 and that the yield of that wool rose steadily from 70 to 90 per cent over the same period.

Wool from South America and South Africa was imported almost entirely 'in the grease'. For the purpose of the calculations and for the want of other evidence it has been assumed that the wool imported from other sources arrived in the grease.

In view of their wide and respected experience of the trade it may be realistic to accept the estimates of clean yield produced by Helmuth Schwartze and Co. as reasonably reliable. It has been pointed out that the yields they estimate are higher than some other contemporary figures but in view of the diversity of such estimates it is preferable to err on the conservative side.[23] They suggested clean wool yield for Australasian wool of about 60 per cent in 1870 and around 50 per cent in the 1880s; there is not much reason to believe that the yield changed significantly thereafter. Average shrinkage on Australasian wools was calculated at 49 per cent by Helmuth Schwartze in 1911;[24] experiments a few years later by the U.S.A. Bureau of Standards gave a somewhat lower figure.[25]

For South American wool Helmuth Schwartze and Co.'s estimates suggest some improvement in the clean wool yield between 1850 and 1880 but in 1885 the yield was put at only 36.8 per cent. This accords with, or is perhaps somewhat higher than, other contemporary estimates. In 1894 the *Textile Manufacturer* estimated a yield of 30 to 40 per cent for River Plate wool.[26] F.J. Hooper gave a figure of 30 per cent for 1900.[27] We assume a constant yield of one-third from South American wool imports to Britain; this may be pessimistic as some later evidence gives a figure nearer 50 per cent,[28] but, as before the First World War these wools never formed more than 10 per cent of British wool imports, slight inaccuracy is of little consequence to the overall calculations.

Schwartze estimated that Cape wools imported to Europe and North America yielded between three-fifths and two-thirds in clean weight in the 1870s with a decline thereafter. Yield was given at only 42 per cent in 1911.[29] We assume a clean yield of 65 per cent in the 1870s and a progressive reduction to 45 per cent in 1910. There were small quantities of wool imported to Britain from other sources which together amounted to a significant amount. Helmuth Schwartze, in his calculations of imports of other wool to Europe and North America, estimated a yield from it fluctuating between 62 and 67 per cent between 1860 and 1885. Although there is scope for error here because of the variations in sources of wool imports to different countries, in our calculations we assume a constant yield of two-thirds for wool imports to Great Britain from all other sources.

Before these various weight losses can be subtracted from the wool import statistics account has to be taken of the very large quantities of wool that were re-exported. The Board of Trade statistics do not permit re-exports of wool to be identified according to their original source, and only rather vague generalisations are possible about their likely composition. Australasian, Cape and Plate wools, as well as many other minor wools, were re-exported. Most South American wool was sent direct to Antwerp, Le Havre and Bordeaux. Of the small quantity sent to Britain, some was re-exported. A substantial proportion of Cape and New Zealand wools may have been re-exported. Although Australian wool was beginning to find its way to Europe late in the century, the majority went through the London wool sales. In general it does not seem unrealistic to assume that the composition of re-exports of wool was in proportion to the sources of imports.

Thus in Table 37 re-exports of wool are subtracted from gross imports in proportion to source, the assumed proportion of washed/scoured wool, adjusted for further weight loss, of Australasian wool and the yield of wool 'in the grease' is calculated and yield adjustments for other types of wool are made. The final column suggests the amount of clean imported wool available to British manufacturers.

The overall yield from wool imports varied from 66 per cent in 1870 to around 50 per cent from 1900 to 1914. Malin suggested that overall loss on washing and scouring of greasy wools averaged 25 per cent, but he acknowledged that this was probably very conservative. The very detailed list of contemporary estimates he produces gives very few examples of greasy wool yielding more than 70 per cent.[30] However, it is possible that the present estimates could be somewhat pessimistic; they may overestimate the amount of wool imported in the grease in particular.

Table 37   *Estimated clean yield of net imports of wool (million lbs.)*

| | Total imports | Net imports | Clean yields | | | | Total yield |
			Austra- lasian	South American	Cape	Others	
1870	263	170	76	3	14	19	112
1880	463	225	93	2	15	33	143
1890	633	291	114	2	24	16	156
1900	559	361	148	8	13	9	178
1910	803	465	169	14	36	24	243

Home Wool Clip

In order to assess the contribution of the retained home wool clip to total raw material consumption it is also necessary to deflate the contemporary estimates to allow for the washing and scouring carried out by manufacturers. The majority of domestic wool was delivered washed, but further washing and scouring was normally necessary by the manufacturer. The Helmuth Schwartze figures estimate a clean yield of United Kingdom wool of three-quarters.[31] In 1903 Hooper estimated from 70 to 80 per cent. The Bradford Chamber of Commerce allowed 78 per cent in 1917. Earlier estimates for the 1870s and 1880 were invariably around the 70 per cent level. Malin, to be conservative, allowed a yield of 80 per cent, but it would seem safe to deflate the retained home clip estimates for the United Kingdom by 25 per cent. Those estimates were prepared by the Bradford Chamber of Commerce and were well regarded for their reliability at the time.

Other Wools and Hairs

The statistics produced by the Bradford Chamber of Commerce include estimated quantities of wool pulled from imported sheepskins. It does not appear to be clear whether the quantities entered are the crude weight of wool or the clean weight. The estimate for 1877 was 23 million pounds. This is somewhat higher than the 22.5 million pounds estimated by Schwartze for the same year. Schwartze believed that clean wool yield was about 70 per cent for fellmongers' wool and adjusted his figures accordingly.[32] We have followed his example and adjusted the estimates of imported skin wool to give a clean weight of 70 per cent of the crude figures.[33] Home produced fellmongers' wool is included in the estimates of total home wool production.

To the estimates of raw wool consumption must be added the imports of alpaca, vicuña, llama, mohair, goat, camel and other hairs. As we have noted elsewhere the Board of Trade import statistics for these raw materials leave a lot to be desired. Moreover there must be some uncertainty about what proportion of the weight of imports of hair was actually available after cleansing for manufacturing. However imports of the various hairs are indicated in Table 38. There was a very small quantity of British goat hair also used in manufacture but it was of insignificant proportions. The figures given are for gross imports; re-exports were of little significance except towards the end of the period. The estimates of the quantity of recovered wool consumed in the United Kingdom do not need any adjustment. Shoddy and mungo were ready for use in their entirety once they had been pulled.

Output

The estimates and calculations brought together in Table 38 undoubtedly give a better perspective of raw material consumption by the wool textile industry than the unadjusted figures in Table 36. The revised figures may only be acceptable as a crude estimate but any conceivable error is not likely to contradict any general conclusions.

Table 38 Raw material consumption in the wool textile industry, 1865–1914 (adjusted estimates, million lbs.)

Annual averages	Foreign and colonial wools		Home grown wools	Skin wool	Recovered wool	Total consumption of all wools and hairs
	Net imports of wool: clean weight	Net imports of hair etc.	Clean weight of retained home clip	Clean weight of imports	Estimated consumption	
1865–9	95	8	112	9	60	284
1870–4	119	11	113	16	89	348
1875–9	126	12	109	14	104	365
1880–4	139	18	89	14	123	383
1885–9	150	23	84	18	101	376
1890–4	173	23	97	23	118	434
1895–9	184	29	86	24	132	455
1900–4	168	37	79	21	145	450
1905–9	202	42	71	25	193	533
1910–14	241	42	72	25	206	586

It would appear that wool and hair consumption rose, on average, in all but two of the quinquennial periods from 1870 to 1914. There may have been a slight decline in the second half of the 1880s, there undoubtedly was in the first few years of the new century. Consumption in the period immediately preceding the First World War was over twice the level of 50 years earlier. The figures clearly portray a picture of continual expansion of the industry through most of the period of so-called depression.

However there are two further complications which need to be borne in mind. Firstly an important raw material for several branches of the industry was cotton. Estimates of the amount of cotton used in the different periods would seem to be impossible to assess but certain trends are examined elsewhere.[34] The movement in fashion towards all-wool worsteds undoubtedly reduced the relative proportion of cotton to wool used in the worsted industry. It seems possible, but by no means certain, that this could have led to a decline in the absolute amount of cotton consumed. On the other hand all the evidence points to a considerable increase in the amount of cotton consumed by the woollen branch of the industry. One indicator would be the export statistics; these of course do not permit exact comparisons over time because of changing widths, possible changing proportions of cotton in mixed cloths and lack of information on the use of cotton in blankets, flannels, carpets and shawls. However, in the woollen cloth category a higher proportion of the increased level of woollen cloth exports in the early 1890s compared with the early 1870s was mixed cloth. Overall it would appear unlikely that the consumption of cotton could have declined in the last third of the nineteenth century; it would appear more likely that there was some increase.

The second problem in using raw material consumption as an indicator of the growth of the size of the wool textile industry results from the changing nature of that industry. By the early twentieth century a much larger amount of wool was leaving the industry in the form of tops, noils or yarn compared with several decades earlier. Exact calculations of the consequences of this are difficult to effect but a number of observations are feasible. Comparing 1875–9 with 1905–9 the weight of yarns exported rose from an annual average in the first period of about 36 million pounds to about 77 million pounds. But imports of yarn for manufacturing also rose in the same period by approximately 13 million pounds. The increase in the net exports of yarn of about 28 million pounds per annum over the period does not materially affect the general conclusions, even bearing in mind that the volume of wool needed for this yarn production was rather more than the weight of the yarn. However when one takes into account the huge increase in the exports of tops and noils which by 1905–9 were averaging over 50 million pounds per annum there is a more significant effect on the assessment. Even so it would still appear that the volume of wool finding its way to final manufacture was absolutely increasing throughout the period.[35] And one should not deny that combing and yarn spinning for export made a valuable contribution to the total output of the industry.

Technological Progress 1870–1914

By 1870 the main processes of wool textile manufacture had been mechanised; it had taken one hundred years to achieve. Further progress between 1870 and 1914 was confined to improvements mainly in the speeding up of machinery.

The most important developments during these years came in the dyeing and chemical fields and can be subdivided into two sections: firstly the improvements that followed from the coming of the synthetic dyestuff industry and, linked with it, that of scientifically prepared chemicals; and secondly the beginning of a real understanding of the structure of the wool fibre. By 1914 the changes coming from the first had been mainly worked out, natural madder and natural indigo had been replaced by the synthetic product and many new dyes had been introduced, some of them much brighter than anything that had been known before. As far as the second was concerned, ideas were still at the drawing board stage and were not to have their full effect until considerably later in the twentieth century.

First, however, we deal with the further mechanisation of the processes. As far as the preparatory ones were concerned there was little change. Machines already mentioned were improved without any new ideas being introduced. The ever increasing use of rags naturally concentrated attention on rag tearing machines, the 'devils' as they had been called, and on the garnetting machines, less severe than the devils and used mainly for tearing up yarn or knitted goods. The early machines of this type were essentially of the same kind as the willeys already used for opening wool and previously described but they, of course, had stronger teeth. Devils and garnetting machines changed little over the years.

Turning to yarn manufacture, the chief developments took place in the worsted section. The main new ideas concerning wool combing had arrived by 1870. Increasingly after that date, particularly for the finer wools now widely used in this section of the trade, preparation for combing was by carding, the so-called worsted carding, which was really a shortened form of woollen carding without the condenser system.

For spinning the worsted spinner increasingly turned to the new methods of cap and ring spinning. Both had been invented in the U.S.A. earlier but their general adoption into the British industry, which essentially now meant the West Riding, only came after 1870. The introduction of the cap spindle in the nineteenth century brought new ideas to the twisting and winding-on section of the spinning process, as much higher speeds of up to 6500 r.p.m. could be obtained and finer yarns could be spun. It should be emphasised that in all forms of worsted spinning, except to some extent with the worsted mule, roller drafting as invented by Paul and developed by Arkwright remained the basis. The various methods (fly spinning, cap spinning and ring spinning) were only concerned with the insertion of the twist and the winding-on to a container of the spun yarn. The principle in all three was the flyer idea of the Saxony spinning wheel: in the original flyer machine as developed by Arkwright the origin of this idea was very clear, in the cap spinning it looked considerably different but in ring spinning, once the traveller is seen as a simple version of the flyer, the basic idea becomes clear again.

In the worsted mule about 90 per cent of the draft was accomplished by the standard four line roller drafting, exactly as used in other types of worsted spinning, but the remaining 10 per cent was inserted by spindle drafting as the carriage ran out and was utilised to remove irregularities in the yarn by drawing out any thick places. Spindle drafting with twist has always had the advantage over the more simple roller drafting in that it does lead to a levelling out, whereas any irregularities in the roller fed into a roller drafting system become worse.

In woollen carding the main concern was with the auxiliary motions of feeding, intermediate feeding and condensing. The endless feed was well known and widely used, indeed carding was hardly practical without it, but the main problem of getting the right quantities automatically onto the feed sheet remained. In 1870 this was probably still done by hand-weighing. The hopper feed which controlled the quantity automatically was invented by Bramwell and was soon widely used in two rather different forms: without a carefully balanced weighing control which was satisfactory for the early processes such as wool scouring and willeying, and the other for feeding the carding set where exact weighing was essential. Intermediate feeds occasioned much discussion, rather more than need have been the case, and the advantage of having the fibres laid traverse on the second feed sheet was fiercely argued. In the end the simpler system, the so-called Scottish, won the day. By 1870 condensing was generally accepted. There were two types of condenser so different in conception as to be almost two different machines. The first invention, the ring doffer, has been described. The period under discussion here brought the tape condenser, where the web of fibres, as taken from the last doffer, was cut into strips by tapes. In the original conception these were steel tapes but leather ones quickly took their place and provided the final solution to this difficult condensing problem that had for so long troubled the woollen spinner. By 1914 the woollen carding machine was complete and was in fact one of the most efficient, perhaps the most efficient, machine available to the industry.

Woollen mules, almost universal in the trade, were very little changed after 1870. Some thought was, however, given to the advantages that would arise if the technique of frame spinning could be applied to woollen yarn. The trouble was the short fibres used and the consequent difficulty of adapting roller drafting to woollen material. Being short, twist needed to be inserted during drafting to prevent breakage and the main difficulty lay in the fact that it was impossible to put permanent twist into a sliver which was held at both ends. Consequently, some form of false twist had to be inserted and the first machine did not appear until after 1900. It was then used to some extent for coarse carpet yarns but the machine's application to most sections of woollen spinning had made little progress before 1914.[36]

The problems occasioned by the increasing quantities of burrs found in wool both from the River Plate and from certain districts of Australia have been mentioned. None of the early methods for their removal was a complete success. The worsted and woollen sections of the trade found the answers in quite different ways. As far as worsteds were concerned, the combing process itself was a reasonably good remover except that the presence of too many large burrs tended to clog the machines. In addition in 1880 a Continental invention by MM Harmel Frères used accurately machined rollers to destroy this vegetable matter. Rather strangely, the woollen trade did not use this simple but excellent idea until the middle of the twentieth century. It preferred to remove the vegetable matter by carbonising, a chemical process discussed in the section on dyeing and chemical improvements below.

Preparatory weaving processes were little changed. Warping bars and the associated creels remained simple mechanisms. Drawing, the pulling of the threads through the heddles, and reeding, the pulling of the threads through the reed, were still hand processes. Weft winding machinery improved, mainly due to the efforts of an American machine-maker, Leesona, who introduced better contrivances for stopping when a thread broke and more delicate mechanisms to control the actual winding of the yarn onto the bobbins.

Turning to weaving, three main improvements, or perhaps one should say developments, occurred: looms were speeded up, the take-up and let-off motions were improved and so-called automatic weaving came very much into the picture. The early power looms had not run much faster than the old hand looms, something like 50 picks per minute being common on the broad loom and about 80 on the narrow. The question of the speed of early power looms is confused by the great variation in different branches of the trade. Looms weaving cotton warps with worsted wefts could go as high as 120 but those weaving cotton warps with shoddy weft had to be slower as there was considerable risk of the weft breaking; in any case, using such thick weft, shuttle changing was much more frequent and this meant that the advantages of higher speeds, even if they could be obtained, was not so great. With regard to all-wool cloths, speeds were higher with worsteds than woollens. With the former 90 picks per minute, or in the Bradford trade perhaps more, were possible but with fine woollens such as were made in the West of England and Scotland, 75–80 was more common.

Two basic types of looms continued to be used: the first was the plain or tappet loom in the Bradford trade; more important generally was the dobby loom, excellent for weaving plain and semi-fancy goods which comprised the main part of the products of the trade. Three loom-makers came to dominate this section: Hutchinson Hollingworth of Dobcross, Hattersley of Keighley and Hodgson of Bradford.[37] All made good durable looms which had the great advantage of being easily adaptable and all could be changed from plain to relatively fancy work, according to fashion demand. Although there were differences in detail they were basically of the same type.

The most useful loom improvements were in the systems involved in letting off the warp (the letting off motion) and winding on the woven cloth (taking up motion). The problem lay in the fact that the warp beam gets smaller as the yarn is woven up and the cloth beam gets larger. Hence, if both are driven simply and positively, an impossible position arises. The cloth would be wound on ever faster and in the end the tension would become so great that weaving could not take place. The winding on of the woven cloth was fairly easily solved by passing the cloth around a positively driven grated roller and then driving the actual cloth beam by a slipping clutch. The yarn take-off motion was more difficult; one could not wind the yarn around a grated roller and for most of the period what was called a negative let-off motion was used, the warp being simply pulled off the beam by the increased tension arising from the positively driven cloth beam working against a weight control. Towards the end of the century more positive, but not necessarily better, let-off motions were evolved. The problem, however, was not really solved and its importance can be gauged by the fact that around 1900 wool textile looms were known as negative or positive, depending on how the let-off motion was operated. Much of the skill of the loom-tuner (i.e. the engineer who looked after the loom) was involved adjusting these motions and many of the faults in cloth especially the tendency for bars to appear in the weft, arose from an unsatisfactory motion.

Automatic weaving was and remains a misnomer. Weaving will not become automatic until all processes in weaving are automated and a weaver is unnecessary; this had certainly not become the case by 1900 and has not, in fact, been achieved by 1982. In late nineteenth-century terms, automatic weaving simply meant that the weft supply was changed automatically, which did relieve the weaver of a very time-consuming job, and obviously led to a speeding up of the loom which did not have to be stopped for the changing of the shuttle. Consequently, even if loom speeds remained static, there was an increase in the actual picks inserted. Automatic weaving also meant that a weaver could have charge of more than one loom. Two or even four were common but in that case an automatic warp stop motion, to stop the loom if the warp broke, was also needed.

Like so many late nineteenth century inventions the automatic loom came from America, invented by Northrop in 1894. The loom was more widely adopted in the U.S.A. than in Britain and much more generally in the cotton trade, for which in fact it was invented. Two points mitigated against its use for wool textiles: first, the yarn, especially woollen and particularly low woollen yarn, was weak and to some extent the use of warp stop motions was counterproductive; second, and probably more important, the automatic weft delivery system had limitations. It was usually fitted on one side of the loom and this meant that single picks from any one shuttle could not be inserted. Indeed the original Northrop automatic loom was essentially one for plain weaving. The possibility of using automatic weaving for semi-fancy cloths did not come until the invention of the Automatic Worsted Loom (as it was called) by Crompton and Knowles in

1911.[38] The problem of having the shuttle changing on only one side still remained but up to four separate colours could be used. This loom was little used in Britain until after 1918. Its limitations have not been sufficiently stressed; designs with single pick colourings could not be woven and the vital single pick weft mixing, very necessary when weaving contrasting warp and weft colour systems, could not be used. There was also a more general limitation in what could be woven arising from the fact that there was only a single box at one side of the loom which, with four at the other side, meant that only four colours at a time could be made and the combinations possible with them were limited. Some traditional designs, such as certain of the tartans, contain more than four colours.

Perhaps a more personal comment is permissible here. One of the authors, who was engaged in the trade from 1930 to 1960, found even then that attempts to introduce automatic weaving to the semi-fancy trade were fraught with problems. Occasionally fashion would demand pick and pick cloths and, as stated above, these could not be woven. Similarly with the type of fabric with a light-coloured warp and a dark-coloured weft, it is quite amazing how much more uneven the cloth will look if the weft is inserted in pairs, not in single picks. Finally, the fact that only four shuttles can be used is a great disadvantage, not only because occasionally more than four colours are wanted but also because if one was weaving cloths with an overcheck it meant that the number of shuttles on the basic ground colour had to be reduced, thereby causing more unevenness to appear in the cloth, and what may appear a small point, single pick overchecking could not be used. The experience gained in the twentieth century certainly leads to the belief that criticisms made that the wool textile industry was slow in adopting automatic weaving are wrong and take little or no account of the problems sketched above. Two others were important: the weft-changing mechanism did put additional strain on the weft yarn and, of course, the more one speeded up the loom, which was one of the reasons for adopting automatic weaving, the more likely the warp was to break. In addition, the fact that the warp had to go through a warp stop motion also made breakage more likely and also made the repairing of this breakage more time-consuming. It was often found that the use of automatic weaving led to a drop, not an increase, in the actual efficiency of the loom. The wool textile trade, given the nature of the product it was manufacturing and the varied needs of the markets that it was supplying, had every reason for not venturing far into this so-called automatic weaving. The price advantage to be gained when suitable plain cloths were in demand would soon be outweighed by the danger of having looms standing idle because they could not manufacture what fashion demanded.

Finishing processes remained the most traditional of all. With the coming of the power loom, mending which had previously been done by the weaver, moved into the factories although of course remaining entirely a hand process. Women menders were usually the highest paid group of female workers and regarded themselves as socially superior to piecers and weavers. This development of mending inside the factory added considerably to the number of people employed. In most woollen and worsted mills, particularly those engaged in the fancy trade, the menders would account for between 5 and 10 per cent of the total labour employed. The cost of this operation had previously been rather disguised, having been done by the weaver. When it came into the factories, attempts were made to transfer part of this cost onto the weaver by fining him for faults in his cloths. Many of the minor strikes in the industry were caused by this problem and when the unions did finally re-establish themselves in the trade, this was one of the issues on which they fought most strongly.

The wet-finishing machines for scouring and milling remained unchanged. Two of these processes however call for mention, namely potting and blowing which were, in purpose at least, somewhat similar. The object was really one of setting the wool so that further shrinking was made more difficult. The concept had begun with the development of potting by the West of England inventor, J.C. Daniell, who had found that if a broadcloth was boiled in water for several hours whilst tightly wound on a roller, then the cloth was set. This was important with the traditional dressed broadcloth as it meant the dress finish, which was so essential, was made more permanent. The process can perhaps be understood if its similarity to the setting of hair is called to mind. Although it was not understood at the time, the physical structure of the wool fibre was changed. Potting was a very severe test for dyestuffs and many which stood scouring and milling well were not fast to potting; indeed, with the exception of the traditional broadcloth, such severe treatment was not needed. Dark indigo cloths were often potted, perhaps because indigo as a dye stood the severe treatment so well. A much simpler and less severe effect could be obtained by blowing steam through the piece either dry or wet. This process was known under a wide variety of names: originally as decatising because of its French origin, as blowing, or, when used for a rather different purpose in worsted finishing, as crabbing. When used for woollens and also for worsteds at the end of the finishing routine, the object was, as with potting, to set the cloth so as to prevent shrinking when the garment from it was being made. When used on worsted cloths before scouring the setting obtained prevented marks appearing in the cloth due to tensioning problems. The wide use of blowing, to give it the more general name, was the main development in wet finishing, indeed in any finishing routine, during the period.

The development of such processes as potting and blowing like other chemically based ones had long term effects which went well beyond the period covered in this volume. The tendency of wool to shrink has both disadvantages and advantages. As far as the latter are concerned, it enables the skilled tailor or dressmaker to mould the cloth at the shoulders and elsewhere. The hand craftsman can adjust this treatment according to the fabric he is handling. Such care became impossible with the growth of the wholesale making-up industry and the general use of the Hoffman Press; this made it much more necessary to be certain that the shrink limits had been included in the cloth by such processes as blowing or decatising.

Turning to the dry-finishing processes, tentering, cutting, raising and pressing, the most important changes were in the more general use of wire raising. The question of when wire raising had first been introduced is an interesting one. There were sixteenth and seventeenth-century prohibitions of its use, but they need not concern us here. It suffices to say that when the industrial revolution came, raising for the wool textile trade still meant raising with teazles. This process had in fact been mechanised earlier, in the sixteenth or seventeenth century, and the machine then used had been illustrated, but not put into general practice. In Britain, rather strangely, the one area which used it appears to have been the Gloucestershire section of the West of England trade. Most raising was still done by hand but, with the mechanisation of other processes, machine raising soon became common. The actual machine introduced was almost exactly similar to the one in seventeenth century illustrations. Obviously the use of wire – it was actually a form of the card wire used in carding – was quite straightforward as this material could easily be wound around a roller and these rollers placed in a machine of a not dissimilar type of that used for gig raising. At first the problem with wire raising was that it was unsatisfactory when done wet. The wires would clearly rust and cause stains. As most raising was, in fact, done wet the handicap was crucial. The coming of stainless steel overcame this disadvantage and more generally, the traditional wet raising finish, the dress finish, ceased to be much in demand. The blanket-like raise obtained by dry processing continued to have a considerable use and as a result wire gradually replaced gig raising, doubtlessly helped by the improved machines manufactured by Tomlinsons of Rochdale. Wet raising did, however, manage to retain a place particularly in the important low woollen trade, because the gigs had a less severe effect on the fabric and the risk of damaging the cloths made from the short shoddy and mungo was an ever-present thought in the finisher's mind.

Chemical Discoveries

It was, of course, in the chemical developments that the real progress took place. Many writers in the past have given insufficient credit to the skill of the wool dyers. When one examines pattern books, particularly those of the late eighteenth century, it is the quality of the colouring that most impresses. This is best seen in the superfine broadcloths of the West of England but equally so in a different way in the brilliantly coloured Norwich worsted materials. Indigo was the most widely used dye, not only for blues but with various yellow dyes for greens, with various reds for purples, and still to some extent for blacks when overdyed with fustic or madder. For blacks, however, more often logwood was used by 1800 and indeed vast quantities of this dye were consumed. Logwood gave an excellent black, when mordanted with iron, and a better one still when chrome mordants were introduced in the middle of the nineteenth century. Judging from pattern books, the main problem facing the earlier dyers was matching one batch to another and this had always been the case with the natural dyes which were not usually standardised.

It was in 1858 that W.H. Perkin, a student under the great German chemist Hoffman at the Royal College of Chemistry, discovered the first synthetic dye – mauve – and started a train of events that by the end of the century had established the great synthetic dyestuff industry. Fresh discoveries, many of them more important than the original mauve, followed. These early synthetic dyes were known as anilines and they coloured wool directly, that is without the complication of mordanting or vatting, but the shades although bright were not fast and for this reason their use was limited. However, the synthesis of madder also by Perkin and by two German chemists, Graebe and Liebermann, meant that this natural dye could be made artificially. This synthesis led to the coming of a wide range of alizarine dyes and these provided many valuable additions to the repertoire of the wool textile trade. But, until the end of the century, natural dyes to a large extent held their position, indigo for the various purposes already listed and logwood as the best black. Then the last years of the century brought two developments: synthetic indigo was introduced and because of its better standardisation soon replaced the natural product, and series of chrome blacks were invented which, after quite a struggle, largely replaced logwood.

What effect did the substitution of these new synthetic dyes have on the wool dyers? First and foremost, it must have made their difficult job rather easier, particularly for the exact matching of shades. The ever growing number of synthetic dyes must also have increased the number of shades available but it should be remembered that the old dyer, by mixing his relatively few natural dyes, did seem to be able to produce almost any colour. Compared with his skill it does not seem that the new discoveries added very much to the beauty or the saleability of the products he manufactured.

The wider chemical knowledge of the nineteenth century, particularly of organic chemistry, had three rather different effects. Improved chemical processing led to cheaper and better chemicals. New chemical processes were introduced, of which carbonising was the most effective; others related to waterproofing, mothproofing, shrink resistance, etc., with the cotton process of mercerisation rather strangely being of no value for wool. Most difficult to interpret at the time but also most significant for the future was the increased knowledge that was gained of the structure of the wool fibre itself.

The wool textile trade has always used large quantities of chemicals other than dyes. Traditionally they were urine for cleaning the wool,[39] olive oil or butter for preparing the wool for spinning, and fuller's earth or potash for cleaning the wool after weaving. During the actual dyeing large amounts of acids and other assistants such as sumach, verdigris, urine and, above all, sulphuric acid or vitriol as it was called, were used. Most of these were replaced during the period being described: soda ash took over for wool scouring, new forms of fatty acid oils such as oliens took over for spinning, and soda ash and soap for piece scouring. Acid, now manufactured in a pure state, continued to be used as the main dyeing assistant with wool. There were, of course, also the vital mordants, amongst which chrome was increasingly superseding alum. There were many others which cannot be considered here. The new chemical industry certainly produced them in a purer and more standardised form than before, and one has a hunch that these new versions of old products were in many cases more valuable to the dyer and others in the trade concerned with chemical processing than the more heralded synthetic dyestuff revolution.

The new chemically based processes were very important. In many cases they were really new; quite a different matter to the change in dyeing, which only involved new synthetic dyes, not new methods of dyeing. As far as processing was concerned synthetic indigo was treated in exactly the same way as natural indigo. From the viewpoint of the actual processing, the development of carbonising probably had the widest application.[40] It had long been known that acid destroyed vegetable matter but the application of this fact to wool processing came comparatively late and may have first been used for removing cotton from rags. Whether this suggested that the principle could just as well be applied to removing vegetable matter from wool is not clear. Certainly during the late nineteenth century it was applied to wool. Increasingly, as more wools with a large percentage of vegetable matter, especially burrs, came into the market, so carbonising became more widely adopted. A difference of approach between the woollen and worsted trades is noticeable. The shorter types of wool for the woollen trade when containing more than 5 per cent of vegetable matter were increasingly carbonised where grown. Firms specialising in scouring and carbonising short wools for the woollen trade became quite numerous. In Britain one firm, Jarmains, acquired a wide reputation. Worsted wools were not carbonised; much of the vegetable matter was crushed by the rollers described above. What remained came away with the noil and consequently noils were frequently carbonised. Finally, particularly in the woollen trade, although there was no reason why it should not have been done with all-wool worsteds, the cloth was quite frequently carbonised. As already stated, all that was needed was treatment with acid; the cloth was run in a machine similar to that used for wool scouring and then dried, usually called baking, which involved hanging in a high temperature for several hours. In this way the vegetable matter was turned to ash. Some mechanical means of removing the ash had to be carried out, and at least in the woollen trade, the best way was to run the piece for a period in a fulling or milling machine. A final wash off completed the process; ammonium sulphate could be used instead of acid.

Showerproofing was probably the most widely used chemical process after carbonising but it was decidedly less successful. The older broadcloth was so thick as to be largely showerproof although if it got really wet it must have been intolerably heavy and uncomfortable to wear. When cloth became thinner in the nineteenth century there came the demand for showerproofing. The arrival of rubber on the scene also affected the position, and cloth could then be rubberised, that is, given a coating of rubber which made it uncomfortable to wear but certainly waterproof. In between, wool textile fabrics could be treated with various chemicals which made the rain more likely to run off. The difficulty was that the more waterproofing material one used, the more sticky and uncomfortable the fabric became.

Finally, washability or shrink-resistance should be considered. Wool naturally shrinks, a result of its surface structure which prevents two way movement of the fibre and it is obviously possible to make it unshrinkable by removing the surface scales. This could be done by treatment with chlorine but only with a considerable effect on the handle. Chlorine could also be used to bleach wool but this was not very frequently done; wool was usually preferred dyed or, even if white, in its attractive, creamy-white natural colour.

These chemical processes, which although in some cases known before 1875 became really important only after that date, probably represented the major technical improvement that took place during the years until the beginning of the First World War.

Finally, how important was the increased knowledge of the structure of wool? The early dye chemists, notably the great Frenchmen of the eighteenth century, had some knowledge; without it they could not have advanced their theories of dyeing. But a really concentrated attack on the subject does not appear to have begun until about 1870 with the work of Professor Bowman, which can still be read with considerable interest. From then progress was continuous but the really great work, that of Astbury and Speakman, only came between the wars. It is doubtful whether what had been done before 1914 had had any great effect on processing the fibre.

The wool textile trade's reaction to these new dyes, chemicals and processes gives the lie to the argument sometimes made that the industry was disinclined to accept new technology. It jumped at the use of the new synthetic dyes as soon as they became available, it made full use of the excellent technical service the German dye manufacturers gave, it welcomed the idea of carbonising to further widen the raw materials available. The comparatively slow use it made of River Plate wools did not depend on the necessity of carbonising these but much more on the fact that the colonial supplies, plus the home-grown, gave them all the wool that they needed. The trade's tendency not to think much of waterproofing or shrink resist finishes rested on a well founded idea that if one wanted these properties, wool was not the right fibre to start with. And it felt with some justification that the complicated structure of the wool fibre did not really affect the processing. Years of craftsmanship had taught the trade how to handle the fibre that has often been described as difficult. If the trade had known that the main results of all this work on the structure of wool was to be a better understanding of how fibres are made and consequently the advent in the twentieth century of its rather arrogant and aggressive rival, the new synthetic fibre trade, it would probably have increased its dislike for the scientific gentlemen at the universities and technical colleges.

The refusal to use this scientific knowledge must, one supposes, be regretted; but is there really any evidence to suggest that a different attitude would have resulted in the production of better cloth or would have achieved better results than those which, by 1914, brought the trade to the highest point of its success?

9 Markets, Products and the State of Trade, 1870–1914

The Interpretation of Trade Statistics

Attempts to follow in detail the course, content and direction of wool textile exports during the nineteenth century are hindered by the complexities of trade statistics and the highly unsatisfactory classifications used. Moreover, changes in those classifications at various times make long-term comparison well nigh impossible in any detail. The variety of measurements, by weight, piece, or linear or square yard and changes over time to measurements used further reduce the usefulness of the statistics.

From time to time manufacturers and Chambers of Commerce battled to improve the methods of classification. With growing trade and the emergence of new types of cloth considerable dissatisfaction was being expressed by the 1850s. For some years the Bradford Chamber of Commerce pressed the Board of Trade to distinguish between woollen and worsted goods, complaining that they were 'mixed up in the strangest and most unaccountable manner, and names applied to goods which, if they have not become entirely obsolete, have long since ceased to represent any important article'.[1] The Leeds Chamber likewise approached the Board of Trade but although the latter was reported as having 'communicated its willingness to adopt, in its printed returns, a more complete classification of textile fabrics', the Bradford newspaper was still moved to record that '. . . the Board of Trade has appeared almost impenetrable to the idea of there being any distinction between woollen and worsted fabrics'.[2]

The pressure from the wool textile districts did however produce a reclassification from 1862. In that year most cloth began to be measured by yard and much more detailed descriptions were recorded, identifying more clearly types or widths of cloth and worsteds from woollens. But the wool textile trade remained suspicious of the published statistics which often did not appear to tally with its own experiences. Jacob Behrens was unwilling, for example, to believe the very high worsted stuff export figures for 1872.[3] It has been suggested that some woollen stuffs continued to be included with worsted stuffs until 1882 and that the separate classification for woollen yarns and worsted yarns, which was introduced in 1862, could not be trusted.[4] A particular problem arose over the method of counting cloth of mixed fibres and it was acknowledged in 1884 that over a series of years 'large quantities of piece goods of mixed materials, in which wool predominated, were erroneously entered as cotton manufactures'.[5] The adjustment in that year would appear to have led to a substantial increase in recorded trade in mixed worsteds.

Behrens was also suspicious of the care taken by Custom House officers and was very critical of them in 1886. He suggested that the exports to Germany during the 1860s and early 1870s showed 'an increase which was too startling to be believed and was, on investigation, found to be altogether wrong' because shippers, at the various ports, had been vying with each other as to who could make the largest returns each week. Behrens argued that there were inexplicable discrepancies between British wool textile export returns and the comparable import statistics of other countries.[6] His clamour for improvements, and other representations, did lead in 1890 to further clarification in the categories for wool textiles. Broad and narrow cloth of various types was further divided into heavy and light and some new descriptive categories were introduced such as worsted coatings; but, although these changes did permit a clearer view of the content of the trade, manufacturers were far from satisfied. A particular criticism many of them made, which is of considerable consequence for an interpretation of the level of trade in the late nineteenth and early twentieth century, was that measurement by linear yard failed to take into account changing widths of both broad and narrow cloth. A merchant, J.A. Godwin, claimed in 1903 that, as well as a higher class of trade being done, '30 years ago we sold narrow width goods from 30 inches down to 21 inches. The average width today is over 40 inches' with some cloth as much as 52 inches to 54 inches.[7] Similar points were made by such contemporary witnesses of the industry as Bowley and Clapham. Clapham commented that 'a yard is a rather vague thing' and stated that Bradford stuffs were getting wider.[8] Bowley, after a detailed discussion of the changes in width and weight of cloth, concluded that 'by the most elementary principles of statistics, we cannot use the results for fine measurements'.[9]

An additional difficulty of the trade statistics that was complained of from time to time was the accuracy of the recorded destination of wool textile exports. Accurate assessment of trade with Germany had been impossible, goods being routed through Holland and Belgium and recorded as trade to those countries. German and French merchants purchased some British goods for resale elsewhere alongside the products of their own manufacturers. Disruption of trading routes through war or other difficulties could divert trade indirectly through other countries and mask the true situation.

The above reservations clearly indicate that the Board of Trade statistics for wool textiles are a minefield that needs to be trodden with extreme care. For many aspects of the trade detailed changes cannot accurately be identified from the figures. Even generalisations about broad trends in content and direction of wool textile exports often have to be qualified to an unsatisfactory extent. The difficulties indicated above should be borne in mind in relation to the discussion of the course, content and direction of trade that follows.

War

The outbreak of hostilities between France and Prussia in the summer of 1870 finally brought to an end the lingering depression and created three years of prosperity for most of the trade. Although markets in France and Germany were somewhat disrupted the decline in competition from those two countries, and their demand for heavy woollens for war purposes, allowed much of the industry to increase output and exports. The woollen branch benefited more than the worsted. The Yorkshire heavy woollen district received orders for army goods from both sides and was able to trade very profitably. However the war was short and French political problems soon curtailed demand from that quarter.

Other parts of the industry had to make adjustments. The, mainly worsted, yarn trade was heavily dependent on German custom and the immediate impact of war caused much manufacturing capacity to be closed down. But the decline in yarn exports to Germany was mitigated somewhat by rising exports elsewhere and, during the following year, the trade gradually resumed a condition of 'extreme buoyancy' with optimism expressed that the development of manufacturing enterprise in Germany would allow continued expansion of yarn exports to that market.[10]

Exports of worsted manufactured goods were initially adversely

Table 39   *Exports of wool textile manufactured goods, 1860–1914*

	Million linear-yards[1]	£ million[2]		Million linear-yards[1]	£ million[2]
1860	190.4	12.2	1888	265.8	20.0
1861	164.4	11.1	1889	270.0	21.3
1862	167.0	13.2	1890	223.2	20.4
1863	217.2	15.5	1891	212.1	18.4
1864	241.0	18.6	1892	203.4	17.9
1865	279.2	20.1	1893	185.4	16.4
1866	281.9	21.8	1894	160.5	14.0
1867	249.5	20.2	1895	233.2	19.7
1868	269.1	19.6	1896	209.7	18.3
1869	303.0	22.7	1897	190.3	16.0
1870	292.7	21.7	1898	152.0	13.7
1871	367.9	27.2	1899	162.1	14.8
1872	412.5	32.4	1900	164.4	15.7
1873	345.9	25.4	1901	148.7	14.2
1874	326.7	22.8	1902	158.3	15.3
1875	317.5	21.7	1903	165.9	15.9
1876	282.2	18.6	1904	180.8	18.0
1877	261.4	17.3	1905	188.0	19.6
1878	257.9	16.7	1906	187.9	20.6
1879	251.3	15.9	1907	192.6	22.2
1880	262.4	17.3	1908	156.7	19.2
1881	272.9	18.1	1909	171.3	20.6
1882	265.2	18.8	1910	199.1	25.1
1883	255.9	18.3	1911	183.9	25.3
1884	290.3	20.1	1912	180.2	26.1
1885	268.1	18.8	1913	176.1	26.0
1886	274.3	19.7	1914	159.6	22.8
1887	282.6	20.6			

NOTES: [1] Excludes all goods not measured in linear yards.
[2] Includes all woollen and worsted manufactures.

affected by the war. Both France and Germany were major markets and the fall in demand from them occasioned a partial halt in manufacturing activity. Although home demand was good in 1870, following the previous good harvests, and commercial confidence should have been high with a low Bank Rate and relatively abundant money, there was the underlying fear that Britain could be drawn into the war. However, the setback to trade and confidence was very short. By the following year stocks were being replenished, prices were rising again and the export trade was very busy. This high level of activity continued throughout 1872 giving rise to the comment that they were the two years in which Bradford 'turned over the largest business it has ever done', although there was a local suspicion that the export figures were just too high.[11]

Other branches of the woollen trade, with the exception of those gaining from war orders, experienced a somewhat similar situation to worsted manufacturers. The flannel trade was reduced. The Huddersfield fancy trade suffered from the curtailment of French demand but was able to maintain manufacturing activity as a result of healthy orders from elsewhere. The union fancy trade was expanding, black doeskins were popular and the home market was brisk throughout 1870 and 1871 for a wide range of goods. There was some recovery in trade with the United States.[12]

In general it may be argued that although the Franco-Prussian war reduced, for a short period, the important British woollen and worsted trade to the two countries, the disruption of manufacturing activity in both countries and their inability to service their established customers allowed British manufacturers to take their place. This was particularly the case as regards France: in Elbeuf and Roubaix production was badly curtailed in 1870.[13] As a result British manufacturers found European, American and other orders being transferred to them. But although it was thought that French wool textiles were utterly disorganised by the war, the recovery of French manufacturing activity appears to have been very rapid so that British gains in French markets were not permanent and British trade with France suffered from the reversal, in 1874, of the post-1860 liberal trade policy.

Whereas rumours of war could cause great concern amongst manufacturers in many areas of the industry, war by no means necessarily had a serious effect on trade. In the last third of the nineteenth century the multifarious conflicts around the world were, on the whole, in areas which were only of minor importance to exports. And it would seem more than likely that the losses through trade disruption and uncertainty were often compensated for by Britain's major role as a supplier of army cloth and blankets. West Riding manufacturers claimed that in every war or conflict they found themselves supplying cloth to both sides. The gains, of course were in the heavy woollen district and were often at the expense of the worsted and better woollen trade. The possibility of war was often sufficient to persuade Dewsbury and district manufacturers to step up production. Merchant orders were quick to arrive although orders could be as quickly cancelled if danger of conflict diminished.

The American Civil War and the Franco-Prussian War were undoubtedly of major consequence to the industry but a host of smaller conflicts from the 1870s had their impact. In 1875 fear of a China war depressed some trade, but created brisk activity in the production of military cloth.[14] The following year news of a potential conflict between Serbia and Turkey began to arouse interest in Dewsbury. A contemporary commentator of the local trade reported: 'Although manufacturers here do not entertain the feeling that induced the Shetland minister and his flock to pray for plenty of wrecks, it is natural that they should look with more than common interest at the contest between Servia and Turkey'.[15] By the late summer of 1876 blankets were being despatched to both sides and many firms were busy with orders; later in the autumn some orders were cancelled when war had still not broken out. But early in 1877 merchants were advising firms in Dewsbury, Batley and Ossett that, should affairs in the East take a warlike turn, they would be prepared to place commissions 'to an immense extent', and local manufacturers admitted the benefits of war to them with such comments as: 'War means more blankets, more rugs, more army clothes; and though none, we believe, would be so vile as to wish that hostilities would begin, so that their particular trades might be benefited, there are numbers of firms who regard the rumours of war with a feeling approaching complacency.'[16]

Table 40   Exports of flannels and blankets, 1860–1914

Annual average	£ thousand	Annual average	£ thousand
1860–4	1237	1890–4	865
1865–9	1057	1895–9	787
1870–4	1123	1900–4	755
1875–9	1061	1905–9	620
1880–4	942	1910–14	810
1885–9	1014		

The Russian-Turkish conflict, when it came, produced vast orders through the rest of 1877, giving rise to full-time working and night working in Dewsbury and district, but the business was not all satisfactory. Turkish defeats led to some countermanded orders and the failure of the large firm of Messrs John Lee and Sons of Cleckheaton, which had had an immense order for blankets placed by a merchant on behalf of the Turkish government. Many smaller firms were subcontracted and were hurt by Lee's difficulties.[17] War, in this instance, whilst to the heavy woollen district's benefit, caused problems for some manufacturers elsewhere in the West Riding of Yorkshire. The war led to the curtailment of German trade with Russia, thereby again reducing German demand for British worsted yarn, and the smaller direct worsted piece trade with Russia and the Middle East also suffered, aggravating the general trade depression. Perhaps there were some mitigating consequences: the trade journal argued that the stoppage of corn exports from Russia would stimulate the grain trade in the United States, which in turn would help Bradford.

Such conflicts as these plus general orders from home and foreign governments for their armed forces occasionally provided the Dewsbury district with very welcome trade in periods of cyclical downturns. However the immensity of the orders, when they came, often created great difficulties. The industry could almost overnight change from a state of inactivity to a situation where its capacity was overstretched. Quick profits could be made but cancellation of orders and delays in the settlement of accounts also from time to time resulted. It was a precarious, risky business.

The Yarn Export Trade 1870–1913

The yarn trade, which had grown during the 1850s and 1860s, was booming, in terms of the volume of its exports in the early 1870s. It declined somewhat later in that decade but from 1880 was, in general, expansionary, to some extent helping to counteract the difficulties in the worsted cloth export trade. As has been noted in Chapter 7, the last third of the century witnessed, in the worsted trade, a movement to specialist spinning firms and a larger increase in spinning capacity than in that for weaving. With the latter being an easier skill for new manufacturing countries to acquire, as their number of looms rose so their demand for yarn increased to the benefit, in particular, of Britain, Germany, France and Belgium. These countries engaged in strong competition with each other and developed specialist skills in different types of yarn and consequent inter-trading.

The yarn trade was in worsted, alpaca and mohair; woollen yarn

Table 41 *Exports of alpaca and mohair yarn*

Annual averages	thousand lbs.	Annual averages	thousand lbs.
1865–9	1 001	1895–9	13 764
1885–9	12 697	1905–9	15 683

exports were of relatively little importance. Britain faced little competition in the alpaca and mohair yarn trade and developed her business in that area very substantially in the 1870s. Thenceforth the value of the trade gradually increased with only slight setbacks in 1887–8, 1898–1904 and 1908–9. Business was not greatly impeded by foreign tariffs; the major market, France, where, it was claimed mohair could not be very successfully spun because of the climate, allowed the yarns in free of duty.[18]

Worsted yarn for overseas markets was spun almost entirely in the West Riding of Yorkshire. Manufacturers in Huddersfield, Glasgow, the West of England and the Leicester hosiery district were also dependent on the Bradford district for various proportions of their needs. Within that district Keighley developed a dependence on worsted spinning, but there was also a general movement from manufacturing to yarn spinning. The result would appear to have been that, although overseas demand was steadily increasing, spinning capacity rose even more rapidly from the 1870s, leading to fierce competition and to profit margins being encroached upon. There was a recognition also that a part of the benefits of the yarn export trade was lost as some of the yarns came back in the form of finished goods, the importation of which reacted upon yarn spinners working for the home market. The transition to greater concentration on yarn spinning within the wool textile industry gradually increased the value of yarn as a proportion of total trade from about 20 per cent in the 1870s to 32 per cent in the peak year of 1898. By that year worsted, alpaca and mohair yarn exports were more valuable than worsted cloth exports.

Germany was consistently the major market for yarn exports, taking over two-thirds, and sometimes over three-quarters. The spinning industry was heavily dependent on the German market and

Table 42   *Exports of wool, worsted, alpaca and mohair yarns*

	thousand lbs.	£ thousand		thousand lbs.	£ thousand
1857–9	23 858	2998	1885–9	56 054	5393
1860–4	29 447	4351	1890–4	60 339	5517
1865–9	35 788	5643	1895–9	76 862	6849
1870–4	40 148	6054	1900–4	72 327	5684
1875–9	35 684	4877	1905–9	77 057	7244
1880–4	40 304	4351	1910–13	88 410	8558

subject to any fluctuations experienced by the German manfacturing industry, particularly as a result of tariff charges in other markets. Marriners of Keighley were in this position, for example. They traded directly, and through Bradford merchants, with Continental firms and had their trade mark registered in Germany.[19] In 1886 Henry Mitchell, a Bradford merchant, was complacently forecasting that Germany would never be able 'to make yarn as good as we can in this country', although he acknowledged she would in due course be able to supply her own manufacturers with yarn.[20] Within only a few years however there were reports that the worsted yarn industry in Germany was rapidly expanding, leading to over-production, and by 1905 there were complaints that British spinning frames could not be kept going, 'even in selling to Germany'.[21] It was suggested that a reason for the yarn trade with Germany surviving as well as it did was that much of it was conducted by German merchants. A trade journal reported. 'We are told if Bradford had depended on English travellers and agents in Germany to push the sale of her yarn, the Germans by this time would probably have been spinning the yarn themselves, and possibly exporting some of it to this country'.[22]

The quality of British yarn was, however, generally acknowledged as very good for the price and its admission to Germany at a mere nominal duty helped the trade to be maintained. Other markets, however, were less stable. High tariffs almost obliterated the United States market for example. Difficulties in some markets were overcome by a broadening of the trade to a wider range including Japan, the Middle East and British Possessions. A large export business developed with Egypt in the 1890s, with 90 per cent of Egyptian imports coming from Britain by the middle of the decade.[23] This broadening of trade is confirmed by the ledgers of E. Posselt and Co., the Bradford yarn dealers.[24]

Whilst the yarn export trade maintained a fairly healthy existence from the 1880s, imports were also, however, beginning to flood in and were causing great concern in some areas of the wool textile industry. Belgium was the major competitor and very successfully gained, indeed overwhelmed, some sections of the British market. The Belgian spinning industry developed particularly in the 1870s and by 1878 was exporting nine-tenths of its production of over 30 million pounds. Although its output was much lower than its counterparts in England, France and Germany, the home consumption of its products was low. By the mid-1890s Belgium was exporting over 12 million pounds of woollen yarn to Britain. Her success arose from her specialisation in mule spun yarn, particularly for hosiery manufac-

Table 43   *Imports of woollen and worsted yarns*

Annual averages	Weaving yarns		Total yarns	
	Million lbs.	£ million	Million lbs.	£ million
1880–4	12.98	1.61	13.86	1.76
1885–9	16.98	2.00	18.24	2.02
1890–4	14.86	1.61	16.16	1.84
1895–9	18.20	1.81	19.37	2.01
1900–4	22.07	2.18	22.70	2.27
1905–9	25.30	2.51	25.88	2.58
1910–13	29.04	3.00	29.66	3.09

ture. The Leicester trade imported large amounts. Huddersfield worsted manufacturers used quantities of Belgian yarn by the 1880s although by no means all manufacturers were convinced of its quality and some after trying it reverted to the British product.[25] Scottish manufacturers by 1905 were also using large amounts of hosiery yarn from Belgium, adversely affecting local spinners, who were also seeing less demand from Yorkshire, as imports were introduced there.[26] There were pleas for tariffs from Scottish spinners, one of whom claimed in 1905 that 'if we could make all these yarns at home we should be giving employment to about 50 additional yarn spinning mills . . .' and argued that a duty was necessary to equalise the British manufacturing disadvantage.[27]

The reasons for the Belgian success were much debated in the trade journals, and in evidence to the Commission on Depression in Trade and Industry and to the Tariff Commission. There was unanimous agreement that lower wages and longer hours were a great advantage to her. There were complaints also of her selling below cost at times of depression, but much of the Belgian success must be put down to her catering for specific and changing needs. Dry combed tops from shorter stapled wool were mule spun to often finer counts and the soft yarn produced came very much into demand in Leicester, Glasgow and Nottingham for what was called cashmere hosiery, replacing to some extent the use of local and Yorkshire yarns. There were attempts to spin similar yarn at home but few manufacturers took up the technique in spite of contemporary criticism that they should be making more effort. Excuses were given that the British climate was not suitable, that markets were insufficient to invest in the new machines and that, with cheaper labour and longer hours abroad, investment in new machinery and in the training of labour would not be fruitful.[28] This would, however, seem to be an area where British spinners were slow to react; there is little evidence that any substantial attempt was made to compete with the Belgian product. It seems to have been very much the case that slowly changing demand for types of hosiery yarn either caught British spinners unawares or was dismissed by them as a passing fashion.

As demand for machine knitting yarns expanded, orders from hand knitters decreased. The teaching of knitting in Board Schools gave some stimulus and demand from the Colonies was rising but at home 'ladies do not knit as they used to', this being explained by one manufacturer as the result of women taking up 'golf and cycling and such things now, instead of making stockings and fancy articles'.[29]

The Course of Trade 1873–1900

The buoyancy of business during the war years had encouraged some optimism. Although there was an acknowledgment of 'exceptional causes' and 'fictitious demand', high expectations gave rise to much new investment, extending manufacturing capacity and thus exacerbating the impact of depression when it descended in 1873. The value of exports of wool textiles which had reached a peak of over £32.4 million in 1872 fell each year in succession until 1880. The experience was less dismal in terms of volume of trade, but exports measured by linear yards and thus taking no account of changes in widths, fell from 412 million yards in 1872 to 251 million yards in 1879. The worsted branch of the industry clearly fared far worse than most woollen manufacturing activity. In value terms, the decline in the overseas trade in worsted accounted for all but 15 per cent of the overall fall. In terms of volume, with the exception of small reductions in the 1870s in the exports of flannels, blankets, carpets and druggets, other woollen cloth exports as a whole increased by nearly 15 per cent. Cotton warped cloth bore the brunt of falling overseas demand for worsted but exports of all-wool cloth also fell substantially. Comparisons with the exceptional years of 1871 and 1872 lead to false impressions but the volume of wool textile exports were about 7 per cent lower in 1877–79 compared with the corresponding period in the previous decade. In the woollen branch of the industry however volume of exports was over one-third higher in the later period.

Gloom descended surprisingly quickly on the trade in 1873 in spite of good wool prices and foreign trade remaining relatively high. General comments of monotonous trade and low profits mask a variety of successful features in 1873 and 1874. The Huddersfield district, on the whole, maintained full time working with continued orders for worsted coatings, black doeskins, woollen cords and fancy union and cheap woollen trouserings. Lower quality union goods were less in demand in the heavy woollen district. Leeds manufacturers encountered only spasmodic demand but the yarn spinners of Halifax and Wakefield, in spite of falling overseas demand and doubts about wool prices, maintained reasonable business.[30]

The following two years brought a steady increase in problems for many sectors of both woollens and worsteds. Trade reports suggest fluctuating business, almost month by month. Early in 1875 there were reports of heavy failures, acute competition and overproduction;[31] by the early summer it was reported that trade was reviving with demand from Canada, France and Germany and reasonable business in tweeds and meltons, but orders were small and spasmodic, creating uncertainty.[32] Attempts to reduce wages in Dewsbury and Batley led to labour disputes. United States business was adversely affected by the higher tariff. Low woollen manufacturers were becoming increasingly aware of growing competition from French manufacturers, particularly those in Elbeuf and Castres. In the autumn home and foreign demand for heavy woollens showed signs of improving, with good orders from Germany, Hungary, Italy and the Levant. Austrian demand revived after duties there were reduced. The mild weather early in the winter held back home demand but frost and snow in December brought improved orders for blankets and overcoatings.[33] The worsted trade continued dull; there were cheerful periods but confidence suffered on reports of overseas failures, notably in New York and Leipzig, and of poor harvest prospects in India, Europe and America, although the trade journal was somewhat out of sympathy with the concern, arguing that the Bradford trade was 'sensitive to almost every influence that moves commerce all over the world – and our merchants are more on the *qui vive* than farmers – they are disposed to grumble and see clouds overhead however favourable the state of things may appear to the ordinary observer'.[34]

The following year, 1876, showed little change. Orders remained small and spasmodic. Stocks built up, failures became more frequent. Home demand compensated for export difficulties to some extent, but another mild autumn reduced winter orders. The Scottish industry maintained regular work and some sections of the Huddersfield trade 'kept exceptionally and profitably busy'. In worsteds, as in woollens, manufacturers of 'specialities' remained very active even complaining of scarcity of hands, but, in general, both in the woollen and worsted trades short time became more common and profits suffered.[35]

From 1877 to 1879 slow, dull and dragging were the adjectives frequently used by the trade press to describe business; and that press gives the distinct impression that manufacturers were becoming more pessimistic in their expectations and more tense in their fears. The value of exports continued in rapid descent, the volume of trade was better sustained. Some of the successful activities of the previous years, such as the manufacture of black doeskins at Huddersfield, disappeared although the search for new successful specialities occasionally brought good results. In July 1877 the *Textile Manufacturer*, reflecting on the causes of the difficulties, was critical of the previous increases in productive power caused often, it suggested, by sons no longer content with the size of mill operated by their fathers and grandfathers and by men hitherto unconnected with the trade launching into it, and forecast an unpleasant outlook. 'How shall business be maintained', it demanded. 'That it will be, no Englishmen will deny, but many dreary paths may have to be trodden before healthiness is again characteristic.'[36]

This prognosis held good for the rest of 1877 and the following two years. Trade remained lifeless but not disastrously low. Occasional worries of looming extra difficulties were, on the whole, proved incorrect. Confidence would appear to have become worse than the volume of trade being carried out should have justified. Reassuring signs were, from time to time, most noticeable in the home market and, even at this stage, it is evident that manufacturers were beginning to follow much more closely the prospects for, and the course of, home demand. Tariffs increasingly aggravated trade. Fashion changes brought the uncertainty of how permanent they were to be. Attempts to reduce wages were widespread, bringing inevitable adverse labour reaction. Perhaps for many individual manufacturers struggling to produce on the barest profit margins the greatest worry was a financial one: the concern that failures elsewhere would pull them down as well.

The Economist's Commercial Review in March 1879, written of course before it was evident that an upturn of trade was beginning, suggests a very despondent wool textile trade. The Leeds woollen trade was described as having gone through the worst year 'that this generation has seen', with diminished turnover, reduced profits and failures. 1879 was described as a year of 'general difficulty, depression and disaster' in Huddersfield and similar gloomy descriptions emanated from elsewhere, but there were also many firms working to reasonable capacity. Trade was less secure, less profitable, less confident, but manufacturing activity continued on a substantial scale with considerable innovating progress. Leeds manufacturers were reported as paying more attention to colour and pattern. The ready-made clothing industry, still quite young in Leeds, was steadily increasing its business, to the advantage of woollen manufacturers. Although Bradford worsted manufacturers had less reason for optimism as they saw their markets become more difficult, Huddersfield woollen and worsted manufacturers were happier, maintaining satisfactory levels of employment and holding markets at home and abroad. Their situation was well summed up by *The Economist*:

> The trade of the district has again largely developed in the direction of greater variety, both in respect of design, fabric and price, and our manufacturers have thereby adapted their productions ever more completely than heretofore to the varied requirements of the masses, for whom they chiefly make it their business to cater.[37]

From the summer of 1879 there were fairly general accounts of improving business. The factory inspector reported that the West Country industry was taking a more hopeful turn.[38] As early as April Bradford manufacturers were wondering whether the worst of the depression was over. Huddersfield was obtaining better business by the following month but comments from Leeds suggest that signs of recovery there were slower to appear.[39]

Recovery was sustained and for the next 10 years the export trade for the industry as a whole and measured by value shows a remarkable steadiness. The average value of exports of wool textile manufactures was £19.4 million per annum from 1880 to 1890 and in no year in the decade did the value fluctuate more than 10 per cent from the average. However, this consistency of performance was to some extent attained towards the end of the decade, by an increase in woollen exports making good a shortfall in worsteds. All the same the worsted export statistics, by value, show considerable constancy from 1880 to 1887, although this was at a level of little more than half the value of those exports from 1864 to 1874. In terms of volume, exports of woollen cloth fluctuated rather more during the decade. The trade improvement of 1879 was sustained until 1882. The next three years brought a slight fall but trade remained above the level of the 1870s. It revived again in 1886 and continued to increase until the end of the decade. The annual average linear yardage of woollen cloth, excluding flannels, blankets and other minor items, exported in 1887–9 was over one-third higher than the corresponding figure for 1877–9.

The worsted trade in the same period had somewhat different

experiences. The value of exports marginally revived to the middle of the decade and then gradually fell until the big revival of 1890. In terms of linear yardage exports showed little recovery before 1884 but in that year there was a big revival. For the next three years they remained above the level of 1877 to 1883 but then, in 1888, resumed a steady fall, which in the early 1890s became increasingly rapid.

Generalisation from the huge volume of commercial reports that were appearing by the 1880s is undoubtedly dangerous. Many of them were recognised at the time as being ludicrously contradictory and gave rise to much debate and dispute, some of which no doubt was a result of the complexity of the industry and its products which could mean that manufacturers even in the same town were experiencing very different trading conditions. However, it is perhaps fair to say that gloomy trade reports seem to have somewhat outnumbered the more optimistic ones.

The continuing recovery of 1880 was aided by the American boom. The reports suggest that in the woollen trade improvement was quite widespread. A movement in fashion towards light or pastel shades encouraged demand for overcoatings and ladies' jackets and mantles. Cheap and medium tweeds continued to become popular.[40] In the following three years comments about the woollen trade develop more optimism but complaints of low profit margins continue to abound. The factory inspectors commented in October 1883 that a large amount of work was being carried out in Scotland and the North of England, with some branches of industry being busier than ever before. But they reported that 'the complaint on the part of employers has been almost universal that they have made little or no profit.'[41] By 1882 there were reports of improving orders for worsted coatings, and a year later manufacturers of other worsteds were aware of some recovery.[42] By 1886 the Factory Inspectors were recording very marked activity with indications of permanent rather than spasmodic improvement in the Bradford trade.[43]

The evidence of individual manufacturers and merchants, and of Chambers of Commerce, in the mid-1880s, to the Commission on Depression in Trade and Industry, provides a mass of contemporary information on the previous problems, current state and future prospects of most branches of the wool textile industry in their various locations. But there was no unanimity about trade improvement by 1885–6. Behrens believed the tide had turned in Bradford.[44] Cleckheaton Chamber of Commerce denied the existence of depression but the Chamber of neighbouring Birstall reported that depression was gradually increasing. Dewsbury Chamber reported no encouraging signs, Heckmondwike wrote of progressively bad and un-profitable business. However, reports of low profits were universal.[45]

As indicated above cloth exports were quite buoyant in 1886 and 1887, with better levels of trade to Europe and both parts of the American continent. European demand slumped somewhat in 1888 but business elsewhere and the home market kept mills busy. Fancy fabrics were popular, worsted coatings were still in demand; the worsted trade generally was busy. Sir Henry Mitchell was reported as saying that a larger volume of trade had been done in the Bradford district than during any of the 40 previous years, and the trade journal mentioned renewed investment in new mills and machinery. The heavy woollen district was busy and the woollen trade elsewhere quite active, except perhaps for flannels.[46]

The next year started with manufacturers in a state of reasonable optimism. Particularly encouraging signs were increasing activity in the Yeadon and Guiseley trade, which had been rather stagnant, an improvement in Eastern markets and a more varied demand from the European continent, which again benefited Huddersfield woollen and worsted manufacturers in particular. Lighter goods were most in favour although many of the monthly trade reports describe manu-facturers in the heavy woollen district as being busy. Complaints of poor profits continued regularly although such figures as we have do suggest profits were being made, sometimes at very respectable levels. Summing up the year 1889 the *Textile Manufacturer* wrote:

> Never was a year so exhaustively reviewed, by pen and tongue, as 1889 has been. Columns upon columns of small type in the woollen district newspapers, after dinner speeches galore, and endless talk on 'Change' and everywhere else, have been more or less helping the general public to arrive at its verdict upon the last twelve months. Writers who have arraigned the last year have differed singularly upon many points of detail, but on the most important fact of all they are almost completely at one. They agree that taking one department of the woollen trade with another, the period under notice was decidedly more prosperous than any twelve months since the famous 'years of plenty'.[47]

The report continued that 'authorities concur in predicting better things still for the year newly dawned'. Initially they were right but 1890 marked the beginning of another substantial downturn in the fortunes of both the woollen and worsted industries.

Thus, on the whole, it seems difficult to deny that much of the decade of the 1880s was a satisfactory period for the wool textile trade. Profits were nowhere near those of the halcyon days of the

1860s. Uncertainties caused by fashion, foreign tariffs and lack of regularity of orders continued but labour stayed at work, manufacturers were persuaded to recommence investment and the earlier despondency of the difficulties faced in some foreign markets were dispelled at least partly by steady improvements in demand from the home population. The ready-made clothing trade continued its progress and from time to time there were encouraging comments that working men were purchasing apparel more regularly and of better quality.

In 1889 the value of wool textile exports reached the highest level for 15 years. But for each of the next five years trade declined to the extent that by 1894 it had fallen to the value of the early 1860s. The decline in value over the five years was 27 per cent; in terms of volume it was nearer 40 per cent. The impact of the McKinley tariff, which was the major factor in the export depression, is discussed below. There were also other problems however. The stoppage of some firms as a result of the shutting off of American trade had broader financial repercussions; in Huddersfield 'several of our oldest and best known manufacturing firms have been obliged to call their creditors together and the enterprise of their neighbours is apparently checked by the wondering enquiry: whose turn will it next be to go down.'[48] Huddersfield manufacturers also blamed the strike in the coal trade for some of their problems.[49] The new French tariff in 1892 hurt many manufacturers in both Yorkshire and Scotland. The revolution in Brazil caused a temporary setback. The heavy woollen district in 1893 suffered from the ban on the importation of rags as a result of the outbreak of cholera on the Continent.[50]

The depression reached its depths in 1894, a year described in the *Bradford Chamber of Commerce Annual Report* as 'one full of disappointments for the wool trade generally and the Bradford trade in particular'. By contrast the value of trade in 1895 almost reached the best levels of the 1880s. The reform of the American tariff was mainly responsible; yardage of cloth sent to the United States rose fourfold compared with the previous year. The home and Continental trades were also quite active. A change in fashion to brighter dress fabrics boosted the Bradford trade, where, it was reported, merchants were buying back goods to resell at handsome profits.[51]

However the recovery was somewhat temporary as trade again declined for the next three years. Over-reaction to the more favourable American tariff glutted that market and exports to the United States in 1896 and 1897 were only about one-half of the peak 1895 level; they sank to less than a fifth in 1898 following the disastrous

Dingley tariff. Trade to Eastern Europe was adversely affected by unsettled political problems but, once again, the home market provided some compensation for manufacturers.[52]

The problems in the major market of the United States, where wool textiles, more than any other industrial goods, were hurt by tariffs, made the industry the odd man out in the general recovery of British industrial output from 1896. It was not until 1902 that long term and rapid recovery was to emerge for the industry. The years 1898 to 1901 were disastrous; home demand did not provide much comfort in the face of the difficulties of exporting to both Europe and North and South America, but yarns exports were the highest ever from 1895 to 1899, although they fell in the following two years. Colonial demand, particularly from Canada and India, was more buoyant.[53]

The change in fashion away from Bradford's staple product of cotton warped stuffs was slightly compensated by a fashion change in favour of Yorkshire worsted manufacturers. From the 1870s onwards exports of worsted coatings became of considerable significance to the trade. The worsted coatings trade was a men's trade. It originated in the late 1850s or early 1860s in the Huddersfield/Halifax area and initially progressed very slowly.[54] No worsted coatings appear to have been exhibited at the international exhibitions of 1862 and 1867, but by the 1870s, they were developing into a substantial business. The trade journal reported in 1877 that there had been 'recent rapid progress of better class worsted coatings in Huddersfield' and that they were superseding black superfine and other woollen cloth. Later that same year it recorded that demand for high class coatings was still rising, with good trade to the United States.[55]

Worsted coatings were exhibited by various Leeds, Huddersfield and Halifax firms at the 1876 Philadelphia Exhibition. Bradford hardly participated but other evidence suggests that Bradford's entry into the worsted coating trade was somewhat late.[56] In evidence to the Commission on Depression in Industry and Trade, Henry Mitchell stated that worsted coatings were not manufactured in Bradford to any extent in 1873. But the trade developed rapidly thereafter.[57] The *Bradford Observer* reported at the end of 1874:

> For some years past, worsted coatings have been made in small quantities by a very restricted number of Bradford manufacturers. Although there are still but a few . . . the trade has undergone a very notable development during the past year and several firms have been gradually adapting their machinery to their production.[58]

Table 44   *Export of worsted coatings*

Annual average	million yards		million yards
1882–4	4.3	1900–4	17.6
1885–9	15.0	1905–8	20.0
1890–4	25.5	1909–13	23.6
1895–9	23.7		

The new product provided severe competition to Leeds woollen coatings and to West of England coatings. It was affecting the market for the latter by 1875 and competition persuaded some West of England manufacturers to experiment with worsted; some firms succeeded, most did not.[59] In 1886 Henry Mitchell forecast that 'it was likely to be a permanent trade'. By that date it had become an important part of the Yorkshire worsted industry, producing reasonable profits.[60] The Board of Trade classified worsted coatings separately from 1882 and thus, as Table 44 shows, the export business may be followed year by year thereafter; exports clearly progressed very rapidly through the 1880s. By 1890, when 27.3 million yards were exported worth £5.3 million, the major market was the United States but only one-third of exports went there. The rest were distributed widely throughout the world with 42 per cent going to European countries and 15 per cent to British Possessions. The McKinley tariff disturbed trade and the proportion going to the United States fell somewhat. The Wilson tariff of 1895 created a fantastic boom with worsted coatings exports to the United States increasing fourfold compared with the previous year. In 1895 57 per cent of exports went to the United States. After that boom the trade gradually declined again and reached a very low level after the Dingley tariff of 1898 and did not to any great extent recover; but this shortfall was gradually made up by other markets in the decade before the First World War. European trade had become of only minor importance but major markets emerged in Canada, Australia, Chile and the Argentine. In 1907 14 per cent of worsted coatings exports went to South America and 47 per cent to British possessions. Thus, except for the slight setback after 1898, Mitchell's prophecy in 1886 that the worsted coatings trade would be permanent was true, at least until the First World War.

After 1900 the Huddersfield district also developed its reputation for all-wool worsted suitings. This was an important fashion trade giving rise to a number of famous firms and also to a host of small specialist weaving firms that bought in yarn.

The Course of Trade 1901–14

The disastrous years of the 1890s were followed from 1901 by a massive export boom for woollen cloth. From the trough of 1901 to the peak of 1912 the value of wool textile cloth and yarn exports almost doubled and, apart from a relatively minor slump in 1908, the period was one of great prosperity for many branches of the trade with high profits and continuing success in new markets. In the home market, although imports of yarns remained high, cloth imports fell very substantially.

As foreign trade began to pick up from 1902 confidence amongst manufacturers was only slowly restored. The trade commentaries of 1902 and 1903 continue full of tales of woe;[61] the drought in Australia was still curtailing wool imports; wool prices were rising although there are few complaints of a great scarcity of wool; the domestic clip of wool was also falling. The industry was becoming aware of very noticeable changes in fashion, the consequences of which were gradually becoming apparent. Exports to most markets were showing increases.

In the woollen industry from 1904 more optimism is evident. Japanese demand for army and navy goods suddenly created great activity in the Colne and Holme valleys, the Heavy Woollen District and the Halifax area. Khaki cloth, blankets and heavy serges were in great demand. Trade to the Far East soared in 1904 and 1905. It has been estimated that the Heavy Woollen district supplied £1.5 million of goods to Japan in those years.[62] Not all wool textile manufacturers shared in the rising prosperity. Firms trading with South Africa suffered from the glut in that market following the ending of the Boer War. Worsted manufacturers had plenty to complain of. The high wool prices and trade uncertainties led to much bargaining within the trade and to margins being cut very fine. Stocks were high and a fall in wool prices was feared. Demand for mohairs was good however and the trade press acknowledged that enterprising manufacturers could do well with novelties. In spite of the gloom in much of the worsted industry it should be pointed out that the volume of exports was somewhat higher than in the previous few years.

In the West of England and the South of Scotland there were clear signs of better times. The former area, having seen fashions move against it, began to see the reverse happening; the few surviving firms received a flood of orders in 1906 and responded with increased overtime and new investment. Rising demand for rainproof coatings, riding tweeds, flannel suitings and motor coatings all benefited the region. Colonial demand for its products was rising but most of its activity was for the home market. It hardly noticed the downturn in 1908 and its trade reports up to the war indicate few problems. It claimed increasing success in continental markets and in South America, and a restoration of some demand from the United States. The reasons for this sudden and welcome revival were manifold. The West of England shared, of course, in the movement of both home and foreign demand away from worsteds towards woollens. Its lighter cloths were popular in the tropics; the new fashion demands resulting from cycling and motoring, cricket and tennis also suited its products.[63] However it also seems apparent that, in this period, there was a better entrepreneurial response to fashion trends and novelties.

Table 45   *Exports of wool textile fabrics, 1900–13 (£ million)*

Annual average	United Kingdom	France	Germany
1900–4	15.8	8.7	11.5
1909–13	24.6	8.2	12.8

SOURCE: *Survey of Textile Industries*, III, 1928, p. 173

In the South of Scotland good reports emerge from 1905 onwards. It too did well in home and colonial demand. Tweeds were in favour and there was enough business for Scotland to secure orders as well as Yorkshire and the West of England, especially as local manufacturing capacity had been reduced in the 1890s. The reports emanating from the Scottish woollen trade do not however portray a consistent picture of commercial success. 1908 was a bad year, but from then until the war a range of factors worked in the area's interest. The death of the King brought heavy demand for black and grey cloth. There was an 'increasing call for wind and dust resisting cloths consequent on the ever increasing use of the motor car for travelling and holiday purposes'.[64] And the district also saw rising activity in the hosiery trade.

In 1907 the value of wool textile cloth exports reached their highest level for over 30 years. The gain was entirely to woollen manufacturers. Canada was continuing to increase its business. South African demand was recovering. Japanese and South American orders remained buoyant as did Continental demand from Germany and Holland. United States orders remained low. There were almost universal reports of satisfactory home business although it seems likely that profits did not rise as rapidly, as rising raw material prices were not always compensated for by a relative rise in finished product prices.

The slump of 1908 was not consistent in its consequences. High world food prices, the failure of the Indian harvest, commercial failures in China and Japan, and the commercial crisis in America caused a fall in demand for woollen and worsted tissues, blankets, carpets and flannels. Worsteds were hit worst. Exports of them, by value, fell by 25 per cent compared with the previous few years. Exports of woollen cloth remained well above the level of the first half of the decade. But home demand was damaged by unsuitable weather and labour disputes in the North of England. Falling raw material prices left many manufacturers having to sell their stocks at a loss.

The following year recovery gradually got under way and in 1910 the increase in the volume of exports was by far the greatest ever for a single year. Almost all classes of woollen goods participated; worsteds experienced a slight revival; blankets, flannels, carpets, rugs and hosiery all saw their overseas markets expand. The commercial review for the year in *The Economist* in February 1911 must have been exceptional because there is hardly a word of reservation about the booming state of the industry. In Bradford 'never have combs put through more wool', yarn demand reached its highest level, profits were better.[65] Rochdale reported the best level of business for years. Home demand throughout the industry was good. A spell of winter weather in November brought early demand for overcoatings and heavy cloth generally.

The prosperity continued for two more years. Favourable reports continued to flow in, although rising prices made some traders jittery. There were a host of potential problems but none of them seems to have come to much.[66] In foreign markets the fear of conflict over the Morocco question, the war between Turkey and Italy, revolution in China, new tariffs in Japan and the uncertainty of potential tariff changes in the United States, all episodes which in previous decades would have led to much uncertainty and pessimism, passed almost unnoticed. At home labour disputes did have some adverse consequences. The coal strike in the spring of 1912 left mills short of fuel. The vogue for the close fitting, narrow hobble skirt did not omen well.[67] And the first reports appear, in relation to furnishing fabrics, of artificial silk replacing natural fibres, particularly mohair. In the 18 months before the outbreak of war business continued high but signs

Table 46   *Net imports of wool textiles, 1900–13 (£ million)*

Annual averages	Fabrics	Yarns
1900–4	8.7	2.3
1909–13	5.8	3.0

of recession did become more and more evident by late in 1913 in spite of the more favourable United States tariff. The trade was probably rightly convinced of the beginnings of a downturn in the business cycle. But after the initial dislocation to markets caused by war the sudden surge of military orders from September 1914 resulted in feverish activity throughout the industry.[68]

Thus the main features of the decade before the war are clear. A rise in the relative importance of woollen goods in home and foreign markets, directed by the fashion movements to tweeds and more 'sporty' goods, was evident. And the export trade as a whole recovered as a result of the success of British woollen cloth. British manufacturers extended foreign business at the expense of their main competitors in France and Germany. The home market was likewise rising and more steady. Fashion changes and the ability of home manufacturers to respond to them led to a reduction in the import of foreign cloth although the expansion of the industry resulted in a rise in demand for foreign yarn.

The Tops and Noils Trade
An extension of the trade in partly manufactured goods began to occur in the 1880s with rising foreign demand, particularly from Germany, for tops and noils. Until 1890 the trade returns do not separately distinguish tops and noils from waste but they would suggest that this particular trade began to develop substantially from 1884. By 1890 exports of them were valued at over £1.25 million, in roughly equal proportions. Table 47 shows the course of the trade thereafter. Whereas exports of noils developed only slowly, the growth of the tops export trade was much more rapid, extending in its peak year of 1912 to almost 45 million pounds, valued at almost £3.5 million. The expansion of this trade had long been forecast, with some trepidation, by worsted yarn spinners who thought, by the 1880s, that the extension of spinning capacity in many of their foreign markets was inevitable. But although the growth of the tops trade was very rapid, particularly in the 1890s and up to 1903, it did not replace

Table 47   Exports of tops and noils

Annual averages	Thousand lbs.	£ thousand	Thousand lbs.	£ thousand
1890–4	10 426	621	9543	639
1895–9	12 300	644	22 403	1325
1900–4	10 400	592	35 163	1884
1905–9	13 013	855	35 050	2751
1910–13	18 478	1171	42 144	3328

demand for worsted yarn, although the latter showed a rather lower rate of growth. One witness to the Tariff Commission in 1905 was anticipating a decrease in yarn exports as tops took over and claimed that the 'tendency was being already felt in a few things', but the overall trade figures do not indicate that the existing yarn trade suffered up to the First World War.[69]

Germany was continually the chief buyer of both tops and noils, accounting for 40 per cent or more of the overseas market for both. In the two decades before the war demand appeared from a wider range of countries including Japan, and expanded particularly from Italy and Scandinavia. There was little business in tops with France which had adequate capacity and capabilities in combing herself. There was some export of noils to the United States but stiff tariffs reduced the flow of tops to a trickle.[70] Most protectionists levied little or no duty on noils or tops. Neither was imported to Britain in any significant quantities.

The Redirection of British Wool Textile Exports

The European Markets

The 50 years before the First World War witnessed very substantial changes in the content and direction of British overseas trade in wool textile manufactured goods. The European and the United States markets declined and were replaced, at least to some extent, by increasing trade with Latin America, the Far East and the British Empire. Reasons for this change of pattern of trade were manifold; fashion changes and rising domestic production in export markets, the latter normally linked with high levels of protection, were of greatest significance.

In the 1860s the major proportion of British wool textile exports consisted of worsted goods. Exact measurement is impossible but roughly 75 per cent in 1860–64 were the latter, excluding carpets. By the last years of peace woollen goods had overtaken worsteds in importance, with almost two-thirds of the trade in 1913 being accounted for by woollen goods. The proportion of wool textile cloth exports going to Europe fell from about 30 per cent in the mid-1860s to around 20 per cent by 1905, much of this being the result of the decrease in trade to the protected markets of France and Germany. Whilst France was making such inroads in the British worsted market, home manufacturers were finding the French market full of problems. The busy trading years of the early 1870s were halted by the reversal of French liberal tariff policy. After 1877 trade picked up again and reached an all-time peak in terms of linear yardage in 1881 but thenceforth exports to France rapidly declined to the extent that by the late 1890s trade was only about one-quarter of the level of the peak years of 1874 and 1881. Decline continued yet further in the following decade.

The expansion of trade with France since the Treaty of 1860 had developed to the extent that a very broad range of cloth was being exported to France by the early 1870s, although mixed worsteds predominated and worsteds as a whole formed roughly three-quarters of the exports, by length. But blankets and woollen broad all-wool and mixed cloth were also exported in quantity. Depression and tariff adjustments in the mid-1870s reduced exports to France and particularly hit sales of flannels, blankets and worsteds. Sales of woollen cloth continued to expand and trade generally picked up again in the closing years of the decade. This renewed growth was brought to a rapid and permanent end by the tariff measures of 1882 which had a disastrous effect on the trade of many types of cloth. The new tariff converted the 10 per cent *ad valorem* duties to specific or

Table 48   *Direction of exports of wool textiles, 1870–1910 (proportion of trade, by value, to various destinations)*

Destination	1870 %	1880 %	1890 %	1900 %	1910 %
United States	21	15	25	9	7
Holland and Germany	32	16	11	16	11
France	11	18	14	10	6
South America	6	6	7	10	13
Far East	6	10	7	9	5
British Empire	15	23	22	33	40

by-weight duties which were particularly disadvantageous to the manufacturers in Britain of mixed goods. Duty on many types of Yorkshire woollen cloths was doubled and in some cases more than trebled. Meltons and pilots were badly affected. A Leeds melton, for example, costing 10*d* a yard before the new tariff would have been taxed at 11 centimes a metre, whereas the new tariff effectively raised the tax to 46 centimes a metre.[71] The Leeds trade generally was seriously damaged leading to a great deal of anger locally. Yeadon and Guiseley and the Heavy Woollen District were also hard hit but the export statistics suggest that the Bradford mixed trade diminished most. Exports of worsteds as a whole fell from 44.5 million linear yards in 1881 to nearly 24 million in 1882 and 1883, and the Bradford Chamber of Commerce was furious about the Government conceding to the new Treaty.[72]

During the 1880s both woollen and worsted exports substantially declined and this trend was given greater impetus by yet further increases in duties in 1892 which were 'virtually prohibitive as far as almost all trades in the Leeds district are concerned'.[73] Cotton warped goods were less seriously affected by the new measures but the Huddersfield and Scottish trades suffered and exports generally continued their downward slide to the extent that by the early years of this century the French market for British wool textiles was only a shadow of its former self.

The tariff difficulties in France were severely aggravated by other problems. The specific tariffs gave rise to difficulties of classifications and descriptions and accusations of 'daily different interpretation of the tariffs by the authorities', and arbitrary decisions, some of which, so it was suggested, arose out of French officials altering 'the classification of goods imported to suit their own financial requirements' as their salaries depended on commission on the money raised.[74] The frustration felt as manufacturers battled to continue trading with France is perhaps summed up by a comment in the *Textile Manufacturer* in March 1887, which accused the French of 'mental irritability' and of harassing trade by petty means. 'To be constantly snarling at your neighbours,' said the journal, 'is both undignified and mischievous and may even become dangerous.'

The statistics of British exports to France are difficult to interpret, particularly because many goods were re-exported to Spain and Latin America for example. However, the trade figures do make clear that the decline in the volume of trade, even allowing for some increase in the width of cloth, was substantially greater than the decline in value, suggesting that the manufacturers of cheaper cloth were worst hit.

Table 49   Exports of wool textile manufactured goods to France

Annual averages	Linear yards	£ thousand
1875–9	48 046	3128
1885–9	29 580	2823
1895–9	17 486	1593

Exports of British wool textiles to Germany slumped disastrously during the 1870s. The abnormally high trade of 1871–2 was halved in 1873 and exports continued to fall during the rest of the decade so that in 1880 exports were only approximately 13 per cent of the level of 1872 in terms of value. Some of this loss arose through rapidly rising efficient home production in Germany but this was more than assisted by a high degree of protectionism which, during the course of the 1870s, substantially curtailed British exports in cheap and heavy goods. The 1879 tariff was disastrous for the trade in low priced North Country goods – cheviots and tweeds. The British Chargé d'Affaires in Dresden reported that the 1881 tariff was particularly severe on heavier low quality goods. He stated: 'they weighed two or three times more than the fine goods, and costing about 5s. a yard, would pay 1s. 6d. in duty, whilst fine cloths, costing £1 a yard, would pay 9d. or 10d.'[75] And the Dewsbury Chamber of Commerce complained bitterly in 1884 that the 1879–80 tariff more than doubled the by-weight duty on their goods leading to sales of woollen goods being reduced by half. The Yeadon and Guiseley trade suffered badly and only manufacturers of fine goods got through relatively unscathed.[76]

Exports to Germany continued to decline in the 1880s, with worsteds suffering rather worse than woollens. In 1886 Henry Mitchell suggested that tariffs had reduced exports of Bradford goods to Germany to one-tenth of their average level of 1870–80.[77] Although there was some recovery of trade in the late 1890s, it slumped again at the beginning of the new century. The interpretation of changes in the German market is complicated by the entrepôt trade through Belgium and Holland, both of which countries were also important markets for British wool textiles. Belgium in particular provided a steady and even expanding market during the 1880s and 1890s, importing a wide range of wool textile fabrics. Trade to Holland, however, was not so buoyant, declining during the 1870s and early 1880s and then not recovering to any great extent.

Italy's demand for British wool textiles likewise declined from the 1870s. In 1883 the British Consul at Genoa commented that the wool textile trade with Italy seemed 'almost menaced with extinction by high tariffs', the greatest blow coming in 1887 when a new tariff abolished two-thirds of the volume of trade in the space of one year.[78] As the Italian weaving industry developed under protection so demand for yarns from Britain grew, but by the 1890s home spinning capacity was meeting much of the demand from weavers and imports of yarn were being reduced, to some extent to be replaced by imports of tops, noils and waste. The decline in Italian demand hurt, in particular, the Yeadon trade in cheap tweeds and manufacturers in the heavy woollen district.

The decline in the wool textile trade to the Iberian peninsular was particularly galling to manufacturers as they thought that here was an area where the British Government should have been able to favourably influence trading relationships. In 1876 Britain supplied about 20 per cent of Spanish imports but the negotiation in the following years by Spain with other European countries of favoured-nation treaties reduced the British proportion of trade to only 10 per cent by 1886.[79] The discriminatory duties and tariffs by weight undoubtedly put Britain at a severe disadvantage: tariffs were, for example, between 30 and 50 per cent higher than on equivalent German goods. The tariffs of 1877 which created the discrimination gave rise to much resentment in Britain and reports of 'incalculable losses' to the home industry.[80]

Some recovery was experienced after 1886 as a result of the conclusion of a commercial convention with Spain, which in return for changes in the wine duties, granted Britain favoured nation status but a general higher level of Spanish duties in 1892 wiped out some of the advantage gained by British manufacturers in the late 1880s.[81] Bradford dress goods were largely unable to compete with the protected home product. Coatings and serges were affected likewise. The trade in high class woollens fluctuated according to changes in the level of duties. Trade with Portugal, although of relatively little importance in the period, followed the general pattern. Duties on Bradford goods were said to be practically prohibitive. Huddersfield goods were also experiencing difficulties early in the 1900s.

The trade with Austria had developed slowly since the 1865 trade treaty, mainly in mixed worsteds. Proposed new duties in 1875 caused some concern in Yorkshire. A Yorkshire deputation to Vienna claimed to have successfully reversed the main adverse aspects of the proposals but a few years later tariffs were increased substantially, leading to diminished trade particularly for Bradford.[82] Some business was maintained in West of England cloth, but the Austrian market was never of great consequence for British manufacturers, although Austrian competition in other markets undoubtedly was. Austrian products gained a reputation for good finishing and by late in the nineteenth century were making some inroads in the British home market in such fabrics as suitings, dress coatings and costume cloths.[83]

The Scandinavian countries provided a small but quite steady market for British wool textile manufactures. In the 1860s Denmark was purchasing broadcloth and all-wool worsted stuffs. Mixed worsteds were finding a market in Sweden and Norway. By the end of the nineteenth century the extent and variety of trade had expanded: woollen broad and narrow cloth was being exported, although in quite small quantities, to Denmark, Norway and Sweden. All three countries were also taking worsted cloths.

Russia was another frustrating market for manufacturers, so much so that some British manufacturers set up mills there to beat the tariff. In the 1860s export of woollen cloth was very low, but worsteds expanded steadily reaching 3.3 million yards by 1875, but heavy protectionist duties thereafter severely reduced trade. There were many complaints to the Committee on Depression in Trade and Industry about the Russian duties. Bradford trade was said to have become merely nominal. Through the 1880s the Russian tariff became increasingly high and wool textiles from all European countries were severely affected, and by the end of the 1880s British wool textile exports to Russia were of no great consequence. A very small trade in heavy woollen broadcloth was maintained and a tiny export of worsted coatings developed. However, exports gradually revived at the beginning of this century for woollen goods and, by 1910, 567,000 yards of woollen cloth were exported, compared with only 42,000 yards of worsteds. The trade fluctuated wildly from year to year.[84]

The United States Market

The market which created the greatest problems and frustrations was that of the United States, and such was the importance of the transatlantic trade that any sudden change in it could alter the state of business almost overnight. The series of tariff changes seriously disturbed exports, particularly in the Bradford trade which was so dependent on the American market. In spite of the tariff changes of the 1860s, wool textile exports to the United States, as we have already seen, on the whole rose steadily in that decade. A peak, both in terms of volume and value was reached in 1872, the exceptional exports in that year arising partly from the disruption of supplies from France and Germany, and perhaps also from the 10 per cent across the board reduction in tariffs. But the volume of exports declined rapidly thereafter, to the extent that in 1878 yardage export was less than one-third of the previous peak level. After 1878 trade fluctuated quite violently, rising in 1889 and 1890 in anticipation of adverse tariff changes and then, following the McKinley tariff, falling to less than 20 million yards in 1894. The moderate Wilson tariff in 1895 produced a short and substantial respite to exporters, but then the Dingley tariff massively reduced trade once again, recovery only gradually occurring in the early 1900s. For most of the period home production was rising successfully in the United States.

The composition of the trade was mainly worsteds so, as fashion turned against cotton warps, British manufacturers found that, to add to intolerable tariffs in the United States, they were at a disadvantage competing in that market with all-wool worsteds from elsewhere. The trade statistics show clearly that the level of exports of all-wool worsteds was maintained better than that of mixed worsteds but, all the same, the former were of far less importance than the latter. Exports of various types of woollen cloth appear to have fluctuated greatly according to the particular provisions of the various tariffs. Some trade was sustained in flannels but the blanket trade fared badly.

The rapid deterioration of trade after 1873 gave rise to critical comment from all sections of the industry about American restrictions. Tariffs were raised again in 1875 leading to accusation that the United States had closed its doors to many British goods. Behrens refused to attend the Philadelphia Exhibition in 1876 as a juror because, he argued, the exhibition was not run on free trade principles, nor was there a real desire for increasing mutual trade. At the same exhibition Leeds manufacturers pointedly marked the prices of their goods to show what they would have been without the imposition of duty. By doing so, they hoped to convince 'the minds of many Americans as to the benefits of a free trade policy'. There were regular complaints also of 'the omniverous appetites of the American protectionists for the most perfect details of the business of their competitors'.[85]

Although there were often claims that the United States market had become closed, between 15 and 20 per cent of British wool textile exports in the late 1870s continued to be sent to the United States. The trade in worsted coatings was expanding, but exporters of heavy woollen goods, for example, faced great problems. In 1877 it was reported that in effect the duty amounted to 225 per cent on some goods, with the average, taking 25 different articles of heavy goods, being 155 per cent.

The slight relaxation of tariff levels in 1883 created only little respite. More optimism was created. Overall Britain benefited more than her main European competitors as a result of the tariff reductions. Exports of worsteds improved but the trade in woollen cloth showed less immediate response. Complaints about the levels of duties continued with much criticism being expressed in evidence to the Commission on Depression in Trade and Industry. There were reports of manufacturers setting up factories in the United States, and exports of textile machinery were buoyant. Scottish tweed manufacturers, who faced a tariff of 35 cents per pound and 35 or 40 per cent *ad valorem*, reported that they could do little business. Bradford makers complained that the specific component of the duties meant that low Bradford goods were penalised.[86]

The volume of cloth exports began to improve in the second half of the 1880s, the benefit being felt perhaps more by woollen manufacturers, although it was claimed by one worsted manufacturer, Swire Smith, the advocate of technical education, that Bradford had regained possession of the American market in spite of the tariffs 'by the exercise of superior skill and design'. Some of the difficulties of the American wool textile industry in the mid 1880s, which led to mill closures, were claimed to be the result of successful British competition.[87]

By early 1889 rumours were spreading of the likelihood of substantial tariff increases.[88] Exports rose rapidly to beat the changes, with reports of consignments avoiding the increases by minutes.[89] The McKinley tariff came into operation in October 1890 and its impositions were severe. The average duty on manufactured wool textiles from Britain increased, according to the Board of Trade, from 67 per cent to 91.5 per cent.[90] The intention of the new tariff was at least partly to readjust duties to take into account the situation where falling raw material prices and manufacturing costs had been allowing high-class cloth to enter the United States under the middle grade duties.[91] Thus better quality goods were hurt most, and worsteds suffered more than woollens. It has been argued that British trade was affected more than European trade as a result of the McKinley tariff,[92] but the United States import statistics suggest otherwise. Comparing 1889 with 1891, thus excluding the inflated year of 1890, Britain's total share of United States imports of cloth rose from 58.6 per cent to 73.2 per cent by weight and from 56.2 per cent to 69.1 per cent by value. For dress goods there was a slight decline in Britain's proportion of trade from 41.7 per cent to 39.7 per cent in volume and from 39.4 per cent to 35.2 per cent in value. The volume of French trade in dress goods declined relatively more, although in value terms the decline was slighter. Taking both groups together the British share of the total wool textile trade rose 3.8 per cent in value terms. Overall the McKinley tariff did reduce the total trade in worsted goods, but not in woollen goods.

The effect of the McKinley tariff was by no means uniform. Scottish manufacturers were badly hurt. Their goods valued at more than 40 cents per pound faced a specific duty of 44 cents per pound, plus 50 per cent *ad valorem*. Border cloth worth 4s per pound was liable to a duty of 3s 10d per pound, a level of 95 per cent. What little trade survived from the West of England was also badly affected. Bradford goods were confronted with a duty of over 100 per cent.[93] In spite of Britain's increased share of the market, the immediate result of the McKinley tariff was to cut the volume of wool textile exports from Britain to the United States by half, and the relative importance of the United States as a market sank disastrously. There were some side effects: more manufacturers attempted to set up factories in the United States, including Salts of Saltaire who established an unsuccessful plant at Bridgeport; cotton goods enjoyed some substitution demand and attempts were made to produce special lines to minimise the effect of the tariff.[94]

The McKinley duties remained in force until 1895. The Wilson tariff of that year, however, brought sudden optimism, described by Clapham as 'lyrical' in Bradford.[95] The *Textile Manufacturer* predicted that the new tariff would give great prosperity to Yorkshire mills, including those of Bradford, and the Colne and Holme valleys.[96] The substantially lower duties did create a rapid restoration of trade. Exports soared to over 88 million yards of woollen and worsted cloth in 1895 compared with an average of only 25 million yards for the previous two years. Britain's share of United States wool textile imports rose by 12.4 per cent overall, the gain in cloth being 6.3 per cent and in dress goods, 9.2 per cent. The Wilson tariff clearly favoured British manufacturers and great gains were made in the export of both all-wool and union broad cloths, flannels, worsted coatings and stuffs. Manufacturers were very active in 1895 servicing the restored United States market, but over-ordering in that year somewhat reduced trade again the next. In the period from 1895 to 1897 many manufacturers found themselves selling to the United States market for the first time in many years but claims of success were not unanimous; one Scottish manufacturer stated that he had seen little new advantage.[97]

Reaction to the flood of imports to the United States was rapid; and in 1898 the Dingley tariff, the third complete revision in seven years, raised duties on wool textiles to above the level of 1890, and thereby reduced trade to its lowest level, in value terms, since early in the century. Duties on yarns were substantially raised.[98] The worsted coatings trade was disastrously affected, and the Bradford trade fared very badly. Comparing 1898 with 1896, exports of worsted coatings to the United States fell from 9,142,000 linear yards to 1,809,000 linear yards. The yardage reduction for stuffs was from 23,824,000 to 12,164,000; for woollen cloth, from 10,913,000 to 1,664,000 and for flannels, from 633,000 to 68,000. Whereas the previous two tariff changes had led to an overall gain in relative trade for British manufacturers, the Dingley tariff had very much the opposite effect. Again comparing 1898 with 1896, the British share of cloth imports to the United States fell by over 7 per cent, by weight and value, and continued to decline thereafter. Dress goods from Britain however managed to maintain their share of the market, and in due course even increased it.

Whereas on average in the years of the Wilson tariff Britain exported over 60 million yards of cloth to the U.S.A., in the five years following the Dingley tariff the amount fell to an average of under 17 million yards. For many manufacturers, trading with the United States became out of the question. As home production of better quality cloth improved there, so even the highest quality British manufacturers could not escape the effect of the tariff. And the effective protection on wool textiles in the United States was amongst the highest for all goods.[99] As a consequence the United States trade as a proportion of Britain's total wool textile exports fell to only 7 per cent in the five years before the First World War.

The problem created for manufacturers by the high tariffs and the frequent tariff changes were also aggravated by petty difficulties in trading with the United States. For example the Dingley tariff included a duty on packing cases, which manufacturers had to avoid by importing cases from the United States. Parcels of exports to the United States had to have an invoice presented in advance to an American consular official in Britain, which created delay and expense and by the 1890s manufacturers were having to go to consuls to swear as to the accuracy of the description of their goods, instead of swearing before a justice of the peace, as they had previously done.[100] But in spite of all these problems for most of this period the British industry maintained a good competitive position with other exporters to the United States.

The Latin American Trade

J.H. Clapham, writing in 1907, described the Argentinian trade in wool textiles as having recently developed most satisfactorily from the point of view of the British manufacturer.[101] Although Argentina was consistently Britain's major market in Latin America, similar growth was apparent in neighbouring markets and Latin American trade as a whole would seem to have been a success story for British manufacturers although the development of the trade in the last third of the nineteenth century and in the first few years of the twentieth century was not smooth.

Wool textile exports to South America had grown only slowly earlier in the nineteenth century although the market was fairly consistently significant. In the mid-1820s between 9 and 16 per cent of total wool textile exports were going to Mexico and South America. At that time the trade consisted primarily of woollen goods but incorporated most of the products of British manufacturers, and was particularly dominated by woollens mixed with cotton for which Latin America was regularly amongst the most important markets. By the mid-1840s between 13 and 15 per cent of British wool textile trade was still going to Latin America. Thereafter, however, as the value of British wool textile exports continued to increase the South American trade did not maintain its proportionate share, mainly it would seem through a lack of expansion in demand rather than Britain being ousted by other competitors.

By the 1870s and 1880s, however, there were widespread fears of the detrimental effect on British trade of French, German and Belgian competition. The British Consul in Argentina expressed his opinion that there was a danger of British trade being lost through the activity of merchants from other European countries. Although he argued that 'we have yet to learn that an Englishman is inferior in either business capacity or industry to a German or any other man', he was clearly impressed by the methods the German merchants were using. Paris merchants were also successfully active, although some of their trade included supplying cheaper British cloth alongside the finer products of French manufacture. Climate and distribution of income in much of South America meant that demand for wool textiles was generally from a wealthy clientele which paid attention to design and European fashion trends, to the consequent benefit of French makers.[102]

In the 1870s and 1880s Britain would appear to have lost out in the competition for the market. Various evidence to the Commission on Depression in Trade and Industry is substantially in agreement. The Consul in Peru commented on the French and German competition in wool textiles and identified an advantage that those countries had through better and cheaper shipping facilities. The Venezuelan Consul stated that British trade there was declining because of stiff German competition and the adverse consequences of a high tariff which particularly hurt imports of heavier cloth. On the other hand trade with Mexico was said to be rapidly growing in spite of much of it being through the hands of German merchants following the breaking of diplomatic relations with Britain in 1867. The Consul in Argentina, the main market, reported a disappointing situation:

> French, Germans and Belgians are striving hard to obtain the control of this important branch of trade and are rapidly improving their position, except in plain goods, in which they cannot compete; but in printed and fancy goods the superior taste of the continental manufacturers is telling very seriously.[103]

In union and mixed goods Britain had been losing ground during the previous nine years with British share of the total Argentinian wool textile market falling from 21 per cent in 1876 to only 11 per cent in 1884. The Consul complained of lack of British representatives in the country to generate business, the unwillingness of British manufacturers to fulfil small orders and he commented on the existence of French and Italian Chambers of Trade in Argentina.

However, although reports continued about the success of European competition in the Latin American markets,[104] gradually a generally more optimistic picture emerged of the success of British cloth in the markets and when wool prices began to rise around 1904 there would appear to have been, in Argentina and perhaps elsewhere, a marked move to cheaper wool textile fabrics, allowing Britain to begin to recapture the market. Consular reports from Argentina, Venezuela, Uruguay and Chile before the First World War all tend to suggest substantial British competitive success, and even as early as the 1890s much better reports than previously were filtering through.[105] Commenting on the Argentinian market in 1898, *The Textile Manufacturer* reported: 'Not very much is heard now of English travellers being without knowledge of the language of the country, but undoubtedly our competitors are far ahead of us as regards circulars and advertising matter.'[106] Figures for Argentinian wool textile imports produced around that time (see Table 50) make

Table 50   Source of Argentine wool textile imports, 1893–6 (average
1893–6, $ thousand of Custom House value)

	Pure wool goods	Wool and cotton mixed
U.K.	2500	1009
Germany	704	166
Belgium	404	282
France	1135	52

SOURCE: *Third Report of Mr. T. Worthington on the Conditions and Prospects of
British Trade in certain South American Countries*, BPP., 1899 (c. 9078)
XCVI, p. 489.

NOTES: The figures exclude blankets, flannels, hosiery, carpets, etc. Germany
dominated the flannel trade, Britain the carpet trade. Blanket imports were
few because of home production. It is possible that the above figures
underestimate British trade and overestimate French and German because of
foreign merchants dealing in British goods.

it clear that Britain dominated the market and exported more to it
than Germany, Belgium and France put together.

In spite of the reports, therefore, of British competitive laxity in
Latin American markets the picture that emerges from the statistics
and contemporary factual reports is one of much success. Many of the
countries were difficult to trade with. Complex tariffs, harsh fines for
inadvertent failures to comply with customs regulations and various
trade treaties to Britain's disadvantage all had to be faced and were.

The Far East Trade

As manufacturers found it increasingly necessary to look beyond
traditional markets for trading outlets so their trade with the Far East
gradually began to expand and there is some evidence to suggest that
the increase in wool textile exports to that area was at least to some
extent the result of manufacturers and merchants actively attempting
to cultivate the market. The Leeds Chamber of Commerce in the
1870s was showing particular interest in Japan. It organised a lecture
on Chinese and Japanese markets and asked the Japanese Ambas-
sador to talk to it. In the following decade the British Consul in Japan
was invited.[107]

The initial expansion of the Japanese market occurred in the 1860s
and was linked with the speeding up of steamship lines. By 1870 the
market however still only accounted for less than 1 per cent by value
of British wool textile exports and was substantially smaller than the
Chinese market. Throughout the 1870s and 1880s the Japanese
market received considerable interest from West Riding manufac-

turers. The market was perhaps particularly attractive through its immunity to the vagaries of European fashion but it was still subject to fluctuations, particularly through war, or the fear of it. There are suggestions in the trade press that manufacturers had difficulty in determining the exact needs of the market and that some aspects of trade were highly competitive, yet by the mid-1880s some Yorkshire manufacturers had established a substantial amount of their business there. Heavy woollen district manufacturers benefited to the extent that in 1900 almost 8 per cent of heavy broad woollen cloth exports went to Japan. The country also became the major overseas market for blanket manufacturers until tariffs reduced it in the 1890s.

For mixed worsted stuffs Japan, by 1890, was the third overseas market, after France and the United States. But the level of this trade was not maintained in the 1890s and by 1905 worsted cloth of all types made up only 16 per cent of exports of wool textile cloth. By that time, however, a broader section of manufacturers were producing for the Japanese market. The flannel trade was rising. Scottish manufacturers who had done little or no trade there in 1886 were receiving orders. And the Russo-Japanese war (1904–5) gave a boost to business through orders to Scotland and the West Riding for khaki cloth. The Dewsbury newspaper reported in 1904:

> Its an ill wind that blows nobody good. The war in the Far East is deplorable but has brought the district good fortune . . . one firm in this neighbourhood is engaged on a contract for no fewer than 800,000 blankets for the Japanese army. Two others at Earlsheaton are turning out 101,000 and a Batley Carr house is producing 60,000.[108]

The Yeadon and district woollen trade was also being kept busy by Japanese orders and the Huddersfield woollen trade was being successful in the market.[109]

Competition however was fierce. Germany in particular paid great attention to the new market. Bousfield's Yokohama agent wrote to him in the 1880s that:

> the Germans are trying hard to bring from Germany imitations of English goods, and they are making great efforts to get in with the Japanese for large contracts. Prince Bismark is writing letters to the Japanese government, not signing, but writing the whole letters, urging the Japanese Government to give whatever business they can to German firms.[110]

And the *Textile Manufacturer* commented in 1889 that 'the presence and influence of the ubiquitous German is felt in Japan as in many

other portions of the world'. Nine years later it argued that inattention to Japanese taste had enabled German competition to secure a
large share of the Japanese market. In some areas British manufacturers certainly lost out. From the early 1880s the Germans were most
successful in the flannel trade,[111] but comment by the end of the
century suggests that British manufacturers were succeeding better in
the market generally and that the wool textile trade there was profitable.[112] Whilst this was happening, however, manufacturers were
receiving many warnings that Japanese home production was developing and threatened trade in the long run. Japanese students were
being sent to European textile schools, Japanese wool purchases
from Australia were rising and continually through the 1890s the
trade press reported on the likely vigorous progress of the 'inimitable
Japanese' in wool textile manufacture. In 1896 it was reported that
the Japanese Government was despatching a commercial mission to
England, America, Germany and India, which gave rise to the comment 'no wonder the Japanese are labelled "the best imitators on
earth" '. New rates of duty in 1898 made the market to some extent
protected but failed to prevent an expansion of imports.[113]

The expansion of trade in wool textiles to China, which had been
substantial in the 1860s, was not on the whole maintained for the rest
of the century. With Hong Kong, China remained the most important
Eastern market until the 1890s but it was a declining market and one
fraught with problems. Famines, droughts, wars and internal disputes
caused regular and substantial fluctuations in demand. Problems of
internal communications hindered the expansion of the market and
although there were occasional exhortations to manufacturers and
merchants to give greater energy to developing trade with China little
progress was made. Business picked up substantially during the war
of 1904–5 and was sustained during the following years. French
merchants were active in China and German competition was said to
be increasing early in the twentieth century.[114] The trade to China
was mainly in worsteds, with all-wool worsteds being in most
demand. However, as worsted exports substantially fell off, so woollen goods began to dominate the trade and the trend was further
stimulated by military demand. There was a consistent small export
of blankets, flannels and other goods with a good blanket trade
emerging in times of war.

Trade with the Colonies
Another major area of market expansion for British wool textile
manufacturers was the colonies. The proportion of exports going to

British possessions rose steadily after the early 1870s to the extent that before the First World War the level reached over 40 per cent; and the colonies took by far the major proportion of exports of some types of cloth.

From the 1870s fears were being expressed in the trade that Britain could be ousted from her colonial markets. The *Textile Manufacturer* reported in 1878 that American manufacturers were gaining some success in the Australian States. Three years later a series of letters from Australia to the journal cajoled British manufacturers to pay more attention to the requirements of the colonies. An ex-York-shireman wrote in March 1881 that 'other nations are doing all they can to push trade' in Australia. A few months later another writer pleaded:

> I would urge the whole community engaged in the textile trade in any way to do their level best to get a firmer grip on this market – I mean the entire colonial market. The great efforts that are being made by the Germans, French and Americans to push trade in these parts is simply astonishing and they must succeed unless more attention is paid to the Australian colonies by the manufacturers of Great Britain.

There were complaints also that Australia was being used as a dump for poor goods by some British firms and this led to demands for greater protection:

> Is the Yorkshire and Lancashire manufacturer to continue sending unchecked his sham material made up from woollen and cotton refuse of all descriptions in order to land it at our ports at prices against which we can never attempt to compete?[115]

In the Australian market in the 1880s French and German manufacturers gained some success as a result of their wool buying houses also acting as agents for sales. In Canada likewise foreign manufacturers found a market but during the 1890s the British industry outstripped its competitors. Contemporary commentators reported that at last Britain was beginning to pay more attention to the needs and tastes of the colonial customers. Imperial preference clearly played its part by giving Britain tariff advantages over her potential competitors.[116]

A clear profile of the content and importance of trade with the colonies emerged in evidence to the Tariff Commission in 1905. For the worsted branch of the industry the colonies were a major market for Bradford dress goods, which found substantial demand in

Canada, Australia and Hong Kong. In 1905 34 per cent of British worsted exports, by value, went to the colonies. Of even more importance was the trade in low woollen union cloth, a trade which arguably helped the survival of the Yeadon and Huddersfield tweed export trades. Scottish manufacturers also benefited from the colonial markets but West of England makers reported little colonial demand for their fine cloths.[117]

For the woollen branch of the industry the trade statistics show very clearly that it was cheaper cloth that was finding a market in the colonies. Taking the average of 1909–13, 40.1 per cent of the export of woollen tissues by length went to the colonies, but in terms of value the proportion was only 26.6 per cent.[118] The blanket trade was more dependent than any other section of the industry on colonial exports. In the decade before the First World War on average over three-quarters of blanket exports went to British possessions, the major markets being South Africa, Australia and Hong Kong. The flannel trade in the same period sent an almost similar proportion of its exports to colonial markets, in its case particularly to Australia and India. The major market for damasks, tapestries and furniture fabrics was, likewise, in the colonies.

Table 51 examines the direction of exports to British possessions in 1909. Canada clearly emerges as the major customer and Australia follows in second place. India was of less consequence because of intense competition from Germany. In 1909–13 only 55 per cent of Indian wool textile imports came from Britain, much of the rest coming from Germany which sent cheap flimsier cloth, stripes and shawls.[119] In 1912 India was Germany's most important market for wool textiles after Britain, Turkey and Roumania. Germany sent £400,000 of goods to India compared with exports of only £154,000 to Canada, South Africa, Australia and New Zealand together.

Thus up to the First World War the colonies were generally an improving market providing a relatively stable outlet for British manufacturers in their staple products. And it should be realised that the trade statistics for cloth exports do not include trade in ready-made clothing a substantial proportion of which found its way to colonial markets. As early as 1886 it was reported that three-quarters of exports of ready-made clothing went to British possessions.

Relative Importance of Home and Foreign Trade

Contemporary chroniclers of the fortunes of the wool textile industry were quite clear that the home market was growing in relative importance in the decades after 1870. This appears to be reflected in the

Table 51   Direction of British wool textile colonial trade in 1909

	Woollen cloth million yds.	Worsted cloth million yds.	Flannels million yds.	Blankets thousand prs.
Canada	8.0	15.3	0.4	43
Australia	10.4	5.6	1.8	94
Hong Kong	2.1	2.6	0.1	84
India	6.0	3.1	1.0	36
New Zealand	1.9	1.1	0.5	21
South Africa	1.6	1.8	0.3	132
West Indies	0.7	0.3	0.8	—
Other	0.9	1.2	0.5	89
TOTAL	31.6	31.0	5.4	499

greater attention that manufacturers were paying to the prospects and state of home demand, as indicated by trade correspondence and reports. The aggregate indicators available, however, only enable a very rough assessment to be made of this trend. Raw material consumption more than doubled between 1860–4 and 1910–14; net exports of yarn rose by about 50 per cent. Exports of woollen and worsted cloth, excluding blankets and other items not included in the main Board of Trade categories, marginally declined over the same period, measured by linear yardage. However, a comparison of 1910–14 with the peak export period of 1870–74 suggests a fall in exports of 47 per cent, although, as already indicated, the figures make no allowance for increasing widths of cloth.

Assessment of the relative importance of the home and foreign markets is possible just before the First World War. The Census of Production of 1907 indicates that about 43 per cent of output of woollen and worsted tissues was exported in that year. The proportion had fallen to 38 per cent by 1912.[120] For yarn the proportion of output exported was 18.5 per cent in 1907 and 15.6 per cent in 1912. These various proportions may be no more than a rough approximation.

The 1907 export proportion accords with the calculations of G.H. Wood. He believed that the best measurement of the extent and division of the trade was raw material consumption and calculated that, in 1905–8, 55.5 per cent of output was for home consumption compared with only 38.5 per cent in 1870–74. He argued that over the intervening period output had increased by 46 per cent, export volume by 6 per cent, home manufactures retained at home by 109 per cent and total home consumption by 113 per cent. His figures are

Table 52   Wool textiles: output and exports, 1907 and 1912

	1907 million linear yards	1912 million linear yards
Production	447.8	475.6
Exports*	192.6	180.2
	255.2	295.4
Retained imports	67.0	58.0
All goods retained	322.2	353.4
Exports:	%	%
Proportion of production	43.0	37.9
Home market:		
British goods	79.2	83.6
Imported goods	20.8	16.4

SOURCE: *Census of Production*, 1924, *op. cit.*, p. 88

NOTE: *includes tissues, flannels and delaines and omits damasks, tapestry, furniture stuffs and plushes

somewhat optimistic as they overestimate the increase in raw material consumption by taking no account of the increased weight loss of wool, but they are not a totally unrealistic reflection of the trends in the industry.[121]

Wood's export trade proportion for 1870–74 is somewhat higher than other contemporary estimates for the 1850s and 1860s but in those two decades export business was rising more rapidly than home business. All the estimates exceed those calculated by Deane who suggests that only in the early 1870s did exports as a proportion of value of output reach 40 per cent and that the level in the three decades before the First World War averaged less than 30 per cent.[122] Her estimates depend heavily on assumptions about the relationship between the value of raw material input and value of final product. The traditional multiplier of three which had been generally assumed earlier in the century had become less realistic by mid-century as wool prices rose and labour and capital productivity improved. In 1857 James suggested:

> It will be quickly observed that whilst in former years the value of the manufactured goods was three or four times that of the raw material, it is now only about doubled. This arises partly from the present excessive price of wool; but of late years the cost of

manufacture has much lessened from the use of combing machines, and the great improvements in the processes of spinning, weaving, etc.[123]

His calculations applied to worsteds. The ratio may have been somewhat less with woollens. The fall in wool prices from the mid-1860s may again have increased the ratio, but this would have been offset to some extent by productivity improvements. It may be that Deane's average ratio of 2.73 for the period 1870 to 1899 is too optimistic and that, consequently the role of the home market is overestimated in her figures.

Foreign Competition in the Home Market

Whereas the value of exports of wool textile manufactured goods on the whole declined after 1870 imports rose very substantially, much to the consternation of many British manufacturers. Comparing the mid-1870s with the mid-1890s the value of exports fell by about 17.5 per cent but that of imports rose by over 130 per cent, so whilst manufacturers were faced with high tariffs in many markets, rising competition from home manufacturers in most developed countries and greater competition in neutral markets so they were also having to battle to maintain their position in some parts of their own home market, which was becoming gradually relatively more important for many branches of the trade.

The volume and value of imports rose somewhat during the 1860s and then very rapidly until the mid-1890s. In that period there were only seven years in which the value of imports did not increase over the previous year. Growth was particularly rapid between 1882 and 1889 and again in the early 1890s, but after 1897 the value of imports fell rapidly to the extent that around 1910 it had returned close to the level of the late 1870s. The imports consisted of a wide range of goods including very miscellaneous items such as rugs, shawls, hosiery, woollen braid and lace but the major part of them was all-wool worsteds from France and perhaps it was only really in this main area that home manufacturers were adversely affected. In some years in the 1880s and 1890s the value of imports of worsted cloth approached the value of exports. In one year, 1889, imports may have exceeded exports. There were often complaints that some of the imports were being dumped in Britain as a result of over-production elsewhere or through tariff charges in other countries suddenly curtailing the market of Britain's competitors, but although examples were occasionally quoted of foreign manufacturers selling in the British market at below cost these instances were rarely substantiated. Wit-

Table 53   *Annual imports of woollen and worsted manufactures into the United Kingdom from various countries (£ thousand)*

Annual averages	Germany	France	Belgium	Holland	Total imports	Net imports
1885–9	336	5533	398	1672	8 450	7840
1890–4	772	5821	488	2572	9 910	8700
1895–9	1061	5896	424	2744	10 550	9790
1900–4	1203	5237	615	2029	9 530	8640

SOURCE: *Tariff Commission*, Table 26

nesses to the Tariff Commission claimed in particular that woollen mantle and costume cloths were being dumped by Germany, Holland and France.[124] But these were cloths subject to sudden fashion changes and both British and foreign manufacturers sometimes found that they had to off-load on to the market at below cost end of season surpluses and outdated fashions. On the principle that 'any price was better than none' Britain did this in some of her Colonial markets, notably Canada and it seems likely that foreign manufacturers found themselves having to do the same at various times.[125] The situation was not new; much earlier in the century merchants and manufacturers on occasions had had to accept losses on sales in North America, Australia and elsewhere.

Besides all-wool worsteds, much of the importation of wool textiles would appear to have been in 'novelties' and 'specialities' not produced in sufficient quantity at home to satisfy needs. The reason for the inability or unwillingness of British worsted manufacturers to produce all-wool worsted cloth to compete with the French is surely one of the major questions about the wool textile industry in the late nineteenth century.

French Competition in All-Wool Worsteds
As long as Bradford was experiencing booming markets at home and abroad for its cotton warped worsteds it was happy to leave the much smaller markets for higher quality, all-wool worsteds in the hands of the French, and it was not really concerned by the unanimous, regular reports of the superiority of the French product. As the export statistics show, the manufacture of all-wool worsteds had not been entirely foresaken but by the 1860s they could have formed only a tiny proportion of total output. British worsted manufacturers can hardly be criticised for having concentrated so much on cotton-warps

and lustre wools. This was the booming mass market of the mid-century, a market which rose far more rapidly than that for the all-wool product. Indeed if criticism is to be levied perhaps it should be against the French industry for making little progress in the use of cotton warps and in the servicing of the mass market.

However, perhaps in the 1860s and certainly by the 1870s, mass market demand began to shift away from the Bradford staple product towards goods made of softer wools, and undoubtedly Bradford manufacturers were very slow and clumsy in their adaptation to the change. That fashion was moving away from Bradford goods was being clearly recognised by the mid-1870s. The factory inspectors included in their 1875 report a letter commenting:

> It is noticeable from the reports of the London sales on the one hand, and from the distribution of orders this season between English and French manufacturing houses, that, in spite of all our efforts the French . . . are simultaneously taking from us a large slice of our wool and of our orders.[126]

The Economist, a few months later, reported complaints from Bradford merchants about the fashion change which, because of the soft and somewhat clinging nature of the all-wool fabric, they said was 'one of the most immodest that has ever been adopted by the ladies of this and other countries'.[127]

There is little initial indication that Bradford manufacturers wanted to attempt to compete with the French. They were used to the fancies of fashion and clearly looked upon the French success as purely temporary, expecting also their own trade to pick up once depression had passed. They did not however doubt that they were capable of adapting to the competition if they wanted to. In a letter to the *Daily Telegraph* in 1881 a Bradford manufacturer wrote: 'Even in all-wools I assert without fear of contradiction, that there is not a single article which cannot be made here as well as in France'.[128]

However, by early in the 1880s concern was beginning to be shown about how permanent the fashion appeared to have become and debate arose about what could be done. On the whole there was still an air of optimism as only a few doubts were expressed that it would not be long before Bradford manufacturers would adapt their methods to produce something comparable to, or even better than, the French product. A contribution to the *Textile Manufacturer* in 1881 perhaps sums up the general view. Its correspondent wrote 'We are sanguine that it is only a question of time when we shall again have the supremacy of the trade over the French . . .',[129] but a lot of time had already passed, allowing the French to make great inroads to the British home market and to overseas markets as well; and as Bradford manufacturers were soon to realise more than time was required to make changes because there were fairly fundamental production difficulties to be overcome.

In Bradford the 'throstle' and 'cap frame' methods of spinning had been universally adopted to produce the yarn required for mixed cloth. The harder and somewhat longer wool that Bradford used for its product had to be oiled in order for it to be worked and the retention of some of the oil in the yarn and finished cloth affected both dyeing and finishing, in particular reducing the brightness of colour. In France, however, the softer and shorter stapled wool was spun on the mule which created less strain and which allowed the spinning to be done 'dry', producing a looser yarn with a softer handle. The throstle in use in Bradford was quite unsuited for spinning the yarn required to compete with the French.

Few mules were in use in the British worsted trade. One estimate suggests there were only 30,000 mule spindles operating in 1884, out of the 2.25 million or more spinning spindles at work in the industry. And although there appears to have been some recognition of the need for the development of mule spinning, the installation of mules in the trade progressed very slowly. In 1904 under 200,000 out of three million worsted spinning spindles in use were mule spindles.[130]

A meeting of manufacturers was held in Bradford in January 1881 'to consider proposals for starting a company to spin all-wool worsted on the mule in the manner adapted by the French'. Attendance, however, was small and although it was unanimously agreed that 'such yarns should be spun at Bradford' very little appears to have resulted from it, although two or three firms 'of long standing, large capital and determined energy' did start tentative experiments, and Platt Bros of Oldham gave attention to producing suitable machinery.[131]

A little progress had been made by the middle of the 1880s. Behrens reported that more manufacturers were setting up the necessary machinery and that one local (Bradford) manufacturer who had begun putting up machinery 'to spin those yarns in which the French have beaten us' had secured good orders for his yarn 'which he would not have got if he could not, with his new machinery, beat the French in quality, in management and in price'.[132] But Behrens agreed with others that the installation of mules was not progressing fast enough.

Why were manufacturers so wary of them? There was a multitude of difficulties, including confidence, capital and labour skills. The installation of mules needed substantial capital outlay at a time when Bradford manufacturers had seen their profits seriously eroded. Mules in use in France had up to 1000 spindles and were very substantial and costly pieces of machinery.[133] With frames being durable and available cheaply second-hand because of the turnover of firms, both old and new manufacturers needed substantial incentive to purchase new mules. They might have been prepared to do so if they had been convinced at the time that the fashion change had become permanent. But the occasional upturn in trade renewed their optimism that a market would soon return for Bradford goods. As Behrens put it, manufacturers 'did not like to fit their plant or their works for a mere fashion' which they thought would revert in due course.[134]

Labour supply and labour skills were also a problem. It was argued that 'to be effectively managed the mule must be minded by men and boys, who are stronger, more suitably clad, and have more staying power than women',[135] and it was believed that the substitution of more costly male for female labour would exacerbate the French advantage in labour costs which many contemporary commentators argued was of considerable advantage to French competitiveness. It was regularly argued that the French through longer hours and lower wages and 'far more patient and tractable labour', were better placed to compete, it being suggested at the same time that the British labour was unwilling to take pains with anything new or troublesome.[136]

It was also clearly the opinion of some, but by no means all, manufacturers that even if Bradford had successfully managed to rival the quality and price of the French all-wool worsted cloth, there would still have been other difficulties. Although some claimed that Bradford designs were as good as any, there was a recognition of a French artistic spirit and, as Clapham put it, unfortunately there was 'difficulty about the acquisition of so intangible a thing as French spirit'.[137] Another attitude expressed in the mid-1880s was that because of their reputation a prejudice had built up for French goods, even where there was no difference in quality.[138]

Some of this explicit contemporary feeling does have a defeatist air about it and with hindsight we may be critical of the slowness of Bradford's reaction to French success but this may well be unfair given the uncertain circumstances of the time. Such contemporary comment as 'our people are the victims of a chronic indisposition to keep abreast with the times' would underestimate the complexity of the forecasting that had to be made in the worsted industry.[139] And one should not overlook that progress was made. Although there was little investment in the mule, existing spinning machinery was to some extent successfully modified to cope with a wider variety of spinning to take more and larger bobbins, thus reducing costs. These modifications by no means solved the problem and complaints about the lack of mule spun yarn continued but by the 1890s the increase in the flow of French imports to Britain was being halted and British worsted manufacturers were doing better in their home market. Clapham could write in 1907 that for 18 years at least all the increase in home consumption 'must have been met by the produce of the home mills',[140] and he later took the view that the British industry in the long run successfully adjusted itself to fashion changes and this view would seem to be supported by the relative export performances of the British and French worsted trades from the 1890s.[141]

10 The Competitiveness of the British Wool Textile Industry

Entrepreneurial Performance

It is unquestionable that in Lancashire and Yorkshire the textile manufactures are carried out in a manner well worthy of the national character. The utmost vigour of judgement, the clearest scanning of the signs of the times, the adaptation to their own purposes of all that can be made useful, indomitable perseverance in pursuing an object to its conclusion, and the most keensighted intelligence have combined in making the cotton manufacturers of Lancashire and the woollen and worsted manufacturers of Yorkshire one of the most important bodies in the country. The qualities and characteristics, by means of which men have achieved this position for their daily occupation, have enabled them to hold an honourable position in the more extended sphere of general society, and to take a useful and a distinguished part in all the great questions of the day.[1]

It was in these words that a factory inspector extolled the virtues of the wool textile manufacturer in the mid-nineteenth century. Yet, later in the century, those entrepreneurs were accused of complacency, lethargy and of using antiquated methods.

The debate about the efficiency of British entrepreneurship in the late nineteenth century has been taking place over several decades. Landes has argued that British entrepreneurship reflected 'a combination of amateurism and complacency' and has accused it of taking markets for granted, of refusing to suit goods to the taste and pocket of clients and of neglecting to promote new products.[2] And Aldcroft has suggested, in an often quoted comment, that 'Britain's relatively poor performance can be attributed largely to the failure of the British entrepreneur to respond to the challenge of changing conditions.'[3] But the original accusations that entrepreneurs were appallingly slow to adjust themselves to changing market conditions and rising foreign competition have been strongly questioned and, in spite of the amount of debate and the studies of various firms and industries, no clear consensus has emerged as to how efficient enterprise was in facing up to the new circumstances of the period. It may be that 'the late Victorian entrepreneur . . . is well on his way to redemption',[4] but he has yet to be completely exonerated. It is, however, perhaps agreed that broad generalisations embracing all industries and all firms within them are ludicrously unrealistic.

What then can one say about the performance of entrepreneurs in the British wool textile industry in the last third of the nineteenth century? Contemporary opinion was very mixed. The trade press abounds with praises of the efficiency and successes of entrepreneurs. The statement that 'We have yet to learn that an Englishman is inferior in either business capacity or industry to a German or any other man' appeared in the *Textile Manufacturer* in May 1882. Two years earlier the same journal had denied the assertion that 'the present race of manufacturers are behind their fathers in the indomitable perseverance that overcame obstacles, and the never failing industry with which they carried on their businesses . . .', and it denied also the charge that 'young men will not stick the business'.[5]

However, intermingled with these favourable comments is a substantial volume of criticism which seems to correspond very closely with the doubts raised in more recent times about enterprise in British industry in the late nineteenth century. Thus one comes across such comments as: 'indifference to the customs and peculiarities of foreign countries (is) so characteristic of many firms'[6] and: 'Englishmen have so long been accustomed to control the markets of the world that they hardly apprehend the true dimensions of the capabilities of their opponents as yet.'[7]

This comment sounds remarkably similar to the warning given in the same journal some ten years earlier: 'It is painfully ludicrous to hear the remarks made by some manufacturers on the prospects of trade. They think and talk as if the foreign manufacturer belonged to an inferior race of beings, and that, as in the past they could command the markets of the world, so will it be again . . .'[8]

The detailed criticisms included such things as: failure to search for orders, and for new markets; inattention to the get-up of goods, to quality, to standard and to presentation; unwillingness to gear production to the specific needs of customers. There were many adverse comments about such matters as trade publicity being produced in English and not in the language of potential customers, and of prices being quoted in British currency. Manufacturers were accused of sending travellers abroad without knowledge of the language and customs of countries in which they were searching for orders. There were stories of antiquated machinery and of an unwillingness to experiment with new methods.[9] And all the criticisms were embodied from time to time in, for example, accusations that entrepreneurs showed 'ignorance, conservative notions regarding processes, want of enterprise, lack of skill or deficiency of training,' resulting in 'sheer negligence'.[10] Some manufacturers, it was said 'hid their heads ostrich-like with their competitors in sight . . . or sit waiting child-like for some good thing to drop into their lap.'[11]

The publication of Ernest Williams' book, *Made in Germany*, in 1896, created quite a stir. He by no means excluded wool textile manufacturers from his condemnations. In relation to them he wrote:

> Where the Englishman is often content to lean on his fattened ledger and give himself an easy time and his wife a new carriage (in the meanwhile reposing comfortable in the bosom of a beneficent Providence), the German grapples the new chance with hooks of steel, and turns it with conspicuous success, to the permanent profit of his business.

and he accused them of being 'the victims of a chronic indisposition to keep abreast with the times'.[12]

However, our examination of the British wool textile industry in the closing decades of the nineteenth century does not lend support to the generality of such criticisms. It may well be that some or all of them are justified in relation to individual firms. It may well be also that earlier in the century, when the industry was doing so well that its business methods were never scrutinised, similar problems existed in some firms. But, in the woollen branch of the industry, at least, there is much to suggest that the entrepreneur was quite dynamic in his approach to changing commercial circumstances. His success in both neutral and many protected markets would seem to do him credit. The extent to which he experimented with his product, both adjusting to fashion changes and stimulating the appetite of his clients with 'specialities', suggests he paid careful attention to his trade. Whether the criticisms of his marketing practices were justified is, likewise, debatable. Many of those criticisms appear to have arisen from consular reports and one must wonder how often these were simply repetitive, rather than the result of considered investigation by the consuls themselves. Moreover the individual wool textile manufacturer was rarely large enough to employ his own representatives in distant markets. He was reliant on merchants and agents in the various countries, who presumably normally spoke the relevant language. Communication between agent and manufacturer may well at times have been at fault but it is difficult to see how the individual manufacturer could either have controlled the efforts and activities of his agent and the agent's representatives or persuaded that agent to provide more detailed information on the tastes and requirements of the markets. Commission agents obtained products from many manufacturers and had their own interests which, Payne has suggested, included wanting variety and comprehensive ranges.[13] The agents had no great incentive to pay attention to the particular queries of one supplying manufacturer. Their efforts may have related more 'to the relative saleability of the lines . . . [they] represented' in order to maximise their own income rather than the sales of a particular manufacturer.[14]

The quality of the entrepreneurial performance of the wool textile industry may, arguably, be judged only by the performance of the industry as a whole.[15] Even if detailed business records survived for a much wider range of firms than is the case, it is most unlikely that those records could adequately throw light on some of the queries raised. But when judging the success of enterprise, it is necessary to take into account the environment in which the individual entrepreneur was working. In an industry where both home and foreign demand were subject to sudden and often unpredictable fluctuations and where other exogenous factors such as fashion could create great uncertainties, good entrepreneurship should perhaps be assessed in terms of a careful and measured response rather than a sudden reaction.

It was an industry also plagued with other difficulties. Regular overcapacity, created amongst other things by the ease of entry in periods of buoyant trade and by the not necessarily very great economies of scale, encouraged a desire for care and moderation in business activities for which, in the circumstances, the entrepreneur could hardly be criticised. Such was the turnover of firms and the fear of failure, which as Sigsworth suggests in due course came to the 'typical' firm,[16] that perhaps risk aversion was sensible. To take the opposite view and to suggest that failure was often the result of poor entrepreneurial practices would need a much more careful analysis of the reasons for failure. But such evidence as there is hardly suggests that many firms failed as a result of the criticisms of entrepreneurs outlined above.

There must, however, be exceptions to the above generalisations. The failure of Bradford worsted manufacturers to adapt their production to French competition, even when it must have become obvious to them that the advantages of French methods in meeting market demand had become permanent, would seem to be inexplicable except in terms of an obstinacy on the part of the manufacturers to recognise the superiority of their French competitors. Perhaps similar obstinacy was inherent in the West of England trade in earlier decades, in its unwillingness to adapt its production to market alterations and new cloths. Otherwise one has to be impressed by the wool textile trade's willingness to experiment with materials and products and a desire to overcome the greater difficulties of trade in foreign markets. Writing in 1911, Graham commented:

> The very existence of Yorkshire manufacturers and merchants depend upon them keeping abreast with the times. No industry in the world has been subjected to so many changes or suffered so much from the vagaries of fashion and no other industry has shown more readiness to throw out obsolete machinery and instal new plant in order to meet the ever changing requirements of the day, and so long as Yorkshire manufacturers, dyers and merchants maintain their present enterprise, inventiveness and vigour they have nothing to fear.

Although one must doubt the claim about replacement of machinery and regret the inaccuracy of the forecast in the long term, the sentiments expressed may not have been far from the truth.[17]

Survival of Firms

Although there were many firms, particularly in the West Riding industry, that in 1900 could trace their ancestry back through two or three generations the overwhelming evidence suggests that the vast majority of firms that existed at one time or another had relatively short lives. How short these lives were is debatable. Various attempts have been made to assess survival using, in particular, trade directories but, as Dr Malin has recently shown, such directories vary in their comprehensiveness and accuracy and it is doubtful if even the most respected of the late nineteenth century trade directories can be assumed to be complete. Malin's study of the directories of the heavy woollen district in Yorkshire, and a comparison of them with the census returns, showed a high level of omission. In 1861 and 1871 over half the rag merchants and dealers in Batley enumerated by the census were not recorded in the corresponding major directories. For Dewsbury the figure was as high as 78 per cent in 1861. Arguably of course the occupational characteristics of rag merchants and dealers and the fact that they were often one man businesses, perhaps without permanent base, might explain their poor coverage in the trade directories. All the same the problem was undoubtedly more general; pirating, haphazard collection and classification of information, and lags between collection and publication all create difficulties in the use of the directories.[18] A further problem in tracing the existence of firms is the recognition of changes in partnership, perhaps leading to new designations, and the identification of changes in location and even product.

However, attempts have been made to use directories, whilst recognising the difficulties inherent in them. Sigsworth and Blackman, by comparing Yorkshire directories for 1870, 1875, and 1912, and checking against other information where possible, found that in the West Riding wool textile industry as a whole only approximately 50 per cent of the firms in existence in 1870 were still surviving five years later and only 9 per cent of the 1870 firms were still working in 1912.[19] Although on the one hand omissions from the directories might mean this level of exit from the industry is too high, the figures could on the other hand understate the extent to which entrepreneurs were changing, bearing in mind the probability of partnership changes within firms. A study by Malin on similar lines and concentrating on the Batley, Dewsbury and Ossett area came to similar conclusions. In the Rochdale flannel and associated trades a similar poor survival record existed. In 1892 only 25 of the 78 firms recorded in 1871–72 appear to have been still working.[20]

Sigsworth and Blackman show that survival rates in the late nineteenth century were low for all sections of the industry but also suggest that those areas of the industry with the smallest firms suffered the greatest losses. But this generalisation is not really substantiated by comparing the survival rate with the average size of firms as indicated by the factory returns. The particular problems of the worsted industry in the 1870s, in spite of relatively large firms, may well have affected the situation.

The year 1875 was one of bad trade and contrasts perhaps unrealistically with the prosperous year of 1870. However, other evidence tends to confirm that such low levels of survival were not uncommon at other periods. Factory inspector R. Baker reported that only 127 out of 318 firms in the Yorkshire trade survived from 1836 to 1846.[21] This level of survival is confirmed by contemporary directories; in Keighley, for example, only approximately one-third of the worsted spinning and manufacturing firms of 1830 were still at work in 1853 in spite of the prosperity of the worsted industry in most of the intervening period. In the neighbouring areas of Bingley, Morton and Haworth, fewer than 20 per cent of the 1830 worsted firms were still recorded in 1853.[22]

These low survival rates in Yorkshire were in an industry which in general was expansionary. In the West of England the gradual decline of the industry makes one less surprised by high exit rates. The factory statistics portray a dismal enough picture but they do not, of course, take into account changes of ownership of mills. In Gloucestershire the number of woollen mills fell from 118 in 1835 to 80 by 1850. A contemporary report claimed that in a few years before 1846 143 woollen manufacturers failed.[23]

The rate of failure of firms may be traced more closely through lists of bankruptcies. These do not, of course, account for all closures or alterations of use nor do they indicate entrepreneurial changes. Moreover in some instances it was possible for firms to continue trading under the supervision of creditors or the liquidator. The bankruptcy gazette, first published in 1828, provides a weekly list of all bankruptcies in Great Britain from 1836. From the 1870s, and occasionally at earlier dates, trade journals and newspapers extracted local names for their own prublications. The lists also include liquidations by arrangement or composition which after 1887 were replaced by deeds of arrangement. Table 54 shows the number of bankruptcies and deeds of arrangement for West Riding woollen firms from 1836 and clearly indicates the periods of the largest number of failures as the late 1830s, the early 1860s, the mid-1870s and around 1890. Some indications of failures in the worsted trade are available from figures published for Bradford industry in the *Bradford Observer* in 1883. They show a high level of failures in the late 1870s but do not distinguish worsted firms separately.[24]

It is possible to examine in more detail the failures of the second half of the 1870s as a result of the attention paid to them by the *Textile Manufacturer*. Rumour and surmise cannot always be separated from fact but a number of features do appear to stand out. Several of the major failures, which brought down other firms, appear to have resulted wholly or partly from speculation of money in other activities. The large firm of John Oldroyd of Britannia Mills, Dewsbury collapsed in 1877 with secured and unsecured debts of £265,000 and assets of £125,000. Oldroyd was regarded as the wealthiest manufacturer in the heavy woollen district, and a man whose advice in matters of business was, to use a homely phrase, 'as good as gold'. His carpet works had apparently been making a healthy profit but he lost £185,000 in a year through speculations in a range of other activities including hops, tea, tin, a Midland soap works and a South Wales colliery.[25] Another Dewsbury firm, Matthew Wharton of Batley Carr went bankrupt through speculation in circuses, shows, fêtes and skating rinks.[26]

Other firms failed through external difficulties. Overseas and London merchants' bankruptcies brought down some. The failure of the London merchant firm of Alexander Collie and Co., which suspended payment in 1875, and associated bankruptcies in London, had serious implications for many woollen firms in the South of Scotland; several leading firms failed. One local newspaper perhaps realistically summed up the situation: 'The failures did not arise from ordinary transactions connected with the tweed trade, which is still in a thriving state, but primarily from certain bold speculations quite foreign to manufacturing enterprise.' The firm of Collie had, in a very short period, built up liabilities of over £3.5 million. Its failure exposed the insecurity of other merchants with little capital and thus dependent wholly on credit. One firm had assets of only £400 but had accepted bills for Collie of £56,000, depending on the commission from them for its income.[27]

Blanket manufacturers, John Lee and Sons of Earlsheaton in Yorkshire, failed as a result of the Turkish Government not settling accounts. They in turn brought down a local shoddy manufacturer, Ab Wilson. But many of these external difficulties simply revealed the lack of financial strength of some Yorkshire firms. As stocks

Table 54   *Failures of West Riding woollen firms, 1836–1905*

Annual averages	Failures	Annual averages	Failures
1836–40	11	1871–5	30
1841–5	5	1876–80	31
1846–50	1	1881–5	25
1851–5	3	1886–90	16
1856–60	5	1891–5	15
1861–5	21	1896–1900	11
1866–70	15	1901–5	6

SOURCE: *Perry's Bankrupt and Insolvent Gazette*, I, 1828 to XXIV, 1861; *Perry's Bankrupt Weekly Gazette*, XXV, 1862 to LV, 1881; *Perry's Gazette*, LVI, 1882 et seq; *Textile Manufacturer*.

NOTES: Includes shoddy firms. Inclusion in the registers did not always mean that the firm ceased trading. We are most grateful to Dr Malin for the figures, which are tentative in that they have been mostly taken from the 'trade classification' section of the *Gazette* rather than from the different headings of 'bankruptcies', 'assignments', etc.

accumulated, settlements were delayed and sources for extensions of borrowed capital dried up, so the weaker firms were forced to declare their insolvency, or in some instances to lie about their position in order to continue business. The trade journal commented in August 1877: 'Men in a hopeless state of insolvency obtained by false representations the property of others and promised payment.'[28] Although the failures were many, however, a report by a Mr R. Seyd in 1877, suggested that overall the trade of Yorkshire, although depressed, was not resting on too substantial a speculative foundation, as the level of failures was low compared with other areas.[29] Detailed analysis of the failures is impossible but the impression the trade reports leave is that many of them in the 1870s were closely connected, the bankruptcy of a few large manufacturing or merchanting firms, spelling doom to their smaller suppliers. It seems probable that many of the difficulties experienced resulted from the foolhardiness of just a few businesses. Rumour played its part and some firms may well have suffered through rumour giving them an undeserved bad name. The Leeds Chamber of Commerce at one stage resolved that:

> Rumours in the newspapers of the financial instability of firms which the newspapers do not cite by name are to be deplored. These are likely in times of excitement, to provoke surmises injurious to respectable houses, and in detriment to the Trade and Character of the Town.[30]

Recorded bankruptcies clearly do not account for the level of disappearance of firms suggested by Sigsworth and Blackman. One can only conclude that, particularly at times of trade depression, entrepreneurs left the industry by choice, liquidating what resources remained to them. The extent to which these, or the failed entrepreneurs, accord with the thesis of a lack of interest or dynamism in third generation firms is debatable. The high turnover of firms might suggest that only very few survived long enough to find their way into the hands of the grandchildren of the original founders. There are several instances of firms being broken up through disagreements between members of the second and third generations of a family.

Marketing

An understanding of the links between the manufacturer and his market is crucial both to an assessment of the reaction of manufacturers to market changes and also to an examination of British competition in all markets. Yet to a very great extent marketing arrangements have been a much neglected area in most studies of British industry in the nineteenth century. In general there is ample information available to suggest the routes taken by goods between their manufacturer and the final purchaser and broad trends in their development are often identifiable. However it is less easy to be specific about the relative importance and efficiency of the methods used.

The marketing methods used by the wool textile industry in the second half of the nineteenth century were quite complex, and varied noticeably in different parts of the industry and for different markets. Of paramount importance to many aspects of trade was the commission agent but wholesale merchants, shippers, commercial travellers, direct tendering and individual contact with retailers and wholesale clothing manufacturers all played a significant role in marketing arrangements.

In both the home and overseas trade the commission agent was a central figure. He was of particular importance in the United States market,[31] but trade to many other parts of the world depended on the efforts of commission houses. The system operated was for manufacturers, or sometimes home merchants, to send goods to foreign merchants either in response to specific orders, or in the earlier period in particular, off their own bat. Orders from commission merchants would be solicited by sending out patterns or samples or by encouraging visits from them. The commission houses then disposed of the goods to wholesale merchants, or directly to retailers. Again in the earlier period the auction house was used in certain instances to dispose of goods, particularly when there was an urgency to do so, perhaps when general sales were not good. In return for their efforts, the commission agents charged typically 5 or 10 per cent of the final sale price, plus any insurance and storage costs incurred, and they demanded varying lengths of credit.

The use of commission houses had advantages for manufacturers. It enabled them to place their goods in the hands of merchants who had close contacts with the local market situation and in whose interests it was to obtain good prices, as the commission depended on these. It meant that manufacturers could save the expense of sending travellers or employing representatives. But there were clearly many disadvantages as well and it may well have been that the greater dependence of British wool textile manufacturers on commission houses, compared with their European competitors, put them at some disadvantage in reacting rapidly to changes in the market. Particular criticism of the commission house system was that goods were obtained from a range of manufacturers. The agents had an interest in keeping a variety of stock so as to be prepared for any possible demand. Thus they had no particular incentive to promote the interests of any one manufacturer and they could be slow to dispose of cloth. This meant that a manufacturer continuously attempting to promote a particular speciality was at a disadvantage.[32]

Other problems for manufacturers using commission houses included the need to finish goods and thus bear the costs and risks thereby involved. Cloth sent to commission houses remained the risk of the manufacturer until it was sold. The latter could not necessarily be guaranteed a quick sale and thus had to bear the cost of waiting. Yet another criticism was that the competitiveness of the product in its final market was likely to be affected by the cost of using a commission house, particularly when the latter acted as an additional middleman rather than a substitute for the wholesale merchant. Commission houses were active in most parts of the world and the records of West Yorkshire firms indicate the extent to which they were used. Firms generated strong links with particular houses but also tested others, particularly in new areas, by sending goods as an experiment.

The major alternative to the commission agent for selling in foreign parts was through direct sales to a merchant at home or abroad. The selling risks were thereby taken over by the merchant but the price was pushed down accordingly. The Bradford piece-trade in particular was mainly conducted through Bradford merchants, many of German origin, who had so successfully established themselves during the middle part of the century. The Fosters of Black Dyke Mills continued to use such merchants for their Continental trade in spite of using commission agents in the United States and foreign agents for their yarn sales. They received many offers to represent them for their Continental piece-trade but always declined. On one occasion they explained why:

we consider it more to our advantage to sell to the large houses in Bradford and leave them to fight it out on the other side than to sell direct to Paris. Our goods are delivered to the merchants in the grey and it is their business to see they are properly dyed and finished, but in case we had an agency on the other side, we should have to do this and the profit is so small it would not pay us, besides which we should have to close many good accounts in this market where the parties take other classes of goods and yarn of importance. For these reasons we have always thought it better not to have representatives in Paris and we still adhere to this.[33]

The popularity of Bradford merchants, which is implied by John Foster's view, would seem to have been agreed generally. The Bradford trade recognised the efficiency of many Bradford merchants and the success of the German merchants, in particular, in Continental markets, because of their contacts and linguistic skills. Manufacturers did not depend entirely on home merchants; many established direct links with Continental and foreign wholesale houses.

Scottish woollen manufacturers also remained wedded to trading with wholesale houses. Initially their links had been with mercantile firms in Edinburgh and Glasgow, but they gradually developed connections with London commission houses. By the second half of the nineteenth century it was more normal for the middleman to act as wholesale merchant, purchasing cloth to order from the manufacturer. The merchants dictated colours and patterns and took much of the financial risk. Cloth was sold under the merchants' name and individual manufacturers were often closely linked to particular merchants. The system had its disadvantages and frustrations; suspicion could affect relationships and there were occasional accusations of merchants giving patterns to other manufacturers to be produced more cheaply. Yet another problem was that the close links with particular merchants could, in difficult trading times, put the manufacturer at a bargaining disadvantage. Later in the century sales were being carried out in other ways. Some firms, particularly those in remote areas, employed agents to sell, on commission, to merchants. But this increased costs and met with hostility from the merchants. Other firms granted foreign agencies but most overseas business remained through the wholesale houses, including some Continental import houses and German merchants based in Britain. Occasionally speculative consignments were sent to distant markets but in general, up to the end of the period, the vast majority of the Scottish woollen trade was entrusted to the wholesale merchants, mainly based in London. Manufacturers sent samples, and occasionally travelled down with patterns to negotiate orders.[34]

West of England manufacturers continued to be dependent mainly on London merchants. Whereas earlier in the century they had often been closely linked with just one or two merchanting firms, the custom did develop for them to distribute their cloths more widely. Occasionally manufacturers tried other sales methods including direct advertising. Some larger firms opened their own warehouses in London, others appointed overseas agents, but the London factor remained of paramount importance to them. A few West Country firms traded directly with America, sending their goods to be packed at Huddersfield, where specialist packers examined goods for faults and accepted responsibility on behalf of the American customer. This ensured that faulty goods did not get imported to America and thereby have to pay the high tariff.[35]

There are very many references, particularly in consular reports, to commercial travellers and their deficiencies, or to the lack of travellers in many markets. However it would seem that such travellers were only rarely employed directly by manufacturing concerns. They were more likely to have been the representatives of wholesale merchants, though there were a few instances of manufacturers employing their own commercial travellers. A trade journal reported in 1876 that those Dewsbury and Batley manufacturers who had their own travellers were getting some orders from the Continent in spite of the poor general demand.[36] Those firms which attempted to combine manufacturing and merchanting sometimes employed travellers. Thus A.H. Hutton of a large firm of woollen and worsted manufacturers and merchants of Leeds, Eccleshill and Bradford sent travellers to the Continent and employed them in Canada and South Africa. They were in a better position to use travellers because of the range of their products.[37]

The criticism of British commercial travellers must therefore have related mainly to those employed by merchants. One wonders, however, what proportion of those representatives were British as there are many examples of foreigners being employed as representatives. The Bradford piece-trade to a great extent was operated by German merchants, using their own representatives on the Continent. Herbert Foster of Black Dyke Mills argued in 1906:

> There is no better travelling done than is done by the Bradford commercial houses. The travellers are mostly Germans who have come and settled there. We have always found them straightforward, and they do their business well, they have done a great deal for Bradford . . . they have the advantages of speaking foreign languages and good connections on the Continent.[38]

Other merchants employed representatives directly in the countries where they were trading. For example, William Thorburn, a Peebles merchant, stated in 1906 that his method had been to employ men of good commercial standing of the country he was selling in. He considered Germans to be more pushing and pertinacious and he argued that in the American market Scotsmen did better as travellers than Englishmen.[39]

The reliance for business on commission agents and wholesale houses, either at home or abroad created a void between manufacturer and consumer that was obviously not easy to bridge; but attempts were made to narrow the gap. Many of the better known entrepreneurs are recorded as having travelled abroad, often to exhibitions or to combine business with pleasure. Members of the Foster family regularly visited their customers in Paris, even though they were not dealing directly with them. Isaac Holden travelled regularly and widely in Europe, North Africa and the Middle East and in the 1880s three Halifax and Keighley manufacturers went on a tour of America and Canada to study the position of manufacturers in those countries.[40]

By late in the century a few manufacturers were selling directly to wholesale clothing manufacturers and to retail shops. The development of the ready-made clothing trade provided a direct outlet although it is probable that the size of the early clothing manufacturers was such that they could not take long runs of cloth at one go. At the same period some of the larger London retailers were bypassing middlemen by ordering their cloth requirements directly from manufacturers; thus Marshall and Snelgrove of Oxford Street, for example, purchased directly from the Fosters and there were various reports that other retailers were going directly to manufacturers.[41] Another means of direct sale was to the Navy Board and the Board of Ordinance. Throughout the century Government purchases of army and navy cloth were made from approved manufacturers, who were requested to tender. Only the larger and established firms could get on the Government approved list, although often work had to be subcontracted.[42]

Thus methods of marketing in the wool textile industry did not undergo very great change during the course of much of the century, but there were some significant small alterations. There was a tendency for manufacturers to produce less for stock from the 1870s, although previously some makers, including those in Scotland, had only produced to order. There was a slight movement to reduce the role of middlemen and there was also a change in the nature of the wholesale merchants. Whereas earlier in the century individual merchants had specialised in different markets, and rarely mixed the home and foreign trades, by the closing decades changes in foreign markets and increased competition had reduced the scope for specialised merchants and most combined many types of business. As Clapham reported, there was little scope left for the specialised merchant as retailers and traders liked to be able to see a wide variety of goods.[43]

International Exhibitions, 1870–1914

The exhibitions of the 1850s and 1860s were reasonably well supported by British wool textile manufacturers. There was always, however, an underlying current of doubt about their usefulness. Bousfield reported some of the criticisms:

> I have heard it expressed as a serious opinion that what we did in 1851 was simply to gather about us all the thieves and bandits in Europe and show them our riches, and that blinded by their obsequious flattery, we asked for nothing better than orders for tools to enable them to break open our strong places and possess themselves of our treasure.[44]

By the 1870s, with exhibitions becoming more frequent and widespread, more general doubts were appearing about their usefulness to manufacturers. Jacob Behrens commented that he was unable to take much interest in those exhibitions that followed, for 'all of them assumed more and more the character of a clamorous bid for custom, and of an attempt merely to extend the sale of the produce of the country holding the exhibition.'[45] There were complaints about a surfeit of exhibitions and that exhibition promoters had become a profession, some exhibitions lacking purpose 'save for employing organizers'.[46]

Various articles in the trade journals in the 1880s included a range of adverse reports. The *Textile Recorder* in September 1884, discussing the 'miserable failures' of some exhibitions, suggest that 'manufacturers, especially those connected with the Textile Industries, are tired of even hearing of the projection of an exhibition'. There were complaints about some exhibitions charging for medals, others being prepared too hurriedly and exhibitions 'being projected for every conceivable thing . . . Ad Nauseam!'[47]

Perhaps much of the dissatisfaction and adverse comment arose initially in relation to the exhibition at Philadelphia in 1876. Many manufacturers doubted that exhibiting there would be of benefit to them because of the level of protectionism in the United States market. Behrens refused to go as a juror.[48] Kidderminster manufacturers declined to exhibit on the principle that 'free trade should be the guiding principle of all international expositions'. Fears of designs being pirated put off other potential exhibitors.[49] The result was that few British towns were well represented: there was only one exhibit from Bradford, four from the Heavy Woollen district although there were rather more from Leeds and Huddersfield. A number of West of England firms made the effort; but overall the comment of the jury that Britain did not do justice to herself at the Exhibition was probably well founded.[50] Manufacturers from various areas of Europe were, however, well represented; the Reims Chamber of Commerce arranged a comprehensive display; the German textile trade was represented by 98 firms.[51] Henry Mitchell in his report of the Philadelphia Exhibition to the Bradford Chamber of Commerce regretted afterwards that English manufacturers had held aloof from the exhibition and suggested that:

> It was a matter of regret that the show of British worsted fabrics, especially from Bradford, was so very insignificant, for a good opportunity was lost of demonstrating to the American people the disadvantages they suffer from the maintenance of prohibitive tariffs.[52]

At yet another Paris exhibition, two years later, British wool textile manufacturers were much better represented although the degree of effort varied much from one district to another. *The Times*, early in 1877, was attempting to encourage manufacturers to exhibit:

> It is incumbent upon the manufacturers of the United Kingdom to show the world at Paris next year that they have not fallen behind the position they once occupied. The competition at Philadelphia was not altogether satisfactory to us.[53]

At the beginning of the next year the *Textile Manufacturer* was doubtful that many had responded to the plea. It suggested that few had taken action about exhibiting at Paris as a feeling prevailed that the individual benefit derived from exhibitions was so minute that it was not worthwhile to incur the labour and annoyance. But some districts were well represented. Huddersfield put on a particularly good display, although, according to Clay, some of the best manufacturers were not represented.[54] Twelve worsted manufacturers from Bradford took part but in spite of the efforts of the Leeds Chamber of Commerce only seven firms from that locality exhibited, and it was commented that their exhibition fell 'miserably short'.[55] A number of Galashiels firms displayed their goods and the West of England was reasonably represented. The latter's exhibits were described in the report of the exhibition in the *Textile Manufacturer* as follows:

> We felt them to be as delicious, as soothing and as refreshing to our heated, jaded and fevered touch as if we had layed [sic] our hands in cool spring water . . . the West is not beaten yet where quality, superiority of fabric and excellence of finish are the test points of standard.[56]

However, in spite of the huge attendance at the exhibition, a very satisfactory tally of awards and reasonable comments on the standards of British goods, not all manufacturers who exhibited were happy with it. There were doubts that it could have contributed very much to trade in the protected European markets and complaints that medals were not fairly allocated. It was reported that one award winner offered his bronze medal as a contribution to a lottery, as he claimed it was awarded to him without any examination of the quality of his exhibits.[57]

In the 1880s exhibitions were being arranged all over the world, often several being held within weeks of each other. In one year the Bradford Chamber of Commerce received official notices of exhibitions to be held at Antwerp, Bordeaux, Lyons, Milan, Santiago, and Hobart but took no action to encourage representatives at any of them.[58] An analysis of the exhibitors at later exhibitions suggests that very few firms made an effort to show their wares, except at the major Paris exhibitions of 1889 and 1900 where British manufacturers were well represented. At the other exhibitions there were a small number of firms which regularly exhibited their goods, and presumably found it worthwhile to do so. Occasionally various Chambers of Commerce organised collective shows. The Bradford Chamber, for example, put on a collective exhibit of 25 glass show-cases containing 1524 specimens at the Calcutta Exhibition of 1884.[59] In general, however, only a tiny minority of firms after the 1870s used the International Fair as a means of drawing attention to their products.

From the amount of contemporary debate in the newspapers and trade press it may well be that this lack of interest was not through apathy, but resulted from more careful evaluation of the potential costs and benefits of undertaking the substantial organisation that was necessary to attend exhibitions. It is noticeable that many of the firms which continued to exhibit were at the upper end of their particular branches of the trade and were noted for their innovatory activity. The 'run of the mill' firm producing standard cloths for the mass market, whose basic products were not likely to receive much attention from the juries and whose goods were heavily taxed in most of the countries where major exhibitions were held, appeared to see little advantage in the exhibitions. The Wool Textile Delegation stated in evidence to the Committee on Trade and Industry in 1926 that 'trade fairs and exhibitions are generally considered to be of no service to the industry'.[60] However, the level of exhibiting from the other major wool textile manufacturing countries of Europe was better sustained. The manufacturers of those countries would, therefore, appear to have had a better opinion of the value of exhibitions.

Textile Education

Throughout the 1850s and 1860s, as manufacturers visiting the great international exhibitions became aware of the improvements in the products of their foreign competitors, there emerged an awareness that the provision of technical education in Britain of benefit to the wool textile industry was well behind that available in most of the other major European countries. And in the minds of some manufacturers, but by no means all, a major reason for the decline in Britain's relative competitive position was to do with the superiority of foreign educational services.

That Britain was poorly provided with technical education institutions giving instruction in manufacturing and commercial methods is undeniable. Indeed the provision of such education was non-existent through the middle decades of the nineteenth century, if one disregards the few local, normally short-lived and to all intents and purposes insignificant attempts that were made to establish schools and institutes. On the Continent, in France, Austria and Germany in particular, a number of institutions were created which gained high international reputations and even attracted English students.

Attempts to establish training courses in textile manufacturing methods, and particularly in weaving, were made in the 1840s and 1850s in Britain. A letter to the Bradford newspaper in 1841 advocated the local establishment of a school of art and design, but nothing transpired.[61] A decade later the Bradford Chamber of Commerce expressed its '. . . strong conviction for the expediency of establishing artisans' Drawing and Modelling Schools . . . as a means highly calculated to foster and improve the staple manufacture'.[62] The demand for education provision gradually spread, perhaps stimulated by the reports on the 1855 Paris Exhibition, a number of which suggested that the progress of French manufacture owed a lot to training in design. No doubt these comments contributed to the establishment in 1859 of a school of design at Bradford, under the patronage of a number of local merchants and manufacturers. But the school faced a problem that later technical institutions were often to encounter, that of finding suitable instructors. The Bradford school appointed James Lobley, who gained an excellent reputation for his artistic ability but not in the application of that ability to the design of textile fabrics. The school developed into a drawing and painting academy for the offspring of gentlefolk.[63]

The exhibitions of the 1860s gave rise to further demands for educational provision in Britain and produced from the ranks of manufacturers a number of champions for the cause, amongst the most notable of whom where the Nusseys of Leeds and Swire Smith of Keighley. In his report as juror to the Paris Exhibition of 1867, Mr Thomas Nussey spoke strongly of the disadvantages under which English manufacturers laboured owing to the absence of technical education.[64] This view was supported by Kitson who went as the representative of Leeds Chamber of Commerce to the Exhibition.[65] Thomas Nussey's report stimulated George, Henry and Arthur Nussey to publish a pamphlet advocating the establishment of 'a centre of manufacturing instruction' at Leeds.[66] They set out a proposal – 'a detailed programme' – for such an institution and their persistent efforts culminated in the foundation in the early 1870s of a school of textile design, which was incorporated in 1874 in the new Yorkshire College of Science as a Department of Textile Industries and was rapidly to gain international recognition as a major textile education centre. Swire Smith was an active promoter of technical education for over 40 years; largely through his efforts a trade school, financed by voluntary contributions, was opened at Keighley by 1870.[67]

The 1870s and 1880s saw very rapid developments in some parts of the wool textile manufacturing districts. Textile colleges or classes were established in Bristol in 1876, Glasgow in 1877, Batley, Bradford, Huddersfield and Kidderminster in 1878, Hawick in 1880 and Morley in 1883. In the West of England, although classes in chemistry and textile design were started in Stroud in 1877 under the auspices of Bristol University College, with the assistance of the Clothworkers' Company, the area as a whole was far behind Yorkshire. In Scotland various attempts were made to run classes, at Hawick and Galashiels for example, but full technical colleges did not emerge until later.[68]

The sudden burst of activity in some areas owed a great deal to the efforts of a few initiators but was further stimulated by the onset of depression in 1873 which gave rise to broader debate about Britain's competitive position. A number of Chambers of Commerce became involved in assisting local education development. The Bradford Chamber, particularly under its Chairman Henry Mitchell, was active in such promotion locally. Batley Chamber organised classes itself in 1878.[69] The President of the Huddersfield Chamber argued in 1877:

> Technical education is a subject fast coming to the front in this country, and one which has long been so with our continental neighbours, and English manufacturers must take up the subject in earnest if we are to maintain our position as the head of commerce in the great markets of the world.[70]

Encouragement was given by the main trade journal, the *Textile Manufacturer*, from its first issues in 1875, and by 1877 it was reporting progress:

> It would seem to be an inherent feature of the English character that long years of strange indifference to any important subject should be suddenly terminated by widespread activity in its promotion.[71]

The long awaited report of the Royal Commission on Technical Instruction, which provided a great deal of detail about foreign colleges and indicated problems in the organisation of some in Britain, was a further stimulus to debate and progress. And progress also owed a very great deal to the enterprise of the Worshipful Company of Clothworkers of the City of London. The Clothworkers' Company provided grants for capital and running costs to many institutions, both large and small. The Textile Department of the Yorkshire College, later Leeds University, had by the end of the 1890s received about £70,000 for equipment and operating costs.[72] In most cases other finance had to be raised locally and in all areas there were active patrons of education but it does seem to be somewhat doubtful whether the 'unexpected enthusiasm amongst manufacturers for textile education', claimed by the *Textile Manufacturer* in 1877 was overwhelming.[73] There were as many, if not more, fierce opponents as strong advocates and relatively few manufacturers would appear to have dipped into their pockets or profits to support their local colleges. The claim by Illingworth of Bradford that 'no one will question the desirability of technical knowledge in every branch of trade, nor the need for culture in every station of life' and that it was 'unanimously agreed' that there was an 'all-round want of technical education' was far from the truth.[74] A pamphlet published in Bradford in 1878 fiercely attacked the rage for 'technical cramming' which it was claimed would give rise to 'spurious superficialism', would divert energy from manufacturing activity, would make the poaching of designs and ideas even easier, and would produce 'a motley crew of half-educated, self-satisfied smatterers flourishing their bits of parchment'.[75]

Opposition was expressed in more moderate tones by many witnesses to the Commission on Depression in Trade and Industry. William Schulze of Galashiels, for example, claimed there was 'no need for improvement of education of workmen',[76] and a prominent Yorkshire manufacturer, J.T. Clay, in a letter to his local newspaper, claimed that workpeople could be far better taught through practical experience in the mill.[77] A letter to the *Textile Manufacturer* in 1883, signed 'Observer', claimed that over-education of millhands would be 'downright mischievous'. A reply from 'a workman' insisted that 'hands will be educated'.[78]

The opposition which continued through the last decades of the nineteenth century is probably largely indicative of disagreements about the content and role of the new education provision. It was claimed by many, undoubtedly correctly, that insufficient thought had been given to curricula and to who should benefit from the training. Most of the early classes were in weaving techniques and design. The availability of training in other industrial and commercial matters came only very slowly, although Jacob Behrens was arguing as early as 1877 that schools should, in addition to weaving, teach machine construction, drawing, the chemistry of dyeing and book-keeping.[79]

Henry Mitchell, also of Bradford complained in 1886 that schools were giving insufficient attention to training in finishing, dyeing and the get-up of goods and there were many complaints of lack of tuition facilities for foreign languages.[80] In the 1890s trade journals were commenting on the trivial and demoralising education in some of the colleges, of mediocrity, of lack of language learning facilities, of out-of-date methods and equipment and of irrelevant examinations. There were suggestions in letters that too many schools were being founded, and that attention was given to quantity rather than quality.[81] The principal of the South of Scotland Central Technical College at Galashiels would have perhaps agreed with some of these criticisms in view of his comments in 1909 that 'we have been playing at technical education for thirty years', and that courses were often designed more for teachers than for artisans.[82]

Much of the criticism about the haphazard development of technical education facilities relevant to the wool textile industry would appear to have been well founded. Some of the problems may well have arisen out of difficulties in recruiting fully competent staff and, in many instances, of insufficient and uncertain funding. However, there were few serious suggestions that the education provided did more harm than good and the reported numbers of students attending the colleges suggest that there was a very substantial demand for training, in spite of few manufacturers being prepared to allow their employees free time to attend. However, one is left with the conclusion that in general, with perhaps the notable exception of one or two colleges, the provision of education for work in the wool textile industry remained seriously behind that available elsewhere in

Europe.[83] The evidence to the Royal Commission on Technical Instruction would also seem to bear out the many complaints concerning the lack of other educational facilities. Industrial museums and
design and pattern libraries which existed in most of the textile
districts of the Continent had few counterparts in Britain.

Design and Fashion
Among the many complaints made against the British wool textile
trade in the nineteenth century, a failure to design well is often heard.
Those complaints which have a general approach can be dismissed as
irrelevant and are usually based on a failure to understand what
textile design is about and in particular a failure to distinguish
between the technical aspects of woven and printed textile design.
The woven designer must work inside the factory and his job is to
produce attractive cloths in the rather limited (design wise) looms
that he has in the weaving shed. Colour sense rather than skill in
making complicated weaves, as is needed for draw or Jacquard
looms, is required. The designer of printed textiles is much less
inhibited and printed designs can be bought from outside 'artists' but
such designs were rarely used in the wool textile trade. After ex-
amining many thousands of patterns the present authors consider
that any criticism of the skill of the wool textile designer in the
nineteenth century is unjustified. Something of the variety of cloths
offered will be described shortly when each area's contribution will
be considered separately.

There is, however, a rather different question or perhaps one
should say, legitimate criticism, namely that the trade did not respond
quickly enough to fashion changes. To answer this criticism completely various questions about fashion would need asking and this is
hardly the place for such a discussion. A number of points can,
however, reasonably be made. Were the comparatively poor section
of the population who were the main buyers of the products of the
low woollen trade, in a position to dictate fashion? Perhaps for the
first time they were able and, one assumes, happy to buy new clothes
and that was about as far as their fashion demand went. Much has
been made of the way in which the West Riding worsted trade went
on manufacturing cotton warp, coarse worsted weft fabrics when
fashion demanded all-wool merino worsteds. As has already been
pointed out, this was much more a machine or technological decision
– the determination to stay with Arkwright's frame – than anything
else. Admittedly it did mean that there was a demand for imported
worsteds and, in retrospect, perhaps more of the worsted spinning

trade should have used mules even if they felt that the frame would triumph in the end, which it certainly did. But of course 'in the end' can be a long time and many firms in the wool textile trade, as in others, had gone to the wall before their point of view was proved right.

Probably the best way to appreciate the response of the trade to changing demand is to consider the area and divisions of the industry one by one, starting of course with the Yorkshire trade. The West Riding woollen trade in the early to middle decades of the century got the answer right. Manufacturers realised that the age-long supremacy of woollens over worsteds in the more expensive end of the trade was passing. The later fortunes of the Gott family as displayed by Crump make this very clear. Men had worn fine broadcloth for too long. The future for the bulk trade in woollen fabrics lay with the cheaper articles, the low woollens as they were unfortunately called. The growth of this trade, as it is hoped this volume has clearly shown, was the great triumph of the Yorkshire industry and surely shows how accurately had been the response to demand – to fashion demand, because fashion should not be regarded as being only high fashion. This cheaper side of the Yorkshire woollen trade has too often been regarded as purely a shoddy trade. There were other branches and the growth of the all new wool Yorkshire tweed, based on the New Zealand cross-bred wools that were arriving in such large weights with the development of the frozen meat trade there, was an excellent example of how to use a by-product in an article which was admirably suited for the wholesale clothing trade when it wanted to move away from the shoddy or low woollen product.

It has already been admitted that the Yorkshire worsted trade did allow the French to capture a large market for all-wool worsteds but, when the Australian merino wools arrived in quantity and were long enough to comb, the area moved into this type of trade. By the end of the century and more particularly in the early twentieth century, the skill of the worsted designers of the Huddersfield trade was the hallmark of excellence and one which enabled the area to maintain a pre-eminent position even during the difficult years of the later twentieth century.

When one turns to the other areas the comparative fortunes of the Scottish and the West of England high-class woollen trade show clearly how impossible it is to make general statements about the response of a national industry to design, fashion or any other stimulus. The West of England could be taken as the perfect example of an area failing to respond to demand whilst the Scottish is completely the opposite: an almost perfect case of a new industry – at least new in the sense of supplying more than local demand – responding with new cloths and new colours, all helped by a judicious use of the general popularity for all things Scottish deriving from such figures as the Queen herself and the great novelist, Scott.

To consider the West of England first, the great days had been before the period covered by this volume although in 1775, and indeed until about 1810, the demand for superfine broadcloths remained good. The trouble was that these cloths had been in fashion for too long and the West of England clothiers (or manufacturers) saw no reason to believe that the demand would cease. They were certainly not the only manufacturers of consumer goods that have fallen into that trap. The selling methods that had arisen in this area – the dominance of the London factor and the consequent lack of contact between the manufacturer and his ultimate customer, may have been all right in the days of steady eighteenth-century demand, but was quite insufficient for the new world of the nineteenth century. It is rather sad to look through the pattern books of nineteenth-century West of England clothiers and see pattern after pattern of drab-coloured cloths in difficult weaves – 2/1 twill, tautz twill or cavalry twill, Bedford cord, etc. – and recollect the work, the traditional skill, that had gone into manufacturing these fabrics that so few people now wanted. If the history of the wool textile trade of Britian in the nineteenth century was only that of the West of England, then all the criticism of the lack of design and lack of response to fashion would be justified, but the whole point of this volume has been to show that this was most certainly not the case.

The Scottish story is completely different and here one has an outstandingly imaginative response to the problem. With a market in high-class woollens that was declining relatively to both worsted and low woollens, the Scottish manufacturers introduced new fabrics which were just what the better off wanted – both the aristocrats on their estates and the new, reasonably well-to-do middle class for their sporting activities. They replaced the West of England as the main producer of the high-class and more expensive woollens and prevented the Yorkshire woollen trade dominating that trade in the way it did the worsted. How was this achieved? How did an area which in the past had catered almost if not entirely for local demands, suddenly acquire this reputation? In the late eighteenth century no one appears to have expected it. At the beginning of the period covered here one of Scotland's greatest sons, David Hume, had commented rather unhelpfully: 'We cannot reasonably expect that a piece of woollen cloth will be brought to perfection in a nation which is ignorant of astronomy or where ethics are neglected.'[84] Yet a hundred years later it could well be maintained that Scottish woven textile design was the best in the world, was known throughout the world, and that Scottish textile designers were going to Yorkshire, to the West of England, to Australasia, U.S.A. and many other parts.

The reasons for this remarkable success were many; perhaps two stand out and provide the starting point for a short account of the achievement. Scottish woollen textile manufacturers by luck or good judgement realised that the future for their relatively high-priced cloths lay not, as had the West of England superfine broadcloths, in the fashionable drawing-room but for leisure wear out of doors. It is worth noting that the two markets where the West of England maintained its position were in the cloths for hunting and the non-apparel cloths for billiard tables, both, it will be noted, leisure pursuits. But for most purposes, whether shooting on the moors, walking in the country or for relaxing weekends, the Scottish trade captured the market; and what was very important, they captured it for both men and women. In the eighteenth century the well-to-do man wore West of England superfine broadcloths when he entered the drawing-room, but the lady accompanying him wore silk. The second outstanding reason for the success lay in the popularity and fame of all things Scottish, which had perhaps been started by Sir Walter Scott's novels and was certainly enhanced later in the nineteenth century by the Queen's passion for staying at Balmoral, for tartans and for other delights of the North.

The development of this successful tradition for woven cloth design can be traced to several factors. Perhaps the most obvious was the coming of the traditional Scottish tartans to the wider scene. Probably more significant, however, in the long run was the adaptation of the shepherd check, for many decades traditionally worn by the Lowland shepherd, to a much wider field. The shepherd check when combined with the many varieties of tartan colourings, produced a range of fabrics sometimes collectively called District checks but perhaps better described under individual names as shepherd checks, dogtooth checks, glen checks and gun club checks. These were the basis of the invasion into the field of leisure wear; by the later decades of the twentieth century no well dressed Englishman, let alone a Scotsman would be without his glen or shepherd check suit, for wear in the country.

The fact that the Scottish native weavers had always used the 2/2 twill should not pass unnoticed. The West of England traditionally used the plain weave which was indeed natural, as it gave them the tight structure they needed to exercise their finishing craft which was where they were so skilled. But the plain weave does not lend itself to colouring like the 2/2 twill. When it came to using the twill weave the West of England, again mainly for reasons of cloth structure preferred the 2/1 twill, another weave not much good for colour effects.

In addition to this expansion of check designs the Scottish mills widened the appeal of the tartan and invented many new non-traditional but very popular colour combinations. These cloths found a wide use for women's skirtings which they have never lost and one that was to spread throughout the world. Scottish designers were also the first to introduce fancy twist effects to the textile fashion world. Twist yarns had always been used particularly with worsteds, but the normal reason was to obtain greater strength and thereby better weaving and stronger fabrics. Such twists were usually self-coloured. The Scottish designer combined two colours in the twist, making such cloths as the Bannockburn – introduced by the firm of Watson in the town of Bannockburn – and the thornproof – a particularly hard twisted fabric made in the plain weave – and the fact that these names have lasted shows how well these cloths met the fashion demand. The introduction of these coloured twist cloths was probably the greatest technical and artistical achievement of the trade and their success came from the fact that they solved the problem of how to introduce a variety of colours into a fabric made on a loom which could weave comparatively few really fancy designs.

Other Scottish successes were the Cheviot suiting based on the native wool, often with elaborate silk stripes, overcoatings of various types invented or perfected by Crombies of Aberdeen and, in a very different field, the coming of Harris tweed. In the face of this development of Scottish woollen textiles, and the sensible decision of the low woollen trade to concentrate on manufacturing the best cloths possible from their cheap raw material without incurring expensive designing, it is unreasonable to believe that the British woollen trade did not respond to fashion or was lacking in designing skill.

The Impact of Protection

The overall effect of foreign tariffs on the British wool textile industry in the late nineteenth and at the beginning of this century was a very emotive question much debated at the time and one which gave rise to very considerable differences of opinion. Within the wool textile industry there were sharply differing views about whether retaliatory duties should have been imposed.

The unofficial Tariff Commission sought evidence to support the view that protectionism was the major cause of the problems of the industry. Unfortunately it appears to have questioned only those who favoured a British protectionist reaction, although a lot of the factual evidence collected is of considerable importance for an understanding of the state of the industry. J.H. Clapham, writing in 1904, acknowledged the severity of foreign tariffs on British goods and congratulated the British export trade for having been so resilient in the face of climbing tariffs and the development of manufacturing on modern lines in previously backward countries. He declined to attempt to consider the relative importance of tariffs and foreign competition on the British industry.[85] Dorothy Hunter, writing of the West of England industry denied that tariffs were the sole, or even major, reason for the decline of that area.[86]

Clearly generalisation is not realistic. Different sections of the industry were adversely affected to different degrees by protectionism in their foreign markets. Some manufacturers in the worsted industry could not hide behind the excuse of tariffs for their poor response to fashion changes. Yet it is realistic to argue that the wool textile industry was more adversely affected by tariffs than almost any other British industry. The duties that it faced in so many markets had in most cases initially arisen through the needs of countries to get their infant wool textile industries off the ground. But as, in many countries, manufacturing capacity and skills reached or exceeded the levels of the British industry, so protectionism remained, effectively excluding many British goods from finding an outlet. The levels of duties in many potential markets were very steep, in the United States for example often exceeding 50 per cent of value. Faced with such levels of tariffs in countries with developed domestic industries it seems quite unfair to criticise the British industry for losing its traditional markets. Indeed the pattern which emerges is one of considerable perseverance on the part of manufacturers. Attempts to beat tariff changes, to alter goods to take the best advantage of tariff categories and efforts in seeking new specialities and different market outlets all would appear to indicate a positive, calculated response by many manufacturers.

It should not be overlooked that in protected markets it was not just the absolute level of tariffs which caused great difficulties for trade; protectionism severely increased the administration or bureaucracy of trading. Manufacturers and merchants had to expend considerable effort and time keeping in touch with the legal requirements of their foreign markets. Goods had to be described in particu-

Table 55   *Exports of wool textile manufactures† from U.K., France, Germany and U.S.A. (£ million)*

Annual averages	U.K.	France	Germany	U.S.A.
1880–4	18.5	14.7	11.3	0.07*
1885–9	20.1	13.9	11.7	0.03
1890–4	17.4	12.3	10.9	0.04
1895–9	16.5	11.0	10.5	0.11
1900–4	15.8	8.7	11.5	0.13
1905–8	20.4	8.6	13.5	0.10

SOURCE: *British and Foreign Trade and Industry* (1854–1908): Statistical Tables and Charts *BPP.*, 1909 (Cd 4896) CII.

NOTES: * Includes wearing apparel for four of the years
† Excludes tops, tails, yarn and apparel

lar ways; disputes over values and descriptions could delay goods and at times mean the expense of returning them. There were frequent complaints of custom houses acting arbitrarily or adopting the least favourable view for the importer. One must have sympathy with the manufacturer who complained about French protectionism:

> Really the intricacies of this tariff make one feel that it was put together, not only to protect the French manufacturer, but to raise so many difficulties for the foreigner as to make him disgusted with the whole.[87]

How can one make an assessment of the performance of the British wool textile industry in the highly protected markets? Indeed, is it justifiable to do so when manufacturers were realistically resigned to a situation where, if they did score success in spite of the tariff, their efforts would soon be curtailed by tariff adjustments. A comparison with other foreign competitors is complicated by the diversity of products traded and variations of tariffs on different classes of goods. However, indications would seem to be that in both protected and neutral markets many parts of the British wool textile industry did rather better than their foreign competitors from the 1880s. Excluding the yarn trade, the development of which can be looked upon as a success story, and comparing 1875–79 with 1900–4 the British industry increased its share of the imports of wool textiles to many protected markets. Britain survived better over that period than other major producers in the United States market for woollen cloth and for dress goods. In neutral markets likewise there is little reason to suppose that overall Britain did any worse than her major competitors although undoubtedly there were areas of less success. Yet a further indicator of the paramount importance of foreign tariffs as an explanation of the decline in overseas trade, rather than a lack of competitiveness and entrepreneurial skill, is the extent to which British manufacturers maintained control of the totally unprotected home market. In woollen goods foreign makers really made very little headway in competing in the British market, although in yarns and particularly in all-wool worsteds they did better.

11 The Wool Textile Industry and the National Economy

In 1803 the value of gross exports of wool textiles was overtaken by the exports of the cotton industry. A decade or so later the value of output of the wool textile industry was likewise exceeded by cotton. The predominant place of wool textiles in the British economy and the national textile industry had come to an end after a period of over four centuries. Just as wool textiles had figured large in the contemporary economic literature of previous centuries so cotton was to dominate in the next. Just as more recent historical analysis has concentrated on the importance of wool textiles in economic and social affairs before the nineteenth century so historians have stressed, and often debated fiercely, the contribution of the cotton industry to the subsequent expansion of the British economy and the consequent economic, commercial, social and institutional changes.

The sudden rise in the supply of raw cotton from abroad, the emergence of a substantial and rapidly growing export trade, and the impact of this newcomer on methods of production and commerce, all from the 1780s, gave rise immediately to widespread fears that the staple trade of the nation, using mainly home-produced raw materials and directly, or indirectly, giving rise to employment on a very substantial scale in all parts of the kingdom, would be rapidly eclipsed and overwhelmed. 'Should those [cotton] mills and engines be suffered to destroy our woollen and stuff manufactures,' wrote Francis Moore in 1782, 'they will prove the most fatal discoveries ever made in Old England.'[1]

However, the fears were not realised. The meteoric rise of cotton continued rapidly to the mid-1840s and then substantially but more fitfully thereafter. Arguably the wool textile industry did not allow itself to be outshone. Deane has estimated that at no stage up to 1870 was the value of the net output of the woollen and worsted industry less than 65 per cent of that of cotton.[2] From 1820 to 1870 the net output of cotton, on a rough average, only exceeded that of the wool textile industry by 22 per cent. There were periods, the 1840s and early 1860s for example, when the rate of growth of net output of wool textiles substantially exceeded that of the cotton industry. In the decades after 1870 the relative role of the wool textile industry in the national economy began to recover. Whereas in 1850 the cotton industry contributed perhaps 5 per cent to national income and the wool textile industry around 3.5 per cent, by 1900 cotton's contribution was rather over 2 per cent whereas wool added another 1.5 per cent.

It is in terms of contribution to exports that the role of the industry can perhaps be most easily measured, but it must be remembered that whereas, again according to Deane's calculation, an average of almost two-thirds of the value of the final product of the cotton industry was exported between 1820 and 1900, the comparable figure for wool textiles was only 28 per cent, although there must be a suspicion that this is a substantial underestimate as her quinquennial figures for much of the second half of the nineteenth century are very low compared with contemporary calculations, including the 1907 Census of Production.

Table 56 suggests that for the first half of the century the proportion of wool textiles in total domestic exports remained remarkably constant at around 16 per cent. As a proportion of the total exports of manufactured goods it was nearer 20 per cent. The relative decline in the industry's contribution commences in the 1850s and save for the exceptional years of the 1860s, continues thereafter, the most noticeable fall being around the turn of the century. In some periods the incremental contribution of wool textiles to exports was quite significant. From the mid-1850s to the mid-1860s almost 20 per cent of the rise in total exports was the contribution of wool textiles, although with wool prices rising and wool exports forming a higher proportion of raw material consumption the import value content of the wool textile exports was higher. Over our period as a whole, however, the industry only contributed less than 6 per cent of the increase in total United Kingdom exports.

The contribution of the industry to national domestic fixed capital investment was never considerable. The slow transition from domestic to factory production, relatively labour intensive methods and the rapid rise of capital goods industries and social overhead investment during the major mid-nineteenth century periods of fixed investment in the industry limited its contribution to gross domestic fixed capital formation. If the estimates in Chapter 2 and 4 are compared with Feinstein's calculations, it would appear that in the 1790s less than 3 per cent of fixed capital investment in industry and commerce was in the factory wool textile industry in spite of its pre-eminent role in industrial output.[3] This was less than 1 per cent of total gross domestic fixed capital formation. By the 1830s the proportions were still only roughly 3.5 per cent and 1 per cent; the level was still very similar in the 1850s but then declined thereafter to a negligible level.

The late eighteenth-century estimates of between one-and-a-half and three million people dependent on the industry no doubt took a broad view of dependancy and included many who received only a small part of their income from wool growing, wool textile manufacture and trade in cloth. It is not until the mid-nineteenth century that a more realistic assessment is possible. In 1851 a little less than 3 per cent of the total national occupied population was engaged in wool textile manufacture; some 22 per cent of all textile workers were in wool textiles. By 1891 only 1.8 per cent of the total occupied population was in the industry although it is possible that the census classifications for both dates underspecify the labour force.

Only in Yorkshire did wool textile labour make up a significant proportion of the local industrial employment. In 1901 the 214,000 wool textile workers there accounted for approximately 12 per cent of the total labour force. In 1851 the proportion had been nearer 18 per cent. In that same year 31 per cent of occupied labour in Lancashire was directly engaged in cotton manufacture. Thus, even within Yorkshire, wool textiles did not take on such a dominant role as cotton was doing across the Pennines.

What of the broader influences of the industry on the national and local economy? Because of the nature of its product, at home its forward linkages were very narrow. The span of its products were broad but the majority of them found their way almost directly to final consumption. A recent appreciative review of a book on the Scottish linen trade asked what was actually done with the linen. Was it worn, eaten off, slept on or wrapped around things?[4] The vast majority of wool textiles were worn; some, blankets and rugs, were slept on; others were used for non-apparel purposes such as curtains, wall hangings, carpets and furnishing fabrics. They were not much used for wrapping – one no longer had to be buried in wool – but they did have some industrial applications. Felts were used for the making of paper, including that used for Bank of England notes.

The main other industries, therefore, which were dependent on the

Table 56 Wool textile exports

Annual averages	Wool textile exports £ m	Proportion of total U.K. exports	Annual averages	Wool textile exports £ m	Proportion of total U.K. exports
1784–6	3.9	29	1854–6	12.7	12
1794–6	5.8	24	1864–6	25.2	15
1804–6	6.8	16	1874–6	26.1	12
1814–6	8.7	18	1884–6	23.8	11
1824–6	6.9	17	1894–6	22.6	10
1834–6	7.3	16	1904–6	24.0	7
1844–6	9.5	16	1912–3	31.9	6

NOTES: Export values include yarn. From the 1830s to 1850s some other textile yarn is included. Figures to 1856 are Davis's real values. Thereafter declared values are given.

wool textile industry for their basic raw materials were clothing, hosiery and carpets. In clothing it was not until the expansion of the ready-made industry late in the nineteenth century that there was any noticeable stimulus to new methods. Carpet and hosiery production undoubtedly both benefited from the development of the industry but for neither can one strongly argue that rising output or new yarns produced any substantial stimulus. Indeed in hosiery it may have been to some extent foreign yarns which enabled expansion and diversification of product.

The major products of wool textile manufacture thus created no major new industry at home. The by-products of the industry were only of minor consequence for other uses. Lanoline, the cholesterin-fatty matter extracted from wool during scouring, was used as a base for ointments and face creams. West Yorkshire rhubarb growing and other agricultural produce, especially hops, thrived on the muck from the mill floor. But abroad forward linkages did develop. As we have shown, the availability of British yarn, and later tops, enabled many other economies to establish weaving, and then spinning, in their first steps to the creation of their own wool textile sectors. In the long run these countries, behind the banners of protectionism, produced severe competition for their parent industry, but their demands for yarn, textile machinery and expertise in the shorter run created a wider general stimulus at home.

As with cotton it was the backward linkages which were more important. Raw material requirements were broader than those of the cotton industry and the implications of the industry's demand on their supply were thus wider. Whilst home supply of wool remained paramount home agriculture reaped the benefit and responded through its breeding experiments, although those were rather over-shadowed by the desire for higher carcase weights for meat. As new and much larger sources of foreign wool were needed so the stimulus was provided first to Europe and then to the southern hemisphere to respond. In Australia, and later New Zealand, the new trade was financed largely by British capital. Likewise capital and entrepre-neurship was provided to experiment with and exploit wool and hairs from many other parts of the globe. The spin-off in terms of influ-ence, more general commercial links and other trade is incalculable.

The demands for additional and cheaper raw materials created the experiments of reclaiming wool from rags. Rag collecting, rag dealing and sorting, and shoddy and mungo preparation developed into a major national, and then international, industry. The rag collector, or 'tatter' as he became known, became a familiar figure on the streets of every major town and city. Rag collecting and sorting enterprises were created in all the main cloth consuming countries of the world in response to the hungry demands for recovered wool from Yorkshire.

The links between the cotton industry and the wool textile industry were manifold. Transfers of capital, technology and entrepreneurship were frequent in both directions. But the wool textile industry, through its very substantial use of cotton in both worsteds and woollens, boosted sections of the cotton trade. Huddersfield emerged as a centre for the doubling of cotton yarn as a result of the needs of the wool textile industry. The successful and stable survival of cotton spinning in Yorkshire was, at least partially, the result of the steady demand the wool textile industry contributed for yarn.[5] The silk industry gained similar benefit.

Other ancillary industries emerged specifically to serve the needs of textile manufacture. Card clothing became a specialised industry in several Yorkshire localities. The firm of Wilson Brothers of Todmorden succeeded in monopolising the world supply of bobbins. Other specialised producers of shuttles, skips and other utensils were established. The need for soap, size, oil, dyestuffs and paper for packing all produced specific spin-offs, most of a local nature but some with broader consequences. The demand for whale oil for the lubrication of textile machinery helped revive the whaling industry and created the expansion of oil refining. The continual search for new and improved dyestuffs had far reaching implications particularly with the innovation of inorganic dyes. Sig collection was just one of several local trades providing minor employment in the wool textile districts.

In Yorkshire and in the West of England mill building and machinery construction requirements produced close connections with a range of other local trades. Although it is unrealistic to claim that many, if any, of them were created or provided with their greatest stimuli directly by the needs of the industry, the linkages were still of local importance. Experimentation in building methods, particularly with the use of iron arose through the desire to construct larger and fireproof mills. Timber, brick, stone, slate, tiles, glass and ironwork were all required in quantity and most were provided by local firms using local labour. Initial experiments with gas lighting in Yorkshire arose from the needs of mills. Developments in steam supply and steam heating were the forerunners of some more general central heating developments.

In Yorkshire an iron industry was already well established before the coming of factories and the iron needs of the latter were by no means dominant, but textile factories required specialist millwrights and machinery engineers and were an important source of demand for the many local steam engine manufacturers who had emerged by the 1820s. An analysis of the engines in the Leeds area at that time indicated that they had come from 13 different suppliers.[5] In 1830 cotton was using about one-third of the coal mined in Lancashire.[6] The coal demands of the wool textile industry were more modest but in Yorkshire the links with the coal industry were close. Entrepreneurial links existed. Some coal mining was carried out by mill owners for their own needs. The machinery manufacturers that established themselves to service the needs of mechanisation in the industry in due course were able to broaden their activities by expanding into overseas markets which they were to dominate until the twentieth century. In some instances they diversified the range of their products to encompass the needs of other industries. Firms such as Hutchinson Hollingworth of Dobcross and Hattersleys of Keighley gained a world wide recognition for their looms. The carding machines and mules of Platts, the mules of Asa Lees and the carding machines of such smaller firms as John Haigh of Huddersfield gained a widespread recognition and role far beyond British shores. Reeds made by Joseph Lund of Bingley and the wool-scouring machines of Petrie and McNaught developed similar reputations. The long traditions of good finishing doubtlessly helped the international sale of the raising machines of Tomlinsons of Rochdale and the cutting machines of Sellers of Huddersfield. No one could compete with the skills of the cardwire makers of Cleckheaton.

The impact of the industry on the development of commercial and financial institutions and its contribution to national economic and political debate were undoubtedly overshadowed by the activities of the cotton industry. Even so in many important local and national aspects it played a major role. The ingenuity of its entrepreneurs in extending and expanding new markets in both the early and late nineteenth century, has already been stressed. Luccock's excursion to South America produced trade in more than wool textiles.[7] Benjamin Gott found himself having to supply other commodities besides cloth to his American customers. In the United States market the trade in raw cotton and wool and cotton textiles was often intricately connected through commercial and financial arrangements as the activities of the Thompsons of Rawdon bear witness.[8]

The predominant role of the London wool market in the sale of Australasian wool and its supply to European manufacturers until late in the nineteenth century brought with it business in shipping, banking and insurance. Although the entrepot trade in wool provided only little direct employment, the financial implications of its existence were broad.

Within the local economics of the wool textile districts the breadth of sources of raw material supply, the range of other goods and services required, the intricate web of credit facilities, the financial requirements, the need to settle trade disputes and to supervise standards of manufacture and the diversity of the markets served required commercial arrangements more complex than for most other industries. The wool textile industry dominated the business of local Chambers of Commerce. Textile entrepreneurs were active in banking in Yorkshire and the West of England. They took an interest in transport development and in the promotion of institutions of benefit to the day-to-day running of the wool textile business. But the impression emerges that, with only a few notable exceptions, they were loath to involve themselves in national issues and their response to local issues and problems not directly connected with their trade was often half-hearted and lukewarm. A few, the Nusseys and Swire Smith for example, were outspoken promoters of education; several raised their voices for consular reform. Few, however, in mid-century, followed Behrens' example of vociferously challenging overseas tariffs and restrictive treaties even though protectionism was more of a curse for wool textiles than most other industries. Some took up local political office for short periods, some provided a philanthropic interest in local schemes and institutions. But of the many thousands of wool textile entrepreneurs during the nineteenth century, including many who gained considerable industrial eminence and wealth, there were only a few who exerted any influence beyond the trade. Most entrepreneurs in wool textiles seem to have made the business their whole life. Those who saw fit to retire rarely took up a life of conspicuous opulence, although they undoubtedly enjoyed their comforts. In the West Riding retirement from the mill did not often mean moving away to a large house or a country estate. Leisure was to be found in maintaining the close circle of previous business friends and through an interest in sporting activities. In the West of England likewise retirement was to the confines of the local gentlemanly society.

Thus in a rather inconspicuous way the wool textile industry continued to maintain an essential role in the British economy of the nineteenth century. Pushed from the limelight first by the rapid rise of 'King Cotton' and then by the innovatory activity of new, more capital intensive industries, it pursued a path of successful, quiet progress, more than maintaining its share of the rising markets of mid-century and adapting, arguably with some success, to the problems of world trade from the 1870s. Perhaps, in general, it followed a path of considered caution. It was rarely at the forefront of any major development in technology, trade and commerce but it was only rarely far behind. Its entrepreneurs surely showed a high degree of acumen in their management of business and much initiative in the pursuance of new markets and the adaptation of their products to changing circumstances. The fruits of their success is indicated by the record levels of their output on the eve of the First World War.

Notes and References

Abbreviations
B.O. *Bradford Observer*
Ec.H.R. *Economic History Review*
J.B.T.S. *Journal of the Bradford Textile Society*
J.E.H. *Journal of Economic History*
L.M. *Leeds Mercury*
T.C. *Tariff Commission Report*
T.M. *Textile Manufacturer*
W.W.C.J. *Wool, Worsted and Cotton Journal*
Y.B.E.S.R. *Yorkshire Bulletin of Economic and Social Research*

Chapter 1
[1] P. Deane, 'The Output of the British Woollen Industry in the Eighteenth Century', *J.E.H.*, XVII, (1957).
[2] Wolrich's calculations are given in detail in J. Bischoff, *A Comprehensive History of the Woollen and Worsted Manufactures*, I, (1842), pp. 185ff and in J. James, *History of the Worsted Manufacture in England from the earliest times*, (1857), pp. 280–5.
[3] D. Defoe, *A Tour Through the Whole Island of Great Britain*, (1927 edn, Peter Davies) p. 605.
[4] Bischoff, *op.cit.*, II, Appendix, Table 4.
[5] J. Aikin, *A Description of the Country from Thirty to Forty Miles Round Manchester*, (1795), pp. 554, 558.
[6] *Ibid.*, p. 559.
[7] A.P. Wadsworth, 'The History of the Rochdale Woollen Trade', *Transactions of the Rochdale Literary and Scientific Society*, XV, (1923–5); Bischoff, *op. cit.*, II, p. 178.
[8] C. Gulvin, *The Tweedmakers: A History of the Scottish Fancy Woollen Industry*, 1600–1914, (1971), Ch. 2.
[9] Arthur Young, *The Farmer's Tour through the East of England*, (1771), II, p. 80; and *A Six Months Tour through the North of England*, (1770), IV, p. 544.
[10] J. Maitland, ed., *An Account of the Proceedings of the Merchants*,

Manufacturers and Others Concerned in the Wool and Woollen Trade of Great Britain in their Application to Parliament, (1800), p. 140; Additional Evidence Relating to Wool, BPP., 1800 (51) 1020, p. 36.

[11] J. Aubrey, Natural History of Wiltshire, edited by John Britton, (1847), p. 113.

[12] S. Rudder, History of Gloucestershire, (Cirencester, 1779), pp. 60–4.

[13] J.H. Fox, The Woollen Manufacture at Wellington, Somerset, (1914); J.H. Fox, Quaker Homespun. The Life of Thomas Fox of Wellington, serge maker and banker, 1747–1826, (1948); S.D. Chapman, ed., The Devon Cloth Industry in the Eighteenth Century, Devon and Cornwall Record Society, New Series, Vol. 23, (1978).

[14] E.M. Sigsworth, 'Wm. Greenwood and Robert Heaton, Two Eighteenth Century Worsted Manufacturers', J.B.T.S., (1951–2); E.M. Sigsworth, Black Dyke Mills: A History, (1958), p. 13.

[15] James, op.cit., p. 324.

[16] Ibid., p. 325.

[17] H. Heaton, The Yorkshire Woollen and Worsted Industries from Earliest Times up to the Industrial Revolution, 2nd edn, (1965), pp. 297, 371.

[18] Ibid., pp. 296–7.

[19] Report from the Select Committee appointed to consider the State of the Woollen Manufacture of England, BPP., 1806 (268) (268a) III, pp. 132, 210.

[20] J.G. Jenkins, The Welsh Woollen Industry, (1969), pp. 183–6.

[21] Gulvin, op. cit., p. 59.

[22] Weight losses from scouring and washing wool are discussed in more detail in Ch. 8.

[23] See H.D. Pawson, Robert Bakewell: Pioneer Livestock Breeder, (1957).

[24] Heaton, op. cit., p. 339n; James, op. cit., p. 312.

Chapter 2

[1] D.T. Jenkins, The West Riding Wool Textile Industry, 1770–1835, A Study of Fixed Capital Formation, (1975); J. de L. Mann, The Cloth Industry in the West of England from 1640 to 1880, (1971); K. Rogers, Wiltshire and Somerset Woollen Mills, (1976).

[2] B. Wilson, Our Village [Bramley], (1860), p. 43; Report from the S.C. [on the] State of the Woollen Manufacture, (1806), loc. cit. III, p. 30.

[3] West Riding Quarter Session Books, West Yorkshire County Record Office, Wakefield.

[4] D.T. Jenkins, op. cit., pp. 8, 15, 17, 118–19.

[5] Ibid., p. 120.

[6] James, op. cit. p. 327; P. Hall, 'Dolphineholme: A History of the Dolphineholme Worsted Mill, 1784 to 1867', Transactions of the Fylde Historical Society, 3, (1969).

[7] D.T. Jenkins, op. cit., Appendix I.

[8] Ibid., pp. 16–18; Quarterly Broad Cloth Accounts, 1805–21, Lupton Mss., 113, Brotherton Library, University of Leeds.

[9] D.T. Jenkins, op. cit., pp. 17, 30–3.

[10] Ibid., pp. 17, 66, 124; Sun Fire Office, Policy Registers, Country Series, Vol. 214, No. 1197383, (1835). Guildhall Library, London.

[11] Reports from the Commissioners appointed to collect information in the

Manufacturing Districts, relative to Employment of Children in Factories, and as to the propriety and means of curtailing the hours of their labour.

First Report *BPP*., (1833) (450) XX.

Second Report *BPP*., (1833) (519) XXI.

Supplementary Reports, *BPP*., (1834) (167) XIX, XX.

[12] *Factory Returns*, (1835), *BPP*., (1836) (138) XLV. See also D.T. Jenkins, 'The Validity of the Factory Returns, 1833–50', *Textile History*, 4, (1973), pp. 26–8.

[13] D.T. Jenkins, *op. cit.*, Ch. 5.

[14] *Ibid.*

[15] *Factory Returns*, (1835), *loc. cit.*

[16] S.D. Chapman, *The Early Factory Masters*, (1967), Appendix A.

[17] J. Tann, *Gloucestershire Woollen Mills*, (1967).

[18] Marshall Mss., Book Four, pp. 286–8, Brotherton Library, University of Leeds.

[19] Foster Mss., Ledger No. 1, Brotherton Library.

[20] Wormalds and Walker Mss., Private Ledgers Nos. 2 and 3, Brotherton Library.

[21] *T.M.*, April 1882, August and October 1883.

[22] Oates Bros (Halifax) Ltd, Notebook, Brotherton Library.

[23] W. & E. Crowther Ltd., Cash Book, Brotherton Library.

[24] G.P. Norton, *Textile Manufacturer's Book-Keeping*, (1889), pp. 233, 236.

[25] D.T. Jenkins, *op. cit.*, p. 165.

[26] Gulvin, *op. cit.*, p. 61.

[27] Sigsworth, *op. cit.*, p. 174.

[28] Maitland, ed., *op. cit.*, pp. 72–3, 100.

[29] P. Hudson, University of Liverpool, is at present investigating capital provision to the Yorkshire wool textile industry between 1770 and 1850.

[30] *Report from the S.C. appointed to inquire into the State of the Laws respecting Joint Stock Companies, BPP.*, (1844) (119) VII, p. 328.

[31] J. Goodchild, 'The Ossett Mill Company', *Textile History*, I, 1, (1968), pp. 46–61.

[32] *Report . . . on Joint Stock Companies, loc. cit.*, p. 328.

[33] See the Committee Book of the Gill Royds Mill Company, City of Leeds Archives Department.

[34] E. Hargrave and W.B. Crump, 'The Diary of Joseph Rogerson, Scribbling Miller of Bramley, 1808–1814' in W.B. Crump, ed., *The Leeds Woollen Industry, 1780–1820*, Publications of the Thoresby Society, XXXII, (1931).

[35] See The Dartmouth Estate Terriers at the Estate Office, Slaithwaite.

[36] D.T. Jenkins, *op. cit.*, pp. 192–6.

[37] R.G. Wilson, *Gentlemen Merchants, The Merchant Community in Leeds, 1700–1830*, (1971), pp. 136–59.

[38] P. Hudson, 'The Role of Banks and the Finance of the West Riding Wool Textile Industry, c.1780–1850', *Business History Review*, LV, 3, 1981.

[39] *Ibid.*

[40] A.H. Cole, *The American Wool Manufacture*, (1926), I, Ch. V.

[41] E.M. Onslow, *Some Early Records of the MacArthurs of Camden*, (1915).

[42] *Report from the Select Committee of the House of Lords on the State of the British Wool Trade*, (1828), *BPP*., (1828) (H.L. 515) VIII, p. 76.

[43] A.T. Playne, *A History of the Parishes of Minchinhampton and Avening*, (1915), p. 154.

[44] Heaton, *op. cit.*, p. 330.

[45] *Ibid*.

[46] Crump, ed., *op. cit.*, p. 7.

[47] D.T. Jenkins, *op. cit.*, pp. 125–7.

[48] Cole, *op. cit.*, I, p. 130.

[49] Heaton, *op. cit.* p. 352.

[50] For examples see D.T. Jenkins, *op. cit.*, pp. 71–4.

[51] James, *op. cit.*, pp. 328–9.

[52] Rogers, *op. cit.*, p. 24, citing the *Salisbury and Winchester Journal*, 12 September 1791.

[53] K.G. Ponting, *The Woollen Industry of South West England*, 1971, p. 161, quoting from William Walker's Journal.

[54] *Leeds Intelligencer*, 17 June 1799.

[55] Rogers, *op. cit.*, p. 25.

[56] James, *op. cit.*, pp. 338–9; P. Hall, *loc. cit.*

[57] F. Peel, *Spen Valley: Past and Present*, 1893, p. 230.

[58] See D.T. Jenkins, *op. cit.*, pp. 81–96.

[59] *Ibid*., pp. 82–3.

[60] P. Mantoux, *The Industrial Revolution in the Eighteenth Century*, new edn. 1964, pp. 333–4, quoting a letter from Watt to Boulton.

[61] T. Turner, 'History of Fenton, Murray and Wood', unpublished Manchester University M.Sc. Tech. thesis, 1966. Ch. II, p. 6.

[62] Mann, *op. cit.*, p. 155.

[63] Rogers, *op. cit.*, p. 39.

[64] Mann, *op. cit.*, p. 155.

[65] Rogers, *op. cit.*, pp. 38–9.

[66] *Ibid*., pp. 41–2.

[67] *Return of Mills and Factories*, (1838), *BPP*., (1839) (41) XLII.

Chapter 3

[1] Maitland, ed., *op. cit.*, pp. 72, 88.

[2] J. Luccock, *The Nature and Properties of Wool*, (1805).

[3] P. Deane, *loc. cit.*, pp. 217–18; Sir J. Sinclair, *General Report of the Agricultural State and Political Circumstances of Scotland*, (1814), III, Statistical Tables, p. 8.

[4] Maitland, ed., *op. cit.*, pp. 137–40.

[5] R.G. Wilson, 'The Supremacy of the Yorkshire Cloth Industry in the Eighteenth century', in N.B. Harte and K.G. Ponting, eds, *Textile History and Economic History: Essays in Honour of Miss Julia de Lacy Mann*, (1973), pp. 225–46.

[6] R. Davis, *The Industrial Revolution and British Overseas Trade*, (1979), pp. 21–4; H. Heaton, 'Yorkshire Cloth Traders in the United States, 1770–1840', *Publications of the Thoresby Society*, XXXVII, iii, (1944), pp. 240–4.

[7] Wilson, *loc. cit.*, p. 240.

[8] Heaton, 'Yorkshire Cloth Traders . . .', *loc. cit.*; Cole, *op. cit.*, I, Ch. VII.

[9] Heaton, 'Yorkshire Cloth Traders . . .', *loc. cit.*, p. 228; 'Extracts from an Old Leeds Merchant's Memorandum Book: 1770–1786', *Publications of the Thoresby Society*, XXIV, (1915).

[10] Wilson, 'The Supremacy of the Yorkshire Cloth Industry', *loc. cit.*, pp. 235–46.

[11] James, *op. cit.*, pp. 304–6.

[12] D.T. Jenkins, *op. cit.*, pp. 15ff.

[13] A.D. Gayer, W.W. Rostow, A.J. Schwartz, *The Growth and Fluctuation of the British Economy, 1790–1850*, (1975 edn), I, pp. 58–61; James, *op. cit.*, p. 375.

[14] 'The Diary of Joseph Rogerson', *loc. cit.*, pp. 77–91.

[15] H. Heaton, 'A Merchant Adventurer in Brazil, 1808–18', *J.E.H.*, VI, (1946); R.G. Wilson, 'The Fortunes of a Leeds Merchant House', *Business History*, X, (1967).

[16] James, *op. cit.*, p. 372.

[17] H. Heaton, 'Non-Importation, 1806–1812', *J.E.H.*, I, 2, (1941).

[18] H. Heaton, 'Benjamin Gott and the Anglo-American Cloth Trade', *Journal of Economic and Business History*, 2, (1929–30).

[19] Heaton, 'Non-Importation . . .', *loc. cit.*

[20] *Ibid.*, p. 181.

[21] Heaton, 'Benjamin Gott . . .', *loc. cit.*, p. 157.

[22] 'The Diary of Joseph Rogerson', *loc. cit.*, p. 91.

[23] *Ibid.*, p. 99.

[24] Heaton, 'Non-Importation . . .', *loc. cit.*, p. 188.

[25] Cole, *op. cit.*, I, p. 146n.

[26] Cole, *op. cit.*, I, pp. 156–60; see also Heaton, 'Yorkshire Cloth Traders . . .', *loc. cit.*, p. 242 and N.S. Buck, *The Development of the Organisation of Anglo-American Trade, 1800–1850*, (1925), pp. 150ff.

[27] James, *op.cit.*, p. 372; 'The Diary of Joseph Rogerson', *loc. cit.*, pp. 110–15.

[28] *Ibid.*, p. 147; Mann, *op. cit.*, p. 154.

[29] James, *op. cit.*, pp. 373–4; H. Heaton, 'An Early Victorian Business Forecaster in the Woollen Industry', *Economic History*, II, (1933), p. 556.

[30] James, *op. cit.*, p. 375; Gulvin, *op. cit.*, p. 39.

[31] Cole, *op. cit.*, I, p. 145; J.B. Williams, *British Commercial Policy and Trade Expansion, 1750–1850*, (1972), p. 237.

[32] Mann, *op. cit.*, pp. 157–8.

[33] See J. Bischoff, *op. cit.*, I, Ch. XI.

[34] James, *op. cit.*, p. 389.

[35] Bischoff, *op. cit.*, I, p. 475; Mann, *op. cit.*, p. 166.

[36] *Ibid.*

[37] Wadsworth, *loc. cit.*, p. 76; J.H. Clapham, '*An Economic History of Modern Britain: The Early Railway Age, 1820–1850*, 1950 edn, p. 45.

[38] See Bischoff, *op. cit.*, II, Ch.II.

[39] *Ibid.*, II, p. 70; Mann, *op. cit.*, p. 165; *Examination of Petitions before the Privy Council against the Tax on Wool imported, BPP.*, (1820) (56) XII.

[40] e.g. Mann, *op. cit.*, p. 158; James, *op. cit.*, pp. 400–15.

[41] James, *op. cit.*, pp. 400–3, 407.

[42] *Report on the State of the Wool Trade*, (1828), *loc. cit.*, p. 285; Williams, *op. cit.*, p. 266.

[43] Heaton, 'Benjamin Gott . . .', *op. cit.*, pp. 158–60.

[44] *L.M.*, 19 November 1825.

[45] W. Hirst, *History of the Woollen Trade for the last Sixty Years*, (1844), pp. 24–5.

[46] *L.M.*, 11 March 1826.

[47] Gulvin, *op. cit.*, p. 64.

[48] Mann, *op. cit.*, p. 170; Heaton, 'Early Victorian Business Forecaster . . .', *loc. cit.*, p. 554.

[49] *Report on the State of the Wool Trade*, 1828, *loc. cit.*, pp. 398, 257.

[50] Williams, *op. cit.*, p. 242; F.J. Glover, 'Philadelphia Merchants and the Yorkshire Blanket Trade, 1820–1860', *Pennsylvania History*, XXVIII, (1961), p. 128; F.J. Glover, 'The Rise of the Heavy Woollen Trade of the West Riding of Yorkshire in the Nineteenth Century', *Business History*, IV, (1961), p. 14.

[51] Glover, 'Philadelphia Merchants . . .', *loc. cit.*, p. 129.

[52] James, *op. cit.*, p. 428–34.

[53] *Ibid.*, p. 450.

[54] Mann, *op. cit.*, pp. 174–5, 180; *Report from the Select Committee appointed to inquire into the present state of Manufacture, Commerce and Shipping in the United Kingdom*, (1833), *BPP.*, 1833 (690) VI, Q. 1104–10. Evidence of Henry Hughes.

[55] James, *op. cit.*, p. 430.

[56] Patent No. 858 of 1766.

[57] Report of the *Assistant Commissioner for Hand Loom Weavers, 1839–40, Part 2. South West England by A. Austin, BPP.*, (1840) (43.1) XXII, pp. 434–5.

[58] See H. Heaton, 'Benjamin Gott and the Industrial Revolution in Yorkshire', *Ec.H.R.*, III, 1931.

[59] See for example pattern book of Stevens and Bailward of Bradford-on-Avon in Bath Reference Library No. W. 677, Dye Pattern Books and Cloth Pattern Books.

[60] Mann, *op. cit.*, p. 129.

[61] See K.G. Ponting, 'The Decline of the Woollen Industry in the Trowbridge and Bradford-on-Avon Area in the Nineteenth Century', unpublished M. Litt. thesis, Bristol University, (1974), especially Salters, pp. 53ff., Clark pp. 67ff.

[62] See stock figure details quoted in R.P. Beckensale, (ed.), *The Trowbridge Woollen Industry illustrated by the stock books of J. & T. Clark*, (1951).

[63] *Minutes of Evidence taken before the Select Committee on the State of Children employed in the Manufactures of the United Kingdom, BPP.*, (1816) (397) III; J.H. Clapham, 'Some Factory Statistics of 1815–16', *Economic Journal*, XXV, (1915), pp. 475–9.

[64] *Returns of Mills and Factories . . .*, (1838), *BPP.*, (1839) (41) XLII.

[65] Personal knowledge.

[66] See C. Gulvin, *The Tweedmakers, A History of the Scottish Fancy Wool Industry*, (1973).

[67] P. Corfield, 'The Size of the Norwich Worsted Industries in the Eight-

eenth and Nineteenth Centuries', unpublished paper given at the Pasold Conference on Textile History, Norwich, (1975).

[68] *Reports, with Appendices, of the Assistant Commissioners on Eastern and South Western England . . .*, (1839), *BPP.*, (1840) (43.1) XXIII, pp. 317ff.

[69] See examples in M.F. Lloyd Prichard, 'The Decline of Norwich', *Ec.H.R.*, 2nd Series, III, 3, (1951), p. 374.

[70] J.H. Clapham, 'The Transference of the Worsted Industry from Norfolk to the West Riding', *Economic Journal*, XX, 1910, p. 200.

[71] J.K. Edwards, 'The Decline of the Norwich Textiles Industry', *Yorkshire Bulletin of Economic and Social Research*, XVI, (1964), p. 38; F. Atkinson, *Some Aspects of the Eighteenth Century Woollen Trade in Halifax*, (1956), p. 18.

[72] Edwards, *loc. cit.*, p. 32.

Chapter 4

[1] See D.T. Jenkins, 'The Validity of the Factory Returns . . .', *loc. cit*; D.T. Jenkins, 'The Factory Returns: 1850–1905', *Textile History*, 9, (1978).

[2] *Wool, Worsted and Cotton Journal*, January 1854, p. 453; *Reports of the Inspectors of Factories for the half year ending October 1889, BPP.*, (1890) (c.6060) xx, p. 11.

[3] James, *op. cit.*, pp. 311, 429, 627.

[4] *Ibid.*, p. 428, quoting *Leeds Mercury*, May 1830.

[5] W.G. Rimmer, 'The Industrial Profile of Leeds, 1740–1840', *Publications of the Thoresby Society*, 50, 1967, p. 176.

[6] 'Account of Failures in and connected with the Wool and Woollen Trade, 1839–48', Robert Jowitt and Sons Ltd. Records, Brotherton Library, University of Leeds. Mss. 62; see also A.M. Patchett family records, Leeds Archives Department.

[7] Sigsworth, *op. cit.*, p. 64.

[8] (Sir J. Behrens), *Sir Jacob Behrens, 1806–1889*, (privately printed, c.1925), pp. 31–4.

[9] J.R. Allen, ed., *op. cit.*

[10] See for example *Exposition universelle de 1851: travaux de la commission française sur l'industrie des nations*, Paris, (1854), Vol. IV.

[11] F. Thompson, *Harris Tweed, The Story of a Hebridean Industry*, (1969).

[12] E.L. Taylor, 'The Early Wool Trade in Rochdale', *Transactions of the Rochdale Literary and Scientific Society*, XII, (1914–16), pp. 71–8.

[13] Wadsworth, *loc. cit.*, p. 107, quoting William Hastings's evidence to the Commons Committee on the Orders in Council in 1812. *Evidence on Petitions against the Orders in Council, BPP.*, (1812) (419) X, p. 206.

[14] Bischoff, *op. cit.*, II, p. 178.

[15] Wadsworth, *loc. cit.*, pp. 136–56.

[16] *Report from the Select Committee into the Laws Regulating the Stamping of Woollen Cloths, BPP.*, (1821) (437) VI, pp. 17–18.

[17] *Report on the State of the British Wool Trade, loc. cit.*, pp. 106, 272, 481.

[18] Wadsworth, *loc. cit.*, p. 155.

[19] *T.M.*, April 1879.

[20] *T.M.*, June 1880.

[21] *T.M.*, January 1882; December 1882.
[22] *T.M.*, January 1882; April 1884.
[23] *Reports of the Factory Inspectors*, October 1886, *BPP.*, 1887 (c.5002) XVII p. 3; *T.M.* May 1888; February 1889; February 1895.
[24] *T.M.*, February 1889.
[25] *Reports of the Factory Inspectors*, (1896), *BPP.*, (1897), (c.8561) XVII, p. 172.
[26] W. Parson and W. White, *History, Directory and Gazetteer of the Counties of Durham and Northumberland*, (1827), I; *Victoria County History: Durham*, (1907), II, pp. 314–19.
[27] *V.C.H.: Durham*, pp. 318–19.
[28] *Report from the Commissioners on the Pollution of Rivers*, (1866), *BPP.*, (1867) (3850–I) XXXIII, Part II.
[29] Parson and White, *op. cit.*
[30] E. Wooler and A.C. Boyde, *Historic Darlington*, (1913), pp. 195–6; *Commission on Pollution of Rivers, loc. cit.*, Part II; James, *op. cit.*, p. 387.
[31] See A.B. Hinds, *A History of Northumberland*, III, Hexamshire, Part I, (1896), p. 270; A.B. Wright, *An Essay towards a History of Hexham*, (1823), pp. 27–8.
[32] *Commission on Pollution of Rivers, loc. cit.*, Part II.
[33] *T.M.*, January 1876.
[34] *T.M.*, July 1883.
[35] J.H. Fox, *op. cit.*; H. Fox, *op. cit.*
[36] Mann *op. cit.*, p. 178.
[37] *Pigotts Directory*, (1842).
[38] A. Plummer, *The Witney Blanket Industry*, (1934).
[39] *Factory Returns*; J.G. Jenkins, *op. cit.*, Ch. III.
[40] P. Rousseaux, *Les Mouvements de Fond de l'économie Anglaise, 1800–1913*, (1938); Mitchell and Deane, *op. cit.*, pp. 471–3.
[41] *Royal Commission on Depression in Trade and Industry*, Second Report, (1886). *BPP.*, (1886) (c.4715) XXI., p. 248.
[42] C.H. Feinstein, 'Capital Accumulation and Economic Growth in Great Britain, 1760–1860', in P. Mathias and M.M. Postan, (eds), *The Cambridge Economic History of Europe*, VII, Part I, (1978), pp. 54–5.
[43] *Royal Commission on Depression in Trade and Industry*, Second Report, *loc. cit.*, pp. 124–8.

Chapter 5

[1] Arthur Young, *Northern Tour* 4., V. pp. 169–90; J. Banks, *Qualified Export*, pp. 55–7.
[2] J.A. Barnard, *The Australian Wool Market 1840–1900*, 1958, p. 21.
[3] There is much interesting comment on the London Wool Sales in S.M. Onslow, ed., *Some Early Records of the Macarthurs of Camden*, (1914). See particularly the letter from Wm. Macarthur to his brother James dated London 28 July 1825 (pp. 409–13) and the letter from William to his father, the great John Macarthur (pp. 419–22). The whole of Chapter XII, 'The Making of the Market for Australian Wool', is both a major source and fascinating reading, especially for anyone involved in the wool market.

[4] See P.L. Brown, ed., *The Clyde Company Papers*, Vols II and III, (1952 and 1958).

[5] We wish to thank Dr P. Chorley, who is engaged in a study of wool growing in Germany, for drawing our attention to much new material on these wools and especially for emphasising that considerable weights of non-merino or merino-x-native wool was sent to England.

[6] See Ch. 9 for further details of the noil trade.

[7] Fettling: the muck removed from the wool during the carding process and which was left deposited on the card wire and had to be removed by hard rakes (or fettlers, as they were called).

[8] Cole, *op. cit.*, II, p. 70.

[9] S. Jubb, *The History of the Shoddy Trade: its Rise, Progress and Present Position*, (1860).

[10] Dr J. Malin, 'The West Riding Recovered Wool Industry, 1813–1939', unpublished D. Phil. thesis, University of York, (1979). We are most grateful to Dr Malin for allowing us to quote from his thesis.

[11] Jubb, *op. cit.*, Malin, *thesis cit.*, p. 6.

[12] *Examination of Petitions before the Privy Council against the Tax on Wool imported, loc. cit.*, p. 76.

[13] *Report on the State of the Wool Trade*, (1828), *loc. cit.*, pp. 158, 257, 397, 450–5.

[14] See Jubb, *op. cit.*, p. 31.

[15] Henry Mayhew, *London Labour and the London Poor*, II, (1861–2), p. 139.

[16] Malin, *thesis cit.*, p. 109.

[17] *T.M.*, July 1881.

[18] Malin, *thesis cit.*, p. 109.

[19] *Ibid.*, p. 123; *Rags – Return of the Names of those countries in Europe which permit the free export or impose a duty; amount per ton of such duty, BPP.*, (1861) (376) LVII.

[20] Quoted by Malin, *thesis cit.*, p. 137 from *Wool and Textile Fabrics*, 19 March 1881, p. 774.

[21] Baines, *op. cit.*, p. 109.

[22] *T.M.*, December 1892.

[23] *T.M.*, March 1889.

[24] Malin, *thesis cit.*, p. 179.

[25] *Ibid.*, p. 42.

[26] See W. White, *Leeds and the Clothing Districts of Yorkshire Directory*, (1853).

[27] Malin, *thesis cit.*, p. 67.

[28] Sykes's patent wool picking machine worked by one woman does as much as twenty women by hand. *Reports by the Jurors of the International Exhibition of 1862. Class XXI. Report on Woollen Goods.*

[29] The condenser plus the Apperley patent feed brings the whole process of scribbling, carding and slubbing into one continuous line that does away with the slubbing billy.

[30] Cole, *op. cit.*, I, p. 102.

[31] James, *op. cit.*, p. 566.

[32] *Ibid.*, p. 568. Our thanks are due to Dr Iredale for information on many aspects of combing. See also J.M. Trickett, 'A Technical Appraisal of

the Holden-Illingworth Papers', unpublished M.Sc.thesis, University of Bradford, (1977).

[33] James, *op. cit.*, p. 569.

[34] The late Air Vice-Marshall Geoffrey Ambler to K.G. Ponting.

[35] Quoted in *Wool Research, 1918–1948*, Vol. 6. Drawing and Spinning. Wool Industries Research Association, 1949, p. 31. Chapter II, The Development of Worsted Drawing, gives a good account of this rather neglected side of worsted spinning.

[36] Mann, *op. cit.*, p. 293.

[37] James, *op. cit.*, p. 414; D.T. Jenkins, *op. cit.*, p. 133.

[38] Sun Fire Office, Policy Registers, Country Series, 172/1085746/1829; 169/1083390/1828; D.T. Jenkins, *op. cit.*, p. 133.

[39] *Ibid.*, 188/1127361/1831; 200/1155688/1833.

[40] *Return of Power Looms in Factories in the United Kingdom, BPP.*, (1836) (24) XLV.

[41] *Hand Loom Weavers: Reports with Appendices of the Assistant Commissioners in Eastern and South Western England, the West Riding of Yorkshire and Germany, BPP.*, (1840) (43–I) XXIII, p. 335.

[42] Gulvin, *op. cit.*, p. 103.

[43] J.G. Jenkins, *op. cit.*, p. 75.

[44] Mann, *op. cit.*, pp. 188–9, 199–200.

[45] *Reports of the Inspectors of Factories*, December 1843, *BPP.*, (1844), (524) (583) XXVIII; May 1845, *BPP.*, 1845 (639) XXV; October 1850, *BPP.*, (1846) (681) (721) XX.

[46] Baines, *op. cit.*, pp. 70–1.

[47] *Reports from the Assistant Hand Loom Weavers Commission*, Part V, *BPP.*, (1840) (220) XXIV, p. 553.

[48] Committee on Industry and Trade, *Survey of Textile Industries*, (1923), p. 167.

[49] *Reports of the Inspectors of Factories*, October 1888, *BPP.*, (1889) (c.5697) XVIII.

[50] Baines, *op. cit.*, p. 71; J. James, *The History of Bradford and its Parish, with Additions and Continuation to the Present time*, (1866), p. 242; R. Whately Cooke Taylor, *The Modern Factory System*, (1891), p. 238.

[51] *Factory Returns* (1861), *BPP.*, (1862) (23) LV.

[52] Sigsworth, *op. cit.*, p. 192.

[53] Cole, *op. cit.*, II, p. 91.

[54] James, *Worsted Manufacture, op. cit.*, p. 482.

[55] *Ibid.*, p. 603.

[56] Sigsworth, *op. cit.*, pp. 190–3.

[57] G.A. Feather, 'A Pennine Worsted Community in the Nineteenth Century', *Textile History*, III, 1972, pp. 64–91.

[58] Gulvin, *op. cit.*, pp. 86, 103, 152, 166, 169.

[59] J.G. Jenkins, *op. cit.*, pp. 75, 79.

[60] A.P. Wadsworth, 'The Early Factory System in the Rochdale District', *Transactions of the Rochdale Literary and Scientific Society*, XIX, (1935–7), p. 154.

[61] Mann, *op. cit.*, pp. 188–9, 200.

[62] *Reports of the Commissioners on the employment of children and young persons in trades and manufactures not already regulated by law*, Fourth Report, *BPP.*, (1865) (3548) XX, pp. 74–6.

[63] R. Baker, 'On the Industrial and Sanitary Economy of the Borough of Leeds, *Journal of the Statistical Society*, XXI, (1858).
[64] J.H. Clapham, 'The Decline of the Handloom in England and Germany', *Bradford Textile Journal*, (1905), p. 45.
[65] *T.M.*, January 1884; January and October 1886.
[66] E.M. Sigsworth and J.M. Blackman, 'The Woollen and Worsted Industries', in D.H. Aldcroft, ed., *The Development of British Industry and Foreign Competition, 1875–1914*, (1968), p. 131.
[67] *T.M.*, May 1886.
[68] Clapham, 'The Decline of the Handloom . . .', *loc. cit.*, pp. 128–9.
[69] *Report of the Jurors in the International Exhibition of* 1862. Class XXI. *Report on Woollen Goods.*
[70] Baines, *op. cit.*, pp. 71–3.
[71] W. Fairbairn, *Treatise on Mills and Millwork*, I, (1861), pp. 233–5; *Wool, Worsted and Cotton Journal*, April 1853.
[72] D.T. Jenkins, 'The Factory Returns: 1850–1905', *Textile History*, IX, 1978, pp. 61–4.
[73] O.N. Greeves, 'The Effects of the American Civil War on the Linen and Wool Textile Industries in the U.K.', unpublished Ph.D. thesis, Bristol University, 1968–9, p. 380.
[74] *Factory Returns, 1871, BPP.*, (1871) (440) LXII.
[75] *Third Report of the Commissioners appointed to inquire into the best means of preventing the pollution of rivers, (Rivers Aire and Calder), BPP.,* (1867) (3850) XXXIII.
[76] Gulvin, *op. cit.*, pp. 96–7.
[77] *Huddersfield Examiner*, 22 October 1864: *T.M.*, November 1884.

Chapter 6

[1] James, *op. cit.*, pp. 444–5.
[2] *L.M.*, Trade Report, May 1835.
[3] Heaton, 'An Early Victorian Forecaster', *loc. cit.*, p. 570.
[4] Glover, 'Philadelphia Merchants . . .', *loc. cit.*, p. 129.
[5] Heaton, 'An Early Victorian Forecaster', *loc. cit.*, p. 570. Many of the following references to the *Leeds Mercury* are from this article.
[6] *L.M.*, May 1837; Glover, 'Philadelphia Merchants . . .', *loc. cit.*, p. 129; James, *op. cit.*, p. 477.
[7] *L.M.*, Trade Report, May 1838.
[8] *L.M.*, Trade Report, June 1839.
[9] Jowitt, Mss. 62. *loc. cit.*
[10] *L.M.* Trade Reports, December 1839; August 1840.
[11] F.J. Glover, 'Government Contracting, Competition and Growth in the Heavy Woollen industry', *Ec.H.R.*, 2nd Series, XVI, 2. (1964).
[12] Mann, *op. cit.*, p. 179 quoting *Gloucester Journal*, 15 January 1842.
[13] *L.M.*, Trade Report, March 1842.
[14] *The Diary of Reuben Gaunt*, Leeds City Reference Library.
[15] *Reports of the Inspectors of Factories*, June and December 1842, *BPP.*, (1843) (429) (523) XXVII.
[16] G. Ingle, 'A History of R.V. Marriner Ltd., Worsted Spinners, Keighley', unpublished M. Phil. thesis, University of Leeds, (1974), p. 134; Bairstow Mss., Leeds City Archives Dept., 3 (26), Copartnership accounts.

[17] James, *op. cit.*, pp. 488–90, 494.
[18] *L.M.*, Trade Reports, October and November 1843.
[19] *Reports of the Inspectors of Factories*, June 1843, *BPP.*, (1844) (524) (583) XXVIII.
[20] Glover, 'Philadelphia Merchants . . .', *loc. cit.*, p. 131.
[21] Heaton, 'An Early Victorian Business Forecaster . . .', *loc. cit.*, p. 561.
[22] *L.M.*, July 1838.
[23] *L.M.* June 1836.
[24] James, *op. cit.*, p. 477.
[25] *Ibid.*
[26] Glover, 'Philadelphia Merchants . . .', *loc. cit.*, p. 131.
[27] *L.M.*, December 1839.
[28] *Reports of the Inspectors of Factories*, December 1842, *loc. cit.*
[29] Glover, 'Rise of the Heavy Woollen Trade . . .', *loc. cit.*, p. 9.
[30] Crump, *op. cit.*, pp. 25, 297.
[31] *Select Committee . . . on the Wool Trade*, 1828, *loc. cit.*, pp. 98, 481.
[32] Clay Mss., Calderdale Archives Dept., Purchase Book 1800–18.
[33] James, *op. cit.*, p. 471; *L.M.*, 21 November 1829; W.B. Crump and G. Gorbal, *History of the Huddersfield Woollen Trade*, (1935), p. 108.
[34] James, *op. cit.*, pp. 472–6.
[35] D.T. Jenkins, 'The Cotton Industry in Yorkshire, 1780–1900', *Textile History*, 10, (1979).
[36] K.G. Ponting ed., *Baines's Account . . . op. cit.*, p. 133.
[37] Sigsworth, *op. cit.*, p. 44 from an analysis of J. Hodgson, *Textile Manufacturers and Other Industries in Keighley*, (1869).
[38] *Bradford Observer*, 6 September 1838; 25 May 1843, cited by Sigsworth, *op. cit.*, pp. 44–5.
[39] James, *op. cit.*, p. 471.
[40] *Ibid.*, p. 476.
[41] Glover, 'Rise of the Heavy Woollen Trade . . .', *loc. cit.*, p. 9.
[42] A.H. Cole, *op. cit.*, I., pp. 33, 165.
[43] Sigsworth, *op. cit.*, pp. 49–50.
[44] James, *op. cit.*, p. 471.
[45] Heaton, 'Victorian Business Forecaster . . .', *loc. cit.*, p. 572.
[46] *Bradford Observer*, 19 September 1835.
[47] Sigsworth, *op. cit.*, pp. 48–9; *Bradford Observer*, 6 July 1843.
[48] *Reports of the Inspectors of Factories*, December 1843, *BPP.*, (1844) (524) (583) XXVIII; Mann, *op. cit.*, p. 195.
[49] Sigsworth, *op. cit.*, p. 227; Ingle, thesis, *op. cit.*, p. 157; Bairstow Mss., Leeds City Archives Dept.
[50] James, *op. cit.* p. 496.
[51] *Reports of the Inspectors of Factories*, December 1843, *loc. cit.*
[52] *L.M.*, November 1843. Trade Report.
[53] *Reports of the Inspectors of Factories*, December 1845, *BPP.*, (1846) (681) (721) XX.
[54] *The Diary of Reuben Gaunt, loc. cit.*
[55] *Reports of the Inspectors of Factories*, May 1846, *BPP.*, (1847) (779) (828) XV; James, *op. cit.*, p. 499; Glover, 'Philadelphia Merchants . . .' *loc. cit.* p. 131.
[56] *Report from the Select Committee on Commercial Distress, BPP.*, 1847–8

(395, 584) VIII, Para. 2678. Evidence of James Morris and H.J. Prescott; Jowitt Mss., *loc. cit.*, 62, Account of failures in and connected with the wool and woollen trade, 1839–48.

[57] *The Diary of Reuben Gaunt, loc. cit.*

[58] *Reports of the Inspectors of Factories*, October 1847, *BPP.*, (1847–8). (900) (957) XXVI.

[59] *Ibid.*, James, *op. cit.*, pp. 500–1.

[60] *Reports of the Inspectors of Factories*, April 1848, *BPP.*, (1849) (1017) (1084) XXII.

[61] *The Economist*, 16 September 1848.

[62] James, *op. cit.*, pp. 504–6.

[63] Glover, 'Philadelphia Merchants . . .' *loc. cit.*, pp. 131–2.

[64] James, *op. cit.*, pp. 504–6; *Reports of the Inspectors of Factories*, April and October 1849; April 1850, *BPP.*, *(*1851) (1304) (1396) XXIII.

[65] James, *op. cit.*, pp. 398, 491–2.

[66] *Bradford Observer*, 8 February 1838 cited by Sigsworth, *op. cit.*, p. 34.

[67] James, *op. cit.*, pp. 524, 540.

[68] *The Economist*, 23 November 1850.

[69] *Reports of the Inspectors of Factories*, April 1851; October 1851, *BPP.*, (1852) (1439) (1500) XXI.

[70] J.E. Cairnes, *Essays in Political Economy*, (1873), p. 28, cited by J.R.T. Hughes, *Fluctuations in Trade, Industry and Finance: A Study of British Economic Development, 1850–1860*, (1960). p. 109.

[71] *The Economist*, 8 November 1851.

[72] James, *op. cit.*, p. 522.

[73] *Wool, Worsted and Cotton Journal*, May, July and September 1853; *The Economist*, 6 January 1855.

[74] *W.W.C.J.*, November and December 1853.

[75] *Ibid.*, January 1854.

[76] James, *op. cit.*, p. 523.

[77] *The Economist* 13 January 1855; *W.W.C.J.*, August, October and November 1854, January 1855; *Reports of the Inspectors of Factories*, April and October 1854, *BPP.*, (1854) (1796) XIX; 1854–55 (1881) XV.

[78] *W.W.C.J.*, February, April, June and September 1854; *Reports of the Inspectors of Factories*, April 1854, *loc. cit.*

[79] *The Economist*, 13 January 1855.

[80] Quoted by *W.W.C.J.*, January 1855.

[81] James, *op. cit.*, p. 524.

[82] Quoted by *The Economist*, 5 January 1856.

[83] *The Economist*, 13 January 1855; see also the *Reports of the Inspectors of Factories*, October 1855, *BPP.*, (1856) (2031) XVIII.

[84] *The Economist*, 5 January 1856.

[85] See James, *op. cit.*, p. 530; *The Economist*, 10 January 1857; Hughes, *op. cit.*, p. 131; *Reports of the Inspectors of Factories*, April and October, 1856, *BPP.*, (1856) (2090) XVIII; 1857 (2153. Sess. 1) III.

[86] *L.M.*, 4 January 1858.

[87] *Ibid.; B.O.*, 7 January 1858 cited by Sigsworth, *op. cit.*, pp. 67–8.

[88] *Report from the Select Committee on the Operation of the Bank Acts and the Causes of the Recent Commercial Distress, BPP.*, (1857–8) (381) V, pp. 373–8.

[89] *Report of the Inspectors of Factories,* December 1857, *BPP.,* (1857–8) (2314) XXIV; A.H. Cole, *op. cit.,* I, p. 338.

[90] *L.M.* 4 January 1858.

[91] *The Economist,* 2 January 1858.

[92] *Reports of the Inspectors of Factories,* April and October, 1858, *BPP.,* (1857–8) (2391) XXIV; 1859 (2463. Sess. 1) XII.

[93] *Ibid.,* October and December 1859, April 1860, *BPP., (*1860) (2594) XXXIV; (1860) (2689) XXXIV.

[94] James, *op. cit.,* p. 514.

[95] *The Economist,* 23 November 1850; 16 August 1851.

[96] *W.W.C.J.,* January 1854; *The Economist,* 9 July 1853.

[97] Barnard, *op. cit.,* p. 54.

[98] Gulvin, *op. cit.,* p. 108.

[99] *W.W.C.J.,* July 1853.

[100] Hughes, *op. cit.,* pp. 102ff.

[101] J & T Clark Mss., Wiltshire County Record Office, Trowbridge.

[102] Cole, *op. cit.,* I, p. 342.

[103] *Ibid.,* I, pp. 344–6.

[104] *W.W.C.J.,* May 1853.

[105] *L.M.,* 11 June 1853.

[106] *L.M.,* 25 June 1853.

[107] Quoted by *W.W.C.J.,* July 1853.

[108] Cole, *op. cit.,* I, p. 342.

[109] *B.O.,* 5 April 1850, quoted by E.M. Sigsworth, 'Bradford and the Great Exhibition, 1851', *Bradford Textile Society Journal* (1950–1), pp. 43–9.

[110] *B.O.,* 13 June 1850.

[111] *L.M.,* 19 April 1851.

[112] M. Bernoville, 'Industrie des Laines Peignées', in *Travaux de La Commission Française sur l'Industrie des Nations,* Paris, (1854), IV.

[113] M.J. Randoing, 'Industrie des Laines Foulées, in *Travaux de La Commission Française, op. cit.,* p. 26.

[114] Bernoville, *loc. cit.,* pp. 209–14.

[115] *Ibid.,* pp. 27–40.

[116] *Ibid.,* pp. 32–4.

[117] See James, *op. cit.,* Appendix, pp. 17–26; E.M. Sigsworth, 'The West Riding Wool Textile Industry and the Great Exhibition', *Y.B.E.S.R.,* IV, 1, (1952), pp. 23–4.

[118] Crump and Ghorbal, *op. cit.,* pp. 128–32.

[119] *L.M.* 23 February 1850. Letter from William Willans, a Huddersfield Woolstapler.

[120] *Official Descriptive and Illustrated Catalogue of the Great Exhibition,* (1851), II, *op. cit.; Reports of the Juries,* Vol. II. p. 775–6.

[121] *Ibid.,* p. 766. The Juries' policy of not awarding medals to merchant exhibitors may have adversely affected them as, presumably, much of the West Country cloth shown by London merchants would not have indicated the manufacturer's name.

[122] Sigsworth, 'The West Riding Wool Textile Industry . . .', *loc. cit.,* p. 27, quoting *L.M.,* 3 May 1851.

[123] *Jacob Behrens, op. cit.,* p. 51.

[124] *Reports of the Deputations to the Paris Exhibition, BPP.,* 1856 (2049) XXXVI, pp. 121–69.
[125] *Ibid.,* p. 138.
[126] *Ibid.,* p. 139.
[127] *Ibid.,* p. 161–7.
[128] *Ibid.,* pp. 159, 168.
[129] *Ibid.,* pp. 121–30.
[130] *Reports of the Inspectors of Factories,* October 1855, *BPP.,* (1856) (2031) XVIII.
[131] *Ibid.,* April 1860, *BPP.,* (1860) (2689) XXXIV.
[132] *B.O.,* 10 March and 6 September 1860; 3 January 1861.
[133] *Huddersfield Examiner,* 15 December 1860; *B.O.,* 3 January 1861.
[134] Huddersfield Chamber of Commerce, Minute Books, October 1860.
[135] *Behrens, op. cit.,* p. 54; *B.O.,* 2 January 1862.
[136] See A.L. Dunham, *The Anglo-French Treaty of Commerce of 1860 and the Progress of the Industrial Revolution in France,* (1930), pp. 215–35.
[137] Reported in the *Huddersfield Examiner,* 4 June 1864; an earlier similar comment had been made by the Factory Inspector, *Reports of the Inspectors of Factories,* 31 October 1861, *BPP.,* 1862 (2923) XXII.
[138] Huddersfield Chamber of Commerce, Minute Books, January 1862.
[139] *L.M.,* 31 December 1864, Annual Trade Review. See also *B.O.,* 1 January 1863.
[140] Dunham, *op. cit.,* p. 231.
[141] *Ibid.,* pp. 215–16, 229–31. See also *The Economist,* 13 July 1861.
[142] Cole, *op. cit.,* I. Ch. XVII.
[143] *Ibid.,* Chs XX & XXI.
[144] *B.O.,* 12 September 1862; *L.M.,* 30 December 1864.
[145] Greeves, *thesis cit.,* p. 207; *Huddersfield Examiner,* 18 April 1863; 6 June 1863; 14 November 1863.
[146] Cole, *op. cit.,* I. p. 377; E.D. Fite, *Social and Industrial Conditions during the Civil War,* (1910), p. 83.
[147] *B.O.,* 3 July 1862.
[148] *The Economist,* 19 January 1861.
[149] Greeves, *op. cit.,* p. 5.
[150] *Report of the Inspectors of Factories,* 30 April 1864, *BPP.,* (1864) (3390) XXII.
[151] W. Smith, *Rambles around Morley, with Descriptive and Historical Sketches; also an Account of the Rise and Progress of the Woollen Manufacture in this Place,* (1866), pp. 60–3.
[152] *B.O.* 4 January 1866.
[153] *Reports of the Inspectors of Factories,* 30 April 1864, *loc. cit.*
[154] *L.M.,* 31 December 1864; *Huddersfield Examiner,* 28 June 1862.
[155] *The Economist,* 19 January 1861.
[156] Greeves, *thesis cit.,* p. 377.
[157] *B.O.,* 13 February 1862.
[158] *Reports of the Inspectors of Factories,* 30 April 1863, *BPP.,* (1863) (3206) XVIII; See also *B.O.,* 5 April 1866; *B.O.,* 13 February 1862; J. Watt, *Facts about the Cotton Famine.*
[159] See *Reports of the Inspectors of Factories,* 31 October 1861; *Hudders-*

field Examiner, 9 November 1861; Bradford Observer, 5 September 1861.

[160] Reports of the Inspectors of Factories, 31 October 1862, BPP., (1863) (3076) XVIII; Huddersfield Examiner, 1 March 1863.

[161] Reports of the Inspectors of Factories, 31 October 1862, loc. cit; B.O., 1 January 1863.

[162] Watt, op. cit., p. 401.

[163] Huddersfield Examiner, 22 April 1864, 3 September 1864, 22 October 1864

[164] L.M., 31 December 1864.

[165] B.O., 11 September 1864; James, History of Bradford . . and Continuation to the Present Time, op. cit., p. 242; Greeves, thesis cit., pp. 138–9.

[166] The Economist, 10 March 1866; Huddersfield Examiner, 12 September 1865, 2 January 1866; B.O., 4 January 1866.

[167] L.M., 1 January 1867; The Economist, 14 March 1868.

[168] Huddersfield Examiner, 4 January 1868.

[169] The Economist, 13 March 1869 (1868 Trade Review). See also the Trade Review for 1867. The Economist, 14 March 1868; see also Huddersfield Examiner, 6 January 1866; 4 January 1868.

[170] L.M., 2 January 1866. See also The Economist, 5 June 1858; L.M. 31 December 1864. Trade was being stimulated by the speeding up of steamship lines to the East. See F.E. Hyde, Far Eastern Trade, 1860–1914, (1973), pp. 23, 30.

[171] Huddersfield Examiner, 1 January 1870; The Economist, 12 March 1871.

[172] Sigsworth, op. cit., p. 74 quoting B.O., 7 January 1864.

[173] See B.O., 2 January 1868.

Chapter 7

[1] See. D.T. Jenkins, 'The Factory Returns, 1850–1905', loc. cit., pp. 69–71; Return of the Numbers of Factories and Workshops, (1874), BPP., (1875) (393) LXXI.

[2] In the second half of the 1890s the factory inspectors produced statistics of employment in the textile trades as part of their regular reports.

[3] Final Report on the First Census of Production of the United Kingdom, (1907); Final Report on the Third Census of Production of the United Kingdom, (1924).

[4] Baines, op. cit., p. 75; see also Henry Forbes, 'The Rise, Progress and Present [1852] State of the Worsted, Alpaca and Mohair Manufacture', in A. Holroyd, ed., Collectanea Bradfordiana, where similar but slightly higher figures are suggested.

[5] D.M. Hunter, The West of England Woollen Industry under Protection and Free Trade, 1910, pp. 46–7.

[6] W. G. Rimmer, 'The Industrial Profile of Leeds, 1740–1840', loc. cit.

[7] J. Thomas, A History of the Leeds Clothing Industry, Yorkshire Bulletin of Economic and Social Research Occasional Paper No. 1, (1955).

[8] F. Hooper, Statistics relating to the Woollen and Worsted Trades of the United Kingdom 1906, (1907). There were a series of editions of this publication.

[9] e.g. T.E. Ashenhurst, *A Practical Treatise in Weaving and Designing*, 2nd edn, (1881).
[10] Gulvin, *op. cit.*, Ch. 5. See also C. Ballantyne, 'The Scottish Tweed Manufacture', *Yorkshire College Textile Magazine*, 1897–8.
[11] F. Thompson, *op. cit.*
[12] *Factory Returns*, 1854, 1874 and 1889.
[13] J.H. Clapham, *The Woollen and Worsted Industries*, 1907, p. 149.
[14] *Ibid.*, p. 148.
[15] *Ibid.*, p. 144.
[16] Sigsworth, *op. cit.*, p. 120.
[17] Clapham, *The Woollen and Worsted Industries*, *op. cit.*, p. 140.
[18] Sigsworth, *op. cit.*, p. 190.
[19] *Ibid.*, p. 130.
[20] *Ibid.*, pp. 92,129, quoting from a report in the *Bradford Observer*, 1 December 1875, of a Bradford Chamber of Commerce meeting.
[21] Sigsworth, *op. cit.*, p. 130, quoting the *Bradford Observer*, 31 December 1883.
[22] We are grateful to Mr James Jones, a director of the Bradford Dyers' Association Ltd, for supplying us with copies of papers in the Association's possession on which much of this discussion is based.
[23] J.H. Clapham, *An Economic History of Modern Britain*, Vol. III, *Machines and National Rivalries*, 1887–1914, *and an Epilogue*, (1938), p. 226; *The Economist*, 29 November 1902; *The Times*, 19 May 1905.
[24] Clapham, *Machines . . .*, *op. cit.*, p. 229; *Survey of Textile Industries*, *op. cit.*, p. 178.
[25] James Graham, 'Wool and the Woollen and Worsted Industries of Great Britain', in F.H. Jackson, *Lectures on British Commerce*, (1911).
[26] *Survey of Textile Industries*, *op. cit.*, p. 177.
[27] Clapham, *Machines . . .*, *op. cit.*, p. 228.
[28] H.W. Macrosty, *The Trust Movement in British Industry*, (1907), p. 140.
[29] Clapham, *Machines . . .*, *op. cit.*, p. 228.
[30] Based on White's *Clothing District Directory*, (1871).
[31] *The Economist*, 31 August 1901.
[32] Clapham, *Machines . . .*, *op. cit.*, p. 226.
[33] *Ibid.*, p. 229.
[34] Mann, *op. cit.*, p. 208.
[35] *Reports of the Royal Commission on Depression of Trade and Industry*, (1886) *loc. cit.*, para. 6791.
[36] Sigsworth, *op. cit.*, p. 187; Hudson, *op. cit.*, p. 454; Gulvin, *op. cit.*, p. 158.
[37] Clapham, *The Woollen and Worsted Industries*, *op. cit.*, p. 153.
[38] H.A. Shannon, 'The Limited Companies of 1866–1883', *Ec.H.R.* IV, 3, (1933).
[39] *Survey of Textile Industries*, *op. cit.*, p. 175.
[40] Bartlett, *op. cit.*, p. 157.

Chapter 8

[1] James, *op. cit.*, p. 463.
[2] J.H. Clapham, 'Transference . . .', *loc. cit.*, p. 208 records the use of mohair in Norwich.

[3] James, *op. cit.*, pp. 461–6. See Bernoville, *loc. cit.*, pp. 38–40, who records that a Norwich firm was employing 1000 persons to spin mohair for French and German manufacturers and comments that French spinners could not spin mohair as well as those of Bradford.

[4] See W. Walton, *The Alpaca, its Naturalisation in the British Isles considered as a National Benefit and as an Object of Immediate Utility to the Farmer and Manufacturer*, 1844.

[5] James, *op. cit.*, p. 453. Alpaca comes in various shades of black, white, grey and brown.

[6] *Ibid.*, p. 454.

[7] Walter, *op. cit.*; Baines, *op. cit.*, pp. 130–1; James, *op. cit.*, p. 453.

[8] James, *op. cit.*, p. 455.

[9] An example of alpaca with a staple length of 42″ was exhibited by Messrs Walter Milligan of Bingley at the Great Exhibition. *Wool, Worsted and Cotton Journal*, April 1853.

[10] Baines, *op. cit.*, p. 131.

[11] See Sigsworth, *op. cit.*, Ch. VIII.

[12] *Ibid.*; see also W.R. Millimore, 'Early Days in the Mohair and Alpaca Trade', *Wool Record*, 79, (1951), pp. 1245–7.

[13] Gulvin, *op. cit.*, pp. 58, 81. Alexander Johnson chartered vessels to obtain rare wools from America.

[14] Crump and Ghorbal, *op. cit.*, p. 128.

[15] Bernoville, *loc. cit.*, pp. 34–5.

[16] A. Sauerbeck, *The Production and Consumption of Wool*, 1878, p. 11; J.R. Hind, *Woollen and Worsted Raw Materials*, 1934, p. 135.

[17] Malin, *thesis cit.*, Ch. V.

[18] *Ibid.*

[19] *T.M.*, March 1882.

[20] Sauerbeck, *op. cit.*, p. 1. See also *T.M.*, April 1887.

[21] Malin, *thesis cit.*, pp. 367–8.

[22] Barnard, *op. cit.*, pp. 7, 196.

[23] Malin, *thesis cit.*, Table V. iii.

[24] *The Wool Year Book*, 1913, pp. 426–7.

[25] Dept. of Commerce, Bureau of Standards. *Technologic Papers of the Bureau of Standard*, No. 57, 1915. W.S. Lewis, 'Difference in Weight between Raw and Clean Wools'.

[26] *T.M.*, May 1894.

[27] Hooper, *op. cit.*, 1903, p. 32.

[28] *The Wool Year Book*, 1913, p. 426.

[29] *Ibid.*,

[30] Malin, *thesis cit.*, Table V. iii.

[31] *Wool Year Book*, 1913, p. 426.

[32] *Ibid.*, p. 427.

[33] The figures derive from the Bradford Chamber of Commerce estimates. Little is known of their source and construction.

[34] See Chs. 6 and 9. Hooper, *op. cit.*, 1903, believed 100 million pounds of cotton was used, 45 million pounds in the worsted trade and 55 million pounds in the woollen trade. See also D.T. Jenkins, 'The Cotton Industry in Yorkshire . . .', *loc. cit.*

[35] It is also necessary to remember that a higher proportion of crossbred,

coarser wools were included in imports later in the period.

[36] A.F. Barker, *Woollen and Worsted Spinning*, (1922), pp. 141–4 for a full discussion of the frame spinning of woollen yarns.

[37] The dobby looms were based on the American Crompton loom. 'The invention of the Crompton fancy loom in 1857, raising the speed from forty-five to eighty-five picks per minute, was an advance greater than any single improvement achieved since that time.' Cole, *op. cit.*, II, p. 91.

[38] The Automatic Worsted Loom as constructed by Crompton & Knowles Loom Works in 1911; illustrated in Cole, *op. cit.*, II, p. 96.

[39] See J.R. Allan, *op. cit.*, pp. 110–11 for interesting details of the process.

[40] 'The method of burr removal called carbonization is of Continental origin, being attributed to a German, Gustav Kober. Introduced abroad first in the fifties; it spread with rapidity coming into general use by the close of the sixties,' Cole, *op. cit.*, II, p. 80. Cole gives as his authority Knecht, *A Manual of Dyeing*, I, p. 152.

Chapter 9

[1] Bradford Chamber of Commerce Minute Books, 31 October 1835, quoted by Sigsworth, *op. cit.*, p. 46.

[2] *Wool, Worsted and Cotton Journal*, May 1853; January 1854; February 1854; *B.O.*, 3 January 1856 quoted by Sigsworth, *op. cit.*, p. 46.

[3] T. Illingworth, *A Sixty Years Retrospect of the Bradford Trade Indicative of Some Causes of the Great Depression*, n.d., p. 62.

[4] A.L. Bowley, 'Notes on the Statistics of the Woollen Industries', *Economic Journal*, XV, (1905), pp. 585–90; Greeves, *thesis cit.*, p. 243. There may have also been some initial difficulties in and after 1862 as the reclassification was carried out.

[5] *Commission on Depression in Trade and Industry*, *loc. cit.*, 2nd Rept, (1886), p. 258. Evidence of Jacob Behrens.

[6] *Ibid.*, pp. 258–9.

[7] C. Ogden and P. Tarbet Macauley, *Gain or Loss? under preference, protection or retaliation: An Inquiry into the Woollen and Worsted Trades on behalf the Yorkshire Ninety-Nine Club*, (1903), p. 58.

[8] Clapham, *The Woollen and Worsted Industries*, *op. cit.*, pp. 274–5.

[9] Bowley, *loc. cit.*, p. 588.

[10] *The Economist*, 11 March 1871, 16 March 1872.

[11] *Ibid.*, 15 March 1873; Illingworth, *op. cit.*, (2nd edn 1883), p. 62.

[12] *The Economist*, 16 March 1872; 15 March 1873.

[13] A. Picard, *Le Bilan d'un Siècle*, (1906), p. 345.

[14] *T.M.*, August 1875.

[15] *Ibid.*, July 1876.

[16] *Ibid.*, April and October 1877.

[17] *Ibid.*, May 1877.

[18] *Tariff Commission*, *op. cit.*, para. 1335.

[19] Ingle, *thesis cit.*, Ch. 4.

[20] *Commission on Depression in Trade and Industry*, *loc. cit.*, 2nd Rept, 1886, p. 127.

[21] *T.M.*, August 1897; *Tariff Commission*, *op. cit.*, Para. 1674.

[22] *T.M.*, February 1897.

324 The British Wool Textile Industry

[23] *T.M.*, May 1896.
[24] E. Possett & Co., Yarn Exporters, Miscellaneous Ledgers, 1863–1912, Bradford Public Library.
[25] *T.M.*, May 1878; January 1883.
[26] *Tariff Commission, op. cit.*, paras. 775, 1563, 1581–8; Gulvin, *op. cit.*, p. 147.
[27] *Ibid.*, para. 1834.
[28] *Ibid.*, paras 1589, 1612, 1701, 1707, 1764.
[29] *Ibid.*, paras 1581–8.
[30] *The Economist*, 14 March 1874. Commercial History and Review of 1873.
[31] *T.M.*, March 1875.
[32] *Ibid.*, April and July 1875; January 1876.
[33] *Ibid.*, November and December 1875.
[34] *Ibid.*, September 1875.
[35] *Ibid.*, December 1875; *The Economist*, 10 March 1877. Commercial History and Review of 1876.
[36] *T.M.*, July 1877.
[37] *The Economist*, 13 March 1880. Commercial History and Review of 1879.
[38] *Reports of the Factory Inspectors*, October 1879, *BPP.*, (1880) (c.2489) XIV.
[39] *T.M.*, April and May 1879.
[40] *T.M.*, August 1880, January 1881.
[41] *Reports of the Factory Inspectors*, October 1803, *BPP.*, (1884) (c.3945) XVIII.
[42] *T.M.*, January 1882, January 1883.
[43] *Reports of the Factory Inspectors*, October 1886, *BPP.*, (1887) (c.5002) XVII.
[44] *Committee on Depression in Trade and Industry, loc. cit.*, 2nd Rept, (1886), p. 248.
[45] *Ibid.*, 1st Report, (1886), Appendices.
[46] *T.M.*, January 1887, January 1888 and January 1889. This would suggest that 1888 was the year of greatest production in the Bradford trade, but even allowing for a large increase in the home market this seems most unlikely from the trade statistics.
[47] *T.M.*, January 1890.
[48] *Reports of the Factory Inspectors*, October 1891, *BPP*, (1892) (c.6720) XX.
[49] Huddersfield Chamber of Commerce, 41st *Annual Report*, (1893).
[50] *Ibid., T.M.*, January 1892; *Reports of the Factory Inspectors*, October 1893, *BPP.* (1894) (c. 7368) XX1.
[51] *T.M.*, January 1896.
[52] *Ibid.*, January 1896, January 1897 and January 1898.
[53] *Ibid.*, January 1899; S.B. Saul, *Studies in British Overseas Trade, 1870–1914*, (1960), pp. 119–20.
[54] J.T. Clay wrote to the *Huddersfield Chronicle* about his involvement in the early development of worsted coatings. See Clay Mss., *loc. cit.*, 274 (52).
[55] *T.M.*, June and November 1877.

[56] United States Centennial Commission, *International Exhibition, 1876 Reports on Awards*. Group IX. See also Sigsworth, *op. cit.*, p. 110, quoting *B.O.*, 20 December 1883. It was claimed that Titus Salt introduced coatings to Bradford in 1868.

[57] 2nd Rept 1886, para. 3787.

[58] Quoted by Sigsworth, *op. cit.*, p. 110.

[59] Mann, *op.cit.*, pp. 216–18.

[60] *Commission on Depression in Trade and Industry*, 2nd Rept, 1886, paras 3795, 3924.

[61] For example, *The Economist*'s Annual Commercial Reviews from 1902 to 1905.

[62] D.J. Sharpe, *A Brief History of the Morley Textile Industry, 1750–1900*, n.d., p. 24.

[63] See Hunter, *op. cit.*, pp. 46–8 and The Annual Commercial Reviews of *The Economist* from 1906 onwards which report the fortunes of the West of England trade.

[64] *The Economist*. Annual Commercial Reviews for 1908, 1909, 1910, 1911 and 1913.

[65] S. Smith, 'Some Lessons from the Brussels Exhibition', *Huddersfield Textile Society*, 1911.

[66] See *The Economist*'s Annual Commercial Reviews and Saul, *op. cit.*, p. 120.

[67] S. Brierley and G.R. Carter, 'Fluctuations in the Woollen Industries of the West Riding', *Economic Journal*, 24, (1914), p. 379.

[68] G.R. Carter, 'Clothing the Allied Armies', *Economic Journal*, 25, (1915); S.J. Chapman and D. Kemp, 'The War and the Textile Industries', *J.R.S.S.*, LXXVIII, March 1915, pp. 206–16.

[69] *Tariff Commission*, *op. cit.*, para. 1692.

[70] Clapham, *The Woollen and Worsted Industries*, *op. cit.*, p. 278.

[71] For details see *T.M.*, April and June 1881, March 1882 and May 1888.

[72] *Ibid.*, March 1882 and May 1888.

[73] Beresford, *op. cit.*, p. 118.

[74] *T.M.*, March 1883, June 1895; *Textile Recorder*, May 1884.

[75] *Account and Papers* – Commercial 26, *BPP.*, (1885) (c.4530) LXXX1, p. 27 quoted by Saul, *op. cit.*, p. 156.

[76] *Commission on Depression in Trade and Industry*, *loc. cit.*, 1st Rept, (1886). Appendices.

[77] *Ibid.*, 2nd Rept (1886), p. 135.

[78] *T.M.*, October 1883. The decline was nearer 50 per cent if one discounts the increased trade in the previous year through attempts to beat the tariff.

[79] Saul, *op. cit.*, p. 139. Much business with Spain was done through French merchants. There were also many reports of British goods being smuggled from France to Spain, sometimes with French labels. For these reasons the trade figures may not be totally realistic.

[80] For details of the tariffs and the reaction to them see *T.M.*, August 1877, February 1879, October 1880 and January 1881.

[81] *T.M.*, January 1892.

[82] *Ibid.*, July 1875, January 1877, March 1882.

[83] *Tariff Commission*, *op. cit.*, paras 1398–9.

[84] *T.M.*, January 1877, June 1882, February 1884, November 1887; *Commission on Depression in Trade and Industry, loc. cit.*, 2nd Rept, 1886, p. 159.

[85] *Behrens, op. cit.*, p. 54; Beresford, *op. cit.*, p. 108; *T.M.*, August 1888.

[86] *T.M.*, March 1881, March 1883; *Commission on Depression in Trade and Industry, loc. cit.*, 2nd Rept, 1886, p. 162 and para. 3798.

[87] *T.M.*, July 1885, November 1888, September 1889.

[88] *Ibid.*, February 1889.

[89] One ship (*The Etruria*), loaded with Bradford goods, was reported as having arrived at New York Customs House 50 seconds before time, saving £36,000 for the importers. *T.M.*, October 1890.

[90] *Board of Trade Journal, IX*, (1890), p. 719 quoted by Saul, *op. cit.*, p. 151.

[91] Cole, *op. cit.*, II. Ch. XXII.

[92] Saul, *op. cit.*, p. 151.

[93] Gulvin, *op. cit.*, pp. 140–3; Mann, *op. cit.*, pp. 217–18; Sigsworth and Blackman, *loc. cit.*, p. 148.

[94] See R.S. Sayers, *A History of Economic Change in England*, 1880–1939, 1967, p. 24 and *T.M.*, March 1891.

[95] Clapham, *Economic History of Modern Britain, op. cit.*, Vol. III, p. 31.

[96] *T.M.*, January 1895, February 1896.

[97] *Tariff Commission, op. cit.*, Vol. II, part 2, para. 1427.

[98] *T.M.*, November 1897.

[99] G.R. Hawke, 'The United States Tariff and Industrial Protection in the late 19th Century', *Ec.H.R.*, 2nd Series, XXVIII, I, (1975), pp. 92–7.

[100] *Tariff Commission, op. cit.*, II, Pt 2, para. 1415; *T.M.*, November 1884 and July 1897.

[101] Clapham, *The Woollen and Worsted Industries, op. cit.*, p. 289.

[102] *T.M.*, May 1882; *Commission on Depression in Trade and Industry, loc. cit.*, 2nd Rept (1886), p. 190; D.C.M. Platt, *Latin America and British Trade, 1806–1914*, (1972), p. 189.

[103] *Commission on Depression in Trade and Industry, loc. cit.*, 2nd Rept, (1886), pp. 59, 66–7, 268.

[104] For example, *T.M.*, January 1895.

[105] Platt, *op. cit.*, pp. 190–2 cites various examples.

[106] *T.M.*, November 1898.

[107] Beresford, *op. cit.*, p. 86.

[108] Sharpe *op. cit.*, quoting the *Dewsbury Reporter*.

[109] *Tariff Commission, op. cit.*, paras 1347, 1433, 1638, 1715, 1743.

[110] *Commission on Depression in Trade and Industry*, (1886), 2nd Rept, p. 230.

[111] *T.M.*, April 1887, June 1889, July 1898.

[112] *T.M.*, July 1898; *Tariff Commission, op. cit.*, para. 1433.

[113] *T.M.*, September 1885, April 1888, October 1895, December 1895, August 1896, November 1898; Clapham, *Woollen and Worsted Industries, op. cit.*, p. 262.

[114] See *T.M.*, October 1884, September 1885, February 1889, September 1890, March 1892; see also the Manchester Chamber of Commerce evidence to the *Commission on Depression in Trade and Industry*, 1st Rept, (1886).

[115] *T.M.*, January 1878, March, August and November 1881.
[116] *T.M.*, December 1899; Clapham, *Woollen and Worsted Industries, op. cit.* p. 290.
[117] *Tariff Commission, op. cit.*, Vol. 11, part 2, paras 1434–45.
[118] Sigsworth and Blackman, *loc. cit.*, pp. 156–7.
[119] Saul, *op. cit.*, p. 201. Britain had no preference in India. See also *Tariff Commission, op. cit.*, Vol. 11, part 2, para. 1445.
[120] *Census of Production*, 1924, *loc. cit.*, p. 88.
[121] G.H. Wood, 'Wages and Efficiency in the Woollen and Cotton Industry', *Huddersfield Textile Society*, (1908–9).
[122] D. Deane and W.A. Cole, *British Economic Growth, 1688–1950*, 2nd edn, (1969), p. 196.
[123] James, *op. cit.*, pp. 515, 543.
[124] *Tariff Commission, op. cit.*, paras 1453–5, (1871–7).
[125] Ogden and Macaulay, *op. cit.*, p. 43.
[126] *Reports of the Factory Inspectors*, April 1875, *BPP.*, (1875) (c.1345) XVI.
[127] *The Economist*, March 1878. *Commercial History and Review of* 1877, p. 36.
[128] Quoted in *T.M.*, March 1881.
[129] *T.M.*, July 1881.
[130] *Textile Recorder*, August 1884; Factory Returns 1905.
[131] *T.M.*, January 1881; Sigsworth, *op. cit.*, pp. 89–90.
[132] *Commission on Depression in Trade and Industry*, *loc. cit.*, 2nd Rept, (1886), p. 255. Evidence of Jacob Behrens. See also the evidence of Henry Mitchell, p. 130.
[133] *Royal Commission on Technical Instructions*, (1884), *BPP.*, (1884) (c.3981) XXIX, 1, p. 314.
[134] *Commission on Depression in Trade and Industry*, *loc. cit.*, 2nd Rept (1886), p. 255.
[135] *Commission on Technical Instruction*, *loc. cit.*, I. p. 368.
[136] Letter quoted in *Reports of the Factory Inspectors*, April 1875, *BPP.*, (1875) (c.1345) XV1; see also the evidence of Henry Mitchell to the *Commission on Depression in Trade and Industry*, 2nd Rept (1886), para. 3883.
[137] Clapham, *The Woollen and Worsted Industries, op. cit.*, p. 304.
[138] *Commission on Depression in Trade and Industry*, *loc. cit.*, 2nd Rept (1886), p. 136. Evidence of G. Gribble.
[139] E.E. Williams, *Made in Germany*, (1896), pp. 84ff.
[140] Clapham, *The Woollen and Worsted Industries, op. cit.*, p. 296.
[141] Clapham, *Economic History of Modern Britain, op. cit.*, III, p. 127.

Chapter 10
[1] *Reports of the Factory Inspectors*, 30 April (1860), *BPP.*, 1860 (2689) XXXIV.
[2] D. Landes, 'Technological Change and Development in Western Europe, 1750–1914', in H.J. Habbakuk and M. Postan, eds *The Cambridge Economic History of Europe*, Vol. VI, The Industrial Revolutions and After, Part I, (1964), p. 564.

[3] D.H. Aldcroft, 'The Entrepreneur and the British Economy, 1870–1914', *Ec.H.R.*, 2nd series, XVI, (1964), p. 113.

[4] D.M. McCloskey and Lars G. Sandberg, 'From Damnation to Redemption: Judgements on the Late Victorian Entrepreneur', *Explorations in Economic History*, IX, (1971).

[5] *T.M.*, October 1880.

[6] *T.M.*, April 1890.

[7] *T.M.*, February 1887.

[8] *T.M.*, January 1878.

[9] For examples of such criticisms see the *Textile Manufacturer* for January 1877, January 1878, February and November 1881, February 1882 and February 1888.

[10] *T.M.*, September 1882.

[11] *T.M.*, January 1878.

[12] E.E. Williams, *Made in Germany*, (1896), pp. 84ff. See also the *Textile Manufacturer*, November 1896 for a discussion of Williams' views.

[13] P.L. Payne, *British Entrepreneurship in the Nineteenth Century*, (1974), pp. 41–4.

[14] *Ibid.*, p. 44. Payne suggests that commission agents deliberately refrained from maximising sales volume for a particular firm in case that firm was encouraged to replace the agent by its own salesman.

[15] i.e. performance in relation to other countries as suggested in D.M. McCloskey, 'Did Victorian Britain Fail?' *Ec.H.R.*, 2nd Series, XXIII, 3, (1970), p. 459, and by S.B. Saul in D.M. McCloskey, ed., *Essays on a Mature Economy: Britain after 1840*. Papers and Proceedings of the M.S.S.B. Conference on the New Economic History of Britain 1840–1939, (1971), p. 394.

[16] E.M. Sigsworth, 'Some Problems in British Business History, 1870–1914', p. 33, in C.J. Kennedy, ed., *Papers of the Sixteenth Business History Conference*, (1969).

[17] J. Graham, 'Wool and the Woollen and Worsted Industries of Great Britain', in F.H. Jackson, *Lectures on British Commerce*, (1911).

[18] Malin, *thesis cit.*, pp. 15–21.

[19] Sigsworth and Blackman, *loc. cit.*, pp. 129–31.

[20] Based on a comparison of Slater's directories for the two years.

[21] *Reports of the Factory Inspectors*, October 1846, *BPP.*, (1847) (779) XV.

[22] Based on a comparison of Parson and White's Directory, 1830 and White's Directory of 1853. One can be even less confident about the accuracy of these early directories.

[23] Timothy Exell, *A Sketch of the Circumstances which providentially led to the Repeal of the Corn and Animal Food Laws and many Custom House Restrictions*, (1847).

[24] *B.O.*, 31 December 1883, cited by Sigsworth, *op. cit.*, p. 77. The Annual Reports of the Leeds Chamber of Commerce after 1884 give the number of receiving orders in the Leeds area. Beresford, *op. cit.*, p. 44. High levels of failures are indicated in 1890, 1892, 1894–5, 1898–1900, and 1902–6. 1905 was a particularly disastrous year.

[25] *T.M.*, August 1877. A later report suggested liabilities of £295,000.

[26] *T.M.*, October 1877.

[27] R.E. Scott, *The South of Scotland Chamber of Commerce, 1860–1960: A*

Century of Commercial History and Progress, (1960); Gulvin, *op. cit.*, p. 131; R. Scott, 'The Collie Disaster', *Transactions of the Hawick Archaeological Society*, (1962).

[28] *T.M.*, May, July and August, 1877.

[29] *T.M.*, January 1877.

[30] Beresford, *op. cit.*, p. 45.

[31] See Heaton, 'Yorkshire Cloth Traders . . .', *loc. cit.*; Heaton, 'Benjamin Gott and the Anglo-American Cloth Trade', *loc. cit.*; Buck, *op. cit.*

[32] Payne, *op. cit.*, p. 43. The British Consul in Germany wrote in 1886 that using a commission agent meant that the cost naturally increased 'not only by the commission of the agent, but also of a great many incidental expenses . . .', which he argued the buyer saved if purchasing direct from a German manufacturer. *Royal Commission on Depression in Trade and Industry, loc. cit.*, 2nd Rept, (1886), Appendix E, p. 169.

[33] Sigsworth, *op. cit.*, p. 340.

[34] Gulvin, *op. cit.*, pp. 117 ff. Because of the nature of the Scottish product the wholesale merchant performed a vital task in cutting pieces for individual orders. Purchasers, be they tailors, makers up, or retailers, rarely wanted full pieces or long runs and thus the merchant was needed to market short lengths to different customers.

[35] *Tariff Commission, op. cit.*, paras 1743, 1809.

[36] *T.M.*, March 1876.

[37] *Tariff Commission, op. cit.*, para. 1579.

[38] *Ibid.*, para. 1678.

[39] *Ibid.*, paras 1841–2.

[40] Sigsworth, *op. cit.*, p. 342; Hudson, *op. cit.*, p. 240; *T.M.*, September 1881.

[41] Sigsworth, *op. cit.*, pp. 345–6.

[42] See Glover, 'Government Contracting . . .', *loc. cit.*, p. 478.

[43] Clapham, *Woollen and Worsted Industries, op. cit.*, pp. 161–4.

[44] *T.M.*, October 1878.

[45] *Sir Jacob Behrens, op. cit.*, p. 53.

[46] *T.M.*, March 1878.

[47] *T.M.*, February 1881 and July 1884.

[48] *Sir Jacob Behrens, op. cit.*, p. 54.

[49] *T.M.*, August 1876 and April 1876.

[50] United States Centennial Commission, *International Exhibition 1876: Reports and Awards*, Vol. 5, Groups VIII–XIV, p. 143. See also *T.M.*, February 1876, February and March 1877.

[51] *T.M.*, November 1875, March 1876.

[52] *T.M.*, December 1877. Six months earlier, however, the trade journal mentioned 'the excellent show made by Yorkshire firms at Philadelphia exhibition', *ibid.*, July 1877.

[53] *Ibid.*, May 1877.

[54] Clay Mss., *loc. cit.*, 274(52).

[55] *T.M.*, March 1877, September 1878.

[56] *Ibid.*, September 1878.

[57] *Ibid.*, March 1879. See also *Report of Henry Mitchell upon the Paris Exhibition together with the Report of the Artisans*, 1878, also pub-

lished as part of *Papers Relative to Industry and Commerce, BPP.*, (1878) (c.2085) LXXVI, No. 18.

[58] E.E. Williams, *op. cit.*, pp. 84ff.

[59] *T.M.*, March 1884.

[60] Committee on Industry and Trade, *Survey of Textile Industries, op. cit.*, p. 181.

[61] *B.O.*, 29 September 1841, cited by Sigsworth, *op. cit.*, p. 57.

[62] Bradford Chamber of Commerce Minute Book, 22 January 1852, cited by Sigsworth, *op. cit.*, p. 57.

[63] B. Wood and W.E. Preston, 'James Lobley, A Bradford Artist', *Journal of the Bradford Historical and Antiquarian Society*, N.S., Vol. III, (1911), p. 257.

[64] See *T.M.*, May 1877.

[65] Beresford, *op. cit.*, Ch. VII.

[66] G.H. and A. Nussey, *A Technical Institution for Leeds and District*, (1867).

[67] Keighley Snowden, *The Master Spinner: A Life of Sir Swire Smith*, (1921); Bradford Corporation, *A History of Education in Bradford since 1870*, (1970).

[68] Mann, *op. cit.*, p. 215; Gulvin, *op. cit.*, pp. 160–1; T. Oliver, *Continued Phases of Textile Education*, (1909). (Reprinted from *The Border Standard*, 18 September 1909).

[69] *T.M.*, February 1878.

[70] *T.M.*, June 1877.

[71] *Ibid.*

[72] *T.M.*, November 1899.

[73] *T.M.*, June 1877.

[74] Illingworth, *op. cit.* p. 9.

[75] *Technicomania and its Cure, addressed to the Merchants, Manufacturers, Spinners, Drapers and Others of the Afflicted and Disrespectfully Dedicated (without consent) to Professor Puff, M.B.T.S., Associate of the Artistic Association of Anthropoid Apes*, by Timothy Tapitnose, Esq., Secretary of the Sublime Society of Scientific Simpletons.

[76] *Committee on Depression in Trade and Industry, loc. cit.*, 2nd Rept, (1886), p. 191.

[77] Clay Mss., *loc. cit.*, 274(52).

[78] *T.M.*, July and August 1883.

[79] *T.M.*, December 1877. The Yorkshire College was considering a course in commercial education in 1887 and in 1903 J.H. Clapham started a new commerce course there. Beresford, *op. cit.*, p. 92.

[80] *Committee on Depression in Trade and Industry, loc. cit.*, 2nd Rept, (1886), p. 131.

[81] See *T.M.*, March 1887, January 1897 and July 1898.

[82] Oliver, *op. cit.*, pp. 7–9.

[83] Published attendance numbers are impossible to interpret as students could be counted more than once if registered for more than one class. Attendance figures give no indication of numbers completing courses.

[84] Quoted Gulvin, *op. cit.* p. 13.

[85] J.H. Clapham, 'Protection and the Wool Trade', *Independent Review*, 1904, pp. 641–50.

[86] Dorothy Hunter, *The West of England Woollen Industry under Protection and Under Free Trade*, (1910), pp. 40–3.

[87] *Tariff Commission, op. cit.*, para. 1501.

Chapter 11

[1] [Francis Moore], *The Contrast; or, a Comparison between our Woollen, Linen, Cotton and Silk Manufactures*, 1782, p. 14.

[2] P. Deane and W.A. Cole, *op. cit.*, p. 294.

[3] C.H. Feinstein, *loc. cit.*

[4] D.T. Jenkins, 'The Yorkshire Cotton Industry . . .', *loc. cit.*

[5] 'No. of Steam Engines in Leeds and area from a Survey made of them by Wm. Lindley. March 1824.' Brotherton Library, University of Leeds, Ms. 18.

[6] D.A. Farnie, *The English Cotton Industry and the World Market, 1815–1896*, (1979), p. 33.

[7] See Ch. 3.

[8] Heaton, 'Yorkshire Cloth Traders . . .', *loc. cit.*

Glossary

Acid Dyes. A class of coal-tar colours, usually themselves colourless salts, but having the property of combining with acids to form colour bases or dyes and widely used in the wool textile trade.

Afterchroming. The method of mordanting by which the chrome is added to the dye bath after the dye itself has gone onto the fibre. It is generally held that this was a development of the nineteenth century but old recipe books show that it had been used previously. It had the advantage over the mordanting before dyeing of taking less time and doing less harm to the wool.

Alizarin. The colouring principle of the important old natural dye, madder; in the middle of the nineteenth century it was produced synthetically and became the basis of a wide range of dyes.

Alpaca. The hair of the alpaca, a type of llama found in South America; very soft handling and used alone or mixed with worsted for superfine lightweight cloths. The use of alpaca was one of the great achievements of Sir Titus Salt.

Alum. A complex salt of great antiquity. It has been very important in the history of the wool textile trade as a mordant, but during the time covered by this volume, was largely replaced by chrome.

Angola. Yarn made of a mixture of wool and cotton.

Angora. The hair of the angora rabbit which has a very soft handle, and was used for making soft fabrics for children's wear and for dresses. It should be distinguished from the angora goat which produces mohair, quite a different fibre.

Aniline Dyes. A name given to the early synthetic dyes, aniline being the basis of them. It is a colourless oil prepared from benzene and unites with acids to form colour salts.

Anthrax. A disease caught, in the past, from handling certain types of wool, particularly those described as East Indian although in fact they usually came from India or Central Asia.

Apperly Feed. An intermediate feed connecting the scribbler to the carder. Invented in the West of England, it became very popular in the later part of the nineteenth century.

Astrakhan. Wool taken from the skins of the Karakul sheep of South Africa, and later from other areas. Very black and curly, the lambs are killed shortly after birth. Sometimes called Persian lamb because the animal appears to have originated there.

Automatic Weaving. Somewhat of a misnomer as, during the late nineteenth and early twentieth century, it essentially meant the addition to a normal power loom of a weft changing mechanism.

Baize (see Bays). A heavy woollen cloth, well felted, and usually raised on both sides.

Bale. Wool pack, the weight varied with the country of origin, usually 200–300 lbs from Australasia and 500–600 lbs from South America. The weights of English bales varied much more widely.

Bannockburn. A design originating in Scotland in the middle of the nineteenth century where a single coloured thread was combined with a marl (i.e. a twist comprised of two distinctive colours).

Barathea. An eight-end weave (actually a twilled hopsack) much used for worsted suitings, notably for evening clothes.

Barwood. One of the most widely used of natural dyes. Easy to apply to wool and the basis of many brown combinations.

Bays (see Baize). Earlier there had probably been a difference. Bays were a worsted warp/woollen weft cloth made in East Anglia in the seventeenth and eighteenth century.

Bearskin. One of the specialised dress fabrics made in the West of England. Apparently lighter weight and finer than beavers.

Beaver. A heavy milled woollen cloth with a raised finish, resulting in a nap like a beaver's skin.

Bedford Cord. A cloth made for trouserings and hard wearing purposes in a distinctive weave giving a well-defined rib in the cloth. This rib was mainly caused by the insertion of a fine cotton end.

Berlins. As far as the woollen trade, the name given to torn up knitwear which was used again in cheap cloths. The derivation of the word is rather mysterious. Berlin yarn was quite different, being a special type of yarn prepared for embroidery and other decorative purposes.

Bichromate of Soda (or Potash). Became, in the late nineteenth century, the most widely used mordant in the wool textile dyeing trade. It is a compound of chrome and soda (or potash) known in the trade simply as chrome.

Big Wheel. The hand spinning wheel for so long generally used in the woollen trade of Britain.

Billy. The slubbing billy, an important machine during the first half of the nineteenth century. The slubbings taken off the carding machine were drafted and given a modicum of twist on the billy before being properly spun on the jenny.

Bird's Eye. A distinctive design which gave, with the two and two colouring, a neat spot effect. Widely used in the worsted trade in the last decades of the nineteenth century and increasingly in the twentieth.

Blending. The mixing together of different qualities and colours and types of raw materials before spinning.

Blowing. A process in wool cloth finishing whereby the fabric is set and further shrinking avoided. Also known under its French name of decatising. In the cotton trade the word is used quite differently and is applied to the opening operation.

Blue Copperas = Copper Sulphate or Blue Vitriol. Widely used in wool dyeing, partly as a mordant but probably more common as an after-treating agent, mainly to brighten shades. An alternative name was blue stone. In old recipes often appears as copperas so can be confused with green copperas (ferrous sulphate) which is quite different.

Bockings. A worsted cloth made in East Anglia in the eighteenth century. The name derived from the town of that name.

Bombazine. A fabric, usually black, made of worsted warp and silk weft. Around 1800 it was a great speciality of the Norwich trade.

Botany. A generic name covering the best wool and the yarns and fabrics made from them. The word derives from Botany Bay, New South Wales, and emphasises the superfine nature of these wools.

Bowing (or **Beating**). The two words should perhaps be separate but the purpose is the same. The raw material, if beaten or treated with the bow, springs apart and in this way vegetable matter can be removed. Bowing was more common with cotton, beating with wool.

Box Cloth. A very heavy milled woollen fabric. As far as the West of England was concerned, the thickest that was made.

Breeches Cloth. Became an important section of the West of England trade. It was made in cavalry (or tautz) twills and whipcords, (also occasionally Bedford Cords) and used for riding and other outdoor purposes.

Broadcloth. Originally any cloth made on the broad loom, but later a fine cloth, usually woven in the plain weave and heavily milled. Yorkshire broadcloths were sometimes called Leeds Cloths where they were chiefly made, but West of England broadcloths were the finest and the best during the period up to 1825 when they became much less fashionable.

Brushing. A finishing process usually done before cutting in order to raise the surface of the cloth so that long fibres can be cut off.

Bumble. A West of England name used for a simple type of willowing machine which opened the wool and removed the vegetable matter.

Burling. The process by which the vegetable matter was removed by hand from the finished cloth. The word also often covered the rectification of certain cloth faults in such fabrics. The meaning of the word varies from district to district. For example, sometimes it included knotting, that is the removal of knots on the yarn from the woven cloth. It should not and normally does not, include mending (sometimes called drawing) which puts right the faults caused by broken ends and other weaving mistakes.

Burling Irons. The implements used for carrying out the burling operation.

Burrs (hence Burring). The spiney seed which contaminated so much wool from South America and also from parts of Australia. It could be removed either by mechanical action or, in the later decades of the nineteenth and during the twentieth century, by carbonising. Burring was the name given to the mechanical process.

Callimancoes. A worsted cloth made originally in Norwich and then in the West Riding.

Camwood. It came from a slightly different species of tree to Barwood but like that dye, dyed wool mordanted with chrome to a brownish colour. It was widely used, notably in combination with indigo.

Cap Spinning. A method of worsted spinning developed by Danforth in America. The yarn produced was soft but strong and much used towards the end of the nineteenth century for hosiery.

Carbonised Noils. The noils removed during the combing process naturally contained a considerable amount of vegetable matter. The discovery of the carbonising process established an important market in those noils that had been carbonised.

Carbonising. A method of removing burrs and other vegetable matter from wool by means of sulphuric acid. It could be done either in the wool, which was usual when heavily contaminated, or in the piece. With the development of the low woollen trade carbonising became very important for removing cotton in rags. The material produced was known as extract.

Card Clothing. The covering, usually leather, or some similar material, into which staples or wires were inserted and then used for covering the carding set.

Carding. The preliminary treatment before spinning to open and mix the wool. Originally done by hand cards which were covered with wire.

Cards See Card Clothing.

Cashmere. The fibre of the Tibetan goat. Probably the finest and loveliest of all fibres. The word has occasionally been badly corrupted to denote certain forms of torn up knitwear.

Cassimere. A fine woollen cloth made in the two and two twill weave, deriving from a patent of Francis Yerbury of 1766. The word comes from the French casimir, that is fine cloth. It should be pointed out that the common twill was very much older, and was certainly not Yerbury's invention.

Cavalry Twill. A fine distinctive cloth with a kind of double twill (technically caused by a faulty stitch in a double weft cloth), and best known as the correct habit for riding. Sometimes called a tautz twill.

Chain. Alternative name for warp, widely used in the West of England.

Challis. A fine fabric made from silk and wool.

Chintz. A finely printed and frequently glazed cotton cloth made in bright designs.

Chlorination. The treatment given to wool with chlorine to remove the surface scales and so prevent shrinking.

Chrome (see Bichromate of Potash or Soda).

Chrome Black. A group of synthetic dyes developed around 1900, at first chrome mordanted but later after-chromed, which were excellent for dyeing black on wool and over the following years replaced the famous Logwood.

Chrome Mordant Dyeing. This method of dyeing was to mordant with the chrome before dyeing. When chrome was first introduced it was widely used but was later replaced by the after-chroming method.

Circular Comb. The type of comb probably originally introduced by James Noble and later developed, probably by another man of the same name which became, in the last decades of the nineteenth century, the most common type of mechanical comb.

Clothworking. This finishing process was closely connected with dyeing. The raising and the shearing, combined with the colour, produced on the super-fine broadcloth one of the highest quality fabrics ever made. The skin-like surface that the wet raising and cutting produced developed the colour. The effect of this combination can be appreciated today by looking at a billiard table covering, the cloth of which is made by the same traditional combination of processes.

Coatings. Generic terms covering all types of lightweight cloth used for making men's and ladies' top coatings.

Cochineal. The scarlet dye obtained from the dried bodies of insects which gave the brightest of all natural dyes, especially when used with a tin mordant.

Cockled. Cloths that, for one reason or another, have become puckered up in manufacture.

Combing. The preparatory process for long wools. The short fibre, the noil, is removed and the product, the top, is spun into worsted yarn.

Commission Combers. Partly as a result of the inventions of Lister, much of the wool combing was done by people working on commission for top makers and others who owned the raw material.

Commission Dyers. Dyeing has always been difficult and although many wool textile businesses had their own dye house, a large percentage of the dyeing was carried out by commission dyers, that is, those working on wool yarn or fabric owned by other people.

Common Twill. The so-called two and two twill, after the plain weave the most widely used of all and particularly good for producing colour and weave effects.

Condensers. The final part of a complete carding set, where the carded web of wool is divided into strips which are rubbed into a kind of twistless sliver. There were two types (1) the ring doffer condenser and (2) the tape condenser (see separate entries).

Cop. The yarn package obtained on the mule.

Copperas. There were two forms important to distinguish (1) Green copperas (2) Blue copperas. (See separate entries).

Cotting. A fault in wool usually caused by malnutrition which meant that fibres tended to grow together.

Cotton Warp Double Twill. An example of the rather odd names developed in the wool textile trade. Obviously such a cloth had a cotton warp and a weave that showed a distinctive type of twill.

Cotton Warp Worsteds. The main product of the Yorkshire worsted trade in the middle decades of the nineteenth century. The warps were of cotton and the wefts of relatively coarse worsteds.

Crabbing. A worsted finishing process. The fabric is treated in boiling water or steam while on a perforated roller and this sets and defines the fabric so that variations will not occur in the following process. Rather similar to blowing for woollens.

Cropping. The cutting of the surface fibres from the cloth, also, and perhaps better, called shearing or simply, cutting.

Cross Cutter. A type of mechanical cutter fairly widely used between 1830 and 1850. The spiral blade cut across the cloth, i.e. from list to list, not as became more common later, lengthwise.

Decatising. An alternative name for blowing.

Devil. A machine by which wool rags are torn up by the shoddy or mungo manufacturer.

Devil's Dust. The waste made during the tearing of wool rags.

Dobby. An arrangement for raising and lowering the harnesses on a loom, hence the dobby loom.

Doeskin. A fine woollen cloth made in a five-end weave and finished by teasle raising and cutting (i.e. dress finish).

Doffer. The last roller on a carding set.

Doffing. Applied to several processes in wool textile manufacture which involved the removing of prepared material from a machine. The most common being the removing of the cops from the mule. But also applied to the removing of the prepared carded material.

Doffing Comb. An ingenious arrangement invented by Hargreaves or Arkwright which removed the material from the last roller (i.e. the doffer) of the carding set.

Dolly. The piece-scouring machine where the fabric is treated in rope as opposed to open width form.

Domett. A plain cloth woven with cotton warp and wool weft made thick and open in texture.

Domett Baize. Presumably a domett that had been raised on one side.

Donegal Tweed. Characteristic Irish tweed, made in the plain weave, with specially prepared knop yarn. Frequently imitated in Yorkshire.

Doublers. Those employed on the yarn doubling machine.

Doubling. The process by which two spun yarns are twisted together. The word is also used in other special senses in wool textile manufacture, thus two slivers are put together in worsted drawing and this is sometimes known as doubling.

Drapery. Another name for cloth, perhaps the most common use being in the two phrases the 'Old' and 'New' draperies, which of course relates to an earlier period than that described in this book.

Drawing. The process, particularly with reference to worsted spinning, by which the combed top is drawn out to a finer sliver ready for spinning. But the word is also used in other senses, notably the drawing of the threads through the heddles prior to weaving and the mending after weaving has been completed.

Draw Loom. The great fancy loom of China and later of the European textile trade. Fabrics of great complexity could be made in this loom and it had a limited use for the making of the finest type of wool (especially worsted) fabrics.

Dress Mending. The name given to the mending of woollen and worsted cloths after other finishing processes have been accomplished.

Drop Box. The type of shuttle box, invented by Robert Kay, which made changing shuttles simpler and ultimately automatic.

Druggets. A coarse woollen fabric, felted and usually raised on one side.

Dry Combing. Combing without the addition of oil, more common on the Continent than in England.

Drying. Generic name covering all processes in wool textile manufacture where wet material has to be dried.

Drysalters. Those who dealt in chemicals needed in cloth manufacture, also in natural dyes.

Dry Spinning. The spinning of tops prepared by dry combing.

Duffel. A thick woollen cloth raised on both sides. Sometimes known as a flushing.

Exeter Serges. As the name implies, made in Exeter with a worsted warp and woollen weft.

Extract. The waste (i.e. a type of shoddy) that has been obtained by carbonising wool/cotton rags. The cotton was of course removed. It was about the lowest type of waste that could be re-used.

False Twist. The name given to the insertion of twist that was not permanently put into the yarn. It was used in machines attempting to produce woollen yarns on a kind of Arkwright-type frame. They were not of any great success or significance before 1914 but later were important.

Fancy. Has several meanings, perhaps the most specific being the important roller on the carding set that lifts the material to the surface of the wire so that it can be removed by the doffer. For further definitions see below.

Fancy Cloth. Generic name given to cloths with a fancy weave and/or colour effect.

Fancy Flannel. Most flannels are in one colour, very often grey, but occasionally they are made with stripes. Striped flannel is really a better term than fancy flannel.

Fancy Waistcoats. In the middle decades of the nineteenth century waistcoats made in very fancy weaves were very popular. Manufactured particularly well in Huddersfield, also in the West of England.

Fancy Worsteds. The name given to the type of fine worsted cloth that towards the end of the period covered in this book, were becoming a main product for the Huddersfield area.

Fearnought. A machine fitted with spiked rollers used for opening and mixing the wool before carding. An alternative name is the willey.

Fellmongering. The removal of wool from the skin of sheep that have been killed for mutton.

Felt. A fabric made by matting or felting together the fibres, there being no separate warp or weft. Sometimes woven cloths that had been heavily felted were used in the same manner and they were called woven felts, which is really a misnomer.

Felted Carpets. Carpets made from felted material, an important product during the middle decades of the century.

Fent. Short, sometimes damaged, lengths of cloth. In certain areas known as bribes.

Fettling. Cleaning of the carding set. Those who did it were called Fettlers and the waste removed was called Fettlings.

Flannel. A woollen, or occasionally a worsted, cloth in a plain colour, usually if a woollen fairly well milled. Often, but not necessarily, grey in colour.

Flannelette. The name given to cotton cloth made to imitate a light weight flannel.

Flock. Very short lengths of wool obtained during processing, particularly during cutting or cropping, but also from rag pulling, where it is really an alternative name for devil's dust.

Flyer. Once the attachment on the Saxony hand spinning wheel that enabled winding and twisting to be done simultaneously, later the little ring on the rim of the ring spinning frame which is, however, better called a traveller.

Flying Shuttle. Kay's method of driving the shuttle across the loom.

French Combing. The method of combing derived from France, mainly from Heilmann's system, and very suitable for treating shorter wools than could be processed by the English combing methods.

French Drawing. A system of drawing where porcupine rollers replace gills. In addition, no twist was inserted until the final stages. Fitted in particularly well with French combing.

French Worsted. Generic name given to worsteds made from Merino wool that were widely imported into Britain from the middle decades of the nineteenth century. At that time the British worsted trade was making cotton warp, coarse worsted weft fabrics.

Frieze. Heavy woollen cloth, usually raised.

Fud. Very short waste, unsuitable for further use as raw material for cloth manufacturing.

Fuller's Earth. A clay once very popular for cleaning cloth. The name, of course, derived from the great use that the fullers made of this material over the centuries.

Fulling. The shrinking and thickening of woollen cloths, sometimes called milling.

Fustic. Sometimes known as Old Fustic to distinguish it from another dye called New Fustic. It was probably the best of the natural yellows and widely used for making dull yellows, browns, etc.

Gabardine. Closely woven twilled cloth, widely used for raincoats.

Garnet Machine. Used for tearing up yarn for re-use. It was much less severe than a devil.

Garnetted Waste. The torn up yarn waste made by the garnet machine.

Gigging. The processing of cloth on the gig.

Gig Mill (sometimes simply a gig). The teasel-covered raising machine.

Glazed Worsteds. Worsteds made in Norwich both plain and fancy, which were given a glazed finish by starching.

Green Copperas = Ferrous Sulphate. The most common iron mordant in the trade.

Guernsey. A type of knitwear originated in the island of that name.

Half Thick. Made in Halifax and presumably less thick than the traditional cloths made in this Yorkshire woollen town.

Half Worsted. A name sometimes given to the cotton warp/worsted weft fabrics made in Yorkshire.

Hand Mule. The type of mule that derived immediately from Crompton in which some of the processes were still performed by hand power. Came before the development of the so called self-acting mule.

Hand Shears. The big clumsy instruments used for cutting the surface of the cloth before the introduction of machine cropping.

Hanks. A length of reeled yarn, often of a standard length for measuring purposes.

Hard Twisted. Yarns that had a large amount of twist inserted during spinning, usually to obtain additional strength.

Harness. The name given to that part of the loom that controlled the raising and lowering of the warp threads.

Harris Tweed. Genuine Harris must be 100 per cent Scottish, and have been spun, dyed, woven and finished in the islands of the Outer Hebrides. This fabric was about to start on its great popularity towards the end of the period described in this volume.

Heavy Woollens. An alternative name for the low woollens of Yorkshire, that is the cloth made from shoddy, mungo or extract.

Heddle (or Healds). The cords or wires that the warp threads passed through in the loom. They are fixed on the harness (q.v.) and the two together are very much the controlling mechanism of the loom.

Hodden Grey. The name given to a coarse woollen fabric made from the Blackface wool. Burns uses the words in a famous poem.

Hopper Feed. The automatic feed used for supplying the carding machine, also for earlier machines such as wool scouring and wool drying. They were of two types, one simply supplied wool at a reasonably regular delivery rate, others had a carefully controlled weighing system so that the yarn coming from the end of the carding machine was of even size.

Huddersfield Worsted. The name given to the fancy worsteds which were developed in the later decades of the nineteenth century and, in the twentieth century, were to become one of the most famous products of the English worsted trade.

Indigo. The most famous of all dyes. It was originally a natural dye but at the end of the nineteenth century was made synthetically. The synthesis of indigo by the great German dyestuff chemist Baeyer was one of the key events in the development of the synthetic dyestuff trade.

Jack. A word used in a number of different senses in the wool textile trade. Perhaps most commonly, the levers on the loom that control the harnesses, but also the name given to a spinning machine rather intermediate between the jenny and the mule.

Jacquard Loom. Loom used for weaving very fancy cloths. It was invented by the Frenchman of that name and replaced the old draw loom.

Jenny. Hargreaves' famous spinning invention. It was essentially a multiple spinning wheel using a spindle, that is twist, with the drafting.

Kersey. An important coarse woolled cloth originally made in the East Anglian town of that name. Later, in the seventeenth and eighteenth centuries, a main product of the Yorkshire woollen trade where it was sometimes known as a Northern Dozen.

Kerseymere. Often regarded as an alternative form of cassimere but this is probably a mistake. The true cassimere was a fine cloth, the kerseymeres were a Yorkshire imitation of these fine cassimeres made from poorer material.

Knop Yarn. Fancy yarn, that is yarns with some distinguishing feature other than the normal colour, fineness, etc. Strictly speaking, knop yarns are that type of yarn where a knop (that is a small lump of fibre or yarn) distinguishes the structure. Perhaps the best example of all is the Donegal Tweed where knops of material are added late in the carding process and these give the well-known spotted effects. But knop yarns can be obtained, and in fact usually are obtained, by special yarn doubling effects.

Lantern Frame. The name given to Arkwright's machine that was used to draw out the combed sliver to a size suitable to go into his spinning (water) frame.

Laps. Waste from the worsted drawing process and re-used by the woollen trade.

Let-Off Motions. the motion of the loom that controlled the delivery of the yarn off the warp beam.

List = selvedge. The edge of a piece of cloth.

Logwood. The most widely used natural dye during the period covered in this volume. Also known as Bluewood or Blackwood. It is an interesting dye for several reasons. It was one, and probably the most important, of the new dyes introduced into Europe following the discovery of America. It is a mordant dye which gives a reasonable black when the material has been treated with copperas. Later it was found that mordanting with chrome was even better and this became the normal method of dyeing black on wool during the nineteenth century.

London Finishing. For many centuries until the middle of the nineteenth, London was the best known centre for the finishing of woollen cloth. See also London Shrinking.

London Shrinking. The finishing process whereby the cloth is damped and then allowed to resume its relaxed state so as to avoid shrinking later. It must originally have been done in London but by the nineteenth century the process was carried out in other centres.

Long Ells. A coarse worsted cloth made in Devon and West Somerset in the early nineteenth century and exported by the East India Company.

Low Woollens. One of the several names given to the great Yorkshire trade based on the re-manufacture of torn-up rags.

Lustre Cloth. Fabric made from the so-called lustre wools which are the English long wool breeds such as the Lincoln, and particularly because of its lustrous nature, the Wensleydale.

Madder. The root of the herbaceous perennial plant *Rubia tinctorum* and during its use as a dye was widely cultivated throughout the world. The synthesis of madder and its replacement by synthetic Alizarin was the great achievement of the early dye chemists, including the Englishman W.H. Perkin.

Marls. Twist yarns made of two different colours.

Mauve. the first of the synthetic dyes. Discovered by Perkin when he was trying to synthesise quinine.

Medleys. The name given to cloths made of mixed coloured wools.

Melton. Heavy woollen cloth, widely used for overcoatings in the nineteenth century.

Mending. The repairing of faults in cloth that arise due to trouble in weaving (i.e. broken ends), offshoots (i.e. missing picks), runches (i.e. collections of ends at the edge of the piece), etc.

Mercerisation. The treatment of cotton in yarn or fabric form of concentrated solution of caustic soda which gave additional strength and affinity for dye-stuffs.

Merino = Merino Wool. That is, the fine wool that comes from the Merino sheep. The word was also widely used to describe cloths made from Merino wool.

Merino Yarn. Yarns made from Merino wool.

Metachrome. Important dyeing process where the mordant and dye are placed in the same dyebath and processed together.

Milled = Fulled. Cloth that has gone through the fulling process. The word milling probably came into general use with the development of rotary milling (or fulling machine) in the early years of the nineteenth century.

Mixed Cloth. A name sometimes applied to cloths made of a mixture of cotton and wool.

Mohair. The hair of the angora goat, produced mainly in Turkey in the nineteenth century, but also later in South Africa and the United States of America.

Moleskin. An alternative name for a fine woollen cloth frequently made in the West of England and lighter in weight than such cloth as beavers, bearskins, etc.

Moquette. A pile cloth used for furnishing fabrics and for carpets.

Moreen. A stout woollen cloth used for curtains.

Moser. The meaning varies from district to district. In Yorkshire a brushing machine. In the West of England the name for the raising machine when fitted with wire instead of teasels.

Mothproofing. The treatment of wool by a chemical which makes it moth-proof.

Mousseline de Laine. A lightweight woollen cloth mainly made in France, but also in Yorkshire and Lancashire.

Mule. Woollen spinning machine. The word, of course, derives from Crompton's famous machine which combined roller and spindle drafting, hence the name. It is, however, worth noting that the woollen mule, the main type known in England in the nineteenth century, used spindle draft only. On the Continent another type of mule nearer to the machine invented by Crompton was used for worsted spinning.

Mungo. The name of the material obtained from tearing felted woollen cloth. It was consequently shorter than shoddy, which came from unfelted cloth.

Nap. Fibrous surface of the woollen cloth. One raises the nap and (or) cuts it down. Hence the word napping. In the West of England, however, the word acquired a specialised meaning, and described a cloth produced in which the nap after being raised up, was rubbed in a special napping (knapping) machine to give it a kind of ribbed or rubbed-up surface.

Napped Coatings. Those produced by the specialised process described under the word nap.

Narrow Cloth. Usually cloth between 27″ to 30″ wide, as was originally made on the narrow as opposed to the broad loom. There were also much narrower cloths made on ribbon looms.

Negro Blankets. A cheap type of cloth made from waste, much sought after by the American market.

Nep. Small knots of entangled fibre, a great curse when processing wools which contain a large amount of short fibre.

Neppy Cloth. A cloth spoilt by having many neps.

New Worsteds. A type of waste made by tearing up worsted cloth that had not been worn. Sometimes and perhaps better called tailor's clippings.

Nip Comb. A type of combing machine invented by Holdon.

Noble Comb. The most common comb at the end of the nineteenth century. It took its name from one James Noble who was a somewhat mysterious character. Much of the actual work on developing this type of comb was done by a leading inventor, Donisthorpe.

Noils. The short fibre from the worsted combing process, which was an important raw material for the woollen trade.

Northern Dozens. The name given, up to the end of the eighteenth century, to the kersey type material made in the West Riding of Yorkshire.

Norwich Worsteds. Expensive and beautifully designed worsted cloth made in Norwich at the end of the eighteenth and beginning of the nineteenth century. Norwich also made plain worsteds.

Olein. An oil consisting mainly of oleic acid, used for woollen spinning. It came into use towards the end of the period dealt with in this volume and could be removed from the cloth by scouring in a bath containing soda ash (called the saponification scour).

Olive Oil. The most commonly used oil for combing until the end of the nineteenth century.

Orleans. A fabric made of cotton warp and worsted weft in which the two were both brought to the surface of the cloth.

Papermakers' Felt. A fabric used in papermaking.

Paramatta. An imitation of Merino, woven with cotton warp and worsted weft. The word derives from Paramatta, a town in New South Wales where John McArthur first began the work that led to the founding of the Australian Merino wool trade.

Peralter Rollers. Rollers set closely together under considerable pressure, which can be used to squash vegetable matter. Although used to some extent in the worsted trade in the nineteenth century, they did not become popular with the woollen trade until well into the twentieth.

Perching. The examination of cloth, particularly after coming from the loom, to find faults which need mending and secondly, after finishing has been completed, in order to see that everything has been put right.

Perpetual Cutters. The name for the cloth cutting machine developed in the early decades of the nineteenth century. Cutting was from end to end, not across the piece.

Perpetuanas. An alternative name for serges, widely made in the Devon trade around 1800.

Petersham. Heavy woollen cloth, the hairy surface of which was usually rolled into little knots. It would seem to have been an alternative and cheaper version of the West of England nap.

Pick and Pick Cloth. Cloths in which different and usually strongly contrasted colours are woven 1 and 1 in the warp and weft. Usually but not necessarily in the common (2 and 2) twill weave.

Pickers. The blocks of leather that hit the shuttle across the loom. They came in with the development of the flying shuttle. There is another, quite different, meaning and the word did, in the later nineteenth century, come to describe the women who picked bits of vegetable matter out of the finished cloth.

Picking. The process by which the thread is hit through the warp.

Piece. A length of finished cloth. Often with wool textile fabrics about 28 yards long in the days of hand weaving, but increasing to as long as 70 yards when power loom weaving became common. The word piece in the plural has a quite different meaning and is used to describe the rather inferior part of the fleece, poorer than the main part but better than the locks. Yet another use of the word as a verb is the name given to the process of repairing the yarns that break during mule spinning (see piecing below).

Piecing. The process by which broken ends are tied or twisted together in the spinning process.

Piecing Machine. A machine, of which several versions were invented, that joined together the slubbings taken from the end of the early carding sets. It was really a kind of mechanised form of the slubbing billy but was never satisfactory and was not widely adopted in the British trade.

Pie Pieces. The name given towards the end of the nineteenth century to the poorest type of wool obtained when pulling the wool from the skins of sheep that had been killed for meat.

Pirn. An alternative name for weft spool, used in both Scotland and the West of England. Could be defined as the wooden, plastic, paper or metal spool on which weft yarn is wound prior to weaving.

Plain Back. A double cloth different on the face to the back with the latter plain.

Plain Weave. The most common weave of all in which every end and pick works exactly opposite to the preceding. The basic type of weave for making standard broadcloth.

Plain Weave Flannels. Flannels made in the plain weave as opposed to the twill. They were normally used for underclothes, particularly vests and shirts. Welsh flannels were of this type.

Potash. Bichromate of potash was a chrome mordant used in the nineteenth century but later replaced by the cheaper bichromate of soda. Earlier the word had meant 'wood ashes'.

Potting (or Roll Boiling). A finishing process in which the pieces were rolled on a roller and boiled in water. This provided a very serious test for dye fastness but gave a silky finish which was surprisingly permanent. Used for traditional West of England fabrics.

Pressing. A final finishing process.

Printers' Felt. See Papermakers' Felt.

Prunelle (2/1 or 1/2) The three-end twill weave much used in the West of England for making showerproof coatings.

Putting Out System. The old traditional system of cloth manufacture under which the clothier gave out the spinning and the weaving to workers in cottages.

Quilly Winding. The quill was an alternative name for the weft pirn, widely used in the West of England, hence also the quilly winding, the process of winding these quills.

Rack. An alternative name for the tenter frame.

Raddle. Rows of pegs used in beaming the warp in order to keep the threads straight and avoid them becoming entangled. Also it enabled the warp to be made the required width.

Rag Grinding. The process by which rags were reduced to a fibrous state for re-use.

Rag Pulling = Rag Grinding

Rainproof Coating. Coating usually made in the 2 and 1 twill but which in addition has been given a chemical treatment to make them, at least to some extent, rainproof.

Raising. The production of the nap on the cloth. Could be done wet, which gave the dress finish, or dry, which gave a blanket finish.

Recovered Wool. An alternative name for shoddy and mungo.

Reed. The name given to the loom part (where it is removable) which consists of wires set between slats. It controls the set of the warp. Hence reeding, the pulling of the threads through the reed.

Regain. The weight of water in a sample of wool or cloth expressed as a percentage of the dried weight. Usually around 16 per cent, but rather strangely the figure officially differs with varying states of the material, that is whether raw wool, combed top or yarn, etc.

Rep. A corded fabric, usually made weft-wise, by putting two picks in the same shed.

Reprocessed Wool (or Re-Used Wool). Another name for shoddy and mungo.

Riding Tweed. Cloths used for riding purposes normally made in the Cavalry twill weave, the Whip cord or the Bedford cord.

Ring Doffer Condenser. The type of condenser on which the last doffer has rings of tape around it and thereby produces continuous narrow slivers of fibre.

Ring Spinning. Method of worsted spinning where drawing, twisting and winding are done simultaneously. It was an important American invention and was destined to become the most common method of worsted spinning.

Rochdale Flannel. Usually plain weave flannel made in the town of that name. Rochdale replaced Newport in Wales as the main centre for the production of this type of flannel in the nineteenth century.

Rolags. The small pieces of carded material produced by the hand carder and then used by the hand spinner. The new processing machines, notably the scribblers, went to quite complicated methods to reproduce these rolags.

Roller Drafting. A system of drafting the sliver invented by Lewis Paul and much improved by Arkwright, in which the material was attenuated between pairs of rollers moving at different surface speeds.

Roving Frame. The name usually given to the last machine in the worsted drawing sequence. Material from this machine goes to the ring spinning frame.

Rovings. The name usually given to the prepared material in sliver form ready for the drawing process in worsted yarns manufacture.

Russel. A worsted cord usually of a fine type and made in Norwich.

Saxony Suiting. A high grade woollen suiting cloth originally made from Merino wools that came for Saxony in Germany. The word was later applied to similar fabrics made from Australian wool.

Saxony Wheel. The hand wheel with the flyer originally developed for flax spinning in Saxony in Germany, hence the name. Later probably used to some extent in worsted spinning.

Scouring. There are two processes: (1) the washing of the wool, i.e. wool scouring, and (2) the washing of the pieces, i.e. the piece scouring.

Scribbler. The first part of the carding process. The wool is opened and then passed to the carder which forms a more thorough opening. Over the decades of the nineteenth century there do appear to have been several changes in the comparative use of the two words scribbling and carding.

Scribbling Mill. The machine upon which the scribbling was carried out.

Self Acting Mule. The fully developed mule. The change from the hand mule invented by Crompton was made by the important Manchester engineer Roberts.

Selvedge. Sometimes selvage, another name for the list, that is the edge of a piece of cloth.

Serge. Originally a worsted warp, woollen weft cloth, widely made in Devon. Later an all-worsted cloth usually, but not necessarily, navy and widely made in the West Riding.

Shalloons. Worsted cloth, one of the first types of worsted fabrics to be made in the West Riding.

Shearing. Alternative word for cropping or cutting. In a quite different sense the word was also used for the removal of the wool from sheep.

Shepherd Check. The four and four colouring on the two and two twill. The name originated in Scotland.

Shoddy. The material obtained by pulling unmilled cloth. Over the decades the meaning of the word tended to change somewhat and later the word sometimes covered all types of pulled material.

Shoddy Duffels. Duffel cloths made of shoddy.

Showerproofing. Cloths that had been given some chemical treatment to make them, at least in part, showerproof.

Shrink Resistant. Name given to fabrics which have been given a treatment that meant they would either not shrink, or only within certain limited standards. In the nineteenth century the main method was dechlorination of the wool before processing.

Shuttle Changing Motion. The main improvement made on the loom introducing so-called automatic weaving. The pirn in the shuttle was changed without stopping the loom.

Sig. The name in the West of England given to the urine collected from the houses and shops.

Single Pick Colouring. The introduction of a single pick of colour usually for a striped effect. This could not be woven in the automatic looms known in the nineteenth century.

Sizing. The treatment of the warp yarn to strengthen it and so prevent breakage during weaving.

Slipe. Skin wool removed from the skin by allowing the skins to sweat in a warm atmosphere.

Sliver. The name given to the loose strands of fibre which come from the carding condenser, or from the drawing frames in the worsted process. The important point to remember is that they did not usually contain any twist.

Slubbers. Those who worked on the slubbing billy.

Slubbing. The process of joining together the slubs made by the carding machines.

Slubbing Billy (see Billy). The machine on which the slubs removed from the carding machine were joined together.

Slubbing Dyers. A word introduced at the end of the nineteenth century to describe, rather misleadingly, those who dyed tops.

Soft Twisted. Yarns that had had less than the normal twist, probably in order to retain a soft handle in the cloths made from them.

Sorting. The first process in preparing the wool for spinning. The various qualities in the fleece are separated.

Spool. Name used to cover almost any type of yarn container.

Square Comb. A type of combing machine developed by Holden.

Standard Condition. The natural condition of the material, especially with reference to the moisture content of the wool.

Steaming. Steaming was widely used in wool textile manufacture. New yarn would be steamed to remove the tendency for the twist to cause snarls. Later in the finishing process the cloth would be steamed before the final pressing process.

Strippers. Those rollers on the scribbling and carding machine that removed the wool from the workers. (q.v.)

Stroudwater Scarlet. As the name implies, a scarlet cloth long made in the Stroud area of Gloucestershire.

Stuffs. Originally an alternative name for worsteds, but later some woollen cloth was also called stuffs.

Sulphuric Acid (or Vitriol). Widely used in dyeing, also in carbonising. Sulphuric acid has very little effect on wool but of course, destroys cotton and vegetable matter.

Sumach. Was the preparation of the dried, chopped leaves of the shoots of the plant of the genus Rhus, much used in tanning as well as dyeing. It was to some extent both a dye and a mordant.

Superfine. The name given to the highest quality of broadcloth, usually made from Spanish Merino wool, in the eighteenth century, and later from German.

Swift. The big roller on the carding set. Also, any large wheel used in cloth manufacturing, for example, the name is sometimes given to part of the warp bar.

Synthetic Dyes. The first synthetic dye is usually held to have been Perkin's mauve but this is not entirely true. There had been earlier ones but they were not important. Perkin made this first synthetic dye from coal tar and it was from this product that the main synthetic dye trade was to be developed. Early synthetic dyes were bright but not fast. Later, with the synthesis of alizarin, the colouring matter of madder, the whole position changed and fast, excellent synthetic dyes were introduced.

Take-up Motion. The motion on the loom that takes up the woven cloth.

Tammies. Cotton warp worsted weft cloth in fancy colours and usually highly glazed.

Tape Condenser. The later type of condenser in which the web of wool is divided by tapes crossing each other.

Tare (or Tear). The allowance in weight given when dealing with wool and to some extent cloth, to allow for small damages, etc. Also the weight of top relative to noil obtained when combing wool.

Tartans. The special type of check, derived of course from Scotland.

Tautz Twill = Cavalry Twill.

Teasels. The head of the thistle-like plant *Dipsacus fullonum*, very widely used particularly in the first half of the nineteenth century for raising the surface of the cloth.

Temples. A means of keeping the cloth the correct width during weaving.

Tenter. The machine used for drying cloth and also for removing any creases and doing any straightening necessary before further processing. Originally done on tenter racks which were such a common sight in all cloth making areas at the beginning of the period covered in this book. Later, tentering machines were introduced. The process was known as tentering and gave rise to other names, for example tenter hooks. These held the cloth whilst it was passing through the tentering machine.

Throstle Spinning. The name given to the bobbin and fly spinning frame which uses the drag of the bobbin for winding on and derives direct from the flyer system developed for the Saxony spinning wheel.

Thrums. The surplus ends of cloth, particularly of warp.

Top Makers. A group of people who, from the end of the nineteenth century onwards, made their living by buying wool, having the tops combed on commission, and then selling the tops to spinners.

Tops. The slivers of fibre produced during worsted combing.

Travellers. The small steel ring that runs on the flange of the ring in the spinning frame acting as the winding-on drag. It enables twisting and winding to be done simultaneously as with the flyer on the Saxony spinning wheel.

Trouserings. An important section of the woollen and worsted trade in the nineteenth century.

Tucking. Originally, and indeed in most areas, the alternative name for fulling. In the West of England the name was also applied to an early process in cloth manufacture, usually called willowing in other areas.

Tucking Machine. Where the tucking was done. Rarely applied to the final fulling but the normal description of the wool processing operation described above (see Tucking).

Tweeds. Originally a cloth made in the lowland area of Scotland, but the term came to be used for a wide variety of woollen cloths having effects produced by colour and design combination. It is worth mentioning the word did not come, as is sometimes said, from the River Tweed but from the misreading of the word twill.

Twill Weave. The common type of weave which shows a line running across the cloth.

Twist Cloth. Cloths made from yarns that have been twisted but usually confined to those where the components of the twist are different colours, thereby giving a distinctive effect. A speciality of the Scottish trade.

Union Cloths. The name given to cloths which contained both wool and cotton. These two fibres could be combined by using a cotton warp or woollen weft but quite frequently in the low woollen trade the cotton fibre was mixed with the wool waste fibre before spinning.

Unions. An alternative name for Union Cloth.

Urine. The common method of obtaining mild alkali, so necessary in wool cloth processing was from stale urine. Used in both the scouring and the dyeing processes.

Urine Vat. The name given to one of the indigo vats where the mild alkali required was obtained by using urine.

Velour. The word has several meanings, but as far as the wool textile trade is concerned, was usually confined to describing any soft handling fabric normally light in weight. The soft handle was obtained by using fine wool and dressing the surface of the cloth.

Velvet. A fabric in which some of the warp or weft threads have been cut so as to give a pile.

Venetian. A distinctive twill cloth widely made in the West of England.

Venetian Weave. A five-end twill (3 and 2 step 2) used for making Venetian cloths.

Verdigris. A green deposit naturally forming on copper or brass but also obtainable by the action of dilute acetic acid on copper plates. It was therefore copper sulphite and was used as a copper mordant in the nineteenth century.

Vicuña. The undercoat, that is the fine part of the fleece, of the vicuña, a kind of llama found in Peru. It produced a remarkably soft and fine fibre, always one of the most expensive in the world although probably not any better than cashmere. The name was also given to the type of fabric made from this fibre.

Virgin Wool. New and unused wool.

Vitriol = Sulphuric Acid (q.v.)

Warehousemen. The name has a rather special meaning in the wool textile trade as indicating those who held stock of cloth for sale.

Warp. The threads that run lengthwise in the cloth.

Warp Creel. The place where the cops or cones of warp yarn are placed ready to be run off to form the warp.

Warping. The arranging of the warp yarns on the warp bar and then their winding on to the warp beam ready for the loom.

Warp Stop Motion. A motion by which the loom stopped if one of the warp ends broke. Not normally used on early power looms but became important when so called automatic looms were introduced and weavers were required to look after a number of them.

Washing Off. The treatment of the fabric in water or some detergent solution to remove substances which was more often than not the soap used in the fulling or milling process.

Water Frame. The name often given to Arkwright's spinning frame, obviously because it was driven by water power.

Waterproofing = Showerproofing.

Weft. The threads that run across the cloth.

Weft Stop Motion (or Weft Fork). The small pronged fork which stops the loom when the weft is missing.

Weft Winding. The winding of the yarn on to the pirn later to go in the shuttle.

Welsh Flannel. A plain weave flannel made in Wales, often from Welsh wool, and used for shirts and underwear. Very popular with miners.

Wet Raising. The raising on the gig whilst the cloth was wet, a standard part of the dress finish.

White Cloth. Should mean the cloth was wanted white, that is for cricket or tennis but also used to include cloth that was to be dyed after weaving.

Willey. There are many types of willey machines with alternative and localised names; all were used for opening wool either in its greasy state before scouring, or more commonly, during the blending process.

Willowing = The process done on the Willey.

Witney Blanket. Fine quality blankets made in the town of that name. The word was sometimes used to describe much poorer blankets not made in Witney.

Woad. The ancient blue dye, which had largely ceased to be used during the period covered by this book.

Woad Vat. Used to describe the vat used for dyeing indigo into which some woad was still added but where basically indigo was the dye. This vat was still used for wool dyeing in the nineteenth century.

Wool Brokers. Those who bought wool on commission for top makers, manufacturers, etc., at wool sales.

Wool Combers. Those who did the wool combing. The name (usually spelt as one word) was also given to a group of wool combers who combined under that title in the later nineteenth century but without success.

Wool Dyed Drab Mills. One of the names for cloth which is more or less self explanatory. The wool had been dyed drab and the cloth was well milled.

Woollen. Traditionally, cloths made from short wool and spun into woollen yarn to produce a cloth which was fulled. In the early part of the period covered by this book, the word woollen was sometimes used to cover all types. of cloths made from wool, i.e. including worsteds.

Woollen Spinning Frame. The machine invented to give continuous woollen spinning. The mule was an intermittent machine. Early attempts were not very successful but towards the end of the period covered in this volume these machines began to be used extensively for making thick yarn for the carpet trade.

Wool Staplers. Those who bought wool from the farmers and sold it to the manufacturers.

Workers. The rollers on the scribbling and carding machines that worked close to the swift, thereby opening the wool.

Worsted. Usually used to define that type of fabric that is made from yarn spun on the worsted as opposed to the woollen principle, in other words where the short wool had been removed and the yarn spun from the tops. The name derived from the Norfolk village of that name but it is important to remember that worsted cloths, that is cloths made from combed wool, were made long before the use of this name. They were sometimes called stuffs. These cloths were not fulled.

Worsted Drawing. The process by which the top is reduced to a sliver fine enough to go into the spinning frame.

Worsted Flannel. As the name implies, flannel type fabric made from worsted yarn. They were not as common as woollen flannels.

Worsted Mules. Were much nearer Crompton's original mule than the so-called woollen mule. They used both roller and spindle draft, and were an important machine in the French worsted trade.

Woven Carpets. Carpets that have been made as woven cloth, not as knotted fabrics which is the commonest type of fabric.

Woven Felts. Cloth that has been heavily felted so that it appears as if it has no woven structure.

Yorkshire Tweed. Tweeds made in the West Riding of Yorkshire. They were of many types.

BIBLIOGRAPHY

Manuscript Sources

A wide range of records have been used in varying degrees of detail. Only the major collections are listed here.

1 Pattern books

Considerable use has been made of pattern books. Many of these have been deposited in various record offices and libraries and constitute valuable sources of information which in the past have not been used with the attention they deserve. Some care is necessary when analysing them for their purposes vary and the conclusions that can be drawn therefrom can be confusing. A note on the varying types may be useful.

One major difference can immediately be seen; there are those which contain samples of dyed wool and those which contain samples of cloth. The latter are by far the more numerous but the former dye recipe books, to give them their correct designation, are valuable in showing how the colours were obtained. Occasionally, as in the case of the records of Stevens and Bailward in the Bath Reference Library, dye recipe books and finished pattern books can be linked together and in such cases a unique picture of manufacturing can be observed.

The actual pattern books can be further subdivided into those containing (a) patterns of actual cloths made and sold (b) patterns of ranges i.e. trials made to show customers with a hope of achieving a sale (c) patterns of varied kinds usually bought from outside as representing future fashion trends. These usually came from France and are comparatively rare. Obviously the relevance of each of these three groups varies, with the first the most important.

Bath
City Reference Library
 Stevens and Bailward, Bradford-on-Avon, Wilts.
 Dye Pattern Books Ref. No. W.677 (for an account of these see K.G.

Ponting, 'Stevens and Bailward –dyers and manufacturers –in 1768–72'. *International Dyer*, October 27, 1978).
Tucker, A.H. Ltd, Wallbridge Mill, Frome, Somerset.
Pattern Books.

Comrie
  Tartan Museum
    Tartan pattern books, notably those from Wilsons of Bannockburn.

Devizes
  Library of Wiltshire Archaeological Society, Devizes
    Waylen of Devizes. Pattern Books.

Galashiels
  Scottish College of Textiles
    A large number of pattern books of several types covering the Scottish Tweed Trade, mainly nineteenth and twentieth century. Very valuable and badly need cataloguing.

Glasgow
  Strathclyde University
    Pattern books. Two pattern books from the Hillfoots area of the Scottish tweed trade.

Halifax
  Halifax Central Public Library
    Clay J.T. & Sons Ltd.
    Pattern Books 1836–1920.
    (A large collection catalogued by P. Hudson, *The West Riding Wool Textile Industry, 1770–1835*. A catalogue of business records from the sixteenth to the twentieth century. 1975. pp. 99–105.
    Walker, Norwood Green Mills, near Halifax.
    Another large collection catalogued by Hudson, op. cit., pp. 463–4.

Huddersfield
  Tolson Museum
    A valuable collection of rather miscellaneous pattern books but including some very attractive fancy vestings. See Hudson, op. cit., pp. 534–7.

Innerleithen
  Scottish Tweed Museum (Ballantynes)
    Pattern books of Ballantynes.

London
  Public Record Office
    Hanson & Mills, London. Blackwell Hall Factors Patterns amongst the business documents.
    (See Gill, C., 'Blackwell Hall Factors 1795–1799' *Economic History Review*, 2nd Series, Vol. VI, No. 3, April 1954)
    Horner & Turner
    Pattern Books from Yorkshire. Reference No. C.108/11.

Norwich
   Bridewell Museum
      A large number of pattern books. There is a valuable manuscript cata-
      logue compiled some years ago by Miss Clabburn.

Trowbridge
   Wilts Record Office
      Applegate Brothers of Bradford-on-Avon. Pattern Books.
      Clark, J. & T., of Trowbridge, Pattern Books.
      Salter & Co., of Trowbridge, Pattern Books.

2   *Other manuscripts*

Bath
   City Reference Library
   Bath and West Society. Letters and Papers, etc., 1783–1815.

Halifax
   Calderdale Archives Department. Clay Mss.

Huddersfield
   Huddersfield Chamber of Commerce. Minute Books.
   Tolson Museum. Clay Mss.

Leeds
   City Archives Department
      Hartley Mss., Bairstow Mss.
      A.M. Patchett Family Records.
   City Reference Library
      J. Bischoff, *Tables relating to Wool and Woollen Manufactures*, c. 1834.
      The Diary of Reuben Gaunt, 1841–1854.
   Brotherton Library, University of Leeds
      Clay Mss. Kellett, Brown & Co. Mss.
      Foster Mss. Lupton Mss.
      Gott Mss. Marriner Mss.
      Jowitt Mss.

Stroud
   Stroud Museum. Sale Catalogue. Trowbridge & Bradford-on-Avon Mills.

Trowbridge
   Wiltshire Record Office.   Clark Mss.
                              Laverton Mss.
                              Salter Mss.

Wakefield
   West Yorkshire County Record Office
   Quarter Sessions Roll and Books.

Newspapers and Journals

Bath Chronicle	*Salisbury Journal*
Bath Journal	*Scotch Tweed*
Bath Observer	*Textile Institute Journal*
Bradford Observer	*Textile Manufacturer*
Devizes and Wiltshire Gazette	*Textile Recorder*
Dyer and Textile Printer	*Trowbridge Advertiser*
Dyers and Colourists, Journal of	*Wiltshire Chronicle*
Economist	*Wiltshire Times*
Leeds Mercury	*Wool Record*
Salisbury Gazette	*Wool, Worsted and Cotton Journal*

Unpublished Theses

Edwards, J.K., 'The Economic Development of Norwich, 1750–1850 with special reference to the Worsted Industry', Ph.D. thesis, University of Leeds, 1963.

Glover, F.J., 'Dewsbury Mills: A History of Messrs. Wormalds and Walker Ltd, Blanket Manufacturers of Dewsbury', Ph.D. thesis, University of Leeds, 1959.

Greeves, O.N., 'The Effects of the American Civil War on the Linen and Wool Textile Industries in the U.K.', Ph.D. thesis, Bristol University, 1968–9.

Hartwell, R.M., 'The Yorkshire Woollen and Worsted Industries, 1800–1850', D.Phil. thesis, University of Oxford, 1956.

Ingle, G., 'A History of R.V. Marriner Ltd, Worsted Spinners, Keighley', M.Phil. thesis, University of Leeds, 1974.

Malin, J.C., 'The West Riding Recovered Wool Industry, 1813 -1939', D.Phil. thesis, University of York, 1979.

Ponting, K.G., 'The Decline of the Woollen Industry in the Trowbridge and Bradford-on-Avon Area in the Nineteenth Century', M.Litt. thesis, Bristol University, 1974.

Roberts, D., 'The Development of the Textile Industry in West Craven and the Skipton district of Yorkshire', M.Sc. thesis, L.S.E., 1956.

Topham, A.J., 'The Credit Structure of the West Riding Textile Industry in the Nineteenth Century', M.A. thesis, University of Leeds, 1953.

Turner, T., 'History of Fenton, Murray and Wood', M.Sc.Tech. thesis, University of Manchester, 1966.

Parliamentary Papers

Additional Evidence Relating to Wool, 1800 (1020) LI.

Report of the Committee on the Woollen Clothiers Petition, 1803, 1802–3 (30) V.

Report of Select Committee on Petition of Merchants and Manufacturers in the Woollen Manufacture of Yorkshire, 1802–3 (71) VI.

Minutes of Evidence on the Woollen Trade Bill, 1802–3 (95) VII.

Report from the Select Committee appointed to consider the State of the Woollen Manufacture of England, 1806 (268) III.

Report from the Select Committee to whom the Petition of Edmund Cartwright, D.D., clerk, respecting a Machine for weaving was referred, 1808 (179) II.

Minutes of Evidence taken before the Select Committee on the State of children employed in the Manufactures of the United Kingdom, 1816 (397) III.

Examination of Petitions before the Privy Council against the Tax on Wool imported, 1820 (56) XII.

An Account of the Total Quantity of Woollen Manufactures Exported, 1800 to 1821, 1821 (443) XVII.

Quantity and Declared Value of British Manufactured Woollen, and British Woollen Yarns exported from Great Britain, 1820 to 1828, 1828 (360) XIX.

Report by the Lords' Select Committee appointed to take into consideration the State of the British Wool Trade, House of Lords Papers, 1828 (515) VIII.

Reports from Commissioners appointed to collect information in the Manufacturing Districts, relative to the Employment of Children in Factories, First Report 1833 (450) XX; Second Report 1833 (519) XXI; Supplementary Reports 1834 (167) XIX, XX.

Account of the Quantities of British Wool, Woollen Yarn, and Woollen Manufactured Goods exported from the United Kingdom in each year from 1820 to 1832 inclusive, 1833 (526) XXXIII.

Report from the Select Committee appointed to inquire into the present state of Manufactures, Commerce and Shipping in the United Kingdom, 1833 (690) VI.

Returns of Mills and Factories. 1833–1905.

Reports of the Inspectors of Factories, 1835–1905.

A Return of the Number of Power Looms used in factories in the manufacture of Woollen, Cotton, Silk and Linen respectively so far as can be collected from the returns of the Factory Commissioners, 1836 (24) XLV.

Reports of the Assistant Commissioners for Handloom Weavers, 1839–40 (43) XXIII–XXXIV.

Statements respecting the Establishment of Joint Stock Woollen Mills in the West Riding of Yorkshire, 1844 (119) VII.

Accounts of Foreign and Colonial Wool imported from 1816 to 1843 inclusive, 1844 (306) XLV.

Statistics of the Woollen Trade with China, 1846 (148) XLIV.

First and Second Reports (and Appendix) from the Select Committee on Commercial Distress, 1847–8 (395, 584) VIII.

Correspondence between the Woollen Manufacturers of Bradford and the Board of Trade, on the subject of their present Distress, and the free Importation of Foreign Merinos into this country, 1847–8 (in 586) LI.

Annual Statements of Trade, 1854–1914.

Report from the Select Committee on the Operation of the Bank Acts and the Causes of the Recent Commercial Distress, 1857–8 (381) V.

Reports of the Commissioners on River Pollution, 1867 (3850) XXXIII; 1871 (c. 347) XXV; 1873 (c. 347–1) XXXVI.

Papers Relative to Industry and Commerce, 1878 (c. 2085) LXXVI No. 18. Woollen and Worsted Trades.

Report of Her Majesty's Commissioners for the Paris Universal Exhibition of 1878, 1880 (c. 2588) XXXII.

Report from the Select Committee on Railway and Canal Charges, 1881 (c.374) XIII.

Reports of the Royal Commissioners on Technical Instruction, 1884 (c. 3981) XXIX, XXX, XXXI.

Reports of the Royal Commission of Depression of Trade and Industry, 1886 (c. 4621) XXI; 1886 (c. 4715) XXII; 1886 (c. 4797) XXIII; 1886 (c. 4893) XXIII.
Opinions of H.M. Diplomatic and Consular Officers on British Trade Methods, 1899 (c. 9078), XCVI.
Census of Production, 1909 (Cd 4896) CII.

Books

Aikin, J., *A Description of the Country from Thirty to Forty Miles Round Manchester*, (1795).
Aldcroft, D.H., ed., *The Development of British Industry and Foreign Competition 1875–1914*, (1968).
Allan, J.R., ed., *Crombies of Grandholm and Cothal 1805–1960*, Aberdeen, (n.d.).
Ashenhurst, T.E., *A Practical Treatise on Weaving and Designing of Textile Fabrics*, 2nd edn, Bradford, (1881).
Aspen, C. and Chapman, S.D., *James Hargreaves and the Spinning Jenny*, (1964).
Astbury, W.T., *Fundamentals of Fibre Structure*, (1933).
Atkinson, F., ed., *Some Aspects of the Eighteenth Century Woollen and Worsted Trade in Halifax*, Halifax, (1956).
Babbage, C., *On the Economy of Machinery and Manufactures*, (1832).
Babbage, C., *The Exposition of 1851*, (1851).
Baines, E., *An Account of the Woollen Manufacture of England*, originally published in *Yorkshire Past and Present*, 1871–2. New edition with introduction by K.G. Ponting, Newton Abbot, (1970).
Barker, A.F., *Woollen and Worsted Spinning*, (1922).
Barlow, H., *The History and Principles of Weaving by Hand and Power*, (1878).
Barnard, A., *The Australian Wool Market, 1840–1900*, Melbourne, (1958).
Beaumont, R., *Woollen and Worsted Cloth Manufacture*, (1888).
Beckensale, R.P., ed., *The Trowbridge Woollen Industry as illustrated by the Stock Books of John Thomas Clark, 1804–24*, Devizes, (1951).
Beer, J.J., *The Emergence of the German Dye Industry*, (1959). *Behrens Sir Jacob, 1806–1889*, c.1925.
Beresford, M.W., *The Leeds Chamber of Commerce*, Leeds, (1951).
Bischoff, J., *The Wool Question Considered*, (1828).
Bischoff, J., *A Comprehensive History of the Woollen and Worsted Manufactures*, 2 Vols, (1842). (New edn. 1968).
Board of Trade, *Working Party Reports: Wool*, (1947).
Bonwick, J., *The Romance of the Wool Trade*, (1887).
Bradford Chamber of Commerce, *Report of the Deputation appointed by the Chamber to visit the Paris Exhibition*, Bradford, (1867).
Bradford Corporation, *A History of Education in Bradford since 1870*, Bradford, (1970).
Bradford Dyers' Association Ltd, Manuscript History, (1950).
Bradley, J., *Wool Carding*, Manchester, (1921).
Bramwell, W.C., *The Wool Carder's Vade Mecum*, Boston, (1881).
Buck, A., *Dress in Eighteenth-Century England*, (1979).

Buck, N.S., *The Development of the Organisation of Anglo-American Trade: 1800–1850*, New Haven, (1925).

Burnley, J., *History of Wool and Wool Combing*, (1889).

Burrows, H., *A History of the Rag Trade*, (1956).

Byrde, P., *The Male Image*, (1979).

Cadoux, G., *L'Influence Française a l'Etranger. Notre Commerce d'Exportation et Nos Consuls*, Paris, (1889).

Carter, H.B., *His Majesty's Spanish Flock. Sir John Banks and the Merinos of George III of England*, (1964).

Carter, H.B., *A Memoir of the Life, Writings and Mechanical Inventions of Edmund Cartwright*, (1843). Reprint with introduction by K.G. Ponting, Bath (1971).

Catling, H., *The Spinning Mule*, Newton Abbot, (1970).

Chapman, S.D. *The Early Factory Masters*, Newton Abbot, (1967).

Chapman, S.D., ed., 'The Devon Cloth Industry in the Eighteenth Century, Sun Fire Office, Inventories of Merchants and Manufacturers' Property, 1726–1770', *Devon and Cornwall Record Society*, New Series, Vol. 23, Torquay, (1978).

Church, R.A., *The Great Victorian Boom, 1850–1873*, (1975).

Clapham, J.H., *The Woollen and Worsted Industries*, (1907).

Clapham, J.H., *An Economic History of Modern Britain*, 3 Vols, Cambridge, 1926–1938.

Clark, W.A., *Manufacture of Woollen, Worsted and Shoddy in France and England and Jute in Scotland*, U.S. Dept. of Labor and Commerce, (1909).

Clow, N. and A., *The Chemical Revolution. A Contribution to Social Technology*, (1952).

Coghlan, S., *Labour and Industry in Australia*, 4 Vols, (1918).

Cole, A.H., *The American Wool Manufacture*, 2 Vols, Harvard, (1926).

Collinson, E., *History of the Worsted Trade and Historic Sketch of Bradford*, (1854).

Committee on Industry and Trade, *Survey of Textile Industries*, (1923).

(Costume Society), *La Belle Epoque 1860–1914*. A Symposium of the Costume Society, (1967).

(Costume Society), *High Victoriana 1860–90*. A Symposium of the Costume Society, (1968).

Crouzet, F., ed., *Capital Formation in the Industrial Revolution*, (1972).

Crump, W.B., ed., *The Leeds Woollen Industry 1780–1820*, Leeds, (1931).

Crump, W.B. and Ghorbal, G., *History of the Huddersfield Woollen Industry*, Huddersfield, (1935).

Cudworth, W., *Worstedopolis. A Sketch History of the Town and Trade of Bradford, the Metropolis of the Worsted Industry*, Bradford, (1888).

Davis, R., *The Industrial Revolution and British Overseas Trade*, Leicester, (1979).

Dawson, H. and Co., *Statistical Review of the Wool and Wool Textile Trades, 1912–1922*, (1923).

Deane, P., and Cole, W.A., *British Economic Growth 1688–1959*, (1962).

Dechesne, L., *L'Evolution Economique et Sociale de l'Industrie de la Laine en Angleterre*, Paris, (1900).

Dobson, B.P., *The Story of the Evolution of the Spinning Machine*, Manchester, (1910).

Duncan, J., *Practical and Descriptive Essay on the Art of Weaving*, Glasgow, (1808).

Dunckley, H., *The Charter of the Nations*, (1854).

Dunham, A.L., *The Anglo-French Treaty of Commerce of 1860*, Ann Arbor, (1930).

Dunsford, M., *Historical Memoirs of Tiverton*, Tiverton (1790).

Du Plessis, A.F., *The Marketing of Wool*, (1931).

Edelstein, S.M., *Historical Notes on the Wet-Processing Industry*, U.S.A., (1972).

Endrei, W., *L'Evolution de Technique de Filage et du Tissage á la revolution industrielle*, Paris, (1979).

English, W., *The Textile Industry, an account of the early inventions of spinning, weaving and knitting machines*, (1969).

Exell, T., *A Sketch of the Circumstances which providentially led to the Repeal of the Corn and Animal Food Laws and many Custom House Restrictions*, (1847). (reprinted 1903).

Fairbairn, W., *Treatise on Mills and Millwork*, (1861).

Farnie, D.A., *The English Cotton Industry and the World Market, 1815–1896*, Oxford, (1979).

Fite, E.D., *Social and Industrial Conditions during the Civil War*, New York, (1910).

Fong, H.B., *The Triumph of the Factory System in England*, Tientsin, (1930).

Forbes, H., *Lecture on the Worsted Industry to the Royal Society of Arts*, (1852).

Forbes, H., *The Rise, Progress and Present State of the Worsted Alpaca and Mohair Manufactures in England*, (1853).

Fox, H., *Quaker Homespun. The Life of Thomas Fox of Wellington, Serge Maker and Banker 1747–1826*, (1948).

Fox, J.H., *The Woollen Manufacture at Wellington, Somerset*, (1914).

Gardner, W.M., ed., *The British Chemical Industry*, (1915).

Garnett, W. Onslow, *Wainstall Mills: The History of I. and I. Calvert Ltd, 1821–1951*, Halifax, (1951).

Gayer, A.D., Rostow, W.W. and Schwarz, A.J., *The Growth and Fluctuation of the British Economy, 1790–1850*, 2 Vols, (1975).

Gibson, H., *The History and Present State of the Sheepbreeding Industry in the Argentine Republic*, Buenos Aires, (1893).

Gilroy, G.C., *The Art of Weaving by Hand and Power*, (1847).

Graham, J., *Memorandum of the Industries of Leeds*, (1906).

Gulvin, C., *The Tweedmakers: a history of the Scottish fancy woollen Industry, 1600–1914*, Newton Abbot, (1973).

Haber, L.F., *The Chemical Industry in the Nineteenth Century in Europe and North America*, (1958).

Haigh, J., *The Dyer's Assistant*, (1778).

Hall, A.J., *The Standard Handbook of Textiles*, 8th edn, (1975).

Harrison, E.S., *Our Scottish District Checks*, Edinburgh, (1968).

Harte, N.B. and Ponting, K.G., eds, *Textile History and Economic History*, Manchester, (1973).

Heaton, H., *The Yorkshire Woollen and Worsted Industries*, Oxford, (1920).

Heaton, H., ed., *The Letter Books of Joseph Holroyd and Sam Hill*, Halifax, (1914).

Hills, R.L., *Power in the Industrial Revolution*, Manchester, (1970).

Hind, J.R., *Woollen and Worsted Raw Materials*, (1934).

Hirst, W., *History of the Woollen Trade for the Last Sixty Years*, Leeds, (1844).

Hodgson, J., *Textile Manufacture and Other Industry in Keighley*, Keighley, (1879).

Hoffman, W.G., *British Industry, 1700–1950*, Oxford, (1955).

The Holden Illingworth Letters, Bradford, (1927).

Holmes, R., *Keighley, Past and Present*, (1858).

Hooper, F., *Statistics Relating to the Woollen and Worsted Trades of the United Kingdom, 1906*, Bradford, (1907).

Horsfall, R.S. and Lawrie, L.G., *The Dyeing of Textile Fibres*, 2nd edn, (1946).

Hoskins, W.G., *Industry, Trade and People in Exeter, 1688–1800*, (1935).

Huddersfield Chamber of Commerce, *Artisans' Reports on Scribbling Machinery and Yarns, Dyeing, Designing Woollen Fabrics and Cloth Finishing at the Paris Exhibition*, (1878).

Hudson, P., *The West Riding Wool Textile Industry: A Catalogue of Business Records from the Sixteenth to the Twentieth Century*, Edington, Wiltshire, (1975).

Hughes, J.R.T., *Fluctuations on Trade, Industry and Finance: A Study of British Economic Development, 1850–1860*, Oxford (1960).

Hummell, J.J., *The Dyeing of Textile Fibres*, (1885).

Hunter, D.M., *The West of England Woollen Industry under Protection and Free Trade*, (1910).

Hutchinson, J.W., *Modern Looms. Their Mechanism and Management*, Bradford, (1934).

Hutchinson Hollingworth & Co. Ltd, *The Dobcross HK Loom*.

Hyde, F.E., *Far Eastern Trade, 1860–1914*, (1973).

Illingworth, T., *A Sixty Year Retrospect of the Bradford Trade Indicative of Some Causes of the Great Depression*, Bradford, (1883).

Illingworth, H. and Goodwin, J.V., *Special Report Prepared for the Tariff Committee of the Bradford Chamber of Commerce*, Bradford, (1876).

Innes, T., *The Tartans of the Clans and Families of Scotland*, Edinburgh, (1950).

James, J., *History of the Worsted Manufacture in England*, (1857).

James, J., *The History of Bradford and its Parish, with Additions and Continuation to the Present Time*, (1866).

Jenkins, D.T., *The West Riding Wool Textile Industry, 1770–1835: A Study of Fixed Capital Formation*, Edington, Wiltshire, (1975).

Jenkins, J.G., *The Welsh Woollen Industry*, Cardiff, (1969).

Jenkins, J.G., ed., *The Wool Textile Industry in Great Britain*, (1972).

Jose, A.W. and Carter, H.J., eds, *Australian Encyclopedia*, 2 Vols, Sydney, (1925–6).

Jubb, S., *The History of the Shoddy Trade: Its Rise, Progress and Present Position*, Batley, (1860).

Knecht, E., Rawson, C. and Lowenthal, R.J., *The Dyeing of Textile Fibres*, (1947).

Lawson, J., *Letters to the Young on Progress in Pudsey during the Last Sixty Years*, Stanningley, (1887).

Lipson, E., *The History of the English Woollen and Worsted Industries*, (1921).

Lipson, E., *A Short History of Wool and its Manufacture*, (1953).

Luccock, J., *The Nature and Properties of Wool*, (1805).

McCloskey, D.M., ed., *Essays on a Mature Economy: Britain after 1840*, (1971).

McLaren, W.S.B., *Spinning Woollen and Worsted*, 2nd edn, (1884).

McLaren, W.S.B. and Beaumont, J., *Report to the Worshipful Clothworkers Company of London on the Weaving and Technical Schools of the Continent*, (1877).

Macpherson, D., *Annals of Commerce*, 4 Vols, (1805).

Macrosty, H.W., *The Trust Movement in British Industry*, (1907).

Maitland, J., ed., *An Account of the Proceedings of the Merchants Manufacturers and Others concerned in the Wool and Woollen Trade of Great Britain in their application to Parliament*, (1800).

Mann, J. de L., *The Cloth Industry in the West of England from 1640 to 1880*, Oxford, (1971).

Mayhall, J., *Annals of Leeds and the Surrounding District*, Leeds, (1860).

Mendenhall, T.E., *The Shrewsbury Draperies and the Welsh Wool Trade in the Seventeenth and Eighteenth Centuries*, (1953).

Ministry of Agriculture and Fisheries, *Report on Wool Marketing in England and Wales*, (1926).

Mitchell, B.R., with Deane, P., *Abstract of British Historical Statistics*, Cambridge, (1962).

Morton, W.E., *An Introduction to the History of Spinning*, (1937).

Muir, A., *In Blackburn Valley: The History of Bowers Mills*, Cambridge, (1969).

Murphy, J., *A Treatise on the Art of Weaving*, Glasgow, 2nd edn, (1827).

Murphy, W.S., ed., *The Textile Industry*, 8 Vols, (1911).

National Association of the Wool Manufacturers of the United States of America, *The Woollen Tariff Defended and Explained*, Cambridge, Mass., (1886).

Nicholson, C., *The Annals of Kendal*, 2nd edn, Kendal, (1861).

Northrop Loom Co., Automatic Weaving. *The Northrop Loom System*, Blackburn, (1949).

Norton, G.P., *Textile Manufacturer's Book-keeping*, (1889).

Nussey, G.H. and A., *A Technical Institution for Leeds and District*, Leeds, (1867).

Official Descriptive and Illustrated Catalogue of the Great Exhibition, 1851, Vol. II.

Ogden, C. and Macaulay, P.T., *Gain or Loss? under preference, protection or retaliation. An Inquiry on the Woollen and Worsted Trades*, Bradford, (1903).

Oliver, T., *Weaving and Designing*, Galashiels, (1907).

Oliver, T., *Continued Phases of Textile Education*, Galashiels, (1909).

Onslow, S.M., ed., *Some Early Records of the MacArthurs of Camden*, Sydney, (1914).

Parson, W. and White, W., *History, Directory and Gazetteer of the Counties of Durham and Northumberland*, (1827), Vol. I.

Partridge, W., *A Practical Treatise on Dyeing etc.*, New York, (1823). (new edition edited by K.G. Ponting, Edington, 1973).

Patent Office, *Subject List of Works on the Textile Industries and Wearing Apparel in the Library of the Patent Office*. Patent Office Library series No. 11 Bibliographical Series No. 7, HMSO., (1902).

Pawson, H.D., *Robert Bakewell. Pioneer Livestock Breeder*, (1957).

Payne, P.L., *British Entrepreneurship in the Nineteenth Century*, (1974).

Peel, F., *Spen Valley Past and Present*, Heckmondwike, (1833).

Picard, A., *Le Bilan d'un Siècle*, Paris (1906).

Pierrard, P., *Tableaux Synoptiques du Commerce de Laines, Fils et Tissus en Angleterre pendant l'année 1883*, (1884).

Platiére, Jean Marie Roland de, *L'art du fabrique d'étoffe en laine*, Paris, (1780).

Platiére, Jean Marie Roland de, *Encyclopedia Méthodique*, (1785).

Platt, D.C.M., *Latin America and British Trade 1806–1914*, (1972).

Playne, A.T., *Minchinhampton & Avening*, (1915).

Plummer, A., *The Witney Blanket Industry*, (1934).

Ponting, K.G., *The Wool Trade, Past and Present*, Manchester (1961).

Ponting, K.G., *A History of the West of England Cloth Industry*, (1957).

Porter, G.R., *The Progress of the Nation*, (1847 edn).

Pressnell, L.S., ed., *Studies in the Industrial Revolution. Essays presented to T.S. Ashton*, (1960).

Preston, J.M., ed., *Fibre Science*, Manchester, (1953).

Priestman, H., *Principles of Wool Carding*, (1904).

Priestman, H., *Principles of Wool Combing*, (1904).

Priestman, H., *Principles of Worsted Spinning*, (1906).

Priestman, H., *Principles of Woollen Spinning*, (1908).

Radcliffe, J.W., *The Manufacture of Woollen and Worsted Yarn*, Manchester, (1950).

Radcliffe, W., *The Origin of the system of Manufacture commonly called Power Loom Weaving etc.*, Stockport, (1828).

Rainnie, G.F., *The Woollen and Worsted Industry*, Oxford, (1965).

Read, J., *Elementary Design and Fabric Structure*, Manchester, (1950).

Rees, A., *Cyclopaedia*, (1819).

Report of Henry Mitchell upon the Paris Exhibition together with the Report of the Artisans, Bradford, (1878).

Report of the Jurors appointed for the Exhibition, 1851, (1852).

Report of the Tariff Commission, Vol. 2. The Textile Trades, (1905).

Report of the U.S. Commission to the Paris Exhibition, (1862).

Report on the Paris Universal Exhibition, 1855. Part I., 3 Vols, 1856.

Report on the Various sections of the Exhibitors in London International Exhibition of 1871, ed. by Lord Houghton. Vol. II. *Woollen and Worsted Fabrics*, by Prof. T.C. Archer.

Richards, M., *An Outline of the Newtown Woollen Industry*, Newtown, (1971).

Rimmer, W.G., *Marshalls of Leeds, Flax Spinners, 1788–1886*, Cambridge, (1960).

Rogers, K., *Wiltshire and Somerset Woollen Mills*, Edington, Wilts., (1976).

Roth, H., *Studies in Primitive Looms.*, Bankfield Museum Notes, 2, Nos. 8–11, Halifax, 1917–18.

Roth, H., *Hand Card Making*, Bankfield Museum Notes 11, (n.d.).

Roth, H., *Hand Wool Combing*, Bankfield Museum Notes 6, (1909).

Rudder, S., *A New History of Gloucestershire*, (1779).

Samuel Bros, *Wool and Woollen Manufactures of Great Britain; an historical account*, (1859).

Sauerbeck, A., *The Production and Consumption of Wool*, (1878).

Saul, S.B., *Studies in British Overseas Trade, 1870–1914*, (1960).

Sayers, R.S., *A History of Economic Change in England, 1880–1939*, (1967).

Schofield, J., *The Science and Practice of Scouring and Milling in the Worsted and Woollen Industry*, Huddersfield, (1921).

Schofield, J., C. and I., *Cloth Finishing: Woollen and Worsted*, Huddersfield, (1935).

Schumpeter, E.B., *English Overseas Trade Statistics*, (1960).

Scott, R.E., *The South of Scotland Chamber of Commerce, 1860–1960: A Century of Commercial History and Progress*, Hawick, (1960).

Shann, E., *An Economic History of Australia*, Cambridge, (1930).

Sharpe, D.J., *A Brief History of the Morley Textile History, 1750–1900*, (n.d.).

Sigsworth, E.M., *Black Dyke Mills: A History. With Introductory Chapters on the Development of the Worsted Industry in the Nineteenth Century*, Liverpool, (1958).

Singer, C., *The Earliest Chemical Industry. The Alum Trade*, (1948).

Singer, C. et al. eds, *History of Technology*, 5 Vols, (1954–8).

Smith, G.R., *Scribbling and Carding*, (1914).

Smith, H.B., *Sheep and Wool Industry of Australia*, (1914).

Smith, S., *Tariff Reform and the Textile Industries: Wool and Cotton*, (1909).

Smith, W., *History and Antiquities of Morley*, (1876).

Smith, W., *Morley Ancient and Modern*, (1886).

Smith, W., *Rambles about Morley, with Descriptive and Historical Sketches; also an account of the rise and progress of the woollen manufacture in this place*, (1866).

South of Scotland Chamber of Commerce, *The Scottish Woollen Trade and Foreign Tariffs*, Hawick, (1903).

Southey, T., *The Rise, Progress and Present State of Colonial Sheep and Wools*, (1851).

Stewart, D.C., *Set of Scottish Tartans*, Edinburgh, (1950).

Suddards, R.W., ed., *Titus of Salt*, Bradford, (1976).

Sykes, D.F.E., *The History of the Colne Valley*, Slaithwaite, (1906).

Tann, J., *Gloucestershire Woollen Mills*, Newton Abbot, (1967).

Tann, J., *The Development of the Factory*, (1970).

Taylour, A.M., *Countess of Bective, The British Woollen Trade*, (1881).

Taussig, F.W., *The Tariff History of the U.S.*, (1881).

Textile Institute, *Textile Terms and Definitions*, 6th edn, (1970).

Thomas, J., *A History of the Leeds Clothing Industry*, Yorkshire Bulletin of Economic and Social Research Occasional Paper, No. 1, (1955).

Thompson, F., *Harris Tweed, The Story of a Hebridean Industry*, Newton Abbot, (1969).

Tomlinson, C., ed., *Cyclopaedia of Useful Arts*, 2 Vols, (1854).

Trow-Smith, R., *A History of British Livestock Industry 1700–1900*, (1959).

Tupling, G.H., *The Economic History of Rossendale*, Manchester, (1927).

United States Centennial Commission: *International Exhibition 1876 Reports on Awards. Group IX and Vol. 5, Group IX*, Washington, (1880).

Ure, A., *The Philosophy of Manufactures*, (1835).
Vickerman, C., *Woollen Spinning*, (1894).
Wadsworth, A.P. and Mann, J. de L., *The Cotton Trade and Industrial Lancashire, 1600–1750*, Manchester, (1931).
Walker, J., *Fortunes Made in Business*, (1884).
Walton, W., *The Alpaca, its Naturalisation in the British Isles considered as a National Benefit and as an Object of Immediate Utility to the Farmer and Manufacturer*, (1844).
Ward, J.S.M., *Cotton and Wool*, (1921).
Watson, W., *Textile Design and Colour*, 4th edn, (1937).
Wells, F.A., *The British Hosiery Trade*, (1935).
Wells, F.A., *Hollins & Viyella, A Study in Business History*, Newton Abbot, (1968).
Weston-Webb, W.F.M., *The Autobiography of a British Yarn Merchant*, (1929).
White, W., *Leeds and the Clothing Districts of Yorkshire Directory*, Sheffield, (1853).
White, W., *Clothing District Directory*, (1871).
Williams, E.E., *Made in Germany*, (1896).
Williams, J., *Batley Past and Present; Its Rise and Progress since the Introduction of Shoddy*, Batley, (1880).
Williams, J.B., *British Commercial Policy and Trade Expansion 1750–1850*, Oxford, (1972).
Wilson, R.G., *Gentlemen Merchants, The Merchant Community of Leeds 1700–1880*, Manchester, (1971).
The Wool Year Book, (1913).
Wool Industries Research Association, *Wool Research*, Vol. IV, *Carding*, (1948), Vol. VI. *Drawing and Spinning*, (1949).
Worrall, J., *The Yorkshire Textile Directory*, (1900).
Wrigley, J. and Bousfield, C.E., *Report on the Woollen Cloth Manufacture of France*, Leeds, (1878).
Young, A., ed., *Annals of Agriculture*, 46 Vols, (1784–1815).

Articles and Pamphlets

Aldcroft, D.H., 'The Entrepreneurs and the British Economy 1870–1914', *Ec.H.R.*, 2nd ser., XVI, (1964).
Ambler, G., 'The Ambler Super-draft', *Journal of Bradford Textile Society*, (1956–7).
Anon., *Letter from A Grower of Long Wool*, (1782).
Anon., *A Comprehensive View of the Present Laws against the illicit Exportation of wool*, (1788).
Anon., (? N. Forster), *An Answer to those who have read Sir John Dalrymple's Pamphlet in support of a tax and permission to export raw wool*, (1782).
Anon., *Plain Reasons addressed to the Peoples of Great Britain against the intended Petition for the Owners and Occupiers of Land in the County of Lincoln, for leave to Export Wool*, (1782).
Anon., *A Letter to the Landed Gentlemen and Graziers of Lincolnshire, etc., by a Friend and Neighbour*, (1782).

Anstey, J., *A Letter to the Secretary of the Bath Agricultural Society on the Subject of a Premium for British Wool*, (1791).

Anstey, J., *Observations on the Importance and Necessity of Introducing Improved Machinery into the Woollen Manufacture more especially as it effects the counties of Wilts., Gloucester and Somerset*, (1803).

Ashworth, W., 'British Industrial Villages in the Nineteenth Century', *Ec. H. R.*, 2nd ser., III, (1950).

Banks, J., *Qualified Export of wool discussed*, (1782).

Bartlett, J.N., 'The Mechanisation of the Kidderminster Carpet Industry', *Business History*, IX, 1.

Baker, R., 'On the Industrial and Sanitary Economy of the Borough of Leeds', *J.S.S.*, XXI, (1858).

Barnard, A., 'Wool Buying in the Nineteenth Century: a Case History', *Yorkshire Bulletin of Social and Economic Research*, VIII, i, (1956).

Beaumont, R., 'The Woollen Industry, 1837–1897, A Contrast', *Yorkshire College Magazine*, V, (1897–8).

Beckwith, F., 'The Population of Leeds during the Industrial Revolution', *Publications of the Thoresby Society*, 41, 2, (1948).

Bernoville, M., 'Industrie des Laines Peignées' in *Travaux de la Commission Française sur les Industries des Nations*, Paris, (1854).

Bolton, C., 'A Contribution to the History of Dyeing', *The Dyer and Textile Printer*, 18.1.35 onwards.

Bowden, P.J., 'Wool Supply and the Woollen Industry', *Ec. H. R.*, 2nd ser., IX, 1, (1956).

Bowley, A.L., 'Note on the Statistics of the Woollen Industries', *Economic Journal*, 15, (1905).

Brierley, S. and Carter, G.R., 'Fluctuations in the Woollen Industries of the West Riding', *Economic Journal*, 24, (1914).

Bright, F.J., 'The American Woollen Trade', *Journal of the Huddersfield Textile Society*, (1909).

Brindett, E., 'Romney Marsh Sheep' in *Sheep Husbandry at Home and Abroad*, (n.d.).

Brooke, C., *Proceedings of the Court of the King's Bench in an action brought by Charles Brooke, Wool Broker, versus Henry Guy, clothier . . . for a libel*, (1743).

Carter, G.R., 'Clothing the Allied Armies', *Economic Journal*, 25, (1915).

Catling, H., 'Evolution of the Spinning Mule', *Textile Institute and Industry*, (1965).

Chaloner, W.H., 'The Cartwright Brothers', in *Wool Through the Ages*, (n.d.)

Chapman, S.D., 'The Pioneers of Worsted Spinning by Power', *Business History*, VII, (1965).

CIBA Review 7, *Scarlet*, Basle, (1938).

CIBA Review 16, *The Loom*, Basle, (1938).

CIBA Review 39, *Madder and Turkey Red*, Basle, (1941).

CIBA Review 59, *The Reel*, Basle, (1947).

CIBA Review 74, *Australia, The Land of Wool*, Basle, (1949).

CIBA Review 85, *Indigo*, Basle, (1947).

CIBA Review 101, *Scottish Highland Dress*, Basle, (1951).

CIBA Review 113, *The Wool Fibre*, Basle, (1956).

CIBA Review 115, *Sir William Henry Perkin*, Basle, (1956).

CIBA Review 124, *Men's Dress*, Basle, (1958).
CIBA Review 130, *The English Wool Industry*, Basle, (1959).
CIBA Review 1966/3, *The Mechanical Loom*, Basle, (1967).
CIBA Review 1968/1, *The Evolution of Mills and Factories*, Basle, (1968).
Clapham, J.H., 'Protection and the Wool Trade', *Independent Review*, (1904).
Clapham, J.H., 'The Decline of the Handloom in England and Germany', *Journal of Bradford Textile Society*, (1905).
Clapham, J.H., 'Industrial Organization in the Woollen and Worsted Industries of Yorkshire', *Economic Journal*, XVI, (1906).
Clapham, J.H., 'The Transference of the Worsted Industry from Norfolk to the West Riding', *Economic Journal*, XX, (1910).
Clapham J.H., 'Some Factory Statistics of 1815–16', *Economic Journal*, XXV, (1915).
Clark, C.O., Ancient and Modern Scouring and Dyeing, *Journal of the Society of Dyers & Colourists*, 61, 3, (1950).
Clark, C.O., *Wool Fabrics and Their Finishes*, (1958).
Coleman, D.C., 'Growth and Decay during the Industrial Revolution. The Case of East Anglia', *Scandinavian Economic History Review*, 2, (1962).
Coleman, D.C., 'Textile growth' in *Textile History and Economic History*, ed. by N. Harte and K.G. Ponting, Manchester, (1973).
Corfield, P., 'The Size of the Norwich Worsted Industry in the Eighteenth and Nineteenth Century'. Discussion Paper at the S.S.R.C./Pasold Conference on Textile History, (1975).
Dalrymple, J., *Whether wool should be exported?*, (1782).
Deane, P., 'The Output of the British Woollen Industry in the Eighteenth Century', *Journal of Economic History*, XVII, (1957).
Edwards, J.K., 'The Decline of the Norwich Textile Industry', *Yorkshire Bulletin of Economic and Social Research*, XVI, (1964).
Edwards, J.K., 'Communications and the Economic Development of Norwich, 1750–1850', *Journal of Transport History*, VII, 2.
'Extracts from an Old Leeds Merchants' Memorandum Book: 1770–1786', *Publications of the Thoresby Society*, 24, (1915).
Fairlie, S., 'Dyestuffs in the Eighteenth Century', *Ec. H. R.*, 2nd ser., XVII, 2, (1961).
Feather, G.A., 'A Pennine Worsted Community in the mid-nineteenth century', *Textile History*, III, (1972).
Fenton, F., 'The Discovery and Early History of the Shoddy and Mungo Trade', *Wool and Textile Fabrics*, 15.1.1881.
Fenton, F., 'Woollen Shoddy: Its Invention, History and Manufacture', *Textile Manufacturer*, April 1881–October 1881.
Flux, A.W., 'British Trade and German Competition', *Economic Journal*, 7, (1897).
Garside, M., 'The Halifax Piece Hall', *Transactions of the Halifax Antiquarian Society*, (1921).
Gill, C., 'Blackwell Hall Factors 1795–99', *Ec. H. R.* 2nd ser., VI, 3, (1956).
Ginsberg, M., 'The Tailoring and Dressmaking Trades, 1700–1850', *Costume*, (1972).
Glover, F.J., 'Thomas Cook and the American blanket trade in the nineteenth century', *Business History Review*, XXV, (1961).

Glover, F.J., 'Philadelphia merchants and the Yorkshire blanket trade, 1820–1860', *Pennsylvania History*, XXVIII, (1961).

Glover, F.J., 'The Rise of the Heavy Woollen Trade of the West Riding of Yorkshire in the Nineteenth Century', *Business History*, IV, (1961).

Glover, F.J., 'A Yorkshire Blanket Maker's Diary', *Journal of the Bradford Textile Society*, (1962–63).

Glover, F.J., 'Government contracting, competition and growth in the heavy woollen industry', *Ec. H. R.*, 2nd ser., XVI, 2, (1964).

Gonner, E.C.K., 'The Survival of Domestic Industries', *Economic Journal*, 3, (1893).

Goodchild, J., 'The Ossett Mill Company', *Textile History*, I, 1, (1968).

Goodchild, J., 'Pildacre Mill: an early West Riding Factory', *Textile History*, I, 3, (1970).

Graham, J., 'Wool and the Woollen and Worsted Industries of Great Britain' in Jackson, F.H., *Lectures on British Commerce*, (1911).

Gulvin, C., (ed.), 'Journal of Henry Brown, Woollen manufacturer, Galashiels, 1828–1829', *Scottish Industrial History, A Miscellany*, Edinburgh, (1978).

Hall, P.P., 'A History of the Dolphineholme Worsted Mill, 1784 to 1867', *Transactions of the Fylde Historical Society*, 3, (1969).

Hawke, G.R., 'The United States Tariff and Industrial Protection in the late 19th Century', *Ec. H. R.* 2nd ser., XXVIII, 1, (1975).

Heaton, H., 'The Leeds White Cloth Hall', *Publications of the Thoresby Society*, 22, (1915).

Heaton, H., 'The Tricks of the Trade: facts and fiction concerning the Yorkshire Textile Industry', *Publications of the Thoresby Society*, 22 (1915).

Heaton, H., 'Benjamin Gott and the Anglo-American Cloth Trade', *Journal of Economic and Business History*, II, (1919).

Heaton, H., 'Benjamin Gott and the Industrial Revolution in Yorkshire', *Ec. H. R.*, III, (1931).

Heaton, H., 'An Early Victorian Business Forecaster in the Woollen Industry', *Economic History, II*, (1933).

Heaton, H., 'Financing the Industrial Revolution', *Bulletin of the Business History Society*, XI, (1937).

Heaton, H., 'Non-Importation, 1806–1812', *Journal of Economic History*, I, 2, (1941).

Heaton, H., 'Yorkshire Cloth Traders in the United States: 1770–1840', *Publications of the Thoresby Society*, 37, (1944).

Heaton, H., 'A Merchant Adventurer in Brazil, 1808–1818', *Journal of Economic History*, VI, (1946).

Heaton, H., 'The American Trade', in Parkinson, C.N., ed., *The Trade Winds*, (1948).

Holmyard, E.J., 'Dyestuffs in the Nineteenth Century', in Singer, C., ed., *A History of Technology. V, The Late Nineteenth Century*, Oxford, (1958).

Iredale, J.A., 'The Last Two Piecing Machines', *Industrial Archaeology*, IV, 1, (1967).

Jenkins, D.T., 'Early Factory Development in the West Riding of Yorkshire, 1770–1800' in Harte, N.B., and Ponting, K.G., eds, *Textile History and Economic History*, Manchester, (1973).

Jenkins D.T., 'The Validity of the Factory Returns, 1833–50', *Textile History*, 4, (1973).

Jenkins, D.T., 'The Factory Returns, 1850–1905', *Textile History*, 9, (1978).

Jenkins, D.T., 'The Cotton Industry in Yorkshire, 1780–1900', *Textile History*, 10, (1979).

Jenkins, J.G., 'The Montgomery Woollen Industry', *Montgomeryshire Collections*, LXVIII, (1963).

Jeremy, D.J., 'Damming the Flood. British Government's Efforts to check the outflow of Technology and Machinery, 1780–1843', *Business History Review*, LI, I, (1971).

Jeremy, D.J., 'Innovation in American Textile Technology during the early 19th century', *Technology & Culture*, 14, I, (1973).

Jeremy, D.J., 'British Textile Technology Transmission to the U.S.: The Philadelphia Region Experience, 1770–1820', *Business History Review*, XLVII, 1, (1973).

Jones, M.J., 'The Merioneth Woollen Industry 1758–1820', *Y Cymmrodor*, (1939).

Kilburn Scott, A., 'Early Cloth Fulling and its Machinery', *Transaction of the Newcomen Society*, 12, (1931–2).

Lemon, H., 'The Handcraftmen in the Wool Textile Trade', *Folk Life*, I, 1963.

Lloyd-Pritchard, M.F., 'The Decline of Norwich', *Ec. H. R.*, 2nd series, III, 3 (1951).

McCloskey, D.M., and Sandberg, Lars G., 'From Damnation to Redemption: Judgements on the Late Victorian Entrepreneurs', *Explorations in Economic History*, IX, (1971).

McCloskey, D.M., 'Did Victorian Britain Fail?', *Ec. H. R.*, 2nd ser., XXIII, 3, (1970).

Mann, J. de L., 'The Textile Industry. Machinery for Cotton, Flax, Wool 1766–1850' in Singer, C., ed., *A History of Technology*. IV, (1958).

Marling, W.H., 'The Woollen Trade of Gloucestershire', *Gloucestershire Archaeological Society*, 36.

Mitchell, J.A.B., 'Brown's Patent Self-Action Feeder. The Prototype of the Scottish Feed', *Scottish Woollen Textile College Students Guide*, No. 3.

Moir, E., 'Gentlemen Clothiers. A Survey of the Goucester Cloth Trade 1750–1831', *Gloucestershire Studies* (ed.), Frinberg, (1957).

Montgomery, F.M., 'John Holker's Mid-Eighteenth Century *Livre d'En-chantillons*', in Gervers, ed., *Studies in Textile History*, Toronto, (1977).

Mudge, E.R., & Hayes, J.L., 'Report upon Wool and Manufactures of Wool', *Paris Universal Exposition, 1867: Reports of the United States Commissioners*, Washington, (1868).

Philpott, B.P., 'Wool Textile Activity and Wool Prices', *Yorkshire Bulletin of Economic and Social Research*, 5, 1, (1953).

Philpott, B.P., 'Fluctuations in Wool Prices, 1870–1953', *Yorkshire Bulletin of Economic and Social Research*, 7, 1, (1955).

Ponting, K.G., 'The Textile Inventions of Sebastian Ziani de Ferranti', *Textile History*, 4, (1973).

Ponting, K.G., 'The Structure of the Somerset-Wiltshire Border Woollen Industry during 1815–1840', Harte, N., and Ponting, K.G., eds, *Economic History and Textile History*, Manchester, (1973).

Ponting, K.G., 'Availability of Capital in the West of England Woollen Industry', in W. Minchinton, ed., *Capital Formation in South West England*. Exeter Papers in Economic History, No. 9, Exeter, (1978).

Randoing, M.K., 'Industrie des Laines Foulées', in *Travaux de la Commission Française sur l'Industrie des Nations*, Paris, (1854).

Reynolds, R., 'The Beginning of the Yorkshire College', *The Gryphon*, II, 2, (1898).

Rimmer, W.G., 'The Industrial Profile of Leeds, 1740–1840', *Publications of the Thoresby Society*, 50, (1967).

Rimmer, W.G., 'The Woollen Industry in the 19th Century: Leeds and Its Industrial Growth', *Leeds Journal*, 30, 1, (1959).

Rothstein, N., 'The Introduction of the Jacquard Loom to Great Britain', Gervers V., ed., *Studies in Textile History*, Toronto, (1977).

Schmercher, J.E., 'State Reform and the Social Economy: an aspect of Industrialisation in late Victorian and Edwardian London', *Ec. H. R.*, 2nd ser., XXXVIII, 3, (1975).

Scott, R., 'The Collie Disaster', *Transactions of the Hawick Archaeological Society*, (1962).

Shannon, H.A., 'The Coming of General Limited Liability' *Economic History*, II, (1931).

Shannon, H.A., 'The First Five Thousand Limited Companies and their Duration', *Economic History*, II, (1932).

Shannon, H.A., 'The Limited Companies of 1866–1883', *Economic History Review*, IV, 3, (1933).

Sigsworth, E.M., 'History of the Local Trade at Morley', *Journal of the Textile Institute*, 40, 10, (1949).

Sigsworth, E.M., 'Bradford and the Great Exhibition', *Journal of the Bradford Textile Society*, (1950–1).

Sigsworth, E.M., 'Foster of Queensbury and Geyer of Lodz', *Yorkshire Bulletin of Economic and Social Research*, III, (1951).

Sigsworth, E.M., 'Wm. Greenwood and Robert Heaton. Two Eighteenth Century Worsted Manufacturers', *Journal of the Bradford Textile Society*, (1951–2).

Sigsworth, E.M., 'The West Riding Wool Textile Industry and the Great Exhibition', *Yorkshire Bulletin of Economic and Social Research*, IV, (1952).

Sigsworth, E.M., and Blackman, J.M., 'The Woollen and Worsted Industries' in Aldcroft, D.H., ed., *The Development of British Industry and Foreign Competition, 1875–1914*, (1968).

Sigsworth, E.M., 'The British Retreat from Pre-Eminence', *The American Benedictine Review*, XXI, 2, (1970).

Sigsworth, E.M., 'Sir Isaac Holden. Bt.: the first comber in Europe' in Harte, N., and Ponting, K.G., eds, *Textile History and Economic History*, Manchester, (1973).

Sigsworth, E.M., 'The West Riding Wool Textile Industry', in *Wool Through the Ages*, (n.d.).

Sinclair, Sir John, *Address to Society for the Improvement of British Wool*, (1791).

Skeel, C.A.J., 'The Welsh Woollen Industry in the Eighteenth and Nineteenth Centuries', *Archaeologia Cambrensis*, Series F, II, (1922).

Smith, S., 'The Woollen Industry', in Cox, H., ed., *British Industries under Free Trade*, (1903).

Southey, T., *Observations to woolgrowers of Australia and Tasmania*, (1831).

Speakman, J.B., 'Wool', Thorpe's *Dictionary of Applied Chemistry*, 5, (1941).

Swain, J., 'Rural Factories in Wales', *Economic Journal*, 24, (1914).

Tann, J., 'The Employment of Power in the West of England Wool Textile Industry, 1790–1840', in Harte, N., and Ponting, K.G., eds, *Textile History and Economic History*, Manchester, (1973).

Taylor, E.L., 'The Early Wool Trade in Rochdale', *Transactions of the Rochdale Literary and Scientific Society*, XII, 1914–16.

Thompson, R.J., 'Wool Prices in Great Britain, 1883–1901', *Journal of the Royal Statistical Society*, LXV, (1902).

Tucker, J., *On the Low Price of Coarse Wool*, 1781–2.

Wadsworth A.P., 'The Early Factory System in the Rochdale District', *Transactions of the Rochdale Literary and Scientific Society*, XIX, 1935–37.

Wild, M.T., 'The Yorkshire Wool Textile Trade', in Jenkins J.G., ed., *The Wool Textile Industry in Great Britain*, (1972).

Wilson, R.G., 'The Fortunes of a Leeds merchant house', *Business History*, X, (1967).

Wilson, R.G., 'The Supremacy of the Yorkshire Cloth Industry in the Eighteenth Century', in Harte, N.B., and Ponting, K.G., eds, *Textile History and Economic History*, Manchester, (1973).

Wilson, R.G., 'Some problems of the Norwich Worsted Industry in the Eighteenth Century', discussion paper at S.S.R.C./Pasold Conference on Textile History, (1975).

Wood, B., and Preston, W.E., 'James Lobley, A Bradford Artist', *Journal of the Bradford and Halifax Antiquarian Society*, New Series, III, (1911).

Wood, G.H., 'Tests of Progress applied to the Woollen Trade', *Journal of the Huddersfield Textile Society*, (1909).

Index

Note: Where an entry refers to a table in the book, the number following the word 'table refers to the page on which the table occurs, not the table number itself